D1110797

SECRETS OF ANGELS
& DEMONS

SECRETS OF ANGELS & DEMONS

The Unauthorised Guide to the Bestselling Novel

EDITED BY

Dan Burstein and Arne de Keijzer

SENIOR CONTRIBUTING EDITOR: David A. Shugarts

CONTRIBUTING EDITORS: Paul Berger, Peter Burstein, Annalyn Swan

CONSULTING EDITORS: John Castro, Judy DeYoung, Anna Isgro,
Gwen Kinkead, Jill Rachlin, Alex Ulam

Weidenfeld & Nicolson

LONDON

First published in Great Britain in 2005
by Weidenfeld & Nicolson

Originally published in the USA in 2004 by CDS Books
in association with Squibnocket Partners LLC

A CIP catalogue record for this book
is available from the British Library.

ISBN 0 297 84871 2

Printed in Australia by Griffin Press,
Netley, South Australia

Weidenfeld & Nicolson

The Orion Publishing Group Ltd
Orion House
5 Upper Saint Martin's Lane
London, WC2H 9EA

For Julie,
The angel who illuminated my experience of Rome circa MCMLXXI
and the rest of my life ever since: "Bella . . . Molto Bella!" Here's to all
the Roman holidays and Italian adventures to come . . .

And for David,
Resident expert on the Bestseller List, Latin, and the
similarities between Harry Potter and Robert Langdon: "Suddenly, it all
became clear."
—DB

For Hannah,
Who dances in my soul,
and to Dick, Steve, Brian, DDJ, Clem,
and my extraordinary extended family.

And especially for Helen,
"If ever any beauty I did see,
Which I desir'd, and got, 'twas but a dream of thee."
—AJD

CONTENTS

EDITOR'S NOTE

Secrets of Angels & Demons: The Unauthorized Guide to the Bestselling Novel follows the same format as our earlier book in this series, *Secrets of the Code: The Unauthorized Guide to the Mysteries Behind The Da Vinci Code.*

Once again we have sought to provide a comprehensive reader's guide by carefully gathering original thought and writing, extensive interviews with experts, and excerpts from books, magazines, and websites. We are again intrigued by Dan Brown's technique of weaving rich and historically important ideas into the heart of his murder mystery plot. At the same time, Brown's blending of real history and invented fantasy immediately sets off the question, what is fact and what is fiction in *Angels & Demons*? We have taken on the task of answering that question, not only in the realm of history and ideas, but in the plot points and devices used by the author. We have taken care to distinguish our editor's voice from the authors' contributions by setting our introductory comments in italics. The text that follows is in the original voice of the author or interviewee. All material is copyrighted by Squibnocket Partners LLC unless otherwise indicated in the copyright notice that follows each selection.

Working with such a wide range of source materials, we have tended to regularize spelling and naming conventions in our own work, while leaving undisturbed the original spellings and conventions that appear in some works that are excerpted here. For example, some experts refer to Bernini as Gianlorenzo and others as Gian Lorenzo. We have tended to standardize on the former.

Words, sentence fragments, or explanatory notes that appear in brackets are ours; those in parentheses are those of the author. Ancillary material prepared for the book but not included here because of the exigencies of publishing—including several essays and interviews we were unable to use—will later appear on our website. To find us on the web, check www.secretsofangelsanddemons.com.

Page numbers in this book referring to *Angels & Demons* are the same for both the US hardcover (Atria Books, a trademark of Simon & Schuster, published in 2003) and the US mass paperback edition (Pocket Star Books, a division of Simon & Schuster, published in 2001).

In giving readers a quick taste of the ideas and writings of a great many experts, we have inevitably had to leave things out we would have otherwise liked to use. We want to thank all the authors, interviewees, publishers, and experts who have so generously made their thoughts and materials available to us. In return, we urge our readers to buy the books written by our experts and pursue all the multitude of ideas referred to within these pages from their original sources.

SECRETS OF ANGELS & DEMONS

INTRODUCTION
ANGELS & DEMONS:
ROUGH DRAFT FOR *THE DA VINCI CODE,*
ROAD MAP FOR DAN BROWN'S
NEXT BOOK

The very first time I spoke to a crowd about *Secrets of the Code,* the book I had published in April 2004 about the histories and mysteries behind Dan Brown's blockbuster best-seller *The Da Vinci Code (DVC),* someone stood up and asked if I would produce a similar book about Dan Brown's *Angels & Demons (A&D).* As I toured the country throughout 2004 with *Secrets of the Code*—fielding questions about whether Jesus and Mary Magdalene were really married, whether a disguised Mary Magdalene appears in the *Last Supper,* and whether the Priory of Sion was a real organization—someone would invariably ask me about *Angels & Demons.* An informal poll I conducted suggested that about one in five readers actually found *Angels & Demons* more interesting than *The Da Vinci Code*—a stunning response, considering that *The Da Vinci Code* was proving to be the one of the biggest, most widely discussed novels of all time.

After experiencing modest sales when it was first published in 2000 (three years before *DVC) Angels & Demons* was, by 2004, riding *The Da Vinci Code*'s coattails as part of the billion-dollar Dan Brown industry. It had nearly five million new copies in print and was pushing ever higher on both the paperback and hardcover fiction bestseller lists.

I decided to sit down and read *Angels & Demons,* so I could give responsive answers to my questioners. Like my experience with *The Da Vinci Code* a year earlier, I stayed up all night reading *Angels & Demons,* fascinated with many of the ideas and issues alluded to in the text, while turning pages as fast as I could to keep up with the murder mystery plot. By the time I closed the book at dawn the next day, I had experienced a series of powerful responses.

First, *Angels & Demons* struck me as a virtual rough draft for *The Da Vinci Code*. Anyone who really wanted to understand *The Da Vinci Code* would need to read *Angels & Demons*. It was in *Angels & Demons* that Dan Brown created the Robert Langdon character. Although Brown had not yet taken to calling him a "symbologist" (the designation Langdon would receive in *DVC*), the Harvard professor was already well on his way there with his specialties in art history and religious iconography.

Structurally, of course, the plots and characters of the two novels are kissing cousins: both books begin in a European city with the brutal murder of a brilliant man who possesses special knowledge. In both cases, the assassin is an unusual character who is part of an ancient or secretive cult. Both murders have unusual forensic characteristics—Leonardo Vetra's gouged eyeball lying on the floor in the corridor of CERN and Jacques Saunière's arrangement of himself naked on the floor of the Louvre as Vitruvian Man.

In both novels, Langdon is awakened by a highly improbable phone call and thrust into action as a kind of postmodern Sherlock Holmes because of his unique insights into occult history and symbology. In each case, Langdon is teamed up with a beautiful, brainy, single European female whose father/grandfather has been brutally murdered and who becomes Langdon's partner in decoding clues and solving apocalyptic mysteries. Langdon will be physically attracted to Vittoria (*A&D*) and Sophie (*DVC*) at various times in each tale, and there will be the promise of a sexual encounter at the end of each. But these books, unlike most of their genre counterparts, spend almost all their time on solving the mysteries of Western civilization—and almost no time on sex.

Each story, despite its peripatetic odyssey of action, is supposed to take place within twenty-four hours. In *Angels & Demons*, the artist of interest whose works contain the clues to understanding the murders is Bernini and the backdrop for almost all the action is Rome; in *The Da Vinci Code* it's Leonardo da Vinci and Paris. In *Angels & Demons*, the ancient mystery sect is the Illuminati; in *The Da Vinci Code*, it is the Priory of Sion. In *Angels & Demons*, Brown imagines lost documents written by Galileo; in *The Da Vinci Code*, Brown mines the very real and authenticated Gnostic gospels and the questionable *Dossiers Secrets*. In *Angels & Demons* it's ambigrams; in *The Da Vinci Code* it's anagrams.

Both books deal predominately with the Catholic Church and the long and complicated history of Christian belief. In *The Da Vinci Code*, Brown explores issues relating to the origins and codification of Christianity; in *Angels & Demons*, he explores a seminal issue facing the Vatican since Galileo: the conflict between scientific and religious cosmologies. In *The Da Vinci Code*, the traditional Catholic Church and the Priory of Sion each believe they are practicing the true version of their religion. In *Angels & Demons*, it is suggested that CERN and the Vatican are two different kinds of churches. In the "Cathedral of Science" (CERN), antimatter is stored deep underground, while in the "Cathedral of Religion" (St. Peter's Basilica), the relics of Peter himself are housed underground (well, maybe not—see Chapter I).

I had a second reaction after finishing *Angels & Demons*. Having spent memorable months of my youth in Rome and knowing its streets and monuments reasonably well; having studied seventeenth-century history in college and being modestly familiar with the worlds of Bernini, Galileo, Milton, Bruno, the Reformation and Counter-Reformation; and having done a fair amount of reading on contemporary quantum physics and cosmology, *Angels & Demons* stimulated my curiosity anew on all these topics. Similar to my experience with *The Da Vinci Code*, my reaction to *Angels & Demons* was to rush out to the local bookstore and buy dozens of nonfiction books on more than thirty different topics (from antimatter to antipopes) that provided the keys to a deeper understanding of *Angels & Demons*'s fictional plot.

Dan Brown is certainly a controversial figure. Theologians have accused him of blasphemy; other writers have accused him of plagiarism. Serious academics have accused him of confusing the masses with his unusual blend of fact and fiction that he insists is all fact (even though these are just novels and are clearly marketed and sold as such).

In my opinion, all these critics are looking at the Dan Brown phenomenon incorrectly. My view is that our culture is starved for intellectual discussion about the big questions of our time. We no longer understand the signs and symbols that were once intuitively obvious to our forebears. We are becoming deracinated from our own cultural heritage. We are torn between the impulses toward faith and spirituality on the one hand, and science and technology on the other. The more logical and technological our society becomes, the more some of us crave spirituality and a return to past values. The more some conclude that God is dead or irrelevant, the more others find themselves returning to church. And the more globalized and materialistic our cultures become, the more small groups seem attracted to the most illogical, untenable, extremist, and dangerous religious dogmas. We are supposed to be living in the information age, and yet we don't know if we are being lied to about basic facts. We know more and more about what happened microseconds after the big bang, yet we still know nothing about what happened before it. We are plunging headlong into a new millennium that is qualitatively different from the two millennia prior. We desperately want to talk about the experience, but there is no forum for doing so.

Dan Brown's books give us the chance to engage in some of this discussion. It may not be the most profound discussion, but what it lacks in profundity it makes up for in accessibility. In most people's daily lives it is not easy to fit in reading a book from cover to cover, thinking about it, talking about it, and becoming stimulated to do additional reading. But *Angels & Demons* and *The Da Vinci Code* have caused millions of people to go through that process. It is for those readers that we have created *Secrets of Angels & Demons*. Dan Brown says some intriguing and tantalizing things about antimatter, entanglement theory, and twenty-first-century cosmology. He gives you a start. He gets you interested, but he doesn't tell you everything you now want to know. That's what our book does.

In *Secrets of Angels & Demons*, you can actually learn the real history of the papal selection process and what might happen when the Vatican's cardinals next go into conclave—and who they might select as the next pope when the time comes. Having become acquainted with the views of some of the world's leading scientists, theologians, and philosophers in Chapter 4, you can then think more critically about your own personal cosmology. Most readers of *Angels & Demons* never heard of the Illuminati before reading the novel. In our book, you can learn the real facts about the Illuminati and how their role in history has been recast by conspiracy theorists of all types. If you are interested in Bernini (and I confess that I was *not* very interested in Bernini when I started the research for this book, but have now changed my mind), in Chapter 5 you will find much enlightenment about his role in creating the look and feel of the "eternal city" that we as tourists experience today. If you think you understand who Galileo was and what happened in his famous trial, take a look at some of the essays in Chapter 2 for some new perspectives. And if you enjoy the game of parsing fact and fiction in Dan Brown's plot, we've got investigative reporters, forensic medicine specialists, technologists, Bernini scholars, and conspiracy theory experts throughout to tell you what Dan Brown got right and what he got wrong in *Angels & Demons.* You can join the debate about whether a "dead eyeball" could still be used to fool a retina-scanning security system. Or whether Bernini's sculpture *St. Teresa in Ecstasy* in Rome's Santa Maria della Vittoria church is meant to depict a women having an ecstatic religious vision, a "toe-curling orgasm" (Dan Brown's phrase), or perhaps both experiences simultaneously.

I had a third reaction to *Angels & Demons.* Just as *Angels & Demons* helped me understand *The Da Vinci Code* even better, I realized that it also helped me understand where Dan Brown was likely to go in his next, as yet unpublished, book, which is expected to appear in 2005. In *Secrets of the Code*, our researchers and experts had already deciphered the coded message on the dust jacket of *The Da Vinci Code* (slightly bolded letters in the copy that, when strung together, spell out "Is there no help for the widow's son?"). Our team had already said publicly that we believed Dan Brown's next book would focus on the Freemasons and probably be set in Washington, DC. Shortly after we issued a press release on this subject in May 2004, Dan Brown announced at one of his now rare public appearances that, yes, he was at work on a new book and, yes, it would involve the history of the Freemasons and be set in Washington, DC.

Careful readers of *The Da Vinci Code* and *Angels & Demons* will recall that, in *both* books, Robert Langdon finds occasion to hold forth on the symbological significance of the eye over the unfinished pyramid on the back of the US dollar bill, attributing this symbol to the Masons and/or the Illuminati, and arguing that it reflects their influence among the Founding Fathers of the United States. Throughout *Angels & Demons*, Brown conflates the history of the Freemasons and the Illuminati. Indeed, when Brown was a little-known struggling writer on his initial book tour for *Angels & Demons*, he played up the Freemason history presented in the book, rather than the Illuminati, and gave many hints that this is a subject that interests him deeply.

As several of our experts point out in these pages, neither Galileo nor Bernini could have been a member of the Illuminati (as Dan Brown suggests they were), if for no other reason than that organization was not founded until 1776—over a century after Galileo's death. But like much else, the point in Dan Brown's work is not the facts (no matter how many times he asserts that everything is factual). The point is to understand his use of myth and metaphor, his uncanny ability to suggest intriguing alternative explanations for historical events, and his talent for mining ideas and symbols that have been hiding in plain sight for years—and infuse them with new thought-provoking interpretations.

If you read Chapter 3 of this book, you are likely to find out more than you ever knew about the Illuminati, the Freemasons, and their real and imagined role in American history. Just as many readers responded to *The Da Vinci Code* by saying, "How come I never knew that?" (about Jesus and Mary Magdalene, about the *Last Supper*, etc.), many will be asking the same question about George Washington, Thomas Jefferson, and early American history after they read Dan Brown's next book.

It appears that Dan Brown has read and studied a variety of occult theories of history and become fascinated with the story line this version of history tells: It starts back in cave-dwelling times with the prominence of the "sacred feminine" and Goddess/fertility cults as the inspiration for the earliest religious and artistic ideas. It comes forward in time through ancient Egypt, where pyramid builders and Goddess cult followers acquired secret knowledge of monument building, alchemy, and magic. It moves through Greece, Crete, and other eastern Mediterranean cultures, including the earliest forms of Judaism, constantly combining the engineering skills of the day (the ability to construct great pyramids and temples, for example), with emphasis on Goddess worship; mystery religious rites; specialized bodies of occult, mathematical, and magical knowledge (such as the Cabala in Judaism); and occasional ecstatic sexual rites practiced as forms of religious devotion.

The thread is then picked up by Jesus (whom Brown calls "the original feminist" in *The Da Vinci Code*), Mary Magdalene, and the Gnostic circles among early Christians. Romans conflate aspects of their pagan beliefs with these new Christian beliefs. The Knights Templar come next, combining the secret knowledge they found during their occupation of the Temple of Solomon with their belief in Mary Magdalene as the "holy grail" and their temple-building skills. After the defeat and massacre of the Templars come all the splinter groups, from the Freemasons, to the Priory of Sion, to the Illuminati, all allegedly carrying forward the tradition of ancient, mystical knowledge, brilliant engineering, and scientific skills, and a belief in the sacred feminine. These beliefs are in counterdistinction to the corrupt, desecrated organized religions of the day. They reach their high tide in the Enlightenment with the American and French Revolutions and the victory of science and free thought over religious dogma.

Dan Brown's next book will likely be set against this story line as well. Indeed, the dark secrets of this version of history, the cover-ups and conspiracies, the buried treasure and relics, the signs, symbols, and artworks lying at the very foundations of the human psyche and human experience, the schism between science and religion, between masculine and feminine—all of this will provide Professor Langdon more than enough material to keep his symbological-decoding practice going through many mysteries and many more books—for years to come.

In our *Secrets* series, we seek to assemble the experts and the ideas that can enrich and deepen the reader's own experience of Dan Brown's themes. I am particularly proud of the resources that my coeditor, Arne de Keijzer, and I have assembled in *Secrets of Angels & Demons*. I wish all our readers good journeys as they undertake the many different voyages of intellectual discovery available through the ideas in this book.

Dan Burstein
November 2004
Join the discussion at www.secretsofangelsanddemons.com.

1: THE VATICAN: AN INSIDER'S VIEW

*Separating fact from clever imagining in the papal succession process •
Handicapping the election for the successor to John Paul II • The ins
and outs of how the Vatican works • Has papal history been lurid as
well as holy? • Were St. Peter's bones really buried under the Vatican? •
How the church's view toward science has changed—and hasn't
changed—from the time of Galileo to the present*

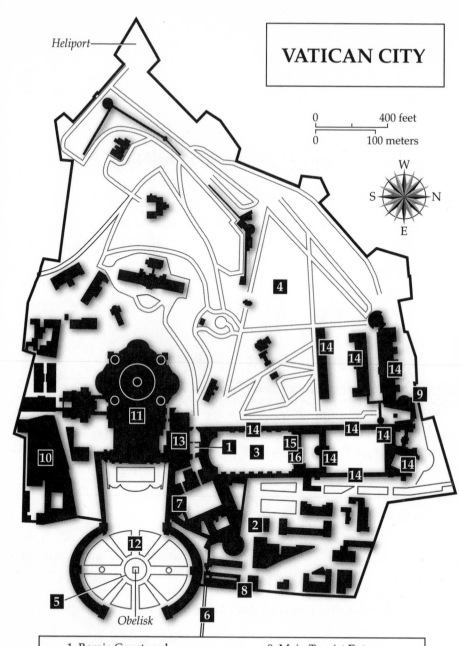

VATICAN CITY

0   400 feet

0   100 meters

Heliport

Obelisk

1. Borgia Courtyard
2. Central Post Office
3. Courtyard of the Belvedere
4. Gardens
5. "Wind Circle," including West Ponente
6. Il Passetto
7. Papal Apartments
8. Porta Sant'Anna
9. Main Tourist Entrance to Vatican Museums
10. Papal Audience Hall
11. St. Peter's Basilica
12. St. Peter's Square
13. Sistine Chapel
14. Vatican Museums
15. Papal Secret Archives
16. The Vatican Library

CONCLAVE 101:
THE PAST, PRESENT, AND FUTURE
OF THE PAPAL ELECTIONS

BY GREG TOBIN

In his bestseller about the death and election of the pope, *Angels & Demons*, Dan Brown writes with brio about ideas and institutions that have been fascinating subjects for people around the world. The novel is a mix of fact and fiction that raises important questions about the structure and internal governance of the Roman Catholic Church and the influences that the church faces in the early years of the twenty-first century. Brown takes imaginative leaps and employs the license of any popular novelist. But informed readers will want to know how closely his vivid picture of the Vatican corresponds to the reality of the popes and the papacy today.

The office of the papacy is nearly two thousand years old, and 261 men have officially held the position of bishop of Rome. It began with St. Peter the Apostle's mission to the capital of the empire in the late fifties or early sixties of the first Christian century and has continued without significant interruption into the current pontificate of Pope John Paul II.

There is no conclusive evidence that Peter was ever in Rome. However, the body

---

Greg Tobin is an author, editor, journalist and scholar who is currently the publisher of *The Catholic Advocate*, the newspaper of the Archdiocese of Newark, New Jersey. He has written two recent novels, *Conclave* and *Council*, as well as a current book about the papal selection process, *Selecting the Pope: Uncovering the Mysteries of Papal Elections*.

of tradition, circumstantial evidence (including his putative grave and remains), and the lack of any claim that he was elsewhere all point to the likelihood, even near certainty, that Peter ministered to Christians in Rome (as did St. Paul) and that he was martyred there in Nero's circus, circa AD 64–67 (at about the same time as Paul). Rome is called the Apostolic See by the Catholic Church in recognition of the "co-founders" of the Christian faith and their position as premier leaders among the earliest church fathers of the so-termed apostolic age (that is, the time immediately after Christ's death through the end of the first century—when the last of the original twelve apostles presumably passed from the scene).

From the very earliest days Christians and their leaders (the *episkopoi*, or "overseers," who came to be called bishops) sought to resolve the issue of authority in matters concerning doctrine and morality. Theological disputes arose amid a climate of intermittent, albeit severe Roman persecution of the Christians. Many churches (such as the African Church) looked to Rome to mediate local conflicts. By about AD 150 the bishop of Rome was the most influential church leader in the Mediterranean world.

From the beginning, after Peter's martyrdom, the leaders of the Church of Rome were elected from among the local clergy there. It was not for several hundred years that a bishop from another diocese was selected for the Roman See: Marinus I (in 882) was bishop of Caere when elected, followed several years later by Formosus (891), bishop of Porto, the second such choice in church history. This has evolved to the point where today it is almost a mandatory qualification to have been a residential bishop of a large diocese.

Throughout the Middle Ages—the period after the fall of the western Roman empire in 476 and up to the time of the Renaissance (in the fifteenth and sixteenth centuries)—papal elections were the ultimate spectator sport for Europeans, with much at stake: by that time the popes had acquired temporal as well as spiritual power. Dating from the gift by Charlemagne's father (in 754), the Roman pontiff ruled much of Italy—known as the Papal States. Rival Roman and Italian families literally killed to position their own as candidates. Emperors and kings attempted (and often succeeded) to control papal elections, through money, military force, and political persuasion. Such political machinations have resonance even today, when cardinals from powerful countries (such as the United States) are deemed unlikely to be elected for fear that global political concerns may overwhelm or taint the pope's ability to govern the universal church.

From 1305 to 1375 the popes (all French) lived in Avignon in splendid exile from Rome and fell under the sway of the king of France. A period of schism followed, from 1378 to 1417. For much of that time, *three* popes simultaneously claimed the throne of Peter. That situation was resolved by the Council of Constance (1417–1418) but not before the Protestant Reformation had been successfully founded. Through the baroque age in which the great basilica of St. Peter was completed in the form we know it today, and into the ages of enlightenment and revolution, the popes were elected for their intellectual capacity and political flexibility, and sometimes for their malleability by the College of Cardinals. Pope Pius VII, elected in 1799 after his predecessor had been forced into exile by Napoleon, set the papacy on its modern course by resisting secular powers and focusing on the internal governance of the church.

Pius VII's successors, which include the longest-serving pontiffs in history (Pius IX logged nearly thirty years as pope), have all been deemed theologically sound and morally worthy and were all elected under fine-tuned conclave rules that allowed the faithful of the church and the cardinals who elected him to serve as primarily a spiritual leader, as *the* primary spiritual leader of Christendom.

From the last four papal conclaves, three of the "winners" have been surprises for one reason or another. In 1958 the cardinals elected a seventy-seven-year-old former diplomat and World War I veteran Angelo Giuseppi Roncalli, who had been marking time on the *cathedra* (bishop's "chair") in Venice. He was widely believed to have been elected to be merely a transitional pope, one who basically was expected to warm the bench for the next pope. He surprised everyone when, as Pope John XXIII, he turned the church on her ear by convoking the Second Ecumenical Council of the Vatican (1962–1965), which resulted in a tidal wave of administrative reform and spiritual renewal.

Pope John's successor, Giovanni Battista Montini, named Paul VI (1963–1975) was not a surprise. A true Vatican insider, Montini had actually received some votes in the 1958 conclave even though he was only an archbishop and not yet a cardinal (the last time in history a noncardinal has received any votes). He was the leading progressive figure of the council and was elected after several ballots in 1963.

On August 26, 1978, the cardinals elected a gentle, intellectual pastor who had been on no one's short list, in the briefest conclave on record: Albino Luciani of Venice. The surprising choice in turn surprised everyone else by choosing the dual name John Paul, a historical first. Unfortunately, he lived for only thirty-three days. The cardinals had returned home patting themselves on the back—and praising the Holy Spirit—for making such a fine choice . . . only to return to Rome to select the third pope within two months.

In a true shocker of a conclave, a "stranger from a far country" was elected on October 16, 1978: fifty-eight-year-old Cardinal Karol Wojtyla, the archbishop of Krakow, Poland. For the first time in 455 years (since the Dutch Hadrian VI, pope from 1522 to 1523) a non-Italian occupied the chair of St. Peter. And the church—as well as the world—has not been the same ever since.

In what is likely to be the near future, the 120 or so cardinals in the conclave (all but a few of whom have been given the red hat by Pope John Paul II) will almost certainly surprise observers—and perhaps themselves—once again.

WHO IS THE POPE?

The papacy, or office held by the pope, is a concept that has developed from the tradition surrounding the apostle Peter's life, ministry, and martyrdom in Rome into its contemporary form through twenty tumultuous centuries. We count 261 men as legitimately elected successors of St. Peter as the bishop of Rome. One way to understand the pope and the papacy is to examine the various titles he holds. The titles of the pope are numerous, historically and theologically significant, and somewhat mind-boggling to the contemporary observer (especially a non-Catholic). Here is a brief description of his official titles:

- Bishop of Rome: First and always, the pope's primary job is overseer of the "Holy See" or "Apostolic See," other names for the local church of Rome. The vicar general of the diocese, usually a cardinal, serves as the pope's chief operating officer.

- Vicar of Jesus Christ: This title supplanted the earlier term "Vicar of Peter," which was adopted by Pope St. Leo I the Great (440–461) in the fifth century. Vicar of Christ is, arguably applicable to any priest or bishop, not just to the pope. Pope Innocent III (1198–1216) stated that he was "*Vicarius Christi* (Vicar of Christ), the successor of Peter, the anointed of the Lord . . . below God but above man, less than God but more than man."

- Successor of the Chief of the Apostles: There are other bishops and archbishops, but only one acknowledged successor of St. Peter himself: "You are Peter. . . . I will give you the keys of the kingdom of heaven," Jesus said in the Gospel of Matthew, Chapter 16. The main altar in St. Peter's Basilica is thought to be built above the apostle's tomb.

- Supreme Pontiff of the Universal Church: The title is adapted from the Roman *Pontifex Maximus* (Supreme or High Priest). *Pontifex* means "bridge builder." The pope is also sometimes called the Roman Pontiff.

- Patriarch of the West: The pope is one of several patriarchs or "fathers" of dioceses that trace their origin directly to the apostles and to centers of Roman imperial government. Other patriarchs preside over Constantinople, Jerusalem, Antioch, Alexandria, Venice, and Lisbon.

- Primate of Italy: By tradition, a number of European and Latin American nations have a chief bishop or primate.

- Archbishop and Metropolitan of the Roman Province: This title reflects a number of factors. A metropolitan exercises ecclesiastical jurisdiction over other bishops within his province (defined geographical area). As metropolitan, the archbishop wears the pallium (a woolen stole—not a "sash," as described in *Angels & Demons*, and not for cardinals only) to signify such jurisdiction—which in the case of the pope alone is universal.

- Sovereign of the Vatican City State: The pope is a political ruler of an independent state. This title was formalized in the Lateran Treaty of 1929 between Pope Pius XI (1922–1939) and Mussolini. From the eighth century through 1870, the pope governed the so-called Papal States in Italy.

- Servant of the Servants of God: Pope St. Gregory I the Great (590–604) adopted the spiritual title *Servus Servorum Dei* to signify that a bishop is one who seeks "to subdue himself rather than his brethren" and to be "a minister, not a master."

WHO ARE THE CARDINALS?

Perhaps even more mysterious, to Catholics and non-Catholics alike, is the concept of a *cardinal*. These somewhat exotic creatures are known as the princes of the church, in part because they form the "court" of the pope as his closest advisers and servants, and in part because in olden days many of them were chosen from noble, even princely families. Most simply put, the cardinals comprise the Holy Father's "cabinet" of advisers and executives, whether they live in Rome and run agencies of the Roman Curia or are residential archbishops in capitals throughout the world. The first cardinals were primarily deacons who helped the pope govern the local house parishes (also called the *tituli*, or "title churches") and districts within Rome (beginning as early as the third century AD). As with any institution, those closest to the power became powerful themselves, and the cardinals of late antiquity and medieval times were immensely wealthy and influential, sometimes vying with the pope himself for the authority to rule the church. But as the College of Cardinals grew in size and became scattered throughout the world—and as Italian cardinals slowly lost their dominance in numbers—it became somewhat less insular and inwardly focused.

Only the pope may "create" a cardinal; it is a personal decision and his alone. Only the pope sets the ground rules for such appointments in terms of numbers (there is currently no maximum number of members in the College of Cardinals, though a maximum of 120 are eligible to be electors, per Popes Paul VI and John Paul II). In times past there were as few as three or four cardinal-electors, and the most ever to participate in a conclave was 111 (both times in 1978, though the composition was slightly different in each conclave due to death and illness).

Traditionally, the archbishops of major cities in the United States, Latin America,

Europe, Africa, and Asia (such as Boston, Vienna, Rio de Janeiro, Dublin, and Bombay) are expected to be given the cardinal's red hat, the sign of his high ecclesiastical status. The pope may choose not to do so, as well: for example Archbishop Montini of Milan (who later became Pope Paul VI) was not elevated to the cardinalate by his mentor Pope Paul XII, even after serving as that pope's closest adviser for many years. On the other hand, John Paul XXIII acted almost immediately upon his own election to name Montini a cardinal—and favored him to succeed to the papacy.

The maximum number of 120 cardinal-electors (those eligible to vote for the new pope) was first set by Paul VI in a statement at a consistory (a gathering or meeting of cardinals), on March 5, 1973, and later included in the formal rules per *Romano Pontificieligendo*. John Paul II maintained that rule in *Universi Dominici Gregis (UDG)*, but he has also appointed so many cardinals that it is theoretically possible that more than 120 could be alive and eligible to enter the conclave—contravening his own rule!

However, it is acutely unlikely that 165 eligible cardinals would ever exist under current guidelines and practice, let alone be permitted to gather in the conclave (as in Chapter 33 *of Angels & Demons*).

Currently (upon publication of this book) there are about 190 total living cardinals, including those age eighty and older, and almost exactly 120 eligible electors. Pope John Paul II has created more cardinals (231) than any pope in history, including the most at one time (including forty-two on February 21, 2001). He startled Vatican observers by naming thirty more cardinals on October 21, 2003, which raised the total membership in the College of Cardinals to the current record level.

WHAT *ANGELS & DEMONS* GOT RIGHT—AND WRONG

I. THE ROLE OF THE CAMERLENGO

The character Father Carlo Ventresca is the *camerlengo*, or "papal chamberlain," in *Angels & Demons*. He is described as "only a priest here. He is the late pope's hand servant" (Chapter 36 of the book). In reality, the camerlengo is a cardinal of the church and assumes full governing power, along with his brethren in the College of Cardinals, during the *sede vacante* ("the see is vacant") period. He enters the conclave to preside at the balloting there and to participate as an elector himself. Unlike what is said in the book, he is also eligible to be elected pope, as was Cardinal Eugenio Pacelli in 1939, who had been camerlengo since 1935 and became Pope Pius XII.

The current cardinal-camerlengo as of late 2004 is Eduardo Martínez Somalo of Spain, age seventy-seven, who was made a cardinal on June 28, 1988, and has been chamberlain of the Holy Roman Church since April 5,1993.

The camerlengo does not lock up the others, then retreat to the "Office of the Pope" (which does not exist, *per se*) to handle accumulated paperwork as the novel suggests. He is one of three cardinals who is not required to resign his administrative position, the others being the cardinal vicar of Rome, who administers the diocese, and the cardinal prefect of the Apostolic Penitentiary, who must remain able to direct the tribunal that grants absolution from grave sins, dispensations, and indulgences on an "emergency" basis. (One can only imagine what such emergencies might entail!)

2. THE ROLE OF THE OTHER CARDINALS

Dan Brown did not delve into detail about procedure and protocols, which are crucial to those involved, the cardinals.

Immediately upon the death of the Roman pontiff, the members of the College of Cardinals from around the world begin to gather in Rome. Although there is much socializing (intimate dinners, national and regional receptions, diplomatic cocktail parties), there is also a lot of work to do. The cardinals meet daily to prepare for the mourning and funeral of the late pope. This mourning period of nine days is called the *novemdiales,* and begins immediately after the camerlengo certifies the pope's death.

Meetings, called *congregations,* are held beginning on the second day after the holy father's death. The dean of the College of Cardinals (currently Cardinal Joseph Ratzinger of Germany, who also holds a number of other important curial positions and is very close to Pope John Paul II) presides at these meetings as well as smaller committee meetings with designated cardinals.

By lot, cardinals are chosen to serve on these steering committees and to take on specified jobs during the period before the conclave, usually for a rotating three-day term of office. Those ineligible to elect, cardinals over the age of eighty, are encouraged to participate in the congregations but are not required to do so, as are the cardinal-electors. Further, these elders are addressed by Pope John Paul II in his constitution:

> In a most earnest and heartfelt way I recommend this prayer to the venerable cardinals who, by reason of age, no longer enjoy the right to take part in the election of the Supreme Pontiff. By virtue of the singular bond with the Apostolic See which the cardinalate represents, let them lead the prayer of the People of God, whether gathered in the patriarchal basilicas of the city of Rome or in places of worship in other particular Churches [i.e., dioceses throughout the world], fervently imploring the assistance of Almighty God and the enlightenment of the Holy Spirit for the cardinal-electors, especially at the time of the election itself. They will thereby participate in an effective and real way in the difficult task of providing a pastor for the universal church. (UDG, No. 85)

There is a huge amount of business to be conducted by the cardinal-electors before the conclave itself actually begins: The College of Cardinals may conduct the ordinary business of the Vatican and the church at large—anything that cannot legitimately be postponed. The *general congregation,* comprised of all cardinals present in Rome, functions as a *committee of the whole* to address such business. The general congregations are held daily, starting within a few days of the death of the holy father. The apostolic constitution that governs their conduct is read aloud and discussed. The cardinals are to take the first of a series of oaths of secrecy. Financial and diplomatic matters are among the issues to be addressed.

Further, a *particular congregation,* which is composed of the cardinal camerlengo and three other cardinals chosen by lot, takes care of housekeeping issues such as funeral and conclave preparations. This group presents to the general congregation the agenda of *urgent decisions* that must be made, such as to fix the day and hour in which the deceased pope's body is brought to St. Peter's Basilica for mourning, to arrange the funeral rites and prepare the rooms for the arriving cardinal-electors, to assign rooms by lot to the cardinals, to approve a budget for expenses to be incurred during the *sede vacante,* to read any document the pope left behind for the College of Cardinals.

All issues are settled upon a majority vote of the cardinals in the general congregation.

3. THE RULES OF ELECTION

Dan Brown's vivid depiction of the papal conclave includes some accurate information, including the fact that the secret meeting in which the voting takes place begins no sooner than fifteen full days after the death of the pope (and no later than twenty days), that the balloting takes place in the Sistine Chapel, and that only the cardinals and a handful of approved staff are allowed within the confines of the Apostolic Palace (the complex that serves as residence and offices for the holy father and key officials).

Perhaps surprisingly to many readers, the rules that govern papal elections are not "ancient forgotten laws" nor "extremely complex," nor can these rules be "forgotten or ignored as obsolete," as stated in Chapter 136. In fact, the rules of the papal election were clearly (if not concisely) revised in a document called an apostolic constitution, written by Pope John Paul II: *Universi Dominici Gregis* was issued on February 22, 1996 and is only the most recent statement on this topic. It also confirms, clarifies, and amends many of the previous rules, eliminates some, adds new ones, and supersedes all previous constitutions promulgated by all previous popes.

The conclave system itself dates from July 7, 1724, when Pope Gregory X published strict rules in *Ubi majus periculum* (at the Second Council of Lyons). The first election under the conclave system occurred on January 21, 1276; the winner, Pope Innocent V, was also the first Dominican priest to be elected as pope.

In the twentieth century alone, the election rules were revised nine times, four times by promulgation of a new apostolic constitution (the most comprehensive form of papal legislation). In 1970 Pope Paul VI raised eyebrows—and cardinalitial hackles— when, on November 21, he stipulated that cardinals must lose their right to elect the pope in conclave when they reach eighty years of age. (Further, cardinals who headed agencies of the Roman Curia were asked to submit their resignations upon reaching age seventy-five.)

The "renowned Vatican scholar from De Paul University in Chicago," named Dr. Joseph Vanek (Chapter 136—who bears no close resemblance to any noted church scholar, living or dead), quotes from *Romano Pontifici eligendo* (*RPE*), the constitution promulgated by Paul VI on October 1, 1975. This document has been nullified by John Paul II's constitution. And the newest set of rules have unique provisions that both reflect the tradition and practice of the previous ten centuries and look forward to the first conclave of the twenty-first century.

For most of the past millennium and a half, there have been various methods of electing the pope allowed by church law. Such methods are designed to be fair and legal and to be open to the influence of the Holy Spirit (whom Catholics profess to be the third person of the Holy Trinity, with God the Father and the Son). Thus, the methods of acclamation, compromise, and balloting were all allowable—until John Paul II's latest constitution and well before the action of the novel.

The holy father very explicitly prohibits two of the three traditional forms of election: *per acclamationem seu inspirationem* (by acclamation or inspiration) and *per compromissum* (by compromise or committee system). He then states that "the form of electing the Roman pontiff shall henceforth be *per scrutinium* [by scrutiny or secret balloting] alone." (*UDG* No. 62)

Election by compromise meant that the cardinal-electors, if deadlocked for any reason, could appoint a committee to make the decision, which would then be adopted by the entire college as its own. Election by acclamation or inspiration provided that any member of the electoral body could rise and declare that, through the inspiration of the Holy Spirit, Cardinal So-and-so was declared to be pope; if agreed by other members of the conclave, such a candidate was chosen as pope. Scrutiny means simply, by a written ballot. The rules for the actual balloting are spelled out in detail in John Paul's constitution, which calls for two ballots in the morning and two in the afternoon.

For the first time ever—and this is the most revolutionary aspect of *UDG*, if the conclave is deadlocked after about thirty ballots the cardinals may vote, by simple majority, to elect a pope by a simple majority vote, abrogating the two-thirds requirement.

There is not, nor has there ever been "Election by Adoration." In my opinion, the author of *Angels & Demons* created this fictional rule to suit the plot of the novel, which it does rather neatly.

There are several other points of variance (some arguable) between the reality of the papal election and Dan Brown's imagined election:

- Choosing a "devil's advocate" is an ecclesiastical practice that deals with the canonization (ratification) of new saints in the Catholic Church—not papal elections. And in recent years it has been discontinued completely.

- It is highly improbable, even in a crisis, that any nonauthorized persons (such as Vittora Vetra and Robert Landon) would ever be allowed to enter the Sistine Chapel when the cardinals are sealed off from the world in the conclave.

- If four leading cardinals were missing, it is very possible that the conclave would be delayed for a period of time in order to determine their whereabouts and availability. A cardinal may join the conclave after it has begun, which would be considered an extraordinary circumstance.

- It would take years (not days) for a dead pope's sarcophagus to be carved and placed over his tomb—in fact, modern popes have not commissioned sarcophagi to be created, but have opted for the simpler, dignified burial containers found in the grotto below the main altar of St. Peter's Basilica.

- "Great Elector" is not an official office or position within the College of Cardinals. Instead, the term *grand elettore* is sometimes given, after the fact, to a "kingmaker" or most influential cardinal within the conclave. The late Cardinal Franz König of Austria (who died at age ninety-eight in 2004) shepherded the candidacy of Karol Wojtyla in this way in 1978.

- A unanimous vote in a conclave would be highly unusual, but not "unprecedented." Under the current rules and in the current climate within the universal church, it would be nearly miraculous in the next conclave.

- It would be a near impossibility for a contemporary pope to father a child in secret. In the early middle ages some popes were married, and in the late middle ages some had mistresses. Pope Hormisdas (died 523) was the father of Pope Silverius (died 537). In the Renaissance era and after, several papal uncles cultivated "cardinal nephews" who were eventually elected in their own right.

At the next conclave, the entire world will be watching for the white smoke (chemically controlled from within the Apostolic Palace) that signals the election of a new pope, the leader of one billion Catholics around the globe. *Angels & Demons* attempts to give us a glimpse into that endlessly fascinating and mysterious process, but the reality—and the results—are often more singular and surprising than anything a writer of fiction can dream up. It has ever been, since the days of Simon Peter the Galilean fisherman to the historic pontificate of John Paul II, one of St. Peter's greatest successors.

KEY DATES AND DOCUMENTS IN THE HISTORY OF
PAPAL ELECTIONS

ca. AD 64	St. Peter martyred by Emperor Nero in Rome.
ca. 150	Office of pope as monarchical bishop emerged under St. Pius I.
ca. 180	St. Irenaeus, bishop of Lyons, published list for first twelve successors of St. Peter.
217	In the first openly disputed papal election, St. Callistus I elected; St. Hippolytus became first *antipope*.
Jan. 10, 236	Fabian elected by sign of the Holy Spirit: a dove on his head.
May 27, 308	Marcellus elected after longest recorded vacancy, nearly four years.
Mar. 1, 499	Oldest text concerning regulation of the papal election, *Ut si quis papa superstite*, issued at synod of bishops in Rome; allowed the pope to nominate his successor, forbade participation of laity in election.
Dec. 16, 882	After the first assassination of a pope (John VIII), the first bishop from another diocese elected pope in contravention of canon law: Marinus I.
Apr. 13, 1059	Nicholas II promulgates *In nomine Domini*.
1179	Alexander III's *Licet de vitanda* requires a two-thirds vote to elect a pope.
July 7, 1274	Gregory X issues *Ubi majus periculum*, establishing the *conclave*.
Dec. 10, 1294	*Constitutionem* of Celestine V allowed three forms of election: acclamation, compromise, and scrutiny.
Oct. 22, 1303	First papal conclave held in the Vatican elected Benedict XI unanimously.

Apr. 8, 1378	Urban VI was the last noncardinal to be elected pope.
Nov. 11, 1417	A papal conclave was held at the Council of Constance to end the Great Western Schism, the last time noncardinals participated in election of a pope.
Dec. 1558	*Cum secundum Apostolum* decreed by Paul IV, forbade canvassing prior to death of the pope.
Oct. 9, 1562	*In eligendis* (also by Paul IV) tightened rules of the conclave.
Sept. 23, 1695	Innocent XII's *Ecclesiae Catholicae* prohibited a candidate from making preelection promises that would be binding upon him as pope.
Dec. 30, 1797	*Christi Ecclesiae regenda* by Pius VI sets rules for conclave and vacancy.
Jan. 10, 1878	Pius IX issued new regulations to be observed during *sede vacante*.
Jan. 20, 1904	Pius X ended the *right of exclusion*, or veto, that had been used in papal elections by Catholic rulers of Austria, Spain, and France.
Dec. 25, 1904	Pius X issued *Vacante Sede Apostolica*, apostolic constitution on the papal election.
Mar. 1, 1922	Pius XI ordered that the conclave must begin fifteen days after the death of the pope, might be extended by the cardinals to eighteen days if necessary.
Dec. 25, 1945	Pius XII, in the second major rules revision of the twentieth century, promulgated *Vacantis Apostolicae Sedis*, calling for a two-thirds-plus-one vote to elect a pope.
Sept. 5, 1962	John XXIII issued the document *Summi Pontificis electio*, slightly modifying Pius XII's 1945 constitution.
Nov. 21, 1970	Paul VI stipulated in *Ingravescentem aetatem* that upon reaching the age of eighty, a cardinal lost the right to vote in the conclave.

Oct. 1, 1975   In the third major constitution dealing with the papal election,
                  Paul VI issued *Romano Pontifici eligendo*, which modernized and
                  clarified some of the rules.

Feb. 22, 1996   John Paul II promulgated *Universi Dominici Gregis*, the substantively
                  revised rules that will govern the next conclave.

Source: *Selecting the Pope: Uncovering the Mysteries of Papal Elections* (Barnes & Noble Books) copyright © 2003
by Greg Tobin and used by permission from the author.

ANGELS, DEMONS, AND THE NEXT POPE

BY AMY D. BERNSTEIN

Parachuting thousands of feet through the sky, as antimatter explodes overhead above Vatican City, the murderous camerlengo in *Angels & Demons* makes a perfect landing on the terrace atop St. Peter's Basilica—and is elected pope on the spot by acclamation. This flight of fancy is one of the more improbable elements in Dan Brown's tale of a papal conclave run amok. But in fact many of the details of Brown's story are drawn, at least in part, from the annals of ancient and not-so-distant skullduggery in the Vatican, found by rummaging around in two thousand years of the Catholic Church's history. As Dan Brown writes, "Conclaves created an intense, politically charged atmosphere, and over the centuries they had turned deadly; poisonings, fistfights and even murder had erupted."

In exploring the dramatic possibilities of how a modern-day papal conclave could survive a threat to its very existence, Brown has created a story that has clearly drawn on some of the more exotic elements of the church's turbulent past, including tales of sexual high jinks. At the same time, he hints at some of the real-life issues that will concern papal electors in the conclave that looms as the health of the current pope, John Paul II, becomes ever more fragile.

Amy D. Bernstein is an author and academic with a specialty in sixteenth-century literature.

From the courageous martyrs who led the church in the earliest centuries, to the medieval papal intriguers, to the poisonous Borgia popes, throughout its long history the papacy has only been as good as the individual human beings who have been chosen to guide it. The list has included a motley succession of saintly, visionary, and statesman-like popes mixed with unscrupulous, corrupt, or simply weak ones. As the papacy has alternated between periods of acute uncertainty and upheaval and times of relative stability, men have fought—and even killed—to occupy the papal throne. Others, however, have done everything to avoid that fate. Many of the earliest popes were martyred, so acceptance of the title then was tantamount to a death sentence. Even without physical dangers, it has always been a position fraught with difficulty.

With the exception of St. Peter—who, as tradition has it, was chosen by Jesus himself—each new bishop of Rome (the pope's original and still most important title) in the early Christian era was elected by a consensus achieved among lay and religious members of the Roman community. Because of the inherent instability and potential fractiousness of a selection process involving so many people, there were a remarkable number of popes during the first millennium of the Christian church who abdicated (two), were deposed (seven), assassinated (possibly as many as eight), or who had competing candidates who declared themselves pope (called *antipopes*, there were about thirty-nine of them in history). Conclaves often involved a crisis, and some conclaves were almost as violent as the one in *Angels & Demons*, with its horrifying murders and threat of imminent annihilation. In the papal election of 366, for example, supporters of rival factions battled until 137 supporters of Ursinus were slaughtered, and Damasus (366–384) was elected pope.

Seven centuries of in-fighting later, Pope Nicholas II, in an effort finally to create a less fractious process of election, decreed in 1059 that cardinals alone would elect the new pope, though with the blessing of other lay and religious members of the community. This helped matters only a little, however, since the cardinals were still at the mercy of secular rulers who had the power to refuse their choice. The rules of the modern conclave were initiated in 1274, after an almost three-year hiatus between popes. Out of sheer frustration, civil authorities first locked the cardinals in the papal palace, and finally, in desperation, removed its roof and denied them food until they chose a pope. Pope Gregory X (1271–1276) went further, promulgating the apostolic constitution *Ubi periculum* (Where There Is Danger), which required all electors to gather in one room and remain there for the duration, completely cut off from the outside world—literally locked in with a key (*cum clave*). Nonetheless, the cardinal-elector system was not always honored until much later. At one point in the early fifteenth century things got so out of hand that there were three legitimately elected popes at once, one at Avignon (Benedict XIII, antipope, 1394–1417), one at Rome (Gregory XII, 1406–1415) and a compromise pope (Alexander V, antipope, 1409–1415) elected by a church council at Pisa.

A HISTORY MORE LURID THAN HOLY

Not surprisingly, given his apocalyptic plot, a number of the sinister particulars used by Dan Brown can be traced to a period when the Roman papacy was at its most corrupt—what the historian Eamon Duffy, in his book *Saints and Sinners*, calls "the dark century." It began with the reign of Sergius III (904–911), who was acclaimed pope after ordering the smothering of his predecessor, Leo V. His pontificate, and those of his immediate successors, were known as the *pornocracy*, being entirely dominated by the abusive and decadent Roman aristocracy. Pope Sergius III sired a son with his beautiful, promiscuous mistress, Marozia. Named Octavius, the boy later became Pope John XII (955–964), "the only recorded instance of an illegitimate son of a previous pope succeeding to the papacy himself," according to Richard McBrien, author of *Lives of the Popes*. (This particular historical detail provides one of the more spectacular plot twists in *Angels & Demons*, when it is revealed that the camerlengo is actually the pope's son.) Once he became Pope John XII, according to Claudio Rendina in *The Popes: Histories and Secrets*, Octavius "continued to gratify his unbridled pleasures, and the Lateran Palace became a real bordello, with the pope surrounded by beautiful women and handsome boys in a depraved lifestyle completely at variance with his ecclesiastical duties."

The ancient real-life fortress Castel Sant'Angelo, where the fictional Robert Langdon rescues Vittoria Vetra from the clutches of the Hassassin, often performed dual service, too, serving as both trysting place and papal dungeon. For a period after Hugo, Marozia's second husband, seized power, it served as imperial residence for the pair—until Marozia's legitimate son by her first marriage, Alberic II (the pope's half-brother), overthrew them. He imprisoned Marozia, his own mother, in the dungeon there, where she remained for fifty-four years. It was a terrible punishment—Robert J. Hutchinson in *When in Rome* quotes the former inmate Benvenuto Cellini as reporting that "it swam with water, and was full of big spiders and many venomous worms."

It took a German emperor, Henry III, in the early years of the second millennium to wrest the papacy from the grip of the Roman aristocracy, and to help launch a reform of the church and its monasteries. At a time when Europe was still divided into feudal fiefdoms, which would eventually coalesce into modern states, monasteries had become strategic centers of political and economic power. In 1066, the year of the Norman Conquest, thirty-five monasteries in England controlled a sixth of the total revenue of the country, according to Duffy's *Saints and Sinners*, and abbots were powerful enough to challenge the king's authority. The same was true of bishoprics. Simony (trading spiritual values for usually substantial material considerations) was a fact of life in the procurement of religious promotions. Pope Leo IX, followed by Pope Gregory VII, led the movement to reform the church, rid it of corruption, and transform it from a parochial institution into a properly international force for constructive change. The internationalization endured, but religious reforms were short-lived.

With the rise of stronger monarchs at the head of the new nation-states came a new threat—competition with Rome for political primacy. Pope Boniface VIII (1294–1303) was particularly good at asserting the power of the papacy, and he clashed with the French king, Philippe IV, on numerous issues. He eventually excommunicated him after the king declared him a heretic. In revenge, the French crown plotted to overthrow him. Though the plot was foiled, Boniface VIII died a month later, a broken man. Philippe IV tried him posthumously for heresy as well as sodomy, fornication, atheism, and simony, though the trial never reached a verdict. Despite his towering arrogance, Boniface VIII was also a great visionary. He founded a university, La Sapienza, in Rome, codified canon law, reorganized the Vatican archives, and catalogued the books in its library. He also instituted the first Jubilee Year in 1300, when hundreds of thousands of pilgrims visited the Vatican, among them Dante Alighieri, who immortalized the event in his fourteenth-century poem the *Inferno*. Brown's depiction of the spectacularly gruesome deaths of the four cardinals in *Angels & Demons* is in fact very reminiscent of the punishments in Dante's *Inferno*. The epic poem includes a description of flames engulfing the feet of Pope Boniface VIII for the sin of simony in the Eighth Circle of hell, while soothsayers have their heads twisted around to face backward—much like the description of Leonardo Vetra's corpse at CERN.

Dante's century and the two immediately succeeding it were crucially important in the history of the papacy in terms of classical scholarship and the flowering of religious art and architecture. Nicholas V (1447–1455), usually thought of as the first Renaissance pope, was a wise statesman and passionate humanist who encouraged the collection, translation, and study of classical texts. His personal library of 807 Latin and 353 Greek books and manuscripts became the basis of a much-expanded Vatican library. One of his successors, Sixtus IV (1471–1484), was responsible for the building of the Sistine Chapel and the creation of the Sistine Choir.

Bringing back the bad old days was a member of the murderous Borgia family, Pope Alexander VI (1492–1503), who has been called "the most notorious pope in all of history" by McBrien in his *Lives of the Popes*. He fathered numerous children with various women, practiced simony, and, by means of assassinations and forced dispossessions, consolidated the power of his and other aristocratic Roman families. Many of his illegitimate children were appointed cardinals (again, resonating with the history of Dan Brown's fictional pope). As a coda to his own violent life, Alexander VI was thought to have been poisoned. In his book *The Bad Popes*, Russell Chamberlin includes an eyewitness description from the contemporary Cardinal John Burchard, which notes the "swollen, blackened appearance" of the pope's corpse—which may have inspired Brown's own depiction of the murdered pope in *Angels & Demons*: "The cheeks had collapsed, and the pope's mouth gaped wide. The tongue was black as death."

Brown delves into some interesting sixteenth-century history by including the *passetto* in his story, the dark passageway along which the unwitting *papabili* (the correct Italian word for what Brown insists on calling the *preferiti*) are led from the Vatican Palace to await their deaths in the Castel Sant'Angelo. Hidden inside a segment of fortified wall, which ran nearly three kilometers, it was built during the papacy of Leo IV (847–855), and was the escape route of Clement VII (1523–1534) when Rome was sacked by the German mercenaries of Charles V in 1527. The 147 Swiss Guards who were left behind to block his escape route were massacred. The anniversary of this tragedy is still observed in the Vatican today, by a ceremony and mass held each year on May sixth.

Brown says in *Angels & Demons* that the *passetto* also served at certain points in history as the secret route from the Vatican papal apartments to erotic assignations in the Castel Sant'Angelo, which was part prison and part princely residence. The papal apartments there, writes Hutchinson, were the scene of numerous liaisons over the centuries. Their walls were "covered by murals of buxom women naked from the waist up, holding their breasts in their hands, like so many Playmates of the Month ... It is plain that some of the earlier popes had more on their minds than merely expanding the papal states." At other times the papacy was so dissolute that the mistresses lived quite openly in the Vatican papal apartments, so that a secret passageway was hardly necessary for popes to attend to their mistresses.

Just as the Castel Sant'Angelo's unsavory past provides a backdrop for the development of the action in *Angels & Demons*, Dan Brown uses four seventeenth-century baroque masterpieces by Gianlorenzo Bernini as clues to the whereabouts of the mortally endangered *papabili* cardinals, and as crime scenes in the Hassassin's trail of bloody revenge. By doing so, he highlights the two elements that define both the church's major strength and its major weakness—its commissioning of some of the most important and daring art in the history of Rome, yet at the same time its silencing of scientific inquiry and intellectual freedom, thereby inviting dissent and revolt. The most infamous example of the church's intolerance of intellectual and scientific inquiry is, of course, the trial and imprisonment of the astronomer Galileo by the Inquisition for supporting the Copernican theory that the universe was heliocentric. Among other things, the church's desire for information control led to the establishment of the Secret Archives, which comprised all the documents removed from the Vatican's Apostolic Library by Pope Pius IV in 1610, and which remained closed to Vatican outsiders until the late nineteenth century. Among the documents in the catalogue of the Secret Archives are the proceedings of the trial and condemnation of Galileo in 1634.

By the end of the eighteenth century, Enlightenment principles of rationalism and free-thinking had gained sufficient momentum to challenge not only the Catholic Church, but the very foundations of the European political system. Dan Brown makes much of this history by choosing as his villain the Illuminati, a secret society which he claims was founded to combat religious thinking and encourage rationalism. As several other experts make clear in this volume, the true Illuminati founded in Bavaria in 1776 obviously had nothing to do with Galileo, who died 134 years before the founding of this group. But Dan Brown uses a fictional, imagined Illuminati history to dramatize the real, nonfiction threat posed to the church by Enlightenment ideas in the seventeenth century, and in a certain sense, ever since.

All along, however, especially in the non-European churches, there have been progressive forces at work, with social ideologies such as the Catholic Workers Movement and Latin American "Liberation Theology" leavening and changing the church's conservatism, with ideas derived from the teachings of the Christian gospel. Over the last century in particular, the Catholic Church has been witnessing the development of two pronounced trends in its midst, social progressivism and doctrinal conservatism, which have spurred debate for some time, most notably since the Second Vatican Council ended in 1965. Dan Brown hints at these real-life differences in the way he describes the opinions and streams of thought of the various fictional cardinals in *Angels & Demons*, and of the recently deceased pope and the camerlengo himself.

While the lurid histories of Vatican events hundreds of years ago are clearly in Dan Brown's mind as he develops his *Angels & Demons* plot, he actually does not have to look all that far back in time for some of his inspirational material.

In the last third of the twentieth century, after the dramatic events of Vatican II, the church was at a crossroads. Under the leadership of Pope John XXIII, the ecumenical council had suddenly transformed the papacy in the space of three years, creating alarm and opposition among the conservative faction in the Curia, and giving hope to the liberals. Paul VI, who succeeded John XXIII, condemned the practice of contraception in the encyclical *Humane vitae*, but continued to implement the findings of the council. After Paul VI's death, an elderly pope was elected, with the expectation that he would be a transitional, conservative figure. In the real-life history of the papacy, the tactic of electing an elderly pope who was expected to die soon was employed on more than one occasion by deadlocked conclaves. In the case of Pope John Paul I, anyone who expected him to be a mere caretaker was soon proven wrong. Despite his many health problems, he sprang into action immediately, promoting ecumenism, peace, and outreach to non-Christian faiths. He embarked on a revision of the Code of Canon Law for the Latin and Orthodox Churches, and ordered an investigation of the Vatican Bank, whose finances were in a shambles.

When Pope John Paul I died suddenly on September 29, 1978, after only thirty-three days in office, there was conjecture that he had been poisoned, much like the murdered pope who died after "a tremendously popular twelve-year reign" in *Angels & Demons*. The official cause of his death was a heart attack while sleeping (similar to the official cause of the pope's death in the thriller, which was a stroke while asleep). Various articles and books have appeared over the last twenty-five years claiming that John Paul I was murdered by conservatives in the Vatican, but no solid evidence has ever been marshaled to support this claim. There were, however, many inconsistencies in the details given by various circumstantial witnesses concerning his death, and no autopsy was performed. In 1984 David Yallop alleged in his book *In God's Name* that John Paul I was poisoned, possibly by digitalis, by Vatican officials who wished to stop an investigation into the Vatican Bank scandal, and its investment in the Banco Ambrosiano in Milan. (In *Angels & Demons* it is not digitalis but an overdose of heparin that is used to murder the pope.)

The election of the current pope, John Paul II, was achieved, as scholar Greg Tobin notes, in one of the most surprising shifts in the history of modern conclaves." It was seen by many as a victory for the Vatican conservatives. The first non-Italian pope since the sixteenth century, this Polish cardinal was deeply spiritual, and, as Eamon Duffy says, "dismissive of the moral and social values of the Enlightenment which, he believes, have led humanity into a spiritual cul-de-sac and have more than half-seduced the churches."

In 1981, three years after John Paul I's death, an assassination attempt on John Paul II's life occurred in St. Peter's Square. This incident may also have served as an inspiration for the murderous behavior of the Hassassin in *Angels & Demons*. John Paul II's would-be assassin was a Turkish Moslem named Mehmet Ali Agca. After the assassination attempt, there was some talk that the Bulgarian secret police had hired the assassin, and that they in turn had been enlisted by the KGB. This claim was never fully substantiated, and no one was prosecuted except Mehmet Ali Agca, who was later pardoned in June 2000, by Italian President Carlo Azeglio Ciampi.

One of the more scandalous events in recent Vatican history occurred in 1998, when Alois Estermann, Vatican commander of the Swiss Guards, and his wife, Gladys Meza Romero, were both murdered in the Guards' barracks by Cedric Tornay, another Swiss Guard, who then committed suicide. At the time the Vatican characterized Tornay's crime as an isolated "fit of madness." It was rumored but never proven that Tornay, a heterosexual, was entangled in a homosexual affair with Estermann, and witnesses remarked that Estermann relentlessly bullied Tornay and blocked his advancement. Both Estermann and his wife were members of Opus Dei, which has helped fuel speculation that another faction in the Vatican, who feared the influence of Opus Dei, were behind the murders. These events were the subject of a recent book by Vatican reporter John Follain, called *City of Secrets, The Truth Behind the Murders at the Vatican*. Published in 2003, it alleges that the pope knew about Estermann's homosexuality, and that he was opposed to his nomination as head of the Swiss Guard. But Cardinal Secretary of State Angelo Sodano, supposedly linked to Opus Dei, lobbied so persistently that the pope, weakened by failing health, finally agreed to the appointment. These 1998 murders were all over the European news as Dan Brown was writing *Angels & Demons*, and, as one thinks about the actions and attitudes of Olivetti, Rocher, and other fictional characters in the novel, one can see the imprint of the Estermann affair and how Dan Brown conjures with it. Opus Dei, of course, would go on to become a major force in *The Da Vinci Code* a few years later.

THE NEXT CONCLAVE

In Chapter 42 of *Angels & Demons*, Dan Brown lists the "unspoken requisites" for papal election: multilingualism in Italian, Spanish, and English, no skeletons in the closet, and age between sixty-five and eighty years. In reality, this would be the barest of lists, and also inaccurate, since Pope John Paul II was elected at fifty-eight years old. Facing an increasingly complex set of issues, the next pope will have to have a range of talents rivaling those of the most skilled modern diplomat.

In writing about the internal debates now engaging the church, Vatican experts such as John L. Allen Jr. in *Conclave*, Francis Burkle-Young in *Passing the Keys*, Greg Tobin in *Selecting the Pope*, and Thomas Reese in *Inside the Vatican*, have identified the issues they think will figure in the election of the next pope. Most experts agree that collegiality, the subject of much debate at Vatican II, has become even more important after Pope John Paul II's lengthy reign, which actually moved toward a recentralization of authority. Collegiality would give more power to the bishops, and require more collaborative decision making among religious and lay people. The church must also confront how the laity, and women in particular, can have more responsibility in the daily life of the church, both in helping to administer sacraments and in making policy.

Vatican watchers also agree the church must continue John Paul II's outreach to other Christians—he has taken steps toward unity with the Eastern Orthodox Church—as well as with non-Christians. Building on the 1965 Vatican II encyclical *Nostra aetate*, which stressed the spiritual patrimony common to Christians and Jews and declared that the Jews were not responsible for the death of Jesus, John Paul II has made a number of pronouncements and symbolic gestures to create healing between the two faiths. He was the first pope to visit the synagogue in Rome in 1986 and established diplomatic relations with Israel in 1994. A penitential service after the Synod of Europe was held in 1986 to atone for the passivity of Christians during the Holocaust. In 1998 the Vatican issued an apology for its silence during the Holocaust, and opened up its archives for examination. David Kertzer, a Brown University professor, was given access to a number of hitherto secret Vatican archives, and recently published a book entitled *The Popes Against the Jews: The Vatican's Role in the Rise of Modern Anti-Semitism*. In the book, he challenges the church's claims of nonintervention, which it will now have to address. The Vatican's office on Interreligious Affairs has spent a great deal of time on improving relations with Islam as well. John Paul II became the first pope in history to visit a mosque, while in Damascus in 2001.

The problems of globalization, and increasing numbers of poor and displaced people worldwide, have intensified the need for social justice. Ever since the debates at Vatican II, where the council members identified the mission of pastoral care to the world's poor and oppressed as among the most important, this issue has become a chief priority.

The recent worldwide scandals over disclosures of priestly pedophilia have created a crisis that must also be dealt with as the church moves forward. The crisis has brought to the fore the debate over whether priests must take the vow of celibacy, which is seen by some as the reason for the large numbers of priestly sex offenders. In *Angels & Demons*, Dan Brown presents the case for the negative effects of celibacy obliquely by showing how the Camerlengo's life has been disastrously affected by his father's and mother's decision to remain celibate. Perhaps the knottiest problems of all facing the church, however—which Dan Brown so adroitly put his finger on—are those of bioethics, sexuality, and all issues related to the technology of birth, contraception, divorce, and the family as an institution. In his 1995 encyclical, *Evangelium vitae*, Pope John Paul II condemned what he calls the "culture of death," reiterating the church's position on everything from contraception and abortion to stem-cell research and euthanasia. A candidate's position on these issues going into the conclave may well prove to be his salvation or his undoing.

With Pope John Paul II's advancing years and deteriorating health has come a wealth of speculation about his successor, despite the fact that canon law forbids the discussion of a papal successor until after the *novemdiales*, the period of mourning following the pope's death. Nonetheless, quite a bit has been written already about which cardinals have the most potential as *papabili*, or possible candidates to be pope. The largest and fastest-growing Catholic populations are now in Latin America, Africa, and China. With two-thirds of the world's billion Catholics living below the Equator; there are some strong voices suggesting that the next pope should come from one of these areas.

Vatican-watcher Pamela Schaeffer, managing editor of the *National Catholic Reporter*, has identified Cardinal Francis Arinze, seventy-one, a native Nigerian who has run the Vatican Office of Interreligious Affairs, as the frontrunner *papabile*. In that role, Arinze has been deeply involved in furthering a rapprochement with the Islamic faith. Steven Waldman, founder of beliefnet, a popular multifaith community website, also thinks Arinze has a real shot, as does author Greg Tobin (further analysis from Waldman and Tobin can be found in this chapter). Paddypower.com, the Irish online betting agent, gives Arinze 6–1 odds.

A Latin American cardinal could also be a likely choice, since the populations of South American and Caribbean churches have become the largest of any worldwide. In this pool of candidates, Oscar Andrés Rodriguez Maradiaga, sixty-one, the conservative archbishop of Tegucigalpa, Honduras, and Cláudio Hummes, seventy, from Brazil, the country with the largest Catholic population in the world, are often mentioned as well. Jorge Mario Bergoglio, sixty-seven, from Argentina has emerged from the pack because of his moral leadership during the 2001 crisis in Argentina, and because of what John Allen calls his "genuine theological and philosophical depth." Norberto Rivera Carrera, sixty-two, is also seen as a possible *papabile*, being both strongly orthodox and a champion of social justice. He has spoken out frequently against the evils of globalization.

Among the Europeans, a witty and engaging Belgian cardinal and a popular choice among his colleagues, Godfried Danneels, seventy-one is Allen's front-runner *papabile*. This media-savvy archbishop of Brussels has a very positive reputation as an intellectual and a pastor, though perhaps too liberal to become pope. Another name which persists, although at seventy-eight he is thought in some quarters to be too old, is Jean-Marie Lustiger, archbishop of Paris. A Jew who converted to Catholicism, Lustiger has presided over a religious renewal in Paris.

Of the Italians, one particularly stands out: Dionigi Tettamanzi, seventy. Archbishop since 1998 of Milan, the world's largest diocese, he is a doctrinal conservative admired by both Opus Dei and progressives alike, according to *Time* magazine. Corriere della Sera calls him a "natural candidate."

Thomas Reese, in his 2003 edition of *Inside the Vatican*, provides an important perspective when he observes that the Catholic Church's Eurocentric foundations are caving in around it. "Western culture is no longer Christian, let alone Catholic," writes Reese. "The Christian message is now countercultural and has to compete for time, attention, and acceptance in a pluralistic environment." Those Americans and Europeans who count themselves as Catholics are clamoring for change on issues such as celibacy and birth control, and demanding more of a voice in the church's decision making. The next pope must set the tone for a consideration of the many important issues that may ultimately determine the church's survival—a theme that Brown underscores in *Angels & Demons*.

Even Dan Brown isn't betting against the church. When the smoke clears at the end of the novel, the Catholic Church, a survivor of countless other catastrophes and misdeeds, and its new pope, the heir of St. Peter, are the only ones still standing, while all the villains have failed, died, or gone up in smoke.

HANDICAPPING THE FIRST PAPAL ELECTION OF THE 21ST CENTURY

Each time a pope is in declining health the handicapping quickly starts on a likely successor. This interest has been heightened in the case of John Paul II, who put the papacy into an unprecedented global spotlight with his support for Polish dock workers, his social conservatism, his worldwide trips in the "pope-mobile," his celebration of Mass in front of thousands, and his admonishments to world leaders. Amplifying a ceremonial spectacle rivaled only by a coronation in Britain, television network anchors with seasoned Vatican experts at their side will cover the unfolding papal succession drama play-by-play. Given the secrecy surrounding the process, this will do wondrous things for the splendor which is Rome, and lend significant symbolic meaning for those of faith—and millions of others. Here, two respected Vatican-watchers preview this process, handicapping a race among those willing to take on challenges which are at once wide ranging and complex: the role of women, ecumenism, the balance of power within the church, the American sexual abuse scandal, declining attendance in Europe, and, as always, issues of theological and structural reform. Who is best qualified to handle these challenges?

WHO ARE THE *PAPABILI*?

BY GREG TOBIN

It is downright foolish to attempt to handicap the papal election, yet journalists and Vatican observers cannot seem to help themselves (myself included). In the May 11, 1998, issue of *US News & World Report*, as but one example of this long-standing guessing game, speculation focused on eleven *papabili*. Today, a half-dozen years later, five of them are over eighty, one is dead, and only two, Schönborn and Arinze, are current contenders. The frontrunner, Carlo Maria Martini, SJ, now seventy-seven and retired as archbishop of Milan, has faded from the pack, due to age and illness.

For detailed analyses of the process and the potential winning candidates, see my own *Selecting the Pope; Conclave: The Politics, Personalities, and Process of the Next Papal Election* by John L. Allen Jr., the highly respected Rome bureau chief for the *National Catholic Reporter*; and *The Next Pope* by the late commentator and papal biographer Peter Hebblethwaite.

The term *pababili* (singular, *papabile*) signifies those who are more likely than others to be elected, those who are "pope-able," so to speak. The term used in the novel *Angels & Demons, preferiti*, is not common or traditional usage among Vatican cognoscenti. And the old, often-repeated adage remains in effect: "He who enters the conclave a pope, leaves a cardinal."

Frontrunners and favorites are not looked upon with particular favor by the electors themselves.

At the time of publication of this book, there are 120 cardinal-electors eligible to participate in the conclave. Of these, the following dozen names might be considered leading candidates, or *papabili*. So here goes . . .

- **Francis Arinze**, seventy-one, prefect of the Congregation for Divine Worship and the Discipline of the Sacraments since 2002 (cardinal since 1985). Arinze has been much mentioned as a leading candidate for the past decade or so. He is considered a very down-to-earth person with a good sense of humor. He is well traveled (making frequent trips to the United States), and the fact that he is a black African is a big plus, as the church is in a major growth phase on that continent.

Greg Tobin is an author, editor, journalist, and scholar who is currently the publisher of *The Catholic Advocate*. Author of *Conclave*, his latest book is *Selecting the Pope: Uncovering the Mysteries of Papal Elections*.

- **Godfried Danneels**, seventy-one, archbishop of Mechelen-Brussels since 1979 (cardinal since 1983). Considered a liberal, and the product of the Catholic University of Louvain (a liberal hotbed, to some). Daneels, often quoted in the press about the pope and the papacy, is the author of several books on theology. He is active in synods of bishops around the world (one way in which the cardinals and other bishops become known to each other—which may or may not pay off in the conclave).

- **Julius Riyadi Darmaatmadja**, SJ, sixty-nine, archbishop of Semarang, Indonesia, since 1983 (cardinal since 1994). Being a Jesuit (Society of Jesus) is considered a strike against a candidate, but he is just the right age if the conclave is held within the next few years. He is probably the leading Asian candidate, now that Cardinal Jaime Sin, seventy, is retired as archbishop of Manila and not in the best of health.

- **Francis Eugene George**, OMI, sixty-seven, archbishop of Chicago since 1997 (cardinal since 1998). Although it is nearly impossible to imagine an American elected as pope in our time—given the superpower status of the United States, the recent scandal within the priesthood and the episcopacy, and general resentment of Americans by Europeans—Cardinal George may be the most respected prelate among the American delegation, well regarded for his spirituality and theological orthodoxy.

- **Cláudio Hummes**, OFM, seventy, archbishop of São Paulo, Brazil, since 1998 (cardinal since 2001). A Brazilian whose family came from Germany, Hummes is a Franciscan and former professor of philosophy who was first ordained a bishop at the age of forty. One sign of papal favor is the fact that he preached the Lenten retreat in the Vatican (for the pope and his advisers) in 2002. He is a strong, not so dark horse who can bring Latin American and European electors together.

- **Jean-Marie Lustiger**, seventy-eight, archbishop of Paris since 1981 (cardinal since 1983). It would be historic to elect a Jew (he lost his mother in Auschwitz) as a pope in this day and age. Lustiger has a strong reputation as a pastoral leader and a "priest's priest" in the hotbed of anticlericalism. He is on the elderly side for serious consideration, but can the cardinals pass up such an opportunity as he presents?

- **Renato Raffaele Martino**, seventy-one, president of the Pontifical Council for Justice and Peace since 2002 (cardinal since 2003). An experienced diplomat (for more than three decades) who has been the Holy See's permanent observer at the United Nations and apostolic delegate to Laos, Malaysia, and Singapore. A member of the newest group of cardinals and now firmly ensconced within the Vatican, where he is as deftly social (makes his own wine) as he is political.

- **Giovanni Battista Re**, seventy, prefect of the Congregation for Bishops since 2000 (cardinal since 2001). For more than ten years Re was a *sostituto* (similar to a chief of staff position in secular government), one of the most powerful positions within the Roman Curia—and now is in charge of presenting candidates for bishop to the Holy Father. He's a friendly and in-your-face type of person who seems to use his influential post to make himself the "insider's inside candidate."

- **Oscar Andrés Rodriguez Maradiaga**, SDB, sixty-one, archbishop of Tegucigalpa, Honduras, since 1993 (cardinal since 2001). A Salesian priest and first ordained as a bishop at the astoundingly young age of thirty-six, Rodriquez Maradiaga is on the young side for election (we'd be looking at a twenty-year pontificate). He is the leading Latin American *papabile*—others being Norberto Rivera Carrera, also sixty-two, archbishop of Mexico City, and Cardinal Hummes (see above)—and among the most conservative.

- **Christoph Schönborn**, fifty-nine, archbishop of Vienna since 1995 (cardinal since 1998). Now the sixth-youngest (once himself the youngest) member of the College of Cardinals, Schönborn is on virtually every list of serious contenders for the papacy. He succeeded to an archiepiscopal see that had been rocked with scandal caused by his predecessor (now deceased), and within recent months more scandal has hit the church in his homeland. He gets high marks for his apparent intelligence and tact.

- **Angelo Scola**, sixty-two, patriarch of Venice since 2002 (cardinal since 2003). One of the leading Italian candidates and from the most recent consistory. Scola is one of the most talked-about Italians (who, as a group, are less numerous and far less powerful within the College of Cardinals). Historically, the patriarch of Venice has been elected pope three times in the past century: Pius X in 1903, John XXIII in 1958, and John Paul I in 1978. Pius X has been canonized, and John will be soon.

- **Dionigi Tettamanzi**, seventy, archbishop of Milan since 2002 (cardinal since 1998). A former archbishop of Genoa, he is the perfect age, ideally orthodox, and in a strong position (as was a previous archbishop of Milan, Giovanni Battista Montini, who was elected Pope Paul VI in 1963). He is also a favorite of the Opus Dei movement, a personal prelature of John Paul II, whom he has in turn supported—which can be a double-edged sword in a papal election that will not favor an Italian.

Papal Chase: Will the Next Pope Be Black, Hispanic, American, or a Jew?

BY STEVEN WALDMAN

So, who will the next pope be—a black, a Hispanic, an American, or a Jew?

No, it's not a joke. All four are real possibilities. Of course, speculating on the next pope in the midst of his twenty-fifth anniversary celebration is disrespectful to the current pope, who is either doing reasonably well physically (in which case we shouldn't talk about him as if he's dead) or else is very ill (in which case we should be offering him our prayers or good wishes).

On the other hand, we just can't help ourselves!

The biggest differences between the papal selection process now and twenty-five years ago are demographic. Of the five countries with the biggest Catholic populations, only one (Italy) is European. Forty-six percent of the world's Catholics are in Latin America; there are more Catholics in the Philippines than in Italy. In 1955 there were 16 million Catholics in all of Africa; today there are 120 million.

The cardinals who will be electing the next pope are a conservative group. All but 5 of the 134 voting cardinals (aka cardinal electors) were appointed by Pope John Paul II, and most share his views. So, we probably won't see a flaming lefty as the next pontiff. Likely factors the cardinals will consider when voting: Do they pick a third worlder to reflect demographics or someone to shore up Old Europe Christendom? Do they want a young (well, under seventy), telegenic man to explain Catholicism to the world? Or an older fellow who won't stick around for quite so long?

John Allen, the Vatican correspondent for the *National Catholic Reporter*, cites an old Italian saying, "Always follow a fat pope with a skinny pope." But if there's a backlash, many analysts believe it will likely be against this pope's penchant for centralizing authority, not against his ideology.

Here are the most frequently mentioned *papabili* among the pope-watching cognoscenti.

Steven Waldman is the editor-in-chief of Beliefnet, the leading multifaith spirituality and religion website. His essay originally appeared on Slate.com. Reprinted by permission of Newspaper Enterprise Association, Inc.

Francis Arinze
Country: Nigeria
Age: 71
Assets: Black! Third worlder. Can go nose-to-nose with Islam.
Liabilities: Black? Maybe too conservative. African Catholic Church too young.

If chosen, Arinze, besides rocking the world as the first black pope, would also be a good pope to have in charge in a time of religious conflict. The former head of the Pontifical Council for Interreligious Dialogue, Arinze is Mr. Interfaith and helped arrange Pope John Paul II's first-ever visit to a mosque. "Theologically, all people come from the same God," he has said.

Deborah Caldwell, senior religion editor of Beliefnet, says of the electors, "They have to go with a Third World cardinal because of the shift of Christianity's vast numbers to Africa, Asia, and Latin America. They just *have* to," she says. "And if you add in the global clash between Islam and Christianity, the clear choice is Arinze."

Ah, but what an exquisite dilemma for liberals. A black pope who, on social issues, makes Phyllis Schlafly seem like Jane Fonda. In a commencement address this year at Georgetown University, Arinze drew protests by saying the institution of marriage is "mocked by homosexuality." If he did become pope and liberals criticized his antigay, anti-abortion views, could conservatives possibly resist the temptation to charge racism? Might be too much to ask.

It's also possible that, deep down, though they wouldn't admit as much publicly, cardinals might fear that the selection of a black pope would alienate some white Catholics. But the biggest strike against him is that the African church, while growing rapidly, is still too young, especially compared to the church in Latin America.

Oscar Andrés Rodriguez Maradiaga
Country: Honduras
Age: 61
Assets: Latin American. Friend of Bono.
Liabilities: Compared media to Hitler. Too young.

"There's a feeling that it's Latin America's turn," says Tom Reese, editor of the Jesuit magazine *America*. It's not just that there are more Catholics there than any other continent—it's a competitive battleground, with Pentecostals chipping away at Catholic market share.

So far, there's no consensus on a Latin American candidate, but the one most often mentioned is Rodriguez, formerly head of the Latin American Bishops group. He's been a strong opponent of Third World debt and an advocate for the church's antipoverty mission. He teamed up with U2's Bono to present a petition at the G-8 meeting in 1999, signed by 17 million people, asking for debt relief.

David Gibson, author of *The Coming Catholic Church* (and also of a forthcoming book on the papal election), describes Rodriguez's assets: "A polyglot, media-savvy Latin American who knows everyone in the College and would represent a powerful statement on behalf of the huge and poverty-stricken Latin American church, as well as the rest of the developing world." John Allen adds that Rodriguez is also a supporter of decentralization, which may be the most important factor of all.

One problem may be his comments that press coverage of the pedophile-priest scandal reflects anti-Catholic views of Ted Turner and other media moguls. "Only in this fashion can I explain the ferocity [in the press] that reminds me of the times of Nero and Diocletian, and more recently, of Stalin and Hitler," he said.

Jean-Marie Lustiger
Country: France
Age: 77
Assets: Jewish? Shore up Old Europe Christendom.
Liabilities: Jewish! Too old.

Lustiger's mother, a Jew, was killed at Auschwitz. If the cardinals wanted to generate excitement in Europe, choosing Lustiger sure would be a dramatic way to do it.

Do Jews consider him Jewish? Technically, yes. As Rabbi Joseph Telushkin, author of *Jewish Literacy*, said, "According to Jewish law, a person born to a Jewish mother is Jewish, and being Jewish is not something a person can renounce. However . . . the Jewish community does not normally relate to such a person as a Jew."

Lustiger is, Telushkin says, popular with Parisian Jews, but other pundits feel that many Jews would be outraged if he were chosen. "Electing him would be a disaster for Catholic-Jewish relations," says Reese. "Some Jews would see this as the church putting him up as an example of what Jews should do."

What probably really rules him out now is his age. Since the mandatory retirement age for cardinals is seventy-five, it might be a bit awkward moral-authority-wise for the pope to bust the cap. So, we probably will never get to find out whether Jewish mothers around the world would have told their children that some day they could grow up to be a doctor, a lawyer, or a pope.

Lubomyr Husar
Country: Ukraine
Age: 71
Assets: Extra holy. Good age. Bridges East and West.
Liabilities: He's American!

Husar is the head of the Ukrainian Greek Catholic Church and has American citizenship. His parents emigrated to the United States, where he attended the Catholic

University of America, was ordained a priest in Stamford, Connecticut, and taught at
St. Basil's College Seminary from 1958 to 1969.

John Allen, who touts him as a dark horse, summarizes the plusses and minuses
thusly: There are three objections to Husar's candidacy. First, he represents Eastern
Europe and, after John Paul, many believe that region of the world will have to wait a
few generations to produce another pope. Second, he is an American citizen, and observers believe it would be diplomatically impossible to elect a superpower pontiff.
Some would suspect Vatican policy was being crafted by the CIA. Third, the pope is
supposed to be the patriarch of the West, and it would be theologically odd for that
office to be held by someone from an Eastern rite.

But, Allen argues, these objections could become positives. "The first two point
to Husar as a bridge between East and West; the third suggests he could be a symbol of
the full catholicity of the church, of its unity in diversity." Finally, Allen says, "He is
also one of the most genuinely Christian men I've ever met."

Dionigi Tettamanzi
Country: Italy
Age: 70
Assets: Italian
Liabilities: Italian

Only 5 percent of the world's Catholics live in Italy. So, why is an Italian even
on the list? Because 35 percent of the voting cardinals either represent an Italian diocese or work for the Vatican administration. There may also be a sense that the church
went through its wacky experimental phase by choosing a Polish pope and needs to get
back to normal. Tettamanzi is conservative and well liked by the very conservative Opus
Dei movement; most of the voting cardinals are conservative, too. Most important, the
leading Irish gambling website, Paddypower.com, rates him as the odds-on favorite.

Christoph Schönborn
Country: Austria
Age: 59
Assets: Intellectual heavyweight. European Christianity could use some excitement.
Liabilities: Europe had its chance.

This cardinal is also a count! A respected theologian, Schönborn was chosen by
Pope John Paul II to serve as the general editor of the revised Catholic catechism.
David Gibson calls Schönborn "a cultured Austrian who is conservative but, true to
his Mittleeuropean roots, can be a bridge between East and West. Maybe a little too
close to a Slavic pope, and maybe a little too young still." His big problem is his age.

Jaime Lucas Ortega y Alamino
Country: Cuba
Age: 68
Assets: Communist country. Hispanic.
Liabilities: Communism no longer a problem.

Picking a pope from a Communist country worked well last time, so why not try again? Alamino has the advantages of being a bastion of faith in a godless land *and* being Hispanic.

Godfried Danneels
Country: Belgium
Age: 70
Assets: Witty
Liabilities: Too liberal

On the off chance that the cardinals want to go with a liberal, Danneels may be the man. "When the bishops and cardinals gather, Danneels is often the center of attention, appreciated for his wit and intellect," says Greg Tobin, author of *Selecting the Pope*. Weaknesses: As a liberal from Belgium, he might be viewed as the Michael Dukakis of the papal race.

Bear in mind, the cardinals traditionally abjure front-runners even more than Democratic Party primary voters do, so there's a good chance it won't be any of the above. An old Italian saying goes, "He who enters the conclave a pope comes out a cardinal."

And there is, finally, what might be called "the God factor." Though it's tempting (and fun) to view the papal selection like the Iowa caucuses—all about voting blocks, spin, and positioning—this is still, on some level, a highly personal and spiritual decision. There may be a cardinal who is all wrong for the political reasons listed above but who's viewed by his peers as a truly holy individual. Many people believe the Holy Spirit will be guiding the cardinals' deliberations, and God may have his own views on this, Paddypower.com notwithstanding.

PONTIFFS PAST, PRESENT, AND FUTURE

AN INTERVIEW WITH RICHARD P. MCBRIEN

Father Richard McBrien is not a Dan Brown fan. "To portray Brown as anything beyond a novelist would be a mistake," McBrien says, pointing out that the author is neither a historian nor a theologian. McBrien is both. A professor of theology at the University of Notre Dame, McBrien literally wrote the book on Catholicism—he is the author of The HarperCollins Encyclopedia of Catholicism. *McBrien does credit Brown with creating a platform to discuss questions like the humanity of Jesus and the role of women in the early church—topics covered in the earlier book in this series,* Secrets of the Code.*

McBrien should also give Brown credit for stirring up discussion about the papacy. One of the main characters in Angels & Demons *is Carlo Ventresco, the psychotic camerlengo who would be pope. While such a character is pure fiction, as McBrien knows all too well, over the centuries the Vatican has been home to both saints and scoundrels. On the saintly side, the martyr Sixtus II (257–258) refused to leave his followers and was beheaded by imperial forces while celebrating Mass. On the other end of the spectrum was John XII (955–964). He became pope while still in his teens, led one of the most immoral lives of any "holy father" in history, and is said to have died in a married woman's bed. In this interview, McBrien, a frequent commentator on church affairs, discusses popes, past and present, as well*

Richard P. McBrien is a professor of theology at the University of Notre Dame and the author of twenty books, including *Lives of the Popes* and his bestselling *Catholicism.*

as his perspective on the ins and outs of the papal selection process. All dates refer to the term of papal reign.

As you've written, over the two thousand years of the papacy some were saints, others scoundrels; some politicians, other pastors; and some reformers and some not.

The greatest pope prior to modern times was Gregory the Great (590–604), who had a genuine concern for the poor and had a lasting impact on the shaping of the pastoral ministry of bishops and priests alike for centuries to come. He was the first to refer to the pope as "the servant of the servants of God." A less well known but no less saintly pope was Sixtus II (257–258), one of the most revered martyrs of the early church. He was beheaded by imperial forces while celebrating Mass, having refused to leave his flock.

Among the so-called scoundrel popes were Sergius III (904–911), who ordered the murder of his predecessor, Leo V, and the antipope Christopher. Throughout his pontificate, he did the bidding of the powerful Roman families. John XII (955–964) was elected at age eighteen and led one of the most immoral lives of any pope in history. He died of a stroke, allegedly in the bed of a married woman. Innocent IV (1243–1254) was the first pope to approve the use of torture in the Inquisition.

The popes of the Middle Ages tended to be more political than the popes of other periods. Innocent III (1198–1216) and Boniface VIII (1295–1303) would be two cases in point. Innocent claimed authority over the whole Christian world. Boniface VIII (1295–1303) made even greater claims of both spiritual and temporal power, declaring that every person on earth was subject to the pope. One of the most prominent reformer popes was Gregory VII (1073–1085). He did his best to address the challenges of simony (buying and selling spiritual benefits), nepotism (placing one's relatives in high ecclesiastical office), clerical corruption (of a financial, sexual, and pastoral kind), and the interference of lay rulers in the internal affairs of the church.

Most of the popes of the first millennium were regarded as saints, although there was no formal process of canonization during that time. There have been only five popes canonized in the second millennium. The great reformer popes, including John XXIII (1958–1963) in particular, had a great impact on the transformation of the church. Indirectly, that had an effect on the world at large, which is why he was so celebrated for his efforts on behalf of peace. Although not yet formally canonized, Pope John XXIII was clearly a saint. Because of his warm, compassionate, nonjudgmental stance toward people, he was able to create a whole new ecumenical atmosphere in the church and inspire even atheists like the Soviet leader Nikita Khrushchev to take seriously the pope's pleas for peace during the Cuban missile crisis. He was perhaps the most beloved pope in all of church history. The former Soviet premier, Mikhail Gorbachev, credited Pope John Paul II with accelerating the collapse of the so-called Soviet empire by his support of the Solidarity movement in Poland and various other initiatives. Other popes, especially Leo XIII (1878–1903), called attention to the plight of workers in the new industrial world and spoke out in defense of their rights to unionize, to fair wages, and to healthy working conditions. Subsequent popes continued to press these points. Did their efforts have the desired effect on the condition of working people? That's a judgment call.

What were the popes like in the time of Galileo and the Counter-Reformation?

In general, several of the popes of the Counter-Reformation period—namely Paul III (1534–1549), Paul IV (1555–1565), and Pius IV (1559–1565)—did their best to address the problems of corruption in the church. These popes also appointed some of the church's leading reformers to the hierarchy, such as Charles Borromeo (d. 1584). As archbishop of Milan, Borromeo held councils and synods, made regular visits to his parishes, reorganized the diocesan administration, established seminaries for the education of future priests, enforced standards of morality for his clergy, and founded a confraternity to teach Christian doctrine to children. His reforms, in fact, were so authentic and far reaching that there was an attempt on his life mounted by disgruntled members of a lay organization that profited from the old system.

Paul III (1534–1549) convened the Council of Trent in 1545 and thereby launched the Catholic Counter-Reformation. Pius IV (1559–1565) reconvened the council after a ten-year suspension and committed his pontificate to reform. Pius V (1566–1572) enforced the decrees of the council, published the Roman Catechism, and reformed the Roman Missal (used for Mass) and the Divine Office (recited or sung by monks and priests). These reforms held up until the middle of the twentieth century when Vatican II ushered in a new era in Catholic liturgy and practice. Gregory XIII (1572–1585) reconstructed and endowed the old Roman College which was later renamed in his honor as the Gregorian University It still exists and flourishes in Rome today. He also reformed the Julian calendar by dropping ten days and adding a leap year. The calendar was renamed as the Gregorian calendar to honor him. Alexander VII (1655–1667) permitted Jesuit missionaries in China to use Chinese rites in the Mass and the administration of the sacraments, but Clement XI (1700–1721) later reversed that decision.

On the other hand, some of the Counter-Reformation popes promoted the work of the Inquisition to root out heresy, and this included the censoring and imprisonment of Galileo, placing the works of Copernicus on the

Index of Forbidden Books under Paul V (1605–1621), and the imposing of a second condemnation of Galileo by Urban VIII (1623–1644) in 1633.

How would you assess the church's relationship with the world of science over the last few centuries?
Better now than before. The church has tended to be initially defensive, and even condemnatory toward new developments that appeared to challenge its traditional teachings on one or another issue. This was true in the nineteenth century and during first half of the twentieth with regard to the interpretation of scripture. The famous Syllabus of Errors issued by Pius IX in 1864 condemned political liberalism (including democracy) and various philosophical views that exalted reason over authority as the norm of truth. In the next pontificate, however, that of Leo XIII, the Vatican archives were opened to scholars because the new pope said that the church had nothing to fear from the truth. During Pius X's pontificate (1903–1914), on the other hand, an anti-Modernist war was waged on Catholic scholars. Historians have argued that those policies set Catholic intellectual life back fifty years, not to be rehabilitated until the Second Vatican Council (1962–1965). The Galileo case, of course, has been emblematic of the church's traditional stance against science. The fact that so conservative a pope as John Paul II admitted that the church had been wrong in what it did is itself an indication of the great change in the church's official stance toward science.

Angels & Demons revolves around the events of the conclave. What is your view on the papal election process?
The papal election process makes Florida's look good. It is defective because it is secret and is confined to a relatively small group of male ecclesiastics, all of whom owe their positions to the decision of one man, the pope, and his closest and most powerful advisers.

Some of the worst examples occurred in the tenth century when the papacy became the plaything of certain powerful aristocratic families in Rome, who controlled the elections from the pontificate of Sergius III (904–911) through that of John XI (931–936). Albert II, prince of Rome, controlled the papacy from 932 to 954. The Holy Roman emperor Otto I (d. 973) controlled the elections of John XIII (965–972) and Benedict VI (973–974), but after his death, power reverted to another Roman family even into the eleventh century with the pontificate of Sergius IV (1009–1012).

The history of papal elections shows that popes—especially long-term and/or dominant figures—are rarely succeeded by photocopies of themselves. After such pontificates, the cardinal-electors seem to prefer some breathing space (which is why they often will elect a so-called transitional pope) or a change of direction. This pattern has been in play for the past 150

years or more: Pius IX was elected as a liberal to succeed the reactionary
Gregory XVI in 1846. Pius IX became himself a reactionary and was succeeded, not by a like-minded cardinal, but by a moderate, Leo XIII in 1878.
Leo XIII was succeeded in turn not by his moderate secretary of state, Cardinal Rampolla, but by the ultraconservative Pius X in 1903. Pius X, in turn,
was succeeded not by his ultraconservative secretary of state, Cardinal Merry
del Val, but by Cardinal Rampolla's protégé, Benedict XV, in 1914. Benedict
was succeeded not by another moderate but by the authoritarian Pius XI in
1922. Here comes an exception to the pattern. Because of the outbreak of
the Second World War, the cardinals looked to someone with diplomatic experience and so they turned to Cardinal Pacelli, who had served as Pius XI's
secretary of state. Pacelli took the name Pius XII. He was succeeded not by
another ascetical and aloof pope but by the warm and jovial John XXIII in
1958. He, in turn, was succeeded by the shy, scholarly Paul VI in 1963, and
he by the gentle, smiling John Paul I in 1978. That pope, as we know, died after only thirty-three days in office. The cardinals elected a young, vigorous
Slav by the name of Karol Wojtyla who continues to serve as Pope John Paul
II. Will he succeeded by another pope just like himself, given the fact that he
appointed almost all of the cardinals who will elect his successor? History
teaches otherwise. But, of course, there are exceptions to every rule.

Is the papal election process likely to change?
    In the future, the electoral process will have to include a wider representation
    of the world's bishops; for example, the presidents of the various national
    conferences of bishops and some meaningful representation of other con-
    stituencies in the church—lay, clerical, and religious. This can only happen,
    however, with a change in current church laws that regulate papal elections.
    According to present church law, only a pope can make such a change. There-
    fore, change can only happen if a pope is elected who is convinced that the
    present system is flawed.

What do you think are the key issues the next pope must deal with over the next decade?
    First, he must restore the papacy as the literal "bridge"—*pontifex* in Latin
    means "bridge-maker"—that it is supposed to be not only between God and
    humanity, but also within the human family itself, and especially within the
    church. The current pontificate has allowed itself to become allied with a cer-
    tain faction in the church—conservative-to-ultraconservative—and in the
    process has made many in the broad center of the church and those of a more
    decidedly liberal orientation feel as if he is not really their "holy father," too.
    Second, he must address openly and without defensiveness the most serious
    crisis the Catholic Church has faced since the Reformation, namely, the

sexual abuse scandal in the priesthood. He must do what the current pope has not been able or willing to do, which is to apologize to the many victims and their families and to meet with a representative group of them to express his apology face to face. He must also require the resignations of any and all bishops who allowed predatory priests to continue functioning as priests and who intimidated those who brought these scandals to the attention of the bishops and eventually the general public. Third, he must uphold the Second Vatican Council's retrieval of the doctrine of collegiality and reverse the trend of the last twenty-six years to recentralize authority in the Vatican. One dramatic way to do this is by mandating each of the national bishops' conferences to prepare plans for a new process for the selection of bishops, one that involves laity and lower clergy and that places the decision essentially in the hands of the local churches rather than the Vatican. Fourth, he must make it clear that he will use the influence of the papal office to champion the cause of social justice, peace, and human rights, and also promote ecumenical and interfaith dialogue and institutional cooperation to address these challenges. Finally, he must urge a thorough reconsideration of the church's traditional teachings on human sexuality, leaving no stone unturned, including obligatory celibacy for priests, birth control, homosexuality, and the like.

WHO IS BURIED IN ST. PETER'S TOMB?

The Illuminati terrorists of Angels & Demons *(and their "insider" mastermind) are keenly concerned with the symbolic meaning of their actions. Although Dan Brown's novel was published almost two years before September 11, 2001, there are eerie parallels between the minds of the Al-Queda-type terrorists and the terrorists in the novel. In both real life and the novel, these particular terrorists do not seek to make demands or to negotiate. They are neither looking for money nor trying to win public support for their cause. Instead, they are carrying out symbolic actions designed to destroy the symbols, as well as the underlying systems, of those they hate.*

In Angels & Demons, *the antimatter that could destroy Vatican City has not just been placed randomly, nor has it been placed at the location where its explosion would necessarily have the most destructive impact. Instead, it has been placed, highly symbolically, precisely on the presumed spot far underground where St. Peter is buried, on the very "rock" at the physical and spiritual heart of the church. There are many interesting questions—historical, philosophical, and theological—raised by this part of the* Angels & Demons *story (not to mention the convolutions of the plot within a plot that leave a trail of loose ends like a Houdini escape scene). Indeed, historians, archaeologists, and theologians have been arguing for years about whether Peter ever went to Rome, whether he is buried under St. Peter's, whether he was buried near Jerusalem, and what theological or spiritual difference these different interpretations make.*

Tom Mueller, a talented travel writer based in Rome, heard about the sheep bones, ox bones, pig bones, and the skeleton of a mouse that investigators have reported finding below the high altar of St. Peter's Basilica. He, too, wanted to try and find an answer to the question, Was Peter himself ever there? Here he shares the results of his investigations.

We also asked Deirdre Good, a noted professor of New Testament studies at The General Theological

Seminary in New York City, to address several of these questions from a scholar's point of view, including whether the symbolism that equates the "rock" with Peter's tomb is accurate. Professor Good is particularly adept at understanding and interpreting ancient languages (she reads Greek, Coptic, Latin, Hebrew, and some Aramaic), shedding new light on biblical passages as a result. She has translated her biblical references from the Greek, but notes the Revised Standard Version is a good reference for those wishing to check the marked passages further.

BEYOND THE GRAVE

BY TOM MUELLER

It was death, aptly enough, that led me to the necropolis. Sitting against the obelisk in the center of St. Peter's Square, I saw the decorous black crosses in the Vatican newspapers that announced the passing of Padre Antonio Ferrua, age one hundred and two, the grand old man of Christian archaeology. One article described Ferrua's many discoveries in the Roman subsoil, including one directly beneath me: a vast pagan cemetery that underlies St. Peter's Square and the basilica itself, containing a grave thought to be Peter's. Another mentioned a long and bitter controversy over the identity of bones supposedly found in this grave, which had reputedly cost Ferrua a cardinalate.

Curious, I decided to visit the necropolis. Soon I was walking down the long dark stair beneath St. Peter's, together with a Vatican guide, as the air grew damp around us, pungent with mold. We emerged on a twilit roadway fronted by stately little mansions of the dead, frescoed with an exotic profusion of the old gods: falcon-headed Horus with his sacred ankh, Venus rising fair and perfumed from the waves, Dionysus and a drunken rout of nymphs and fauns brandishing phallic wands. My guide, a young archaeologist with clear blue eyes, a blond bob, and a patter polished by many tours, explained that these mausoleums had once stood beneath the open sky. Some had courtyards for graveside banquets, with terra-cotta pipes leading down into the graves, through which banqueters poured wine to slake the thirst of the dead. As we proceeded, grates overhead revealed a distant, luminous ceiling of coffered gold. We were directly beneath the nave of the basilica, approaching the high altar.

At the end of the roadway, under the altar itself, was a rough block of masonry. Through a crack in the brickwork a slender column of white marble could be seen,

---

Tom Mueller is a writer based in Italy. This article originally appeared in a slightly different version in *The Atlantic*. Used with permission of the author.

like a bone laid bare. "This is the tomb of the apostle Peter," the guide announced, "marked by the so-called *aedicula*, a memorial to Peter with two marble columns, raised in the second century." The other side of the masonry block was covered with a web of ancient graffiti, left by pious visitors to the tomb. She indicated the strata of stonework built up over the *aedicula*, a neat core sample of the site: the fourth-century masonry of Constantine the Great, who built the first church of St. Peter; an altar of the seventh century; another of the twelfth; and finally the present high altar, raised in 1594, after Constantine's original church had been demolished and New St. Peter's had been built in its place.

"We should not be surprised that Peter's grave is surrounded by pagan tombs," she said. "Remember that in AD 64, when Peter died, Rome's Christians were an obscure Eastern cult, a tiny enclave in a predominantly pagan population." In that year Nero, the reigning emperor, rounded them up in the Vatican circus. Striding among them dressed as a charioteer, he watched as some were wrapped in animal skins and savaged by dogs, others crucified and set alight, human torches to illuminate the spectacle. Peter, their leader, died that hellish night, she continued. He was buried on a slope of the adjoining Vatican Hill, which once rose where the basilica now stands; in time an extensive pagan necropolis grew up around his simple grave. Two hundred fifty years later, when Constantine decided to erect a basilica over Peter's grave, his workmen buried part of this necropolis in a million-cubic-meter landfill, to create a level foundation for the church. This was the area, preserved beneath a thick blanket of earth, that Ferrua's excavation had revealed.

The guide's story matched the official Vatican account of Peter's martyrdom and grave. But she had never mentioned the question of Peter's bones.

In 1939, when workmen unearthed a stretch of sumptuous Roman masonry below the high altar, the scholarly Pius XII ordered a systematic excavation. It was a courageous decision (previous popes had prohibited such exploration), though courage had its limits. The excavators he chose—Antonio Ferrua and his three colleagues—were Vatican habitués, who worked under a solemn vow of secrecy. The decade-long investigation was closely overseen by Pius XII's longtime collaborator Monsignor Ludwig Kaas, and the actual digging was done by the *sampietrini*, the hereditary corps of Vatican City workmen. It was an inside job.

In 1951, after twelve years of silence from the site and feverish speculation in the world outside, Ferrua and his colleagues published their official report. It caused an immediate uproar. Critics accused them of faulty and haphazard archaeology and the loss of valuable artifacts. Evidence emerged of a running feud between the four excavators and Monsignor Kaas, and of nocturnal meddling at the work site. Kaas had even begun cutting the power to the dig when he and the *sampietrini* were absent, to prevent the archaeologists from making any unsupervised discoveries.

In fact, Ferrua and his colleagues had worked with remarkable objectivity. For, despite intense pressure from the Vatican community, they reported no trace of Peter—not one inscription that named him, not even amid the graffiti on his supposed tomb. Strangest of all, they stated that the earth under the *aedicula* had been empty.

Pius XII soon authorized further research in the necropolis by Margherita Guarducci, an eminent classical epigraphist and another fervent Catholic. Guarducci rapidly overturned the previous findings, and admitted a sultry breeze of Italian-style *polemica*. She discovered inscriptions and drawings in Peter's honor that Ferrua and his colleagues had, in her view, inexplicably omitted from their report; the most important of these, an inscription near the *aedicula* that she read as "Peter is within," she claimed Ferrua had removed from the site and secreted in his monastic cell. In the snarl of graffiti on Peter's tomb she discerned a "mystic cryptography," with countless coded messages about the apostle. At length she even produced Peter's remains. A *sampietrino* had given her a wooden box of bones, she explained, which were inside the *aedicula* when the archaeologists first discovered it. Somehow they had overlooked the precious relics, and Monsignor Kaas later tucked them away for safekeeping. Scientific tests arranged by Guarducci indicated that the bones had been wrapped in a cloth of royal purple stitched with gold, and were those of a man of sixty to seventy years with a robust physique—the bones, she argued, of the apostle.

Guarducci's results, which she published in a steady stream of articles and books, were criticized by the scholarly community in tones ranging from derision to outrage. Her mystic cryptography was widely questioned, as was every scrap of logic and science she had used to link the bones in the box to Peter. Her most caustic critic was Antonio Ferrua, who subjected each of her publications to a withering and sarcastic review. Some time after Guarducci announced the discovery of Peter's remains, Ferrua wrote a ferocious memorandum to put Pope Paul VI on his guard. Having methodically dismantled Guarducci's account, he reviewed with high irony the contents of the famous box, which in addition to human remains held sheep, ox, and pig bones, and the complete skeleton of a mouse.

Paul VI apparently believed Guarducci, for he soon announced that Peter's authentic relics had been found. But Padre Ferrua had the last laugh. Shortly after Paul's death in 1978, Guarducci was banned from the necropolis, and subsequently from the basilica archives. The presumed relics, which had been reinstalled with great fanfare in the masonry surrounding the *aedicula*, were removed from sight. In later years a bitter Guarducci implied that the forces of darkness, in the person of Antonio Ferrua, had sabotaged her work.

This is only the most recent episode in the age-old mystery of Peter's tomb. In 1624 Pope Urban VIII ordered the work for Bernini's towering bronze canopy over the high altar to begin. No sooner was ground broken, however, than the excavators started dropping dead. Urban himself fell ill, and all Rome whispered of Peter's curse, said to strike down those who disturbed the apostle's rest. Meanwhile, horrified eyewitnesses watched a steady stream of pagan relics issue from the church's holiest soil, some so scandalous that the pope ordered them dumped in the Tiber. One of the finds, a funerary statue of a man reclining bare-chested on a dining couch with a gentle epicurean smile, fortunately survived the papal wrath, together with its inscription:

> *Tivoli is my home town, Flavius Agricola my name—yes, I'm the one you see reclining here, just as I did all the years of life Fate granted me, taking good care of my little self and never running short on wine. . . . Mix the wine, drink deep, wreathed in flowers, and do not refuse to pretty girls the pleasures of sex. When death comes, earth and fire devour all.*

In Urban's time speculation about what lay beneath the high altar was already a thousand years old. Writers of the early Middle Ages mentioned terrifying apparitions, caves, and secret passageways beneath the church, as well as the odd notion that Peter lay buried in a pagan temple. Such ideas may have stemmed in part from chance discoveries in the pagan necropolis that we now know underlies the basilica. But they also arose from a deeper uncertainty about Peter's grave, rooted in the Bible itself.

The New Testament, which contains the only roughly contemporary account of Peter's life, makes no reference to his having been in Rome or to his martyrdom. In the Acts of the Apostles, which chronicle the apostles' deeds after Jesus died, Peter last appears around AD 44, in a Jerusalem jail, from which he is released by an angel. He then disappears from the biblical narrative, with such finality that some scholars take the delivering angel to be a euphemism for death. Paul, writing to and from Rome in the years Peter was reputedly there, omits him from the lists of Rome's prominent Christians that conclude his letters. I Peter, an epistle attributed to Peter himself, is addressed from "Babylon," which may mean Rome. The obliquity of the reference aside, however, the epistle's theology and high Greek style are wrong for Peter, an unschooled fisherman from Galilee. Many scholars reject his authorship.

Literary evidence for Peter's presence and martyrdom in Rome remains ambiguous through the late second century. Some researchers see hints in I Clement, probably written in Rome about AD 96, and in the letter of Ignatius of Antioch to the Romans, composed a few decades later. But these references are extremely vague, in contexts that seem to demand clarity. And no one ever mentions Peter's grave.

With good reason. Even if we grant that Peter was martyred in Rome, his body is unlikely to have been recovered for burial, or his grave ever marked. The Neronian persecution made being a Christian a capital crime. Under Roman law the body of such a criminal, particularly a foreigner like Peter, was often denied burial, and might be summarily dumped in the Tiber. To recover it, someone would have had to petition the Roman authorities, thereby identifying himself as a Christian—tantamount to suicide.

What is more, few of Peter's fellow Christians would have troubled about his bones. Christians around AD 64 anxiously awaited the Parousia, Jesus Christ's imminent Second Coming. Martyrs' relics and graves seemed of little moment in a world about to be consumed by fire. It wasn't until a century or more after Peter's death that the cult of the martyrs developed in the West.

The first explicit mentions of Peter's Roman sojourn, martyrdom, and grave appear around this same time. From 170 to about 210 three authors—Dionysius of Corinth, Irenaeus of Lyons, and Gaius of Rome—state that Peter and Paul founded the Roman Church. Since Paul clearly denies this in his letters, their claim is problematic. Yet it is intriguing. Dionysius adds that Peter "gave witness," evidently through martyrdom. Still more significant, Gaius says that a *tropaion* ("trophy" or "memorial") to Peter stood in the Vatican in his day. Many scholars, including Ferrua, believe this is the *aedicula* at the heart of the Vatican necropolis, dated by archaeological evidence to circa AD 170, making Gaius's the first reference to Peter's tomb.

Gaius, however, wrote 150 years after Peter's death. Christianity was no longer an isolated sect but an empire-wide movement. The hope of an impending *Parousia* had faded, and the cult of the martyrs had arisen, presumably from a desire for tangible links with a heaven that had come to seem more distant, but for more practical reasons as well. Church unity was now threatened by mystical, speculative heresies practiced by Gnostics and Montanists, who claimed access to new divine revelations. Against these dangerous innovators, conventional Christians like Dionysius, Irenaeus, and Gaius insisted that the only valid beliefs were those taught by Jesus and his hearers. They compiled bishops' lists for the major churches, to demonstrate an unbroken chain of leaders back to an illustrious early founder. The presence of an apostle, confirmed by his tomb and relics, became an ideal pedigree of orthodoxy for a local congregation, and a source of enormous prestige. The remains of Peter, Prince of the Apostles, were the most prestigious pedigree of all.

Sitting in St. Peter's Square today, I imagine the Vatican before all this—before the Baroque basilica with Michelangelo's soaring dome, before the majestic edifice of the papacy. I picture Constantine's original church, age-worn and austere, and then look back further still, to the Vatican as Constantine first saw it in AD 312, punctuated by great monuments in various stages of decay: the ruined circus, with the obelisk still standing at its center; the neighboring Vatican Hill, with its noble house tombs and silvery grove of olive trees at the summit; a white marble pyramid more than thirty-five meters high; a watertight stadium for gladiatorial sea battles; and the enormous white drum of Hadrian's mausoleum, long before it metamorphosed into the Castel Sant'Angelo.

Above all I imagine the temples for which the Vatican was famous. In ancient times, Roman historians tell us, this swampy region beyond the Tiber was an eerie borderland of fevers and giant snakes, where the voices of the gods could be heard. These historians derived the name "Vaticanum" from *vates*, a holy seer who understood these voices. Pliny described an ancient oak, still standing here in his day, on which were bronze Etruscan letters of religious significance. Later, extravagant temples and sacred compounds were built to Eastern deities. The ecstatic rites celebrated here fascinated the Romans, but were too wild to be held within the city itself. Small wonder that Peter, hero of another marginal Eastern cult, was believed to have come here in the end, or that Constantine built a glorious new temple in his honor. The Vatican has always been sacred soil.

"UPON THIS ROCK"

BY DEIRDRE GOOD

In his book *Angels & Demons*, Dan Brown describes a short and intense dialogue between Robert Langdon and the camerlengo on the interpretation of Jesus' words (see p. 480 of the novel). They are trying to find a canister of antimatter before it blows up the Vatican and most of Rome. The camerlengo declares that its location has been revealed to him by Jesus' words to Peter in Matthew 16:18: "You are Peter (Greek: *petros*), and upon this rock (Greek: *petra*) I will build my church." Langdon, in contrast, understands Jesus' words to Peter as metaphorical. He exclaims: "The quote is a metaphor, Father! There is no actual rock!" But the camerlengo declares: "Peter is the rock" and he identifies this "rock" as Peter's tomb and the location of the antimatter, saying, "The Illuminati have placed their tool of destruction on the very cornerstone of this church. At the foundation ... On the very rock upon which this church was built. And I know where that rock is."

The camerlengo is apparently taking Matthew 16:18 literally. In this passage from Matthew, Peter is identified by name and place and his tomb is under St. Peter's. Dan Brown sweeps many alternative interpretations aside to suit his plot. The text is made to conform to the author's note at the beginning of the book stating that references to works of art, tombs, tunnels, and architecture are entirely factual and can be seen today.

But has Dan Brown interpreted the words of Jesus, as quoted in Matthew, correctly? Did Jesus identify Peter's burial place (body) in Matthew's gospel as the place where the church would be built? Or was he commending Peter's *recognition* of him as the church's foundation? Was there a specific, physical "church" Jesus had in mind?

Deirdre Good is professor of New Testament at The General Theological Seminary in New York City. She reads Greek, Coptic, Latin, Hebrew, and some Aramaic.

This often-quoted passage occurs in the broader context of Matthew 16:13–19:

Now when Jesus came into the district of Caesarea Philippi, he asked his disciples, "Who do people say that the Son of man is?" And they said, "Some say John the Baptist, others say Elijah, and others Jeremiah or one of the prophets." He said to them, "But who do you say that I am?" Simon Peter replied, "You are the Christ, the Son of the living God." And Jesus answered him, "Blessed are you, Simon Barjona [son of Jonah]! For flesh and blood has not revealed this [it] to you, but my Father who is in heaven. And I tell you, you are stone [Peter], and on this rock I will build my church, and the powers of death shall not prevail against it. I will give you the keys of the kingdom of heaven, and whatever you bind on earth shall be bound in heaven, and whatever you loose on earth shall be loosed in heaven."

How does this wider context help us interpret the "Upon this rock . . ." text? What is the role of Peter in Matthew's gospel? What is the meaning of "it" in the phrase "flesh and blood has not revealed this or it to you?"

To be sure, the tradition that St. Peter's Basilica in Rome is built on Peter's tomb endures to this day. This tradition relies on identification of a first- and second-century burial site located next to Nero's circus where Christians were martyred during his reign (AD 54–68). There is no specific account of Peter or his burial in Rome but his martyrdom and crucifixion are traditionally located on the Vatican hill. By mid–second century, a shrine appeared over Peter's grave and Nero's circus fell into disuse. Constantine the Great (306–37) built a basilica over the necropolis in which Peter was believed to have been buried. The shrine in the chancel area (the space around the altar of the church) rested on a marble platform raised above the transept floor, and a canopy or *baldacchino* rose above it supported by four spiral columns. In the sixth century Gregory the Great (590–604) raised the floor level and added a crypt. Prior to Michelangelo's commission from Pope Paul III (1534–49) to design a new basilica, the troops of Charles V stabled their horses in the old one. Eventually, in the seventeenth century, Bernini's baldacchino would rise above this hallowed spot.

On December 23, 1950, Pope Pius XII made a startling announcement. St. Peter's tomb had been discovered beneath the altar of St. Peter's basilica! This was the result of archaeological investigations made from 1939 to 1949 under the basilica. A small monument marking the tomb of Peter was said to have been uncovered, and was believed to be dated as early as AD 160. The investigations were supervised by Monsignor Ludwig Kaas.

But was this really Peter's tomb? And can the bones be identified definitively? There was also, in fact, a second burial unknown to the excavators. Monsignor Kaas, frustrated by the work of archaeologists under his supervision, had taken to visiting the site alone and in secret. On one occasion, he had noticed an unopened second tomb in the monument, and ordered the workman accompanying him to open it. The tomb was not empty, and Kaas ordered the remains removed and stored for safekeeping. Margherita Guarducci, an epigrapher studying tomb graffiti, discovered these events by chance after Kaas's death. When Paul VI, a family friend of the Guarduccis, was elected pope, she informed him of her belief that in fact these remains were the true remains of Peter. The bones were found where Kaas had stored them. Analysis showed that they did indeed belong to a man in his sixties, enabling Paul VI to announce on June 26, 1968, that the relics of St. Peter had been discovered!

Although the scant remains of bones found in the tomb were initially identified as those of a man in his late sixties, more extensive study later revealed that they actually belonged to an older man, a younger man, an older woman, a pig, a chicken, and a horse.

Many scholars, including John Curran of the Queen's University, Belfast, are unconvinced by Guarducci's arguments that these bones are indeed those of St. Peter. Thus, the fact remains that there is no undisputed documentary evidence that Peter was buried in a specific spot.

Let us return to Matthew's text. Interpreters from the first century onward have read the text in other ways. Some, for example, who focus on the literary interpretation of Matthew believe that Jesus' words to Peter are metaphorical, and that they refer to the importance of Peter's recognition of Jesus as "Son of the Living God" (Matthew 16:13–18) rather than to an actual building. It is a feminine pronoun that connects back to *rock*, which is a feminine noun in the phrase "on this rock."

In spite of Dan Brown's reading of Jesus' words in Matthew, and, to be fair, most modern translations, Peter (Greek: *petros*) did not exist as a pre-Christian Greek name. It translates the Aramaic word *kepha* meaning "stone" and may well have been meant as a designated surname in Matthew 16. Simon son of Jonah is to be known as Simon Stone, no longer son of an earthly father but the "stone" at the community's base. The word also connotes "gem," or it could be an allusion to Peter's hard character.

The Greek word *ekklesia*, translated as "church," connotes "assembly" or "gathering" rather than a building. The early reformer Tyndale translated it "congregation" in 1524. By the term "community," Matthew's Jesus indicates the existence of Matthew's community, distinguishing it from other assemblies or synagogues. At this point in the gospel, after preaching to different groups who accept and then reject his message, Jesus identifies disciples and followers as a group built on the foundation of Peter. A house built on a rock remains firm (7:24–25).

Peter's authority of "binding and loosing," cited in the above Matthew passage, probably refers to "forbid and permit" in a context of rabbinic halakic or legal decisions. In 18:18, the same phrase describes community judgment, so Peter's authority is balanced by that of Matthew's community. Thus, Peter's task as holder of keys is to open the kingdom of heaven for believers by means of his binding interpretation of the law. Peter represents a disciple's dependence not just on understanding Jesus' teaching through interpretative teaching within and without the Matthean community (especially after the resurrection), but also, and perhaps more importantly, by means of revelation. At the same time, there is something distinctive about a foundation that is unique from what is built upon it. An edifice grows. A foundation does not. So the notion of office exists within a context of local community at first. Peter's ministry continues in that of the community as we have seen.

In the second century, Origen first connects Peter as prototypical disciple with "the building of the church in him, effected by the word." By the third century, Cyprian sees in Peter the prototype of every bishop. Bishop Stephanus (254–57) seems to have been the first to connect "rock" with the Bishop of Rome. Thus from the third century on, Jesus' words in Matthew were used in Rome to legitimate claims undoubtedly made earlier. In the new interpretation of scripture from the third century onward, the term "stone" is understood to connote authority located in a particular place (Rome). It continues in the fifth-century sermons of Pope Leo the Great for whom in Peter rests the authority of the pope. Augustine, on the other hand, interpreted Christ as the fundamental rock of the church. Peter's fallibility made it possible for Christians of the Middle Ages to identify with Peter. In the East, by contrast, Peter's confession itself is the rock of the church.

All these interpretations of Jesus' words in Matthew are readings of the biblical text in tension with each other and with differing implications. How do we hold all these interpretations together? By recognizing that no single interpretation is true. Hence, one interpretation may not be stressed if it excludes all the others. Dan Brown's fictional camerlengo proposes one reading that excludes all others for the sake of the plot of *Angels & Demons*, and the resonances of placing the antimatter on the presumed literal and figurative foundation of the church. However, given the wealth of interpretation on this key passage from Matthew, readers of *Angels & Demons* should not think that Jesus' words to Peter can be shrunk to fit only this meaning cited by the camerlengo. Robert Langdon may also be right! And so may a myriad of other interpretations.

THE VATICAN IN THE ERA OF
GALILEO AND BERNINI

AN INTERVIEW WITH JOHN O'MALLEY, SJ

The era that anchors Angels & Demons—*the time of Bernini, Galileo, and antipapist conspiracies—was a period in history when Rome was challenged in new ways and which changed it and its relationship to society forever. As we learned in the essay by Greg Tobin earlier in this chapter, during the sixteenth century the Vatican had been engaged in a struggle for political as well as ecclesiastical primacy; by the end of the seventeenth century the popes, while still deeply involved in European politics, put a renewed effort into providing spiritual leadership.*

What forced this transition was not just the emergence of the science versus religion debate. In 1510 the priest Martin Luther had come to Rome, only to find deep corruption within the institution. Seven years later his proclamation of protest were posted on the doors of the cathedral in Wittenberg. The Vatican's epochal battle with Protestantism had begun. Reformers like Martin Luther and John Calvin called for the church to reevaluate itself, claiming that it was morally and spiritually bankrupt. Protestantism spread not only through Germany and much of northern Europe, but even to the Italian and southern European heartlands of Catholicism. In response, the Catholics launched what became known in history as the Counter-Reformation—of which Galileo was both beneficiary (the church

John W. O'Malley, a Jesuit priest, teaches church history at the Weston Jesuit School of Theology in Cambridge, Massachusetts. Among his prizewinning books are *The First Jesuits* and *Trent and All That*.

wanted to be seen as attuned to the emergence of the new science of the heavens) and victim (the church could brook no fundamental challenge to its view of creation).

One of the most notable institutions of the Counter-Reformation was the Council of Trent. First convened in December 1545 by Pope Paul III, it continued to meet, on and off, through the next five pontificates. The Council of Trent proved highly influential during the next two centuries of church history, even though as an exercise in internal democracy, it was relatively unrepresentative. Only 31 bishops attended its opening and, even at its largest session, there were never more than 200 bishops present. Attendance by bishops from Germany, where the Reformation had its roots and made the most inroads, was particularly spotty. There were never more than thirteen Germans involved in the council's deliberations.

The Council of Trent was given two principal charges: curbing corruption, such as the selling of indulgences, and reinterpreting the church's theological doctrine. In his book Trent and All That: Renaming Catholicism in the Early Modern Era, *Father John O'Malley, a professor of church history at the Weston Jesuit School of Theology, concludes that the results were significant—and somewhat mixed. The most egregious abuses were successfully eliminated, but the retooled religious message—that only God's grace saves mankind, even though individuals are active in this process—remained somewhat obfuscated to all but the church's most theologically sophisticated followers. Nevertheless, O'Malley argues, the Counter-Reformation served its purpose and laid the groundwork for a stronger, though more repressive, Catholic Church. The church that emerged from the Counter-Reformation felt itself victorious. Popes celebrated this victory by glorifying their faith: they commissioned new churches and hundreds of works of art around the Vatican. Bernini would work on many of these new churches and monuments— and several would become the scenes for the brutal murders in the fictional world of* Angels & Demons.

It is this Vatican—the Vatican of the sixteenth and seventeenth centuries—that is the backdrop for much of Dan Brown's novel. In this interview, O'Malley, one of the leading experts on this period of church history, discusses the issues that confronted the church, focusing on its attitudes toward science and art. He also asserts his informed opinion that the Secret Archives of the Vatican, which Dan Brown makes so much of, contain no real secrets after all.

Can you describe the overall political climate that the Catholic Church found itself in during the sixteenth and seventeenth centuries? What led to the Counter-Reformation?

In the sixteenth century the church faced one of the biggest challenges in its history with the Protestant-Reformation launched by Martin Luther that soon spread to parts of Germany, all of Scandinavia, England, Scotland— and, for a while, Poland. The Protestant era erupted because Marin Luther and John Calvin felt that the basic Christian message had been deformed by the church, that the "old church" had suppressed the true message of the scripture, and that the principal culprits were the popes. The Protestant groups differed among themselves on many points, but they all agreed that the papacy had to go, that it was even a creation of the devil. The Reformation may not have had the success it did if certain political leaders had not decided to use it for their own political advantage. For example, King Francis I of France severely repressed Protestant movements in France, but he gave aid and comfort to German Protestants in order to cause trouble for his political rival, Emperor Charles V.

The Counter-Reformation is the efforts of Catholic leaders such as popes, kings, princes, dukes, bishops, etc., to counter the Protestant-Reformation in one form or another. They did it by giving a good example of Christian living (often preached, not so often practiced), but also by mounting armies and navies, like the Spanish Armada, to try to defeat the enemy. In the same vein, Catholic monarchs (including the pope) promoted Inquisitions to dig out dissenters. It must be remembered though, that Protestant leaders used similar tactics. In Geneva, for example, John Calvin established an institution known as the Consistory, whose purpose was to seek out and, when warranted, punish misbelievers. In the England of Elizabeth I, the Court of Star Chamber did the same, although it preferred to label them traitors rather than heretics. In the sixteenth century, correct religious belief was a concern of both Protestants and Catholics, and governments believed it was their responsibility to assure it and to protect their subjects from error.

Why was the Council of Trent such a turning point in religious history?

The Council of Trent was in part a Catholic attempt to answer the theological questions and disputes that Luther and Calvin had raised. The term that I think is best for the period, the one that I use in my books, is *Early Modern Catholicism.*

From the very beginning of the Reformation in 1517, a council was seen as the traditional and most equitable way of dealing with the emerging religious crisis. Had the council been able to meet, say, in the early 1520s it might have stemmed the Reformation before it built up such momentum. But political forces (including the papacy, which feared a council might try to curb its powers) coalesced to prevent an early meeting. The first session of the Council of Trent was not until 1545, a good generation too late!

Nonetheless, the council, through many difficulties over a seventeen-year period, answered the doctrinal questions raised by the Protestants. The bishops wrote a justification document that concluded: it's God's grace that saves us, we don't save ourselves, but we are active in this process, we're not just puppets being pulled on strings, predestined to heaven or hell as Luther and Calvin seemed to be saying. The problem with the justification document was that it was so complicated that people didn't get it—it had an effect on theologians, but didn't translate into the pews and preaching. And you ended up with the following characterization of it: do good works and God will take care of you. That's not what was decreed.

Perhaps more important than the doctrinal issues, the Council of Trent took effective steps to reform the bishops, principally by forcing them to re-side in their diocese and do their traditional job. It also insisted that no one could be bishop of more than one diocese at the same time, an abuse that had made for absentee bishops. Such "pluralistic" bishops collected the money for the job, hired a vicar, and led a pleasant life at a place of their choice. Many bishops, of course, were conscientious and sincere, but a disturbingly large number were careerists.

No pope ever set foot in the Council of Trent—one reason is that it was so far from Rome, in the foothills of the Alps. The other reason is that the German emperor, Charles V, did not want the pope to attend because it was to be bishops making the decisions. At the end though, they did bring documents to the pope to sign off on. Papal ambassadors were there—so the papacy had a loose control over the deliberations. At the council, a cynical French bishop said, "In previous councils, the bishops were inspired by the Holy Spirit. At this council the inspiration arrives in letters from Rome."

By the seventeenth century the quality of bishops had improved and the quality of preaching had improved. To a considerable extent, the problems had been taken care of. One of the ironies of the Council of Trent, however, is that it really wanted to emphasize the authority of bishops and limit the way the papacy was operating. But as things worked out, the council actually provided support for papal authority because it met under the auspices of the pope, came to a successful conclusion under the pope, and then the pope claimed the right to interpret and implement the conclusions of the council. In the long run, that served to enhance papal authority.

What was the state of scientific investigation at this time?
By the middle of the seventeenth century, faith in Aristotle's texts was being replaced by faith in controlled experimentation. The scientific revolution was under way! There was no real opposition between science and religion, though. Until Galileo, most scholars were agreed that since God created the world and since we could understand it, there could be no conflict between what God said in the Bible and what he said in creation. But with the crisis over Galileo, the conflict began, as we see better in retrospect.

Galileo is an emblem of the conflict. But what you have to realize is that it started as disputes among academics. The church was only peripherally in-volved. There were those scientists who were convinced that Aristotle and Ptolemy were right, that it was an earth-centered system. Then there were those eccentrics, beginning with Copernicus, who began to question this. It was a series of accidents that Galileo was eventfully condemned for his posi-tion. Some say to this day it was his own fault—he was doing things that so irritated people. He was a good friend of Pope Urban VIII and they had had a number of conversations. Urban was open to his ideas in a casual, friendly way, but Galileo had been told that he was not to propose his ideas as true, though he could propose them as a theory. He ignored that advice and published his book. The pope was told he'd been made a fool of. Even so, the pope abstained from the whole controversy. But the bureaucrats in Rome were more aggressive. The trouble with Galileo's theory was that it seemed to contradict scripture, so how could it possibly be true? The pope still didn't intervene but there were a lot of bad practical results for the church: bit by bit people were coming to see that Galileo was right.

How is it that the popes became so deeply interested and connected to art?

The "Vatican"—the Vatican quarter of what was once just Rome—has only been the regular residence of the popes only since the fifteenth century (and their exclusive residence only since 1870). The Vatican as we know it today is basically a Renaissance product—the Sistine Chapel, the "new" St. Peter's, etc. The basis for its importance is the certainty that the spot was venerated as the tomb of St. Peter from the second century forward (and there is solid archeological evidence that indicates he was in fact buried there after he was executed in the first century).

By the baroque era, the popes were secure and there was a certain sense of serenity and a desire to glorify Rome. The popes were interested in making Rome the most beautiful and advanced city in Europe. Rome was the artistic center of the world. It's where everything was happening in the sixteenth and seventeenth centuries. One of the great projects in Rome at the time was completing the "new" basilica of St. Peter, which had been begun a century earlier and on which Raphael and Michelangelo had worked. Then in the seventeenth century, Bernini, along with several other important artists and architects, worked on it.

The popes became great patrons of art for several reasons. Perhaps the most important was the long tradition that held bishops responsible for providing beautiful places of worship. Bishops, as the chief citizens of their cities, were also responsible for enhancing artistically even the more secular aspects of urban life, such as laying out good streets, constructing fountains to supply water, and so forth. Especially beginning in the fifteenth century, the popes patronized artists also to enhance their prestige and the prestige of their city, Rome.

Of all of Bernini's artistic accomplishments, which are the greatest?

Bernini designed the Piazza of St. Peter's. It's an incredible engineering feat, finished in the seventeenth century. When it rains today, there are still no puddles. It's a spectacular entrance to the church—commissioned under several different popes. Once you get inside the church, Bernini did a number of things, but the two most spectacular are the Baldacchino, the bronze tent over the papal altar at the nave of the church, and the so-called Chair of St. Peter at the apse of the church. The Baldacchino is over the altar, which is over the traditional place where St. Peter is believed to be buried. It was done for Pope Urban VIII and the symbol of his family, the Barberini's, is the bee. If you look closely, you'll see bees are crawling all over the Baldacchino. The Chair of St. Peter was a wooden chair that by tradition was supposed to be the chair from which St. Peter taught in Rome—that's not true, but it is an old, old relic. So Bernini encased it in bronze with gold leaf and surrounded it with four saints and above it put an alabaster window with a dove representing the Holy Spirit.

In Angels & Demons, *Dan Brown writes about the secret Vatican archives. Are there really secret archives and what is in them?*

The Vatican has a number of archives. The best known and most extensive is the so-called Secret Vatican Archives. The word *secret* is in this instance badly misleading. It means simply "private," that is, it is the official, diplomatic correspondence of the pope (usually through some office of the Curia). In other words, it is no less nor no more secret than the archives of the US State Department. Those "secret" archives were officially opened to the public in the late nineteenth century, and qualified scholars of any religious persuasion are free to use them. This library, perhaps the most extensive in the whole world, goes back to antiquity. It contains the archive of the Inquisition, which contains records of trials for heresy, denunciations, and so on. But, of course, most of the documents are from the modern era. As with all archives, "recent" documents (records that might touch living persons) are still closed, and are opened as time marches on.

So, what's your overall assessment of the period since the Council of Trent in the history of the papacy? Has the pope's power grown through the centuries?

The pope as bishop of Rome has from the earliest centuries claimed special prerogatives. These claims have grown over the centuries. The pope now runs the church as a whole, rather than the earlier practice of really independent units just loosely bound together. The pope claims to speak infallibly and makes decisions without seeking the consent of the church. As the pope's power has increased, so has the power of the Curia, the collective name for the Vatican bureaucracy. Especially with the ease of communications since the invention of the telegraph, then the telephone, and now email, more and more issues have been referred to the Vatican for a decision. And those decisions are handled by the different bureaus, which means that the decision-making power has—especially in the past hundred years—shifted more and more to the center and away from the local authorities, especially away from the bishops. The Catholic Church is now a highly centralized institution. The advantages are obvious, but the disadvantage is that initiative is stifled on the local level.

THE CHURCH SINCE GALILEO: PROBLEMS THEN ARE STILL PROBLEMS NOW

AN INTERVIEW WITH JOHN DOMINIC CROSSAN

The interaction between science, religion, and the search for truth has often been contentious—dating back to the days of the earliest "heresies" and reaching a major new focal point in the trial of Galileo. John Dominic Crossan, an author of over twenty books on Christianity and frequent commentator on church affairs, believes that Galileo's trial by the Inquisition was more about the church asserting itself to maintain its authority than it was about scientific theory or theology. He also believes that the two major problems facing the church today—fundamentalism and the abuse of authority—are the same problems that existed in Galileo's time. The fundamentalists, then and now, Crossan believes, read the Bible too literally, often missing its deeper meanings. His harshest criticism is directed at the lack of accountability within the church. Being responsible to no one, Crossan argues, the pope is increasingly estranged from the church and its followers. This is similar to the climate of belief in Galileo's day, when heretics were punished as much for questioning papal authority as for their specific beliefs. The issues today are different—birth control, pedophiliac priests, and the like—but the underlying argument about papal authority still reverberates. Crossan isn't optimistic that things are likely to change now any more than they were in the sixteenth century. The next pope, he points out, will be elected by cardinals who are fiercely loyal to the old pope—and the status quo.

Like Robert Langdon, the scholarly hero of Angels & Demons *who tries to solve his high-stakes*

John Dominic Crossan, a former monk and priest, is the author of over twenty books and a frequent commentator and lecturer on church issues.

puzzle at the intersection of historical documents and baroque monuments, Crossan tries to find religious truths among the "texts and the stones," often combining sophisticated readings of the Bible with historical information from archaeological finds. A preeminent expert on the historical Jesus and coauthor of the forthcoming book In Search of Paul: How Jesus's Apostle Opposed Rome's Empire with God's Kingdom, *he is a former monk—a member of a thirteenth-century order called the Servites—and priest. Here, he discusses the role of the church since Galileo's time in general, and its position on science in particular.*

How, historically, has the church treated science, scientific discoveries, and scientists? Was Galileo wronged?

There is no actual conflict between the church and science. But there is a serious conflict between the authority of the church and anyone, from any field or discipline, who disagrees with its authority. Galileo said, in effect, that the book of Joshua was wrong in imagining the sun as circling the earth. The proper answer to that should have been either the Bible is wrong or the description is metaphorical. But the dispute was not about scientific research. It was about biblical and papal authority. I was a priest in 1968. I said the pope was wrong to be against birth control, but he was still my pope even when he was wrong, just as I thought my country was wrong to be in Vietnam, but it was still my country. I was forced out of the priesthood for saying that. It's the same kind of thing but even more with theology. You cannot question papal authority.

There are those who believe the church finally put the Galileo controversy behind itself with its review of the Galileo matter in the 1990s and those, on the other hand, who call the "apology" that was issued half-hearted.

I thought it was a huge joke—three hundred years later to admit you were wrong. Really, three hundred years is a little bit slow. It's not like it was a hidden thing that no one knew about. To say that Galileo versus the church is about science is bunk! I'd much prefer to see a papal statement now admitting that there was and is a general abuse of power by authority within the church.

Let's discuss some other historical matters. Was the Council of Trent effective in dealing with the issues facing the church four centuries ago?

The Counter-Reformation against Luther triggered the Council of Trent. The Council of Trent cured the symptom—corruption—but not the problem, the abuse of authority. It was over the latter, not the former, that the church ultimately split into Catholic and Protestant wings. The Reformation and Counter-Reformation were a combined disaster. Not that the church did not need reform—it did then and still does now. But after that period the

Roman Catholic Church had no valid loyal opposition from within. And Protestantism, having no Roman Catholicism to oppose, splintered internally again and again into a multitude of sects. The Council of Trent removed the immediate symptoms but left the cancer to continue its work.

How has the church handled weighty scientific questions like evolution and cosmology?

If someone reads Genesis and takes it literally, you can't accept evolution. I would never read it literally, not just because of evolution, but because it was clearly intended as a magnificent hymn to the Sabbath. The Sabbath is even bigger than God—not even God can create the world without being finished by Friday evening. It's not that the world was really created in any set of six days. It was created in six days so that God could rest on the Sabbath. Genesis I is a divine message for the sanctity of the Sabbath. That's what the person who wrote it meant. Evolution helps you see it should have been read metaphorically all along. Once you accept evolution, the whole cosmology of the universe doesn't represent a threat any longer. The old cosmology was a common sense one—like we still say that the sun "rises" or "sets." Since at least the beginning of the last century the church has read Genesis I more metaphorically—and more accurately. Why? The argument for evolution had too much evidence, so they had to find another way to view the Bible. Once you do that, you don't get locked into a fight between the fundamental and literal interpretation. The biblical writers told magnificent stories. Before the Enlightenment, people always knew the difference between literal fact and metaphorical fiction but they also had a far greater capacity to take a story seriously and accept it programmatically. After the Enlightenment, we took these stories too literally and thus created our own problems.

In your writings, you have taken on what you consider to be some of the "deceptions" that have been perpetuated by the church: that Jesus was never buried, for example, and that the Shroud of Turin is a fake. Are these symptoms of a larger problem facing the church?

There is a basic problem endemic to Roman Catholics and most other religions in deciding what is metaphorical and what is literal in their sacred texts or constitutional laws. That is the central problem of religion that makes fundamentalism so dangerous: the fundamentalists take literally what was intended metaphorically or they take as permanently relevant what was temporarily valid. The irony is that Dan Brown writes a book that mirrors and magnifies that very problem. Most people reading him do not have the slightest idea where the literal fact ends and metaphorical fiction begins in his work.

At the beginning of the twentieth century, a number of theologians and philosophers tried to adapt Catholic thought to a new age—Modernism, as it was called. But these efforts were crushed by the rule of Pius X (1903–1914). How and why did this happen?

In one sense Modernism was the first attempt to have the Second Vatican Council, which wasn't convened for another fifty years. Modernism was accepting the spirit of the age. In every era, people of faith have to decide what changes and what doesn't. But Pius X dug in his heels and wouldn't change. He condemned anything that he thought threatened the habits of the church. He lost some of the best minds in the church and the church sacrificed its influence on what was changing. It lost its ability to criticize by saying that everything was wrong.

How did the Vatican relate to the great dictators of the twentieth century—Hitler and Stalin?
The church was peculiarly unready to handle the dictators. If you have no accountability like the church, then that makes you very weak in dealing with a dictator. The pope didn't recognize a quantum leap in human evil. Hitler and Stalin were trying to control the minds and hearts of people. The church absolutely miscalculated with Hitler. Pius XII didn't have a clue how dangerous Hitler was. He signed a pact with Hitler, thereby emasculating the Catholic Church in Germany, which was the only strong opposition to Hitler. The church needs to say that action was dumb and disastrous.

How much has Pope John Paul II changed the direction of the church?
He's not changed the direction of the church in any significant way. Pope John XXIII, convened the Second Vatican Council (1962–1965), which set out to bring the church up to date. It was the modern equivalent of Council of Trent—but it wasn't fighting against the threat of reformation. It was an ideal situation to re-create the church, to modernize it. But there was no structural change. There was cosmetic change. The Second Vatican Council brought together all the bishops of the world. But they don't run the church, the pope does. Unfortunately, John Paul II dismantled the progress of the Second Vatican Council and reversed whatever headway had been made. He increased greatly the number of cardinals, but the College of Cardinals is an institution that has no basis in scripture and, as an institution, I'd put it up there with Disney World and the British monarchy—a heck of a show.

As for Pope John Paul's attitude toward science, he has no problem understanding Genesis, Chapter I, but he doesn't go the next step. If the Bible, the inspired word of God, can be outdated (but not wrong), couldn't the pope's position on some issues be outdated, too? He's not open to the message that something needs to change. How many priests have to go and how many have to stay that are pedophiles before the pope says there is something seriously wrong? Pope John Paul II has split the church down the middle. Sure, a huge number of people will turn out to see him in the United States when he visits, but then they ignore him when he' s gone. That's not leadership, that's entertainment.

What do you believe to be the major issues today's Vatican must deal with? Are they any different now than they were a few decades ago when you were still a priest?

The most important issues are the ones that the Vatican is still trying to avoid. First, fundamentalism. Second, what type of authority the pope should have or, to put it in a broader context, what style of authority is appropriate for the church as the People of God. What is lacking in the current system is any kind of accountability. How does the pope know when he's wrong?

There is no accountability for the pope. He can do whatever he wants and if people do not follow him, he can simply say they are bad people. Consider, for example, the fact that so many Roman Catholics in the United States do not follow the church's rules on sexual matters. That might not mean they are bad people. Instead, it might be a message from the Holy Spirit that the pope himself is out of touch with God. But how does God get through to a pope? How should power be exercised in the modern Catholic Church? The church leaders say they listen only to God, only to the Holy Spirit. What they really mean is that they listen only to themselves.

These problems of leadership authority are not new—they've been there for at least a thousand years. It is the problem that split the church East from West. The East had no problem with the pope as first among equals, but said that he should not and could not act alone: alone–he must act with the bishops and the whole church. The West itself split again later over the same issue of papal authority, between Protestantism and Catholicism. And now there's a covert split in the church between those who attempt to follow and extend Vatican II and those who resist it and seek to reverse its trajectory.

In my memoir, *A Long Way from Tipperary: What a Former Irish Monk Discovered in His Search for the Truth,* I wrote, "I make this suggestion for the future of the church I love. It is a proposal that will not solve everything but without which we may not be able to solve anything. I imagine something like this. There is a Third Vatican Council. The pope convenes all the bishops of the entire world. Then, in a solemn public ceremony in St. Peter's Basilica they all implore God to take back the gift of infallibility and grant them instead the gift of accuracy."

Dan Brown devotes a large part of Angels & Demons *to describing the inner workings of a fictional papal selection process. How do you think the next real life papal selection process will work?*

The present pope has been in charge for twenty-five years and so he has appointed most of the cardinals. Think of them as a cabinet. It's like President Bush being president for life and then also appointing a cabinet that will select his successor. How can change occur under these circumstances? The cardinals are not even representatives of the bishops, they are hand-picked by the pope. When anyone in authority appoints those who choose his own successor, there's no accountability. In the case of the Vatican, it's a good way to control the future and it shows a disastrous lack of trust in the Holy Spirit. Once upon a time in the Bible, people trusted in the Holy Spirit. Judas was replaced by casting lots among the possible candidates. That's the way the twelfth apostle was chosen. I'm not suggesting it as a new conclave procedure, but I admire its spirit and appreciate it as graphically showing trust in the Holy Spirit. If you stack the conclave that elects your successor, you are preempting the power of God. Why make it so hard for God?

What other issues will come into play at the conclave that picks the next pope?
There is a gap between social justice and ecclesiastical justice. The present pope calls for justice and dignity for all, but won't even allow a discussion of women serving as priests. I prefer justice that applies both socially outside the church and ecclesiastically inside it.

The next pope will be someone who was probably appointed a cardinal by the present pope. I would not be surprised to see a black pope from Africa. That would send a tremendous message of openness to the third world. Such a pope would probably be socially more radical, but religiously more conservative than even the current pope. He will talk about social justice, but the critical religious questions facing the church—about birth control, population control, etc., and above all, questions of papal authority—will remain unasked and therefore unanswered.

2: Galileo: The Pious Heretic

Combative yet compliant: the contradictory nature of a pioneer scientist • Copernicus, originator of the heliocentric theory, upon whose shoulders Galileo would stand • The emerging conflict between the Book of Nature and the Book of God • The battle for control over "truth" and how man comes to know it • Was Galileo's trial to some degree his fault? • How Dan Brown—and many others—have turned Galileo into a myth

Galileo Opened the Skies to the Mind of Man

BY JOHN CASTRO

Galileo Galilei's life was a study in contradictions. The future martyr of science was educated in a monastery until the age of fifteen, and passionately wanted to be a monk. But his father, Vincenzo, wanted him to train in medicine instead, a money-making, worldly profession. He wrested his son from the church before he could take vows. After two years Galileo abandoned medicine to pursue a new passion: mathematics. He entered the far less cloistered life of Pisa and its university, developing a worldly, gregarious nature in the process. Stillman Drake, translator and famed scholar of Galileo, summed up his worldly persona:

> *He thrived on companionship, and his mistress bore him three children . . . he delighted in wine . . . He took pleasure in conversing with artisans and applying his science to their practical problems. . . . Galileo was personally skilled in art, talented in music, and devoted to literature.*

Galileo's greatest early intellectual influence, his father, was an iconoclastic court musician and music theorist who attacked those who blindly followed theory. "It seems to

---

John Castro is a New York City–based writer, editor, researcher, and theater director with a particular love of Shakespeare. He also contributed to the previous book in the series, *Secrets of the Code.*

me," Vincenzo once said, "that they who rely simply on the weight of authority to prove any assertion, without searching out the arguments to support it, act absurdly." Galileo not only inherited his father's empirical bent but also his bellicose style. He vociferously offended his rivals, not hesitating to skewer them in public debates. "Galileo was nothing if not combative," Drake says. This trait won him many enemies. Yet Galileo's worldly side helped him become a skilled flatterer and courtier. He cunningly plied the great ecclesiastical and secular leaders of Italy for their backing, offering them scientific inventions in exchange for favors and appointments.

By entering academic life, young Galileo seems to have transferred some of his religious zeal into his intellectual discipline. He came to believe that mathematics unlocked the secrets of the world. "This grand book the universe," he once said, "is written in the language of mathematics." If mathematics was "written" into the world, God was its author, revealing himself in nature. This gave Galileo's inquiries into physics a religious sentiment: "Holy scripture and nature proceed equally from the divine word . . ."

The tension between these worldly and intellectual tendencies is reflected in Galileo's scientific and technical achievements. He was a consummate inventor and artisan. He constantly experimented with and invented many practical devices, including water pumps, highly accurate balances, military compasses, thermometers, and navigational aids. He developed a keen eye for developing devices to benefit his patrons.

It was in theoretical sciences, however, that Galileo made his greatest mark. While he is famous for his observation of the heavens, his most significant contribution to the sciences was his willingness to make detailed observations to test theory. By closely reading God's "grand book of the universe" without prejudice or bias, he introduced the world to experimentation. This is why, in Einstein's words, he was the founder of modern science: "All knowledge of reality starts from experience and ends in it. Because Galileo saw this, and particularly because he drummed it into the scientific world, he is the father of modern physics—indeed, of modern science altogether."

What was it about these endeavors that landed Galileo before the Inquisition? What was at stake for the church? Galileo believed that the Bible was not a source of knowledge about the natural world, but rather a moral guide written in sometimes figurative language. If science contradicts scripture, then the scripture in question needs to be seen as a figurative moral lesson, not a description of the natural world.

Galileo's accusers, the philosopher and Galileo scholar Richard J. Blackwell explains in his essay "The Scientific Revolution," would not have disagreed on this point, but would have "insisted on a critically important modification. Since God is its author, every statement in the Bible must be true . . . the loyal Christian believer is required to accept it as true as a matter of religious faith." Therefore, judgments about whether scripture was literal or figurative would fall under the final authority of the church.

By insisting on the truth of the Copernican doctrine, Galileo "claimed that science could force theologians to change their views, rather than vice versa," according to Charles Seife, author of *Alpha and Omega*. Galileo was implicitly declaring himself a theologian superior to the leaders of the church. Unfortunately there were greater challenges to the church than Galileo's astronomical revolution. The Protestant Reformation and the threat of open warfare between Protestant and Catholic forces throughout Europe had placed the Holy See on high alert for any breaches in doctrine. The fundamental strength and influence of the church was being called into question in every sphere, literally and figuratively. Armies were on the march, and neither political nor intellectual rebellion would be tolerated.

Surprisingly, Galileo retained a devout attitude toward the Catholic Church. Before his abjuration (renunciation) before his tormentors, Galileo insisted on removing from the formal declaration of guilt an abhorrent clause that "suggested he had lapsed in his behavior as a good Catholic," writes Dava Sobel, author of *Galileo's Daughter*. Galileo could deny his most closely held scientific beliefs, but he could not surrender his Catholicism to any kind of blemish. The clauses were stricken, and, freed from this ultimate indignity, Galileo abjured "with a sincere heart and unfeigned faith ... the said errors and heresies, and generally all and every error and sect contrary to the Holy Catholic Church."

"He was a Catholic who had come to believe something Catholics were forbidden to believe," writes Sobel. "Rather than break with the church, he had tried to hold—and at the same time not hold—this problematic hypothesis, this image of the mobile earth."

In 1992 the Catholic Church, under the leadership of Pope John Paul II, issued a "formal recognition of error" in the Galileo affair. Ironically, the commission declared that Galileo had been "more perceptive" in his scriptural interpretations than the theologians who had judged him. Galileo's accusers had mistaken which scriptures needed to be believed literally and which needed to be interpreted figuratively. Galileo, in short, was right—not because the church had unjustly persecuted him for his science, but because he had a keener insight into the way the Bible should be interpreted in the light of science. In its own way, the Vatican's recognition marked little or no change from theological attitudes of Galileo's time. Statements about the natural world still fell under church authority. The only difference was that Galileo's interpretation was now deemed superior.

Prominent thinkers have made the case that Galileo should shoulder much of the blame for the tragedy that befell him. He was certainly wrong about human nature. He could not understand the impossibility of reversing the direction of the academic and ecclesiastical culture of his time, and he could not restrain himself from trying. But he was right. No matter how provocative his disobedience to the church, his impulse was correct: despite the incompleteness of his proofs, or the vagaries of his personality, he created the modern notion of scientific inquiry.

It can be argued that the scientific mind is valued more in the Western world today than religious authority; but it was Galileo's tragedy to be kept from exploring that intellectual freedom fully. Despite this, and despite the eight years that he lost to the Inquisition—years in which he could have pursued and refined his astronomy—Galileo won. Galileo was right. Unencumbered by doctrine or prejudice, he opened the skies to the mind of man, and in so doing, inaugurated the modern age.

ON THE COPERNICAN TRAIL

AN INTERVIEW WITH OWEN GINGERICH

In Angels & Demons, Dan Brown draws a quick sketch of Polish astronomer Copernicus as an outspoken scientist condemned by the Catholic Church for flagrantly advancing the notion of a solar-centered universe. How accurate is Brown's rendering? Was Copernicus attacked by the church? Did he brazenly promote heliocentrism? Was his book the burning bestseller of the times?

To set the record straight, we talked with astrophysicist Owen Gingerich, a research professor at Harvard and one of the world's foremost authorities on Copernicus. Gingerich has been on the Copernican trail for a good part of his long career. He spent thirty years scouring the globe for sixteenth-century editions of Copernicus's On the Revolutions of the Heavenly Spheres—*the book that got Galileo into hot water with the church.*

Gingerich started his journey in Scotland in 1970, when he spotted an original copy of Revolutions *that had once belonged to Erasmus Reinhold, a prominent astronomy teacher in the 1540s. The richly annotated copy reminded him of a comment once made by novelist Arthur Koestler—that* Revolutions *was "the book nobody read." If Reinhold had scribbled so profusely in his copy, thought Gingerich, how many other minds had been roused by Copernicus?*

After tracking down and studying six hundred copies of early editions, a journey he recounts in

Owen Gingerich is a research professor of astronomy and of the history of science at Harvard University and author of *The Book Nobody Read: Chasing the Revolutions of Nicolaus Copernicus.*

The Book Nobody Read: Chasing the Revolutions of Nicolaus Copernicus, *Gingerich says without a doubt that Copernicus's book was not just widely read, it was also revolutionary. Gingerich's search turned up original copies owned and annotated by a number of other significant historical figures, such as German astronomer Johannes Kepler and even Galileo, who entered their notes with great care. Ironically, a copy owned by Giordano Bruno, the mathematician burned at the stake by the Catholic Church for heresy, showed no proof that he had even read the book.*

We asked Gingerich about the real Copernicus, his relationship with the religious hierarchy, and the role Revolutions *played in fueling the conflagration between Galileo and the church.*

⌒

A central theme in Angels & Demons *by Dan Brown is the conflict between religion and science. Brown and others believe the battle began with Copernicus and his vision that the planets, including the earth, revolved around the sun. How would you describe the evolution of the debate?*

By the beginning of the sixteenth century, a sacred geography had become thoroughly entwined with the understanding of the Bible: the earth, home of corruption and decay, housed within its bowels hellfire (did not belching volcanoes give occasional evidence?) while high above the pure crystalline celestial spheres was the eternal, incorruptible home of God and the abode of the elect. To propose a radical new cosmology was to challenge the very foundations of Christian understanding.

Probably the Catholic Church could have taken a revisionist sun-centered, moving-earth cosmology in its stride, except that shortly before Copernicus proposed it, a different challenge had set the world on fire. Martin Luther, a German monk, had visited Rome during the jubilee year in 1500, and was shocked by the corrupt opulence built on the unscriptural sale of papal indulgences. His debating theses, posted on the Wittenberg church door in 1517, ignited the Protestant Reformation. The newly introduced art of printing fanned the flames. Rome launched a counterattack, demanding that its own members show a united front with respect to biblical interpretation. Their theologians opted for a literal anti-Copernican reading of scripture's Psalm 104:4, "The Lord God laid the foundation of the earth that it not be moved forever." They refused to admit that an unauthorized "amateur" theologian such as Galileo could make an acceptable alternative suggestion about how to understand that verse.

Why do you think the public is so fascinated with the theme of science versus religion today?

Today the idea of a literal eternal abode of the damned deep within the earth seems just as ridiculous to us as the notion of the earth spinning on its axis and rushing a mile a second around the sun did to nearly every educated person in the 1500s. But the history of the intellectual transformation brought about by the scientific revolution is one of the great stories of the past half millennium, and it becomes so much more palpable when the clash of ideas can be dramatized in black and white terms, as in the case of Galileo. The picture of warfare between science and Christianity, resulting in "martyrs of science," became well embellished in the nineteenth century. Today the best historians reject these metaphors and opt for a more nuanced portrayal of the actual events, but seeing the struggle in terms of good guys and bad guys or angels and demons is an embedded part of popular mythology. The public gets the impression, from the retelling of the lives of Galileo, Copernicus, and Johannes Kepler, that they are confronting the formation of our modern world. Most people are unaware that it's fictionalized history.

I think it's mostly the pathos of the so-called Galileo affair that fascinates today. It's a story that almost tells itself. But I know from personal experience that many people view it in terms of black and white and get quite agitated when the picture is painted in shades of gray.

Can you describe the overall content of Copernicus's Revolutions *and the tone of his description of a sun-centered cosmos?*

Copernicus's four-hundred-page *Revolutions* is divided into six books. The first book contains the major presentation and defense of his heliocentric cosmology, which made the earth a planet and literally created the solar system as a concept. Essentially, he was redrafting the blueprint of the planetary system, taking the major step toward our modern astronomical view. He does not say what steps led him to propose such a radical notion. It was clearly for him a "theory pleasing to the mind," and although he had good philosophical arguments in its favor, he had no observational proofs, so he was obliged to fall back on rhetoric and persuasion.

The remaining five books are essentially full of technical specifications, mathematically dense and not suitable for bedtime reading except, perhaps, as a cure for insomnia. In these latter parts, Copernicus shows in detail how to compute the positions of the sun, moon, and planets based on a scheme that uses combinations of uniformly moving circles. Copernicus was much taken by this aesthetic ideal which, however, eventually proved to be a dead end.

Why was Copernicus reluctant to publish Revolutions *and under what circumstances was it finally published?*

Copernicus states quite candidly that he feared he would be hissed off the stage for presenting an idea that at first glance seemed so contrary to common sense. But at the same time, though he had worked for many years on his manuscript, even while he was serving as administrator and legal officer of the Catholic Frauenburg cathedral chapter, he knew the work was still plagued by minor inconsistencies.

He might never have published *Revolutions* except that in 1539 a young German mathematician, Georg Joachim Rheticus, a Lutheran lecturer at the University of Wittenberg, arrived to learn about his astronomical ideas. Rheticus brought along some useful books and data, and probably helped Copernicus put the finishing touches on his treatise. He persuaded Copernicus to allow him to take a copy of the manuscript to Nüremberg, where there was a printing establishment whose international clientele could make such a technical publication financially feasible.

The manuscript went to Nüremberg just in the nick of time for, as Copernicus was finishing the proofreading, he suffered a stroke, and when the final pages were brought to him (the title page and other front matter), he was probably too ill to fully comprehend what it included. He died in May 1543, just after the printing of his book was completed.

Once the book was published, what was the immediate reaction in the scientific and religious communities?
The initial scientific reaction, and one that became almost universal throughout the sixteenth century, held that the book was a manual of computation, and well done, but that its heliocentric cosmology was merely a device to organize the concepts. This interpretation was reinforced by an anonymous introduction added in the print shop to the effect that the cosmology was simply a hypothesis that need not be true or even probable. Very few readers of the book caught on that Copernicus had not written the introduction and that he probably did not accept it.

The introduction was actually written by Andreas Osiander, the learned clergyman who served as the in-house proofreader of the pages before they were printed. Though today many people consider his action reprehensible, in fact, it prevented ecclesiastical criticism and allowed the book to circulate for several decades without objections from the religious communities.

How well known were Copernicus's ideas in Galileo's time? How ready were scholars, and even the common man, to accept Copernicus's view, which would later become Galileo's view?
Although *Revolutions* was considered too advanced to be taught in beginning astronomy courses, schoolboys must have heard about it. In 1576 a widely reprinted popular almanac, which must have circulated in thousands of copies, gave an English translation of the central cosmological chapters of Copernicus's book, so his ideas became popularly known even if few people actually accepted the heliocentric system as the real description of the world.

In 1970 I started a search to examine as many copies of *Revolutions* as possible to see what evidence of readership the margins contained. I soon discovered that the book had been widely distributed and that it had a substantial number of readers, but the great majority of those who examined it really carefully seemed to think it was a great handbook for computing the orbits of the planets, but not a physically real description of the universe. So far I have examined nearly six hundred copies of the first and second editions, in libraries from Australia and China to Russia and Sweden and from New York to San Diego (and to Guadalajara, Mexico). *The Book Nobody Read* is my personal memoir about the adventures of searching for the books plus the stories of what I found.

During your study of sixteenth-century copies of Revolutions, *as you tell in your book, you found comments jotted in the margins by some illustrious owners. Whose annotations did you find most interesting?*

I assigned the copies stars as in a Michelin travel guide; three stars are "worth the trip." I awarded three stars to about a dozen copies, and of these I would say that, owing largely to the depth and significance of their notes, the four most fascinating copies are one owned by Johannes Kepler, who found the elliptical form of the planetary orbits; the copy thoroughly annotated by his teacher, Michael Maestlin; the copy with extensive marginalia by Erasmus Reinhold, the astronomy professor at Wittenberg (which was the book that got my search started); and a copy richly annotated by Paul Wittich, an almost unknown itinerant astronomy tutor.

Both Kepler and Maestlin were in the small minority who accepted the Copernican cosmology. Reinhold and Wittich belonged to the majority who were fascinated by Copernicus's handling of the small circles to produce the planetary motions by using only combinations of uniform circular motion, but they ignored the heliocentric cosmology.

You have seen and studied Galileo's personal copy of the Copernicus book. What notations did Galileo make in the book?

I was at first disappointed that the margins of Galileo's copy didn't include any technical analysis, or even any evidence that he had read it, so much so that I refused to believe it was his copy. Later, when I became more familiar with his handwriting, I realized it was indeed his, and I had to face the fact that he was a physicist not much interested in the fine details of calculating planetary positions.

What Galileo marked in his copy of *Revolutions* were the ten "corrections" required by the Catholic Church's Holy Office of the Index. This involved crossing out some phrases or sentences and generally replacing them with statements that made the text appear to be entirely hypothetical and not a description of physical reality. But it's lovely to see that Galileo crossed out the original text only very lightly. He could demonstrate to the Inquisition that he was being good and had corrected his copy, but nevertheless he made sure that he could still read the original formulation.

In your research, you tried to calculate how many copies of Revolutions *were printed. What figure did you arrive at? Do you also have an estimate of how many copies of Galileo's* Dialogue on the Two Chief World Systems *were printed and how many may have survived?*

My best estimate for the print run for the first edition of *Revolutions* is between four hundred and five hundred copies. We know that one thousand copies of the *Dialogo* were printed, and it seems the Inquisition could not suppress very many of them. I suspect that when the *Dialogo* was placed on the church's Index of Prohibited Books, people hung on to them and kept much better care of their banned copies. Thus, today Galileo's book is by far the most common of the great treatises of the scientific revolution.

A commonly held belief is that Copernicus was persecuted by the Catholic Church. In Angels & Demons, *two characters observe, "Outspoken scientists like Copernicus—" and "Were murdered . . . murdered by the church for revealing scientific truths." What was the true relationship between Copernicus and the Catholic Church?*

Unfortunately, Brown is reinforcing a false stereotype here. Copernicus was a servant of the Catholic Church. He dedicated his book to the pope, and never suffered any personal reproach or persecution.

Popular media productions are fond of including Giordano Bruno's fiery death at the stake because it adds drama and tension to the story. It is true that Bruno was interested in some of Copernicus's ideas—I actually found his copy of *Revolutions* when I was making my worldwide search—but there was no evidence that he had studied it in any detail or understood the astronomical arguments. In any event, Bruno was condemned possibly for being a spy and for a series of radical theological ideas, of which his Copernicanism and the plurality of inhabited worlds was at best only a minor part.

In truth, it is extremely difficult to document anyone put to death as a heretic for introducing new scientific ideas.

Why heliocentrism? Of all the issues science could challenge church doctrine on, why was this one such a focal point for Galileo and others?

But what were the other possible issues where science could challenge church doctrine? The age of the earth? Evidence for animals now extinct? These were future issues, but science did not begin to pose problems until late in the eighteenth century. Atomism? This could challenge the Catholic view of the Eucharist, but alchemy was too rudimentary to provide a theoretical framework to argue boldly for the existence of atoms. By the time chemistry got there, atomism was a non-issue between science and religion.

The dichotomy between the incorruptible heavens and the totally different terrestrial physics? Aristotle taught that natural celestial motions were circular, whereas on earth natural motions were only up or down—in other words, an entirely different physics of motion was involved. Furthermore, the earth, in contrast to the heavens, was a place of decay, death, and rebirth. The evidence that the new stars of 1572 and 1604 lay far above the earth's atmosphere, in the supposedly unchanging celestial realms, posed a challenge to traditional Aristotelian doctrine, something exploited by Galileo, but this did not directly threaten church teachings. So that more or less just leaves heliocentrism impinging on the whole cozy picture of the central earth and the not-too-distant heaven, together with a specific conflict with a handful of scripture passages that could most readily be interpreted as speaking against the mobility of the earth.

Remember that what ensued was primarily a turf battle. Theology was "the queen of the sciences" and in the universities theologians outranked medical doctors, and doctors outranked astronomers. Who held the keys to truth? Theologians would not willingly allow their status to be eroded by an outsider who claimed that the Book of Nature could trump the Book of Scripture when it came to understanding potentially ambiguous statements in the Bible. It seems almost obvious that there would have been something of a battle between the papal insiders and those outside, and this was all complicated by the fact that some of the outsiders were not just theologians, but Lutheran and Calvinist theologians. It's no wonder that the Roman authorities felt embattled, and in a sense Galileo was caught in the crossfire.

Copernicus, Kepler, and Galileo were all religious men whose astronomic discoveries clashed with church teachings. How did they personally rationalize their discoveries with their religious beliefs?

In two out of three cases there is very rich material addressing their religious beliefs. This is especially true for Kepler, who was trained at the Tübingen University seminary to become a Lutheran theologian. He saw the Copernican system as the embodiment of the Holy Trinity (with the sun as God the Father, the outer shell of stars as Jesus Christ, and the intervening space as the Holy Spirit). In the introduction to his greatest book, the *Astronomia Nova*, he wrote:

If someone is so dumb that he cannot grasp the science of astronomy, or so weak that he cannot believe Copernicus without offending his piety, I advise him to mind his own business, to quit this worldly pursuit, to stay at home and cultivate his own garden, and when he turns his eyes toward the visible heavens (the only way he sees them), let him with his whole heart pour forth praise and gratitude to God the Creator. Let him assure himself that he is serving God no less than the astronomer to whom God has granted the privilege of seeing more clearly with the eyes of the mind.

Galileo was much more aloof in mentioning his personal religious beliefs, but he was a staunch Catholic supportive of his two illegitimate daughters, whom he had sent to a convent. In his letter to Grand Duchess Christina of Tuscany he outlined an approach to reconcile the Book of Scripture to the Book of Nature, which he felt were two avenues to truth that should not conflict with each other. He opposed a form of scriptural literalism that excluded consideration of certain physical possibilities, and he endorsed the view that "the Bible teaches how to go to heaven, not how the heavens go."

For Copernicus, we have little record of his path to the heliocentric cosmology, nor do we have explicit mention of his personal piety. He apparently felt no personal conflict between his cosmology and his Christian beliefs, though he was surely aware that many people would have problems with it. His book was dedicated to the pope, and we know he played a very active role in the cathedral chapter at Frauenburg, the northernmost diocese in Poland. At one point his colleagues encouraged him to become the bishop, which would have required his ordination, but at that juncture in his life Copernicus preferred to devote his efforts to finishing his book *Revolutions*.

As you just mentioned, Galileo famously said, "The Bible teaches how to go to heaven, not how the heavens go," that is, that the Bible speaks idiomatically and is not a scientific textbook. In light of that comment, do you think the Catholic Church censured Galileo for accepting heliocentrism or was he a victim of church politics?

This all took place during the Thirty Years' War and at the time of the Counter-Reformation when the Catholic Church was trying to maintain a unified approach against the Protestant heresy (as they saw it). As part of their strategy the Roman hierarchy had ordered Galileo not to hold or teach the Copernican system, which the conservatives believed undermined their interpretation of scriptures such as Joshua at the battle of Gibeon commanding the sun, and not the earth, to stand still. Galileo essentially got into trouble for disobeying orders, though it seems to us today that his punishment, house arrest for the rest of his life, was unduly harsh. Of course, we see this sort of thing going on in many places today for political reasons. The Galileo affair was essentially a political maneuver for Pope Urban VIII, who was walking a tightrope between the political aspirations of the French cardinals versus the Spanish cardinals; he needed to assert his authority conspicuously in a power move.

How widely known was the attack on Galileo among other scientists and among other intelligentsia? Is there any evidence that it slowed down the progress of science in general?

The English poet John Milton wrote about Galileo's troubles in *Areopagitica*, his defense of the freedom of speech. Milton described his visit to Florence, saying, "There it was that I found and visited the famous Galileo, grown old a prisoner to the Inquisition, for thinking in astronomy otherwise than the Franciscan and Dominican licensers thought." Probably the most notable ef-

fect on a scientist, to use an anachronous word not invented until the nineteenth century, was the action of Descartes, who suppressed for some time
his *Philosophia Principia* and then rewrote parts of it to be more masked in its
Copernicanism.

In the decades following the Galileo affair, the Catholic Church continued to be the largest financial supporter of astronomy, largely through the Jesuits, but Catholic astronomers were heavily circumscribed in the ways they
could teach or think about cosmological issues. Partly as a consequence, creative science seems clearly to have moved to more northern, Protestant climes,
although the genius of Isaac Newton and of Christiaan Huygens may con-
siderably distort our evaluation.

*Do you have any reason to believe that Galileo, again as Brown states, was a member of a secret society
opposed to the church, such as the Illuminati or Freemasons?*

Very occasionally one sees insinuations that Galileo might have had connections like this, but I suspect this is wishful thinking on the part of Freemason
fans. I know of nothing substantial that involves Galileo with those secret societies.

Brown suggests that Galileo wrote a secret last book called the Diagramma, *so controversial that it was
quietly published in Holland. Is there any truth to this or is it pure fiction?*

This isn't even speculation—it's pure fantasy!

GALILEO: RIGHT MESSAGE AT THE WRONG TIME

An Interview with Steven J. Harris

In Angels & Demons, Camerlengo Ventresca agonizes over the Catholic Church's "defeat" in the face of science's advances in understanding the natural and cosmological worlds. He is articulating a hundred-year-old thesis that became the predominant view of science's relationship to religion in the early twentieth century, as America and Europe became more secularized. Simply put, it says that religion and science are inevitably opposed. Why else would the Catholic Church have persecuted Galileo?

In the popular mind, this idea has proved hard to deconstruct. Historian of science Steve Harris represents a recent countertrend in the study of how science and religion relate to each other. He rejects the notion that they are natural enemies and argues for a more complex, nuanced view of their interaction, a view that emphasizes the church's indifference to, and later patronage of science's discoveries, with Galileo's inquisition being the big exception. This he terms the church's greatest mistake in its approach to the new methods of investigating the natural world.

Harris believes Dan Brown misrepresents Galileo as a member of the Illuminati in Angels & Demons*—and also disputes the accuracy of Brown's treatment of the scientists Johannes Kepler and Georges Lemaître.*

Noted historian of science Steven J. Harris has taught at Harvard University and Wellesley College. He has written extensively on the history of the Jesuits and their relation to science and is the coeditor of the two-volume *The Jesuits: Cultures, Sciences, and the Arts, 1540–1773*.

Dan Brown's Angels & Demons *is surprisingly intellectual in that it employs ideas as leverage for the plot. It also involves a lot of scientific name dropping. How accurate do you find the latter?*

Part of the problem is the obvious one that Dan Brown and I represent two different genres, fiction and nonfiction, and two very different ways of approaching the past. A novelist has much greater freedom in putting together a story than does a historian. As a historian of science, I am interested in what scientists actually did.

Even allowing for the creative freedom of the novelist, however, I'm troubled by how Brown uses historical figures in motivating the central plot. He mentions Copernicus, Galileo, Lemaître, among others. I must say there are factual problems with almost all of them, and some exaggerations as well. More critically, however, Brown seems willing to use the historical authority of their names without fully understanding the historical context of their lives.

Why don't we start with the book's central thesis, which is that science and religion are arch enemies. The book says science and religion have always been at war. But were they before the 1500s and 1600s, the time of Copernicus and Galileo?

Well, my position would be that they weren't "at war" before, during, or after. It's a complex story. Overall, I would say that there have been long periods of indifference, accommodation, and cooperation punctuated by episodes of tension and occasionally even of conflict. Put simply, the "conflict" thesis is ham-fisted and much of my scholarly work is an attempt to develop the nuances and contexts of science-religion interactions.

The chief problem with the conflict thesis is that it assumes both a monolithic "religion" and a monolithic "science." And it assumes, or implies, both a temporal and an institutional continuity for religion and science. Yet the post-Reformation Catholic Church of the seventeenth century was a different creature from its medieval ancestor, just as modern science has become a very different enterprise from ancient and medieval science. Within Christianity, there are now many churches and sects; within science there are many fields, disciplines, and institutional settings.

In Brown's representation of science and religion, there is a pronounced tendency to stereotype, conflate, and exaggerate. For example, Brown has CERN's director, Maximilian Kohler, declare that "the Church may not be burning scientists anymore, but if you think they've released their reign over science, ask yourself why half the schools in your country are not allowed to teach evolution."

As I understand it, the creationist movement in America is overwhelmingly Protestant, not Catholic. Recent rules passed in a few school districts in a few states require the teaching of creationism alongside evolution, not the prohibition of evolution "in half the country." Nor is it clear that the Catholic Church ever burned a single scientist at the stake. The most likely candidate would be Giordano Bruno, but he was no scientist—though he did support Copernican astronomy and argued, on theological grounds, for an infinite universe—and he was burned for denying, among other things, the Holy Trinity.

The only scientist I know of who was burned at the stake by religious authorities was the physician and anatomist Michael Servetus (1509–1553), although he was killed for theological heresies. He was burned to death in Geneva in 1553 by Calvinists under the authority and in the presence of John Calvin himself.

So Angels & Demons *overinflates the conflict between religion and science, making it much more sweeping than it actually was?*

As I look over the history of interactions between the various branches of Christendom and the various branches of science, points of tension have been relatively few and far between. But when they do erupt, they have broad cultural implications. If you go back to the twelfth and thirteenth centuries, the tension would have been between reason and faith, where reason would have been represented in the newly recovered works of Aristotle and other ancient Greeks and faith represented in the early medieval theology of the Latin Church. But interestingly enough, by the end of the thirteenth century, you have a rather profound synthesis between ancient pagan Greek natural philosophy and medieval Christian theology. What's more, Greek natural philosophy came to the Latin west largely through Arabic translations and Jewish mediators—about as non-Christian as you can get.

That's what Thomas Aquinas (1225?–1274) and his generation was about. He worked his way through the details of Aristotle and said this works and that doesn't. For example, Aristotle said the universe was uncreated and unending. Well, that just doesn't fly in the Christian story of creation. So Aquinas said, well, Aristotle was a pagan, he lived a long time ago, he got that wrong. We know from the Bible that the world was created. So on that point, Aristotle is wrong. But when Aristotle says the earth is made out of earth, air, water, and fire—the four elements of ancient Greek matter theory—Aquinas can accept that.

So there were already some intellectual tensions before 1500 between science as it was then and the Catholic Church?

Yes, the Greek and especially the Aristotelian texts challenged, stimulated, and even threatened Latin Christian ways of thinking. But after several decades of genuine struggle, you have a profound synthesis in which some of the most basic doctrines of the Catholic Church are now articulated in the language of Aristotle. What is remarkable for me is that the Catholic Church was eventually able to integrate a wholly alien philosophical system into its theology.

And that explains in some ways why Copernicus's ideas were so explosive?

Yes, because Aristotle's view of the world was geocentric—or more precisely, geocentric, geostatic, spherical, and finite. What is more, Aristotle's world picture was fully endorsed by almost all other surviving Greek authorities, including Plato, Galen, and especially Ptolemy, the chief architect of Greek geocentric astronomy. Thus, the consensus view of ancient Greeks was that the earth was at the center of the cosmos, and everything else—the sun, moon, planets, and stars—whirled around the earth in enormous crystalline spheres arranged concentrically, all embraced by a final, finite stellar sphere.

There is nothing in the Bible that depicts the world in such detailed terms. So that's the other important part of the synthesis. Again, by about the fourteenth century, almost all Catholic intellectuals understood the world to be geocentric, as Aristotle described it. They accepted and embraced "foreign" knowledge about the structure and operation of the natural world. If the medieval Catholic Church had really been "at war" with Greek science, there never would have been a geocentric astronomy for Copernicus and Galileo to contemplate and criticize.

In fact, I think the most eloquent expression of this synthesis isn't so much Aquinas as Dante. When you travel with the pilgrim through Dante's imagined world, you're traveling through an essentially Aristotelian architecture. The earth is at the center, the planets travel in their concentric orbits, and the sphere of the stars marks the outer limit of the physical cosmos. There's no biblical precedent for that. Even the rings of hell are arranged concentrically.

Then, of course, what Aquinas and Dante do is to Christianize that world picture. The earth, physically speaking, is situated at the center of God's creation but at the point most remote from the starry heavens. Human beings, morally speaking, are suspended on the earth, with hell below and heaven above—more precisely, with the Christian heaven (the Empyrean) located in the nonphysical space beyond the last sphere of the stars. So now when Copernicus proposed and Galileo vigorously advocated a heliocentric cosmos, you don't need to be a prophet to see trouble on the horizon.

So Angels & Demons *correctly depicts Galileo, the first real popularizer of Copernicus, as being an enormous threat to the church.*

Yes, but even there it's a lot more complicated than Dan Brown would have you believe.

What were the central issues in that confrontation between Galileo and the church?

I'd back up just one step to Copernicus. Copernicus himself was a priest and a canon. He was educated by the church. He received an excellent humanist education at the height of the Renaissance at three different Italian universities. He returned to Poland and became an important administrator in the Catholic Church. He first developed his idea of a heliocentric system about 1512, which he wrote up as a manuscript and circulated among friends. But he doesn't publish his great work, *On the Revolution of the Heavenly Spheres*, until 1543.

On his deathbed.

Yes, literally on his deathbed. Now, if you want to misunderstand the story, you'd say the reason why he hesitated was he was afraid of what the church would do to him for presenting a different cosmology. In fact, two bishops, a cardinal, and a pope encouraged him to publish. The book he did eventually publish was dedicated to the reigning pope, Paul III. What he feared—and he states this explicitly in his introduction—were people who didn't understand mathematics. In order for this theory to make sense, his readers had to understand the complex geometric arguments he presents.

Early on in Angels & Demons, *Maximilian Kohler, the head of CERN, says the Catholic Church murdered Copernicus. True?*

No. He was seventy when he died—certainly a ripe old age for the sixteenth century. The church did not murder Copernicus. But he was certainly concerned about how his book would be received. He knew he was presenting a big idea with big implications. And it was a novel idea—though here he sought to underplay its novelty by citing ancient Greek precedents for a heliocentric universe. Of course he was concerned.

Now, if you take the next step and ask, what was the reaction to Copernicus in the latter half of the sixteenth century? you encounter one of those delightful quirks of history. Despite being one of the most controversial ideas of the seventeenth century, in the sixteenth century, one finds barely a murmur. It was, after all, essentially an esoteric, technical treatise on mathematical astronomy. As Copernicus suspected, few could follow the argument. In fact, only a handful of theologians and astronomers even commented on Copernicus's heliocentric theory.

It took Galileo to bring it to the front stage of history.

Yes, and what makes Galileo interesting is that he makes telescopic observations accessible. People—mathematically untrained people—could look through the telescope and see for themselves what he was talking about. In order to follow Copernicus's argument, in contrast, you had to study mathematics for years. Now, the twist there is that none of Galileo's telescopic observations provide any compelling proof for the Copernican theory. There is nothing in his observations that could not be explained in other ways.

But nonetheless, the Roman Catholic Church wished to silence even discussion of it, right?

Not quite. There's an important qualification here. Galileo brought the "Copernican question" to the forefront. But we need to keep in mind that the Catholic Church had been in a bitter, bitter war—literally as well as theologically—with Protestants, and the Catholic hierarchy was very sensitive to questions that challenged, or even appeared to challenge, Catholic doctrines. You have to place this in the context of the times.

Where does Galileo fit in this war?

Galileo is a very different personality from Copernicus. He thrives on controversy; he loves the limelight. He starts speaking and writing about the Copernican theory in and around Rome. And there are some conservative Catholics, mostly Dominicans, who try to get him and the theory in trouble with the Inquisition. And they partially succeed. This leads to a decree by the Inquisition in 1616, during the pontificate of Paul V, that condemns the heliocentric theory as "philosophically absurd and false and formally heretical."

That same year—seventy-three years after its appearance—Copernicus's treatise was placed on the Index of Prohibited Books. It was not condemned outright but only prohibited until corrected, and the corrections consisted of only a handful of paragraphs. Fewer than 10 percent of the surviving copies show signs of actual correction.

Galileo isn't directly implicated in the Inquisition's decree, but he is told by Cardinal Bellarmine not to teach the Copernican theory as *true.* He may, however, teach it as a *hypothesis.* Evidently, Galileo agreed to abide by this.

Before we get into how Galileo forced the confrontation in 1633, let's establish what in the Copernican theory would have riled the church fathers? What's at issue?

Again, I think the better way to think of it is not in terms of Aristotle, but Dante. He popularizes, as it were, a worldview that is profoundly Christian and geocentric. Where is hell? Hell is underneath your feet. There are many paintings of Judgment Day from the period which depict the earth opening up and demons grabbing people by the ankles and dragging them down to hell. By the same token, there are many paintings of the ascension of Mary and the ascension of Christ. *Up* and *down* have a profound theological meaning as well as an absolute physical meaning in the Christianized Aristotelian cosmos of the sixteenth century.

If you relocate—or better said, dislocate—the earth from the center of the universe and place it in orbit around the sun, you not only make a mess of Aristotelian physics and cosmology, you make a mess of the stage on which Christian drama plays out. Now, it must be said that the tensions between Dante's picture of the Christian cosmos and Copernicus's mathematical cosmos were there in 1543, but no one really explored them.

Was the trial of Galileo also about the church's right to say who could interpret the scriptures?
Yes. That's the other important thing, especially with Galileo. Galileo invokes the medieval truism that there are two books: the Book of God, the Bible, and the Book of Nature, God's creation. And, of course, since both have the same author, neither book can contradict the other.

What Galileo said was that the only people who are really qualified to interpret the Book of Nature are mathematicians. In a famous passage, he says the Book of Nature is written in the language of geometry. And so he is saying, indirectly, to theologians that they lack the technical knowledge—mathematics—necessary to understand the natural world. To Catholic theologians struggling in the wake of the Protestant Reformation to retain their cultural authority, this probably sounded like one more attack on their credibility. In a word, Galileo was making waves at the wrong time.

So the Catholic Church's reaction was somewhat understandable in the context of the times?
The bottom line is that the church condemned Galileo's defense of Copernicanism, so they don't get off the hook. They condemned an astronomical theory that was essentially true. And as everyone knows, that was a big mistake—I would say the single biggest mistake the Catholic Church has made as far as the history of science is concerned.

That said, it is important to note that some members of the Catholic hierarchy understood at the time that this was a mistake. Rivka Feldhay, a historian of science (*Galileo and the Church: Political Inquisition or Critical Dialogue?*), has looked closely at the climate of opinion, especially among Dominicans and Jesuits at the time of the trial, and found a range of interpretations. Generally speaking, Dominicans felt that Galileo's arguments were wrong because they are based on mathematics and mathematics cannot deliver truth about the physical world. Jesuits, on the other hand, believed that mathematics can deliver truth about the physical world but decided that Galileo did not have such mathematical proof in hand. Still others agreed with the Jesuits about the power of mathematical physics but accepted Galileo's arguments. Although a "silenced minority," this last group saw that condemnation of the heliocentric worldview would have serious repercussions. Their day would come only much later.

According to Robert Langdon, the fictional hero of Angels & Demons, *the Illuminati, which included Galileo, were scientists who met in secret in the 1500s to oppose the church's "inaccurate teachings" about the physical world and its "monopoly on truth." Is that true?*

I am not an expert on the Illuminati. As far as I know, the first historical Illuminati were religious figures—mystics and enthusiasts mostly—who lived in Spain and Italy in the first part of the sixteenth century. *Illuminati* was initially a pejorative term. They weren't organized and, at least in Spain, did not have a discernible interest in science.

There was no Illuminati as depicted in Angels & Demons—*that is, a secret sect bitterly opposed to the church?*

No, not that I know of. Now, Galileo did belong to a scientific society, The Academy of the Lynx. (The lynx, according to Greek myth, was especially sharp-sighted, presumably like the members of its namesake society.) It was organized by Federico Cesi, a young Roman aristocrat, and modeled in part on the Society of Jesus. He intended it to be a group of well-educated, morally upright, and spiritually pure men dedicated to a life of learning. Galileo was elected a member about 1611. He was very proud of his membership and openly declared it by including the academy's emblem on the title pages of his publications. The Academy of the Lynx was by no means secret. And it was not established in opposition to the Catholic Church. What's more, it dissolved upon the death of its founder in 1630, three years before Galileo's trial.

Is there any evidence, as Dan Brown claims in the novel, that Galileo knew English and used it to avoid Vatican scrutiny?

No. Indeed, I would be surprised if he did, since England then was something of a scientific backwater and virtually nothing written in English would have interested Galileo scientifically.

You've written that after Galileo's trial, the church became a patron of some branches of science. Can you elaborate?

Yes. This is what I mean about the conflict thesis not being a good guide for historians. It doesn't encourage a broad enough perspective.

If you think about science in all its glory, it is hardly a monolithic enterprise, either in its methods, theories, or domains of study. There's theoretical physics, observational astronomy, computational meteorology, experimental psychology—all kinds of sciences that the Catholic Church has encouraged, tolerated, or been indifferent about. The two major areas in which religion and science have clashed are heliocentric astronomy, which we've talked about, and evolution broadly defined (i.e., biological evolution, geology, human evolution, etc.).

Has the Catholic Church in Rome banned Catholics from accepting evolution?
No, at least not when put so bluntly. After Darwin published *On the Origin of Species* in 1859, official Catholic response was decidedly cool. In 1909 a pontifical biblical commission reaffirmed the "literal and historical meaning of Genesis" and prohibited a purely scientific (materialistic) account of human origins. By 1950, though, Pope Pius XII had issued an encyclical (*Humani generis*) that, while cautious with regard to questions of human evolution, said that "the teaching authority of the church does not forbid that, in conformity with the present state of human sciences and sacred theology, research and discussion on the part of men experienced in both fields take place with regard to the doctrine of evolution." Not exactly a ringing endorsement of Darwinian evolution, but by no means was it a prohibition of the theory of organic evolution.

As one who believes the historical relationship between science and religion is highly nuanced, do you agree, as the camerlengo says in Angels & Demons, *that science has destroyed the Roman Catholic Church?*
"Destroyed," no, not by a long shot. "Encroached," yes, but only in a certain way. Most of the cultural functions performed by religion—any religion—have little to do with most of those performed by science. But when it comes to understanding and interpreting the workings of nature, the scientist now has more authority in most of Western culture than does the priest, the theologian, or saint. In this sense, scientists have, over the last three hundred years or so, encroached on the cultural authority of religious leaders.

Turning to modern physics, does Angels & Demons *portray the big bang theory of Georges Lemaître correctly? And was the big bang seen as proof of a supreme being who created the world?*
Well, yes and no. By about the middle of the twentieth century, people at the highest levels of the Catholic hierarchy—including a couple of popes—were indeed fond of big bang cosmology, though in ways Lemaître himself didn't like.
First, a couple of minor factual corrections. In 1923 Lemaître interrupted his doctoral work on Einstein's general theory of relativity to attend seminary. He was ordained as a Catholic priest that same year. (When asked later why he took this unusual step, he replied, "I was interested in truth from

the standpoint of salvation, you see, as well as from the standpoint of scientific certainty.") He continued his studies in Cambridge, England (1924), and Cambridge, Massachusetts (1925). He then learned of Edwin Hubble's empirical research on galactic velocities from the Harvard astronomer Harlow Shapley.

In any event, Lemaître published his theory of the primeval atom (only later was it given the derisive label of big bang) in 1927 in a short paper in a rather obscure Belgian journal. So, rather like Copernicus's theory, its initial impact was almost nil. Only when he sent a copy to Arthur Eddington in England in 1930 did word spread. In 1932 Einstein himself attended a lecture by Lemaître and declared that "this is the most beautiful and satisfactory explanation of creation to which I have ever listened."

How does Brown misuse Lemaître's theory?

In the book, Leonardo Vetra serves as a fictional link between Lemaitre's primeval atom–big bang theory and Genesis. It is Vetra who performs the miracle of creating something out of nothing, thereby promising—or, for the antagonists of the novel, threatening—to bind the worlds of high-energy physics and biblical hermeneutics. First of all, I don't think Lemaître had anything to say about what happened before his primeval atom underwent spontaneous radioactive decay. Strictly speaking, then, there is no Genesis, no creation of matter out of nothing in Lemaître.

How does antimatter fit into all this?

Antimatter exists, both in theory and in fact. But it doesn't figure into Lemaître's theory at all. His primeval atom is simply a huge atomic nucleus composed of plain old matter—neutrons, protons, electrons, etc.

Lemaître himself expressly rejected the sort of commingling of cosmology and Genesis that drives Brown's story line, which is yet another delightful twist in the actual history. He warned against precisely what some Catholic theologians were openly hoping for, namely, a scientific theory that would vindicate Genesis. This is what Lemaître had to say: "As far as I can see, [the primeval atom hypothesis] remains entirely outside any metaphysical or religious question. It leaves the materialist free to deny any transcendental Being. . . . For the believer, it removes any attempt at familiarity with God . . . It is consonant with the wording of Isaiah speaking of the 'Hidden God,' hidden even in the beginning of creation."

So in your view, the church would have no reason to act as the camerlengo does in Angels & Demons, *because it does not feel threatened by science?*

No. I'm sorry to say that the underlying premise of the book simply does not work for me. My imagination is too burdened with facts of the past.

So nothing in Angels & Demons' *intellectual ideas concerning the relationship of science and religion is historically accurate?*

Well, as I've said, the idea of a conflict between science and religion has become a fixture of sorts, with the trial of Galileo being its oft-cited emblem. What I've tried to say is that that emblem does not accurately represent the historical record. The interactions between the many parts of Christianity and the many fields of science are infinitely more nuanced and intellectually subtle than the conflict thesis allows for.

Tell us about the secret archive in the Vatican containing Galileo's banned writings where Robert Langdon nearly dies.

There's the Vatican Library, the Vatican Archives, and the Secret Archives. The Galileo trial documents were kept in the Secret Archives. As the name implies, the Secret Archives were secret and so virtually no one could examine the trial documents for more than a century and a half after Galileo's death in 1642.

Consequently, no scholarly work on the trial existed before 1800. But in the nineteenth century, a number of events conspired to give historians a chance to examine the documents. Here's the story in a nutshell. Napoleon's armies invaded the Papal States in 1809 and confiscated, among other things, the trial documents. They were eventually returned to Rome in 1846, some say on condition that the Vatican publish them and/or make them available to scholars. Over the next few years, the Vatican did publish parts. But omissions and judicious editing raised suspicions.

For the next thirty years, a small but steady stream of scholars, not always dutiful sons of the church, made pilgrimages to Rome to examine the documents for themselves. The best Galileo scholars of that generation were German. One of the big themes in Germany at the time was the Kulturkampf—the "culture war"—which pitted secular, progressive, modern culture against the priestly, traditional, medieval culture of the Catholic Church. The pioneers of Galileo scholarship were, almost to a man progressive positivists.

As I see it, the "Galileo industry" and the conflict thesis arose contemporaneously. Both exploited the recent availability of the trial documents (which, I believe, were again sealed sometime after 1880) and the growth of both coincided with the rise of industrialized, secular nation states bent on limiting the political authority of the Catholic Church. The conflict thesis has as much to do with nineteenth-century positivism and national politics as it does with the Catholic Church. It is important—but not as a guide to what happened in the sixteenth or seventeenth centuries.

Why Does Dan Brown allude to Giordano Bruno in Angels & Demons? *Here's what Steven J. Harris says about the philosopher's significance.*

Giordano Bruno is certainly an interesting figure in the history of science and the conflict between science and religion. He was born in 1548 in Naples (about a generation before Galileo) and joined the Dominican order as a teenager. Suddenly, and for reasons not entirely clear, he broke his vows, left the order, and fled Italy. He openly rejected the geocentric cosmology of Aristotle and vigorously promoted Copernicus's heliocentric theory, yet proclaimed himself to be "an enemy of mathematics" when applied to the physical world. This, of course, was an attitude directly at odds with the emerging trend of mathematical physics.

More surprisingly, he argued for an infinite universe and imagined an infinite number of heliocentric worlds like our own, distant stars being likened to our sun. His reasoning had more to do with theology than astronomy, since he thought only an infinite cosmos could express the infinite power and creativity of God. He also espoused a number of overtly political ideas that made him the object of considerable controversy. He was perhaps best known and most respected among his contemporaries for his method of teaching mnemotechny, or the art of memory (which had a long tradition in the Dominican order) and for his advocacy of the Hermetic philosophy, a sort of philosophically grounded magic supposedly having its origin in the body of writings attributed to Hermes Trismegistus. After several years of wandering, he returned to Italy, hoping perhaps to assume the chair in mathematics at the University of Padua. (In fact, it was none other than Galileo who was called to the chair in 1592.) Bruno was arrested in Venice, extradited to Rome and, after seven years in prison, refused to recant his heretical religious beliefs—as well as his heliocentrism and belief in an infinite universe—and was condemned to death. He was burned at the stake in 1600.

What's interesting about Bruno, apart from his rich and original philosophical speculations, is how he has been used by various parties over the years. In the eighteenth century, his ideas were still thought of (in some circles) as eccentric, extravagant, and impertinent. By the nineteenth century, and especially after Italian unification, he became a hero for liberals, a cause célèbre for advocating freedom of thought, and—somewhat incongruously given his views on mathematics and embrace of magical practices—a precursor of modern science. As Voltaire once said, history is a trick we play on the dead. I suppose what is relevant in connection with *Angels & Demons* is that Galileo certainly knew of the fame and fate of Bruno and learned from Bruno's mistake: obstinacy when before the Inquisition does not pay.

THE MYTH OF GALILEO

AN INTERVIEW WITH WADE ROWLAND

Popular history holds Galileo up not only as a master astronomer but as a champion of conscience who takes on intolerant clerics bent on stopping the march of progress. It's the same view that Dan Brown adopts in Angels & Demons, *basing the novel's plot on the premise that the Catholic Church condemned Galileo for promoting Copernicus's theory that the sun, not the earth, was at the center of the universe. But Wade Rowland, a Canadian journalist, television producer, university lecturer on science, religion, and ethics, and author of more than a dozen books, challenges that view as largely a historical myth.*

In his book Galileo's Mistake: A New Look at the Epic Confrontation Between Galileo and the Church, *Rowland argues that Galileo was hardly a "paladin of truth and freedom," nor was the church so "venal and close-minded." Moreover, the basic conflict between the scientist and the church, Rowland maintains, wasn't even about Copernicanism. Rather, it was a battle over the nature of truth and how man comes to know it. Galileo insisted that nature holds the secrets of the universe, and that science and mathematics alone could unravel them. The church countered that science can be helpful but it doesn't have all the answers: God, morality, and ethics can also teach a few lessons. Rowland sees merit in both positions. "We should admire Galileo," he writes, but at the same time we should "recognize*

Wade Rowland is the author of *Galileo's Mistake: A New Look at the Epic Confrontation Between Galileo and the Church,* and more than a dozen other books.

the important truths championed by his adversaries in the church, who drew from a much deeper well of philosophical experience."

This dramatic reassessment of the controversy sheds a more sympathetic light on the seventeenth-century church and a harsher one on Galileo. In the interview that follows, Rowland eloquently makes his case.

The generally accepted view of Galileo is that he was condemned by the Catholic Church for confirming Copernicus's discovery of the "truth," that is, that the earth revolved around the sun.

To begin with, the word *discovery* is a misleading concept here. Earth-centered and solar-centered systems had been in competition since at least the time of classical Greece, so even Copernicus was drawing from a very old well of speculation.

In Galileo's time there was, within the church, and especially among Jesuit astronomers, a strong suspicion that Copernicus was right. Galileo's telescopic discoveries provided *indirect* confirmation of that suspicion in several ways. They showed, for example, that celestial objects were not perfect and flawless, but appeared to be made of the same ordinary stuff as earth. The moon was rugged and mountainous, and the sun itself showed imperfections called sun spots. Mars, seen through the telescope, varied in size at different places in its orbit. And then there was the discovery of Jupiter's moons. The Copernican system arranged the planets neatly around the sun according to the speed of their revolutions—Mercury fastest and closest, Saturn slowest and farthest—and here was Jupiter, a miniature solar system with satellites arranged sequentially by period in exactly the same way. It had also been argued by proponents of the ancient astronomer Ptolemy that, if the earth moved at a high rate of speed in orbit, it would quickly leave the moon behind. Galileo was able to show that that had not happened with Jupiter and its moons, which further undermined the Ptolemaic belief in a (necessarily) stationary earth orbited by the sun.

It is important to bear in mind that the church neither persecuted nor prosecuted Copernicus himself for his speculations—in fact he was thanked by the pope for helping to simplify calendar-making, which relied on accurate astronomical observations. Nor did the church complain of Galileo's telescopic "confirmations." He was in fact welcomed in Rome by the church hierarchy and asked to present his discoveries to Jesuit astronomers, who immediately set about confirming them from their own observatories in Rome.

Clearly, something other than Copernicanism must have been at the root of Galileo's dispute with the church.

If the traditional view is a myth, then what was at the core of the conflict between Galileo and the Catholic Church?

The core of the dispute was something more complicated than orbital mechanics, and at the same time much more interesting. The disagreement was over two conflicting views of the nature of truth and reality, on where one ought to look for authoritative truth about the world. One way to summarize this subtle and complex debate is to look at it in the context of Galileo's famous description of scripture and nature as being two different texts revealing God and his works—providing truth about the universe. Galileo insisted that science should always take precedence over scripture (or more broadly, metaphysical insight) in all matters that were susceptible to scientific inquiry. His reason was that the meaning of scripture was open to interpretation by humans, and therefore vulnerable to error. Science, on the other hand, dealt directly with nature, which, he said, *is its own interpreter.* The Book of Nature, Galileo said, is written in mathematics, for which there is always an unarguably correct interpretation. In other words, he believed that, in a very real sense, nature was constructed of numbers, and therefore subject to final and definitive understanding by mathematics-based science.

Now, think of this in terms of church authority. According to Galileo, the church's intellectual authority ought to be confined to areas of knowledge in which science could offer no insights. He had also written that science, given time, was capable of progressively unraveling *all* the mysteries of the universe. That left religion and moral philosophy—the intellectual domain of the church—in the position of filling in the gaps in scientific knowledge, temporarily, until scientific progress would eventually make these error-prone disciplines unnecessary. The church could not accept, either on political or philosophical grounds, such a radical challenge to its authority.

The church was also concerned with the additional problem that there was no place for moral values in the purely mathematical world that Galileo perceived. Morality, in the church's view, ought to be at the core of inquiry and understanding, not tacked on somehow at the periphery, as an afterthought. In the church's view, the universe operated according to moral, as well as mathematical, precepts.

So, the church was willing to believe that the earth was not the center of the universe?

The record clearly shows that the church's position was that if Copernicanism could be shown to be correct, then those passages in scripture which seemed to indicate that the sun revolved around the earth, and that the earth did not move, would have to be reinterpreted. Cardinal Bellarmine, head of the Collegio Romano and senior Vatican theologian, spelled it out in no uncertain terms in 1615, when he wrote that if there were real proof that the sun is the center of the universe and the earth moves around the sun, "then we should have to proceed with great circumspection in explaining passages of scripture which appear to teach the contrary, and rather admit that we do not understand them, than declare an opinion to be false which is proved to be true."

But if this was to be done without calling the church's intellectual authority into question, it would have to be done circumspectly, in consultation with the proper church authorities. And that would take time. Galileo had, in effect, been asked to respect the church's need for time to adjust to the new reality being proposed by science. It is important, as well, to remember that Galileo had not been able to prove the validity of Copernicanism. Definitive confirmation through stellar parallax measurements would have to wait until the nineteenth century.

Why was the church so afraid that heliocentrism would take root?

There were a number of reasons, both political and theological. One of the most interesting is that Copernicanism, if it was right, appeared to mean that the universe was very much larger than had been thought. If the earth moved around the sun in orbit, then it had to be possible to detect a perceived shift in the position of the so-called fixed stars as the earth moved from one side of its orbit to the other. Had those stars been close by, the shift would have been prominent and obvious. But no one, using the technology of the day, had been able to see any shift at all. That could mean one of two things: the Copernican hypothesis was wrong, or the stars were so incredibly far away that the angle of shift was undetectable. The universe that for thousands of years had seemed a cozy place now seemed, potentially at least, to be unimaginably vast—perhaps even infinite.

What problems did an infinite universe pose for the church?

An infinite universe posed serious theological problems. If the universe was not finite, where were hell and purgatory to be located? How could God be separate and distinct from his creation, as Christian dogma claimed? If the universe was infinite, God must by definition be a part of it, since it included everything. Where could order and harmony and purpose reside in an infinite, and therefore formless, universe? The entire Aristotelian-Thomist-Ptolemaic cosmology that had served Christianity well since its birth would collapse, and with it the thousand-year-old hierarchy of interdependent existence that linked, in an unbroken chain, the inanimate to plant and animal life, to man, to angels, to God. And if that happened, what would become of the painstakingly crafted systems of morals and values built on those assumptions?

The idea of an infinite universe nevertheless eventually took hold, and was accepted for the next three hundred years. Twentieth-century astronomers, physicists, and cosmologists then had to face similar foundational questions, with similarly profound psychological angst, when science concluded that the universe is indeed finite, having had a definable beginning in the big bang.

In Angels & Demons, *one character calls Galileo's* Dialogues *"the ultimate scientific sellout" because he tries to take both the scientific and religious positions to keep himself out of trouble with the church.*

The *Dialogues on the Two Chief World Systems* presents, in the form of a discussion among three friends, arguments for and against both the Copernican and Ptolemaic systems. Ptolemaic, or earth-centered, cosmology is represented by a character called Simplicio, which gives you some idea of where the author's sympathies lay. Taken as a whole, the book is a clear and trenchant defense of Copernicanism, which is why it angered church authorities who had ordered him to remain quiet on the subject. Remember, Galileo had no proof that the Copernican hypothesis was correct, only strong suspicions and some indirect confirmations. His defense of Copernicus seems especially courageous in this context.

In your view, what was Galileo's mistake?

Galileo's intellectual mistake was his naive materialism, to use the philosophical term. As the prototypical modern scientist, he had formulated the view that when a scientific hypothesis (like Copernicanism) had been tested and shown to fit with evidence of scientific observation, it should then be taken as a definitive statement of reality. He believed that science discovers truths about the world *that exclude all other explanations.* Furthermore, he believed that it was within the power of science eventually to know all there is to know about the world, to know, in his words "what God knows."

The church held the view that there were limits to human understanding, and that what science does is build models of nature (usually, as in Galileo's case, mathematical ones) and examine those. To mistake the models for the reality of nature as God had made it, was to mistake the map for the territory. Pope Urban VIII summed it up nicely when he warned Galileo not to "force necessity on God," in other words, not to presume that science's explanations are the *only* valid explanations for the workings of the world.

The church, and in particular Cardinal Bellarmine, tried to convince him that science did not reveal nature, but rather constructed models which with varying degrees "saved the appearances," or provided useful, workable explanations for a more complex and inscrutable authentic reality. The church's long-standing position had been eloquently expressed by Nicholas of Cusa, who might have supplied the model for the Renaissance man. Cardinal, mathematician, philosopher, physician, and experimental scientist, Cusa wrote in 1440, in his influential book, *De docta ignorantia*:

> *This is how things stand with respect to truth and with respect to our understanding, which is not truth itself. Never will our understanding lay hold of truth in so exact a manner that it may not grasp it still more exactly, and it will do so indefinitely. What conclusion can we draw from this? That the very essence of things, that which is the true nature of being, cannot ever be reached in its purity, not by us. All philosophers have sought it, none have found it. The more profoundly learned we become in this ignorance, the closer we approach to truth itself.*

Intellectually, Galileo was simply mistaken: nature, as we understand today, is *not* "its own interpreter." The describing of nature by science—that is, by human scientists using instruments and techniques of human manufacture, answering questions defined by human needs and aspirations—is not simply a form of stenography or transcription. Scientific knowledge, by its nature, is contingent to a significant degree on the cultural milieu in which it is developed. It therefore cannot make a legitimate claim to preeminence as a source of truth.

What was Galileo's motive in trying to prove the church wrong? Was his reputedly large ego a big factor?
Doubtless Galileo did have an ego to match his oversized intellect. But one can sympathize. Imagine the power he must have felt on making his telescopic discoveries, on seeing things that, as he boasted, no man had seen before. Imagine his sense of intellectual superiority when physical experiments he conducted disproved key aspects of Aristotelian science, which had been the gold standard for a thousand years and more. It would have taken a person of extraordinary humility to have remained patient with opposing views, especially ones as subtle as those presented by the church—and Galileo was not such a man.

It's my belief, and this is admittedly controversial, that in the end, Galileo learned a little humility. He had begun by insisting on complete intellectual freedom for science and scientists, and ended by accepting the position that there is a need for the kind of morally informed intellectual discipline provided by the church. This, at least, is what is implied by his statement of abjuration at his trial, most of which he wrote himself. I think he was genuinely contrite, and in *Galileo's Mistake* I spend considerable time supporting this view with historical evidence.

Do you believe the church of the time deserves the reputation of being irrational and anti-intellectual?

Remember that for the first fifteen hundred years of its existence, the church claimed ultimate authority in all fields of intellectual and spiritual endeavor, including what we now call science. There is many a weighty tome detailing the scientific accomplishments of the medieval era and little or no evidence that I am aware of to indicate that the church deliberately thwarted scientific enquiry. The consensus view today is that the scientific revolution of the seventeenth century happened because a critical mass of knowledge had been accumulated, thanks to the efforts of medieval thinkers.

At the same time, it is not completely accurate to say that the medieval church *encouraged* science. The church's position on science was that it was valuable, and interesting, and a useful adjunct to scriptural knowledge, but that one should be careful not to get too wrapped up in its fascinations, because that could lead to distraction from what was really important—that is, matters of the soul. It is an undeniable fact, for example, that there were Jesuit astronomers every bit as adept as Galileo, who made similar observations, but claimed no credit.

Pope Urban VIII favored Galileo at first. But, after Galileo published the Dialogues *in 1632, the pope turned against him. Why the change of heart?*
I have already referred to the overriding problem of Galileo's having disobeyed a direct order not to preach Copernicanism, but there is also some thought that the pope took the buffoonlike character of Simplicio in the *Dialogues* as being a deliberate personal attack. However, there is no documentary evidence for this, nor is it likely to me that Galileo would have gone out of his way deliberately to alienate such a powerful friend and ally.

Galileo was insistent that the once unified field of *science* or knowledge of the world be split in two, in a very literal sense. What we now call science and was then called *natural philosophy* was to be the exclusive domain of the scientist (of whom Galileo is the modern forerunner), while *moral philosophy*, including theology, was to be the realm of the church and its philosophers and theologians. The clear implication of this—one that the church understood but Galileo seems not to have grasped—was that as science steadily expanded its (potentially all-inclusive) knowledge of the workings of the world, the domain of moral philosophy would, of necessity, steadily shrink into irrelevance. This represented a threat to church authority—and to the status of Truth—that church leaders were simply unwilling to accept.

Cardinal Bellarmine was considered among the most intellectual and scientific-minded of the cardinals in Galileo's time. Yet he was involved in the trial and burning at the stake of mathematician Giordano Bruno. At first he tried to protect Galileo but then became the point man used by the pope to censure him. How do you explain Bellarmine's behavior?

Bellarmine died in 1621, twelve years before the trial of Galileo. However, at the trial a letter from Bellarmine, written to Galileo in 1616, was introduced. It made it clear that Galileo had been warned at that time about keeping his views on Copernicanism to himself. The same letter affirmed that a rumor that Galileo had been asked to abjure his views on Copernicanism was false. At the time of his death, Bellarmine was on good terms with Galileo, and so it is simply not accurate to characterize the cardinal as in any way having actively assisted in Galileo's conviction. Bellarmine's only problem with his friend Galileo was the scientist's insistence on treating Copernicanism as fact, rather than hypothesis. After all, it had not been proved.

What effect did the Inquisition have on Galileo and possibly other scientists of the time? Did the threat of torture and murder hang over their every thought and word?

The role of the Inquisition, I believe, has been overstated. It was certainly an iniquitous institution, particularly from the modern point of view of universal human rights (a concept born in the eighteenth century). But, with possible exceptions, such as fifteenth-century Spain, where it was corrupted and abused (against papal complaints) by the monarchs of the time, it was not an all-pervading, omniscient force like some modern secret police agency. It concerned itself almost exclusively with doctrinal heresy and its suppression, and only rarely did scientific thought fall into that category.

One exception was speculation about whether the universe was infinite or finite. Giordano Bruno fell afoul of the Inquisition for preaching an infinite universe, along with many other heresies, and was eventually burned at the stake at Campo dei Fiori in Rome in 1600. (Bruno had been excommunicated by the Calvinist and Lutheran Churches as well, after leaving the Dominican fold.)

Bruno's case is often produced as evidence that the Inquisition tried to suppress science, but the historical record makes it clear, in my view, that this was not the case, that his "science" would have been tolerated had he not also crossed so many doctrinal boundaries. The truly great scientists of the era—Copernicus, Kepler, Galileo—all managed to conduct their observations and publish their findings despite, as in Galileo's case, eventual objections from the Inquisition.

In short, while the Inquisition certainly did not assist the advance of science, it did not seriously impede it, either.

It is also worth remembering that charges of heresy were a risk faced not just by Roman Catholics, but throughout Protestant Europe. (Holland is the single, honorable exception.) Even in liberal England, Thomas Hobbes faced threats of the burning of his books, and his person, for his philosophical views.

What about the Inquisition's use of torture?

Torture was rarely used by the Inquisition (Spain again provides the exception, particularly under the notorious Dominican, Tomás de Torquemada). The preferred approach was a kind of long-term forced psychoanalysis aimed at convincing the victim of the error of his or her ways. Certainly, no serious scholar thinks it was ever a real threat in Galileo's case. Far from being caged in a dungeon in Rome during the period of his trial, Galileo was comfortably ensconced in the luxury of the Villa Medici, which is not, of course, to say that it was a pleasant experience for him. He was clearly under great mental and emotional stress.

So, you would consider Galileo's punishment from the church a firm slap on the wrist?

Given the circumstances of his case, and the surrounding historical contingencies, Galileo's punishment—house arrest at the pleasure of the pope— seems to me to have been reasonably even-handed. It was certainly more than a slap on the wrist, but it was not Bruno's fate, either. While confined to his villa outside Florence, Galileo wrote his greatest contribution to science, *Discourses on Two New Sciences*. He met with the English philosopher Thomas Hobbes and the poet John Milton, and other intellectual luminaries of the day. He was able to visit his daughters at the nearby convent where they lived. He died of natural causes at age seventy-five in the company of his son, friends, and students, and was given the church's last rites. His remains were interred in the magnificent Franciscan church of Santa Croce in Florence (though not without some bureaucratic haggling over the details), where Dante and Michelangelo also rest.

Dan Brown refers to a supposedly lost manuscript called Diagramma della Verita, *written by Galileo while under house arrest. Brown also says that Milton wrote around the margins of the book. Do scholars believe Galileo wrote such a book or is the whole notion fiction?*

I have seen no reference to any such document in the scholarly literature, or anywhere else, for that matter. As for the Milton annotations, it's a nice fictional conceit, nothing more. Milton met with Galileo in Florence just before the scientist's death, but there is no record of their conversation. Milton does refer briefly to their encounter in *Areopagitica*, his famous polemic for freedom of the press in the face of Puritan censorship. He uses Galileo as an example of how censorship had "dampened the glory of Italian wits," bringing learning among them to a "servile condition."

Is there any evidence that Galileo could have been involved with the Illuminati, Freemasons, or other secret, anti-Vatican societies?

As far as I am aware, there is no such evidence, and given Galileo's well-documented respect for the church and his friendships with popes and cardinals, it seems unlikely, though not impossible. Certainly, there is no record of Freemasonry in Tuscany, the region of Italy where Galileo lived and worked, prior to 1735, when it came under the scrutiny of the local Inquisition for the first time. This was of course long after the scientist's death. The Masons do seem to have played an important part in having built the second, and more imposing, sepulcher to honor Galileo in Santa Croce. His remains were transferred there from their original, less conspicuous place of interment within that church in 1737 (when a second skeleton was found with his, possibly that of his eldest daughter).

What purpose has the myth of Galileo served over the years and how should we think of Galileo?
The myth of Galileo is one of the defining narratives of modern Western culture (or to be technical, of Modernism). The moral lessons it teaches are a cornerstone of our belief in the supreme power and validity of reason, and in science's exclusive access to reliable knowledge of the world. It teaches, in short, that religion and spirituality are but superstition. It also vividly illustrates the dangers and arbitrariness of religious authority, and the futility of resistance to the advance of science.

We should admire Galileo for what he was: an inspired but fallible progenitor of the scientific enterprise, understandably bedazzled by its power. We should at the same time recognize the important truths championed by his adversaries in the church, who drew from a much deeper well of philosophical experience. Not the least of those truths is that moral and natural philosophy cannot survive as separate and exclusive fields of knowledge without each running the risk of becoming a grotesque and dangerous parody of itself.

BLIND AMBITION AND SINCERE PIETY

AN INTERVIEW WITH MARCELO GLEISER

In Angels & Demons, *Dan Brown refers to Galileo as an "ill-fated astronomer." Marcelo Gleiser, a physicist, professor, and author of* The Dancing Universe: From Creation Myths to the Big Bang, *paints a more nuanced portrait, calling the great scientist a "pious heretic," a man possessed of a rare combination of blind ambition and sincere piety. Gleiser maintains that it was Galileo's ambition— and the belief that he was destined to save the church from ignorance—that ultimately antagonized the church hierarchy.*

Gleiser regards this early fissure as "a schism between science and religion that is still very much alive today." He doesn't see an end to this split, in our lifetime: "The poison is dogmatism," he says. Only a more conciliatory approach, on the part of both the spiritual and the secular forces involved in the great debate, will help resolve the conflict.

Here Gleiser sheds historical light on Galileo, his clash with the church, and Brown's depiction of the larger debate. In a subsequent interview (see Chapter 6), he delves into more scientific matters, discussing how the study of physics has evolved from Galileo to the big bang.

Marcelo Gleiser is the Appleton Professor of Natural Philosophy at Dartmouth College and the author of *The Dancing Universe: From Creation Myths to the Big Bang*, scheduled to be reprinted in early 2005. He is also the source for the phrase "pious heretic" used in the title for this chapter.

A central theme in Dan Brown's Angels & Demons *is the incompatibility of science and religion, starting from the clash between Galileo and the Catholic Church, and extending to a modern-day war between the Vatican and physicists at CERN, a Swiss research lab. What makes this science versus religion theme so compelling?*

Most people in the world are religious. The Bible is by far the all-time best-seller. The need to believe in a supernatural reality that transcends our earthly existence is as old as history. Death, and our awareness of it, renders us helpless in the hands of time. It's not easy to accept that our days are numbered, that random accidents happen, that there is no higher purpose to existence other than what we make of it with our own choices. So we look up for answers, creating deities of all kinds to guide us, to offer us solace, to bypass, somehow, our limited time span.

In came science, and, in four hundred years, proceeded to explain "mysteries" that were once attributed to gods or miracles, making it harder for people to believe. There is no doubt that the secularization of society brought much freedom to humankind. But to many it also left a spiritual void in its wake. To the believer, science is seen as a threatening force that will take away the comforting promises of paradise, eternal life, reincarnation, etc. A world without God is too hard to endure. To the nonbeliever, religion is seen as an archaic structure devoid of any meaning; the idea that there are supernatural forces ruling the cosmos and our lives is considered utterly absurd and fantastic.

It was Dan Brown's clever idea to bring the conflict into CERN, the "sacred church" of science. In the novel, one of CERN's leading scientists, Leonardo Vetra, wants to use science to prove the existence of God. If he succeeds, religion wins. Quite ironically, it wins through science, with a small-scale creation repeated in the laboratory; the big bang as a reproducible event. This experiment is not something science can actually contemplate doing anytime soon or perhaps ever, as there are problems with its conception. But it makes for a great story: a religious scientist trying to reconcile the age-old schism between science and religion—and within his own soul as any good creative work should—through his scientific research.

You write that it's "surprising" that science and religion are thought of as being so disparate in modern times.

There isn't a clear-cut point in history where science and religion parted their ways for good. There is, however, a trend, which began during the seventeenth century with the work of Galileo, Johannes Kepler, Isaac Newton, and others. At the time, science, or better, natural philosophy, was seen as inferior to theology. Kepler and Newton, both very religious, thought of their science as a way to approach God, to understand his ways. They believed that nature was a blueprint of God's mind, and that our reason was the bridge; unveiling nature's mysteries was a path to God. Galileo saw his work as separate but complementary to his religious beliefs. He kept the two apart in print, although his intentions were quite clear: the church *had* to embrace the new science (his science!) to avoid certain embarrassment. In his book *The Assayer* he wrote, "It was granted to me alone to discover all the new phenomena in the sky and nothing to anybody else." Clearly, he thought of himself as the one chosen by God to reveal the truth about nature to a world stuck in Aristotelian dogma. This is not very different from a prophet, who believes that he or she is chosen by God to reveal his words and wisdom to the world.

Copernicus's model of a sun-centered universe was a radical departure from the thinking of the time. What led Copernicus to propose such a theory? And why didn't the church oppose his discovery at first?

Copernicus was what I once called a "reluctant revolutionary." He was, in many ways, a product of the Renaissance, having studied in Italy in the early 1500s. His sun-centered model clearly reflected that. He wrote of the beautiful harmony achieved through his arrangement, where the order of the planets is dictated by the time they take to complete a circle around the sun: Mercury, with three months, the closest, and Saturn, with twenty-nine years, the farthest. (There were only six planets known at the time since Uranus, Neptune, and Pluto are not visible to the naked eye.) But there was another less groundbreaking reason behind Copernicus's idea: around 150 CE, Ptolemy had developed an earth-centered model where the earth was slightly displaced from the center and planets moved with regular speeds about a fictitious point called the *equant*. By Copernicus's time, Ptolemy's model was *the* accepted model. The problem is that it clashed with one of the rules laid down by Plato some eighteen centuries earlier, that any model describing the motions of the planets had to use circles *and* regular velocities. Copernicus wanted to make astronomy once again compliant with the Platonic rules. His sun-centered model did exactly (or almost exactly) that. So, one may say that he moved astronomy forward while trying to move it backward. He had no intention of causing a "revolution."

Copernicus's great book, *On the Revolutions of the Heavenly Spheres*, included a preface that advised the reader not to take the sun-centered hypothesis seriously as it violated the holy scripture; it was only to be considered a mathematical construction to aid in the calculations of planetary motions. It turns out that this preface was *not* written by Copernicus but by one Andreas Osiander, a Lutheran theologian who oversaw the publication of the book while Copernicus lay in a near coma on his deathbed. Osiander's preface, even if

somewhat sneaky, softened the blow: the church would not take offense on
Copernicanism until much later, and that thanks to Galileo.

Why, then, was Galileo's acceptance of the Copernicus model an outrage to the Catholic Church?
When Galileo came onto the scene defending Copernicus, he took a con-
frontational approach, challenging the church to revise its theological interpretation of the Bible as it conflicted with what he was observing in the skies.
Galileo's diplomacy and timing couldn't have been worse; the Protestant Reformation presented a serious challenge to the church's authority. It certainly
didn't need a new one to emerge, especially in Italy.

*Brown writes that Galileo believed that "science and religion are not enemies, but rather allies—two
different languages telling the same story, a story of symmetry and balance." Is that an accurate description
of Galileo's thinking, and if so, does it suggest that the church did not want science and religion to be
unified in any way?*
It is clear that Galileo did not want to be at war with the church. At least
openly. He tried, even if somewhat heavy handedly, to forge a compromise
with church leaders. First in 1615, when he was told by Cardinal Barberini
(who was to become Pope Urban VIII, the same one who condemned Galileo
later) not to go "beyond the arguments used by Ptolemy and Copernicus,"
that is, to consider a sun-centered cosmos as a mathematical construction
only and not the real thing. At about the same time, the master of controversial questions of the Roman College, the all-powerful Cardinal Bellarmine,
challenged Galileo to find irrevocable proof that the sun was indeed at the
center. Galileo's answer came in the famous *Dialogue on the Two Chief World Systems*, the book that got him into trouble with the Inquisition. It portrayed the
church's position (in particular that of Pope Urban VIII) in the voice of
Simplicio, a simple-minded and old-fashioned Aristotelian. Galileo had gotten permission to publish the book from Urban, as long as he included the
church's position that even if evidence pointed toward a sun-centered cosmos,
God could, by a miracle, move the skies and everything else around a fixed earth
daily as opposed to having the earth turn around itself like a spinning top.
Galileo thought he could outsmart the church leaders, as he had many others in
his life. That was his big mistake. The church had no interest in aligning itself
with a new science that constituted a challenge to its authority. Galileo's intentions may have been toward reconciliation, but his approach was disastrous.

*So you believe the church couldn't tolerate Galileo's arrogance in trying to portray himself as purveyor of
the sole truth?*
Exactly. In 1615 Cardinal Ciampoli, expressing the views of Cardinal Barberini, wrote to Galileo to leave theology to the theologians: "To explain the

scripture is claimed by theologians as their field, and if new things are brought in, even by an admirable mind, not everyone has the dispassionate faculty of taking them just as they are said." In other words, don't step on our turf. But Galileo did.

Did Galileo harbor any desires, secret or overt, to retaliate against the church and, if so, did he act on them?

Not in any obvious way. The notion that he founded a secret society, although very interesting, is probably a fiction. However, while he was in house arrest, he did write another book, the *Discourse Concerning the Two New Sciences*, which was smuggled out of Italy and published in Leyden in 1638. The fact that he wrote the book and that it got printed in Europe proves that he still nurtured a rebellious interest in pushing his "new science" forward. The book is, perhaps, Galileo's most important contribution to science, in which he returned to his youthful explorations and obtained, through a remarkable combination of experimentation and geometrical deduction, the laws describing the motions of falling objects and projectiles. It was of key importance to Newton's studies of gravity and motion, and a deadly blow to Aristotelian science.

How did the conflict between science and religion manifest itself after Galileo?

The success of Newtonian science broadened the split between science and religion; it became increasingly clear that the more one understood nature, the less one had to invoke God to explain this or that. God became a solution to questions the new science couldn't yet explain, the so-called God of the gaps. As science progressed, the gaps got tighter. During the eighteenth century, the deists, such as Benjamin Franklin, relegated God to the role of creator of the world and the laws that rule its behavior: he was no longer a constant presence in the universe. This is the "watch-maker" God, an image that became increasingly popular in the nineteenth century. The church's reluctance to follow and accept the emerging scientific view of the world didn't help; science was seen as the ultimate rational pursuit of knowledge, devoid of any spirituality. It led men away from God. Its power to explain natural phenomena threatened the church's hegemony. On the other hand, an increasing number of scientists looked at religion with suspicion, as most couldn't accept faith-based knowledge. To them, it was clear that nature's mysteries were accessible to the human mind, and that it was absurd to assume the existence of supernatural forces ruling the cosmos. The two camps became entrenched. Scientific works no longer had room for any reference to religion for the simple reason that faith didn't help one understand natural phenomena or stop an epidemic.

Can a person approach understanding the world through science and still be religious?

Certainly. I know many scientists who are also very religious—Muslims, Jews, and Christians, to cite only monotheistic religions. To them, science illuminates the path to God, helps them appreciate his masterwork, nature. There are also less conventional ways to find religiosity in science. Take, for example, Einstein. He had great disdain for the authoritarian structure of organized religion, claiming that the pursuit of science is the only truly religious experience one can have. To him, and many others, science helps express a deep sense of spiritual communion with nature without the need to invoke any supernatural being or beings.

Can you give us a few more examples of prominent scientists who have managed to reconcile science and religion in search of answers about the universe?

Dan Brown gives us an excellent example, that of the Belgium cosmologist-priest Georges Lemaître. In 1931 Lemaître proposed a model that became known as the *primeval atom*. His idea was that the universe appeared out of the radioactive decay of a giant nucleus. Although he didn't propose the big bang model per se as Brown suggests, Lemaître's ideas clearly influenced George Gamow, the real architect of the big bang model. Perhaps surprisingly, Lemaître never openly mixed his science and his faith. Even the question of where the primeval atom came from was, he believed, a scientific question. He was disconcerted when, in 1951, Pope Pius XII compared the big bang with Genesis. To him, science was perfectly deterministic and didn't need supernatural causes. Mixing the two would only cause confusion and strife. His faith transcended the material description of nature achieved by science.

There are many other examples. Abdus Salam, a Nobel Prize–winning physicist, was also a Muslim. He kept his religion and science in different compartments of his public life. Arthur Eddington, the leading astrophysicist of the early twentieth century, was a Quaker. It is in the intimacy of a scientist's private life that you may find the dynamic interplay of science and religion in action. To many, faith is what fuels their creative work in science.

Do you believe this schism between science and religion can be resolved, or will be resolved in our lifetime?

I believe it can, but don't think it will. The only way to resolve this schism is to greatly improve the quality of science education. There is widespread confusion as to what the goals of science are. Unfortunately, religious people see science as a threat to their beliefs, that the more science explains about the universe, the less room there is for faith in the supernatural. This is partially the fault of certain scientists, especially the ones who adopt a "no-dialogue" attitude toward religious people. A colleague once told me that the mere act of sitting at a round-table discussion with creationists gives them credibility they don't deserve. Although I understand my colleague's position, I don't think it will help things get any better. You may not convince the people at the table, especially those who believe that the Bible can be used as a scientific text, but you may open the minds of some in the audience. I'd like to believe in the ability we have to learn from each other.

So neither side has all the answers?

The problem springs from the belief that science will one day have *all* the answers and that, once that day comes, religion will be obsolete. I find this to be complete nonsense. First, science will *never* have all the answers; nature is much smarter than we are. We will always be scrambling to catch up with new discoveries, as we peer deeper and deeper into the very small and the very large. It would be quite arrogant of scientists to presume that we can and will have all the answers, although some do believe that. Second, science is not designed to address the spiritual needs filled by religion. Humans are spiritual creatures, who search for gods to become better than they are. To the atheist, this "god" may be nature and its mysteries, or the belief that there is a rational explanation to everything.

Science is a language, a narrative that describes the world we live in. It is an evolving process, constantly corrected by new knowledge. It is limited by its very structure, based as it is on empirical validation. There are certain questions and issues that simply don't belong to science, at least not science as we understand it nowadays: questions of moral choices, of emotional loss, even events that cannot be quantitatively tested or observed methodically. As Dan Brown wrote in the voice of Sylvie, the secretary to CERN's director general, "Did [scientists] really believe quarks and mesons inspire the average human being? Or that *equations* could replace someone's need for faith in the divine?" This is precisely the general perception, that science is a replacement for religion. That is *not* what science is about.

Believers should accept the fact that one does not need religion to be a moral person. On the other hand, one should always have the choice to believe, so long as this belief does not infringe on the freedom of others not to. Unfortunately, religious extremism often has a blinding effect, rendering the faithful unable to understand and respect the other, or to listen and learn from scientists. Until the blinds are lifted and difference is not perceived as threat, the schism will remain.

AVENGING GALILEO

BY STEPHAN HERRERA

Those who believe that Galileo's sacrosanct place in history cannot be overstated haven't read *Angels & Demons*. Many of the scientists and historians who have reviewed Dan Brown's depiction of Galileo as a vengeful, scientific zealot who aids and abets a secret, conspiratorial society called the Illuminati, find it nothing short of pure science fiction.

It's not just that Brown takes science and history and twists them to advance his plot. Like many fiction writers, he does—with aplomb. It's that Brown, in one plot twist and secret revelation after another, ends up turning Galileo into a character only a conspiracy theorist could love. And by casting Galileo as an intentional martyr who would risk everything for the sake of science, this great and complex figure is turned into a one-dimensional character, which he certainly was not.

Academic critics tend to protest too much about the liberties that fiction writers take to tell their tales. But, Dan Brown critics do have a point: although Galileo really "was a thorn in the side of the Vatican," the broader truths about Galileo's life and legacy are much more interesting than the fictional biography ascribed to him in *Angels*

Stephan Herrera is Life Sciences editor at MIT's *Technology Review* magazine in Cambridge, Massachusetts. His book, *Closer to God: The Fantastic Voyage of Nanotechnology*, will be published in the fall of 2005.

& Demons. Brown unwittingly pushes Galileo further into the realm of mythology and martyrdom. The more this image grows, especially in pop culture, the more it eclipses Galileo's real contributions to science and perpetuates the silly and cynical notion that science and religion are natural enemies. What should be abundantly clear is that nothing suffers more from this false premise than science itself.

DEEP IMPACT

To scientists, Galileo gave the world new insights into the laws of physics. To this day, scientists at places like CERN and NASA still talk of "Galilean transformations." Brown contributes to the transformation of Galileo from a scientist to a martyr. There is a reason why Galileo is more famous and revered than physicists like Fermi, Bohr, Newton, even Einstein: history loves a martyr.

The romantic view of the man shows no sign of disappearing. Alas, Galileo was just a man. To be sure, he was a great man of science—certainly one of the best—but he was human, imperfect. He fathered three illegitimate children. He was not always as smart as Brown's characters seem to think. In fact, in a sense, he was playing a dangerous game with the Vatican and the Medicis by using their patronage to push for the acceptance of Copernican theory. But then again, in addition to being a man of science, he was an entrepreneur, a bit of a hustler, and a man who wanted it all.

His treatment at the hands of the Inquisition, while Draconian and frustrating, was better than the fate the Inquisition usually meted out to its enemies and perceived heretics during that era. Although Galileo spent his final years under house arrest, he was spared the fate meted out to so many others convicted of heresy by the Inquisition at that time. He was not killed, thrown in a dungeon, or tortured. He was not denied creature comforts or contact with colleagues, admirers, or family, or medical attention. In fact, he spent his final years in a villa in Arcetri, under the Tuscan sun—and, as Dava Sobel so beautifully detailed in *Galileo's Daughter*, very close to the center of the universe of his doting daughter Sister Marie Celeste.

Galileo was a late bloomer and began his career first as an educator before branching out as a writer, historian, mathematician, cosmologist, and inventor. He did not, as many believe, invent the telescope. But in 1609, in his mid-forties, just a few years after the telescope was invented in Holland, he refined its design significantly. He spent many more years after that making additional refinements that greatly advanced celestial observation. If he wasn't the first to use a telescope to view a super nova, Jupiter's moons, Saturn's rings, the mountains on the moon—and most historians believe he was—he was certainly the first to create mathematical proofs of their existence from his observations, which is why space probes are named after him these days.

"G," as physicists like to call him now, seemed to get smarter and more curious and observant with age. He gave lectures on the shape, location, and dimensions of hell as described in Dante's *Inferno*. He gave private tutorials on Euclidian geometry, arithmetic, fortification, surveying, cosmography, and optics. He was in his forties when he first published and formulated mathematical explanations for the isochronism of the pendulum, and the speed of falling objects, the rate of which he surmised was a factor of their density, not their weight as Aristotle had theorized. He invented a crude thermometer to measure air and water temperature and a hydrostatic balance to measure the gravity of objects.

His observations and calculations of gravity, ocean tides, and the interplay between the moon's orbit around the earth, and the earth's elliptical path around the sun, validated the Copernican theory that the sun, not the earth, is the center of our solar system. Dan Brown correctly notes that "NASA's current model of planetary orbits, observed through high-powered telescopes" really is astonishingly close to what Galileo predicted four hundred years ago.

The Robert Langdon character in *Angels & Demons* is right in thinking that Galileo was a man who could turn mathematics into poetry. Brown refers to Galileo writing in "ancient Italian." Actually, he wrote in Tuscan, a dialect or linguistic approach that, while not appropriately termed "ancient" (Dan Brown seems to describe anything old as "ancient"), lends itself particularly well to poetry, as in Dante's use of Tuscan dialect, and as in Galileo's preferred format: the dialogue. The Tuscan dialect is also well suited to sarcasm, which Galileo exploited fully in nearly all of his writings that dealt with debunking Aristotelian and Platonic reasoning.

LOST IN TRANSLATION

Contrary to what is implied in the novel, Galileo did not try to sneak things under the noses of his benefactors in the Vatican. Galileo believed that science had to be transparent. Unlike Aristotle and Plato, Galileo knew that reason alone, without the support of observation, tabulation, and experimental replication, would not suffice for scientific evidence. While it is certainly true that "Galileo was a thorn in the side of the Vatican's," as Brown describes him, he did not set out to be a thorn, much less a martyr for the cause of science and the scientific method.

Scholars like the late Stillman Drake of the University of Toronto theorize that Galileo did not anticipate the negative response of the Vatican to his 1614 letter to Grand Duchess Christina of Tuscany and later to the publication of his 1632 book, *Dialogue on the Great World Systems, Ptolemaic and Copernican*. After all, *Dialogue* had been vetted and cleared by no less than four of the Vatican's own censors prior to publication. Some theorize that either the censors did not fully grasp what Galileo was arguing or they simply did not read it. Some believe that the explicit tract on heliocentric theory was "buried" toward the end of the book when it was submitted for review, and then relocated to a more prominent section at the front of the book for publication.

Richard Landon, director of the Thomas Fisher Rare Book Library at the University of Toronto, which houses the Stillman Drake collection of Galileana, says that the letter to Christina and then the *Dialogue* were Galileo's attempt to reconcile religion with science. "Citing Copernicus in an over-simplified way, Galileo was asserting that there are many things we don't understand perfectly and the fact that we seek more perfect understanding of the unknown reflects the beneficence of God."

Far from explicitly trying to upend centuries of Christian doctrine, and put himself at odds with Pope Urban VIII and the Inquisition, Galileo thought it would have been abundantly clear at that point in time that his main gripe was with Aristotle and Ptolemy—not the church. Like all scientists at the time, as Robert Langdon and Vittoria Vetra note, Galileo was not fond of the church putting a religious spin on his discoveries. What Brown fails to note, however, is that this did not drive Galileo underground or bring out his dark side. Galileo thought he understood how to manage the politics of the Vatican, so why bother with cloak and dagger? As the scholars at the Galileo Project at Rice University note, Galileo had a series of close relationships with popes and cardinals. For twenty-two years, even before he became Pope Urban VIII, Cardinal Maffeo Barberini, for example, was an enthusiastic benefactor of Galileo's and even sided with Galileo on controversial matters such as his theory on the motion of the tides.

Urban VIII thought he and Galileo had an understanding that, because of the changing winds of politics in the Vatican (which translated meant the imposed insecurity of the Inquisition and the rise of Protestantism), Galileo should frame his support for Copernicus's heliocentric theory over Aristotle's geocentric theory as a hypothesis. Galileo badly miscalculated the depth of his friendship with Urban versus the powerful political imperatives of the day for the pope. As a Rice University Galileo scholar explains it, "It appears that the pope never forgave Galileo for putting the argument of God's omnipotence (the argument he himself had put to Galileo in 1623) in the mouth of Simplicio [Galileo's *Dialogue* character, whose name might be rendered in English as "the simpleton"], the staunch Aristotelian whose arguments had been systematically destroyed in the previous four-hundred-odd pages."

DEMYSTIFYING DAN BROWN'S GALILEO

Stillman Drake barely gave conspiracy theories about Galileo's role in the Illuminati a second thought. No serious scholar pays much attention to this conspiracy theory—his role in creating or sustaining it was dramatically exaggerated. Still, as Brown seems to be suggesting, Galileo could certainly be forgiven if he supported the spirit, if not necessarily some of the cultish methods, of groups such as the Illuminati. And Galileo devotees, then and now, could be forgiven if they harbored some resentment about the way the Vatican and Pope Urban VIII handled their disagreements with Galileo. No doubt about it: the Vatican behaved badly, threatening to torture, imprison and burn him at the stake unless he agreed to get down on his knees "to abjure, curse and detest" his belief in Copernicus's heliocentric theory.

Hal Hellman, the Galileo historian and bestselling author of *Great Feuds in Science*, is among the skeptics who say that although Galileo certainly had a right to, he did not play a part in a secret vendetta against the Vatican and probably never lost his religion. To the contrary. "Galileo remained a believer, in spite of his treatment by the church," said Hellman. Very much as the character Robert Langdon opines, Hellman reckons that Galileo's Illuminati would have been a secret society, but a sane and tame one, dedicated only to scientific discussion and research, not violence, revenge, and humiliation.

But suppose Galileo had been just as naive about the unintended consequences of creating and encouraging a secret society of "enlightened" thinkers to hold forth and press ahead with their scientific discoveries as he had been about the Vatican's response to his dialogues on Copernican theory. Certainly one can imagine that things might have turned out badly in this case, too. One can imagine that Galileo might have thought he was helping the cause of science by organizing a secret cadre of scientists and rationalists, producing for posterity a secret handbook written in a language not easily deciphered by Vatican censors, filled with riddles for the ages penned in a secret script whose answers rely upon a reader's grasp of the great Archimedes-inspired language, mathematics.

"Brown has done his homework here," Hellman said. "Brown's use of Galileo as the generator of the obscure booklet, *Diagramma della Verita (Diagram of Truth)*, was very clever. This booklet is the kind of thing Galileo might have written—if indeed the Illuminati had been 'Galileo's Illuminati,' which they weren't—because Galileo appreciated burlesque poetry and low comedy." Still, like most historians of the period, Hellman counts himself among those who suspect that the Illuminati only came into being in substantive form in 1776—close to 150 years after Galileo's trial at Inquisition headquarters in Rome.

What Dan Brown's Robert Langdon neglects to mention is that Galileo guilt has caught up with the Vatican. In 1992 Pope John Paul II apologized for the church's treatment of Galileo and acknowledged what more than a few in the Vatican felt even during the time of Galileo that science and religion need not be enemies.

3: OF CONSPIRACIES AND CONSPIRATORS: THE ILLUMINATI ILLUMINATED

One man's search for the inheritors of the conspiracy said to rule the world • Separating the myth and reality of the Illuminati • The origins and activities of Dan Brown's Hassassin • Did the Assassins serve as "mystical aspirants" for the Knights Templar and Masons? • Are the Illuminati still active in one form or another? • Skull and Bones: America's enduring bent toward the secret and powerful • The Illuminati as the ultimate source for science fiction . . . maybe

ON THE TRAIL OF THE ILLUMINATI: A JOURNALIST'S SEARCH FOR THE "CONSPIRACY THAT RULES THE WORLD"

BY GEORGE JOHNSON

Many readers encounter the history and mythology of the Illuminati for the first time in the course of reading Angels & Demons. *They typically wonder if the Illuminati is a real organization in history and, if so, how much of Dan Brown's description is accurate. To help answer that question, we turned to George Johnson, the well-known* New York Times *science writer. Johnson shares several interests with Dan Brown and fans of* Angels & Demons: *He has written extensively about the conflicts and confluences of science and religion, including contributing an essay on that topic elsewhere in this volume. He has written about quantum physics and antimatter. And, as it turns out, he has written a book that deals extensively with the Order of Illuminati, its history, and the uses of myths and legends about the strange organization by (mostly right-wing) modern conspiracy theorists. That book,* Architects of Fear: Conspiracy Theories and Paranoia in American Politics, *was published in 1983 and remains a veritable gold mine of hard fact and analysis about the real history of the Illuminati. Even more important than the factual history presented by Johnson is his description of the vast web of myth that has grown up around the Illuminati and similar organizations of the past and present and the negative political uses to which the myth is sometimes put.*

For Secrets of Angels & Demons, *Johnson wrote a mini-memoir of the experiences more*

George Johnson writes about science for the *New York Times* from Santa Fe, New Mexico, and is winner of the AAAS Science Journalism Award. His seventh book, *Miss Leavitt's Stars*, will be published in the spring of 2005 by Norton.

than two decades ago that drew him into the Illuminati, conspiracy theories, and political paranoia and its
impact on American politics.

Twenty years later, the boxes are still stacked in my shed, stuffed with pamphlets, newspapers, books, magazines, cassette tapes, even a few educational comic books, all describing in numbing detail the connections of a conspiracy as invisible and dense as the wiring on a computer chip. The writers of these tracts include anti-Communists, anti-Semites, anti-Catholics, anti-Protestants, antisecular humanists—so many things to be against! There are Christian fundamentalists who believe they, not the Jews, are God's chosen people, that America, not Palestine, is the promised land; there are British Israelites who insist that the people of England are the lost tribe of Israel; there are right-wing Catholics intent on overturning the Vatican II reforms; there is an Orthodox rabbi condemning Reform Judaism as the source of all modern evil.

What all these tracts have in common is the belief that the world is in such a mess because of a conspiracy. Never mind what you are told by the press. The events we see unfolding on the television news shows and across the pages of newspapers and magazines are stage-managed distractions, a shadow play for children, diversions to hide from us the true driving force of history: a centuries-old struggle for world control by a secret society called the Illuminati.

Egyptian sun worshipers and ancient Greek mystery cults; Gnostics, Cathars, Knights Templar, and other medieval heretics; mystical societies like the Spanish Alumbrados and the German Rosicrucians; European Freemasons, the Communist party, the Federal Reserve, the World Bank, the Council on Foreign Relations, and, of course, the Trilateral Commission, a kind of Rotary Club of the extremely rich and powerful—all have served as "Illuminati fronts" in somebody's conspiracy theory. A picture is worth a thousand words and the symbol of this group—an eye hovering above a pyramid—says it all: a small elite of enlightened beings sits at the top of the heap, controlling all that happens below. They also control the money supply, hence the appearance of their emblem on the back of the one-dollar bill along with the Illuminati motto: *Novus Ordo Seclorum.* For that is the ultimate aim of the conspiracy: a new secular order.

I stumbled across the legend, recycled yet again in novelist Dan Brown's *Angels & Demons* (bits and pieces also appear in *The Da Vinci Code*), back in the early 1980s when I was working as a newspaper reporter in Minneapolis. A reader named Frank had been struck (for all the wrong reasons) by an article I had written, something about politics. He called and promised me the biggest scoop of my life.

So on a very slow day (anything to get out of the office), I drove to the western suburb where Frank lived by himself amid the acres of asphalt and shag carpeting that had replaced the cornfields. He invited me into his modestly furnished living room, offered me coffee, and then launched into an increasingly angry disquisition on the horrors of modern life: wars, famines, the rise of totalitarianism, drugs, crime, venereal disease, the gyrations of the stock market, inflation, interest rates, atheism—all were soaring beyond control. Then he posed his question: *"Do you think all of this could be happening accidentally?"* The answer was in the hard glare of his eyes. Impossible. There had to be a master plan. Someone was benefiting—the people at the top of the pyramid. The Illuminati. He asked me to pull a dollar bill from my wallet and look at the back. Maybe he had a point. What was that weird shining eyeball doing there?

Frank turned out to be right in an unexpected way: this was the scoop of a lifetime. The story was not that everything was controlled by something called the Illuminati, but that, all over the world, people like Frank fervently believed that it was. Where did this strange story come from and why had I not heard it before?

I quit my job, moved into the library, and started my search.

They probably didn't mention this in your high school history class, not (I'm pretty sure) because of a nefarious cover-up but because of the relative obscurity of the event: on the ninth of May in 1798, a prominent leader of New England's powerful Congregationalists, the Reverend Jedidiah Morse (father to Samuel F. B. Morse, inventor of the telegraph) stood at the pulpit of the New North Church in Boston and warned of a secret plot to destroy Christianity and overthrow the newly formed government of the United States. Religion would be replaced with atheism, faith in God with faith in human reason. The name of this seditious force, he declared, was the Order of the Illuminati. Hiding inside Masonic lodges—a secret society coiled inside a secret society—the conspirators were waiting for the perfect time to strike.

The reverend's suspicions had become aroused by a book that had just been published and was, in its day, as popular as a Dan Brown thriller is today. It was called, in the unwieldy manner of the time, *Proofs of a Conspiracy Against All the Religions and Governments of Europe, Carried on in the Secret Meetings of Freemasons, Illuminati and Reading Societies*, by John Robison, a mathematician and professor of natural philosophy at the University of Edinburgh. As was clear from the title, he intended the book not as fiction but as an exposé. More accustomed to writing about scientific subjects (telescopes, magnetism) for publications like the *Encyclopaedia Britannica*, the professor had recently been shaken to hear that a secret society called the Bavarian Illuminati had infiltrated the Masonic lodges in France and was responsible for fomenting the bloody French Revolution. Far from a popular uprising of oppressed countrymen, Robison had concluded, the revolution had been stage-managed by this group of puppeteers, conspirators bent on overthrowing the French monarchy and its ally, the Catholic Church. Having toppled this holy alliance, the *ancien régime*, the Illuminati were spreading across Europe and possibly beyond. Their ultimate aim was world domination.

Reverend Morse had picked up his copy of *Proofs of a Conspiracy* in a Philadelphia bookshop. Intently turning the pages, he read how the plot had been hatched some two decades earlier in Bavaria, a principality in southeastern Germany, by an atheistic young professor named Adam Weishaupt. Hyped up on the ideas of Enlightenment philosophy—the superiority of reason over religion; the equality of all men—his Order of the Illuminati tried to overthrow the Bavarian government. The revolution failed and the group was disbanded, or so the authorities believed. In fact it had survived underground, spreading like the flu through the Masonic lodges of Europe. That was the story, anyway. Robison was a Freemason himself—he considered it a harmless diversion, a social organization aimed at instilling the virtues of brotherhood and charity. He was shocked to read what had been happening on the Continent. Recently, he warned, the tentacles of the Illuminati had reached into lodges in England, Scotland, and even the United States.

That was enough for Reverend Morse, who immediately took to the pulpit to warn of "dark conspiracies of the Illuminati against civil government and Christianity" emanating from an "illuminated mother club in France." Everyone, he said, must read Robison. "We have reason to tremble for the safety of our political, as well as our religious ark."

Late-eighteenth-century New England was a land ripe for paranoia. Since the fall of the Bastille in 1789, Americans had watched in wonder and then horror as the French Revolution, with its call for a "reign of reason"—fraternity, liberty, and equality—had given way to the Reign of Terror. In the churches, statues of the saints were toppled, replaced with depictions of atheist philosophers like Voltaire. Priests, noblemen, and other dissenters were dispatched to the guillotine.

Morse was terrified that the same sort of thing was about to happen in America. New England in those days had its own, milder form of church-state establishment: the Standing Order, consisting of Morse's Congregationalists, the upper-crust descendants of the Pilgrims, and their political allies, the Federalists. With Napoleon's armies now marching across Europe, President Adams, the leader of the Federalists, feared that the United States would soon be the target of a French-controlled insurrection, an attack from within. Rallying to the threat, Congress passed the Alien and Sedition Acts, reining in civil rights. Jefferson's Democrats were eyed suspiciously as French sympathizers. Who knew? Maybe the Illuminati were behind the plan.

Even the wildest tales become easier to believe when they hit you from two different directions. Around the time Robison's book appeared, some local newspapers began excerpting the recently translated writings ("the ravings of a Bedlamite," Thomas Jefferson called them) of a French Jesuit, Abbé Barruel, who traced the Illuminati plot back to the medieval Cathars and Templars. Before long his four-volume book on the Illuminati conspiracy was translated into English. (President Adams's wife, Abigail, considered the work must reading, recommending it to friends.)

Actually, it turns out, Robison and Barruel were cribbing from the same sources, a mass of pamphlets and articles that had been circulating in Germany and France, portraying the eighteenth century's various upheavals—political and ideological—as secret plots by a society of "illuminated" men. Whether this inner light was sparked by impious philosophy or, as some of the tracts argued, occult mystical powers, seemed unimportant. Either way it was a black light of pure evil.

It wasn't just the wackos who believed these things. In the midst of the hysteria, the president of Yale University, Timothy Dwight, warned the people of New Haven about the threat: "Shall we, my brethren, become partakers of these sins? Shall we introduce them into our government, our schools, our families? Shall our sons become the disciples of Voltaire, and the dragoons of Marat; or our daughters the concubines of the Illuminati?" His brother, Theodore Dwight, suggested in a public speech that Jefferson himself might be an Illuminatus. Reverend Morse listed Thomas Paine as a coconspirator.

When he took to the pulpit the following year, he was ready to name names: "I have now in my possession complete and indubitable proof ... an official, authenticated list of the names, ages, places of nativity, possessions, of the officers and members of a Society of *Illuminati* ..."

It is impossible now to read these words without thinking of a later demagogue, the Red-baiting Senator Joe McCarthy, as he spoke in 1950 of another nefarious plot: "I have here in my hand a list of 205 members of the Communist party ..."

Morse's evidence was as flimsy as McCarthy's: the names of some one hundred Virginians—mostly French immigrants—who belonged to a Masonic lodge with ties to one in France. Who knew what kind of radical ideas might be fermenting inside those walls? To Morse and other leaders of the Standing Order, the secular ideals of Enlightenment philosophy seemed as threatening as Communism would 150 years later. And France, in the grip of an ideology, its armies marching across Europe, had all the makings of an evil empire.

The human race has blundered on as long as it has because our brains have evolved into precision instruments for seeing order in the world, even when it isn't there. As I read about the New England Illuminati scare—the primary source is Vernon Stauffer's 1918 history, *New England and the Bavarian Illuminati*—and about the confusing role of Freemasonry in the French Revolution, I felt the neuronal hum of ideas clicking together to form a structure. It's a seductive feeling—that everything is connected, that this mad, mad world can be embraced by a single theory of everything, a tight network of cause and effect with a prime mover in control ... that there is a secret history in which everything you know turns out to be wrong.

Individually the facts check out. There was indeed a struggle in the eighteenth century between the Catholic Church and Freemasonry, whose secretive lodges served in those days as safe houses for gentlemen interested in new ideas—science, philosophy, politics, a cosmopolitan government, a secular society, a brotherhood of man extending across the boundaries of nations. Amid the claptrap of secret rituals and ceremonies, dangerous ideas were being entertained.

Some of these "free thinkers," as they were called, naturally became involved in the French Revolution. A few pursued more dubious interests: spiritualism, mesmerism, the cabala, alchemy. There was a thin line then between hardcore science and what we now dismiss as the occult. If all that seems hard to reconcile with Masonry today—conservative middle-aged businessmen raising money for charity and marching in patriotic parades—then remember: these were tumultuous times. The world was in upheaval, everything was up for grabs.

Whether or not, as legend has it, this unlikely consortium descended from traveling guilds of ancient stonecutters is a mystery. In any case *operative* masonry—the real kind, involving hammers and chisels and flying chips of rock—provided the inspiration for *speculative* Masonry: just as a rock can be shaped to fit sturdily within a wall so can a man be shaped into a better citizen, not just of the country but of the world.

Those who felt threatened by the phenomenon had no tools for understanding it, except as a conspiracy. Add in the spurious myths that Masons had concocted about themselves—that they inherited their traditions from the builders of the pyramids and biblical stonecutters, that their rituals have been protected for centuries by secret societies (this is where the Cathars, Templars, Rosicrucians, and so forth come in), and it all makes for a tantalizing tale. Each of these groups had, at one time or another, been branded by the church as heretics, dabblers in the occult; some had been dragged before the Inquisition. Spice up the tale with some of the Vatican propaganda that had been floating around for centuries and you had yourself a conspiracy theory: the history of the European Enlightenment stripped of its subtleties and contradictions, milled and hammered into rectilinear form.

Swept along by the intellectual free-for-all, an idealistic (and somewhat megalomaniacal) professor—the real Adam Weishaupt—started his Order of the Illuminati on May 1, 1776. (Conspiracy theorists just love this date: May Day, when the Communist Internationale is celebrated, grafted onto the birth year of the USA. Weishaupt wasn't the first to use the Illuminati name. Long before, a mystical society called the Alumbrados (Spanish for "Illuminati") had been targets of the Inquisition. There is no evidence that the Bavarian order shared anything with the Spanish Alumbrados except the name. But to the paranoiacs, there had to be a connection.

Viewed from the twenty-first century, Weishaupt's aims sound noble enough: to smuggle philosophy books—Voltaire, Diderot, D'Alembert, Montesquieu—past the Jesuits who ran the Bavarian school system and to arm a generation of scholars intellectually against the repressiveness of a country paralyzed by dogma. Weishaupt, however, was not the man for the job. It is human nature, perhaps, for one to take on the worst qualities of his enemies. The Jesuits, the soldiers of the Vatican, were known (partly through their actions and partly through Protestant propaganda) for their wiliness, as the pope's CIA. So ingrained is this image that the second definition of *Jesuit* in *Merriam-Webster* is "one given to intrigue or equivocation." Maybe Weishaupt felt that he was up against so formidable an opponent that he had to fight it on its own terms. In any case, his first order of business was to invent an array of secret rituals and codes that gave his new Illuminati the appearance of a cult of reason. Members in the lowest ranks were not allowed to know even the identities of their fellow initiates, much less that of their highest superiors. They were required to spy on each other and write intelligence reports. (Sometimes Weishaupt comes off as an eighteenth-century Bavarian version of Lyndon LaRouche.)

This weird combination of scholarship and skullduggery apparently had an appeal. The more illustrious members included Goethe, the German poet and natural philosopher, and the author of *Faust*. The movement spread throughout universities and Masonic lodges in Germany and Austria, becoming influential enough to engender a high degree of paranoia among keepers of the status quo. It was not a violent revolution Weishaupt and his acolytes were hoping to foment, but an intellectual one. Thomas Jefferson probably had it right when he later wrote:

> *As Weishaupt lived under the tyranny of a despot and priests, he knew that caution was necessary even in spreading information, and the principles of pure morality . . . This has given an air of mystery to his views . . . and is the color for the ravings against him of Robison, Barruel, and Morse.*

In the end, the church and the royalty easily triumphed. Responding to all kinds of fantastic accusations, the government quashed Weishaupt's order less than a decade after it was founded. The Illuminati conspiracy, such as it was, ended. And the Illuminati conspiracy theory had begun.

I still remember the evening in 1982 when I drove my rental car to the Los Angeles suburb of Van Nuys to hear a talk called "Adam Weishaupt, a Human Devil." I'd finished the library research for my book and was now on a fact-finding mission in the land of paranoia, southern California. Outside the meeting room, people sat at card tables selling tracts about the great conspiracy: *Secret Societies and Subversive Movements*, published in 1924; *None Dare Call It Conspiracy*, a classic of right-wing paranoia from the 1960s; a booklet called "The Cult of the All-Seeing Eye." There was even an edition for sale of Robison's *Proofs of a Conspiracy*, reprinted by the John Birch Society with a new introduction pointing out the parallels between the Illuminati and the Communist party.

For the next hour, the speaker, an electronics engineer for an aerospace company, laid out the twentieth-century version of the Illuminati legend. By now the tale had taken on a fundamentalist Christian flavor. The original Illuminatus was Lucifer himself—of course! the angel of light—and the mischief began in the Garden of Eden when Eve was tempted by the serpent and mankind fell from grace. From there the satanic plot was carried forth by the usual chain of cults, secret societies, and European philosophers, culminating in the Bavarian Illuminati staring at us insolently from the back of our own dollar bills. Light, Lucifer, Enlightenment, Illuminati—the words rang with a sonorous resonance. Maybe the deepest of mysteries is how ideas and images, these *memes*, as some scientists now call them, take on a life of their own. We are just the vectors, disposable receptacles, brains equipped with arms and legs for spreading the infection around.

From Van Nuys I drove to Rancho Cucamonga—what a perfect name for this town!—where I met Alberto Rivera, a disturbed little man who claimed to be a former Jesuit priest. He had left the church in horror when he learned that it was actually controlled by the Illuminati. Now here was a curious twist: a legend started by paranoid priests had mutated into anti-Catholic propaganda. The conspiracy theory had come full circle. The details were all there in a lurid Christian comic book, *Alberto*, part of a series in which the Catholic Church, invented by Lucifer and descended from pagan worship, uses occult powers to secretly control the world. The Vatican had fomented the Bolshevik Revolution, it had recruited Hitler to exterminate the Jews.

This was all becoming drearily familiar by now, as was the version of the tale in which the Jews are the Illuminati, with the plan for world domination laid out in *The Protocols of the Meetings of the Elders of Zion*. Was the Christian ecumenical movement a Catholic-Illuminati plot to subsume Protestantism (Alberto Rivera again) or a Protestant-Illuminati plot to undermine Catholicism (as in *Conspiracy Against God and Man* by Father Clarence Kelly)? Take your pick. I'd read in *The Occult and the Third Reich*, by the pseudonymous Jean-Michel Angebert, how the Nazis were an Illuminati front and, in *To Eliminate the Opiate* by Rabbi Marvin S. Antelman, how the Illuminati were Reform Jews.

Everyone was part of the conspiracy.

It turns out that there is a perfectly innocuous reason for the staring pyramid on the dollar bill. The very same symbol appears on the back of the Great Seal of the United States, as adopted by the Continental Congress in 1782. (On the front is the familiar eagle with *E Pluribus Unum* dangling from its beak.) Egyptology was all the rage back then—a pyramid already appeared on the Continental fifty-dollar bill. When he designed the Great Seal, Charles Thomson adopted a similar image to signify strength and duration. The eye, he explained, was that of Providence, looking benevolently over the new nation. *Novus ordo seclorum* is Latin for "a new order of the ages," referring, Thomson said, to "the new American era."

A century and a half later, Henry Wallace, a member of Franklin Delano Roosevelt's cabinet, suggested (with a bit of a stretch) that the motto could also be taken to mean "the New Deal." Roosevelt liked the idea and had the whole seal, front and back, emblazoned on the dollar.

As it happens, Masons do count both FDR and Wallace among their illustrious past members, along with George Washington, Benjamin Franklin, James Monroe, James Buchanan, Andrew Johnson, Theodore Roosevelt, William Taft, Warren G. Harding, Lyndon Johnson, and Gerald Ford—and for that matter Davy Crockett, Buffalo Bill, Douglas Fairbanks, and John Wayne.

Such are the coincidences that serve as the glue for conspiracy theories—and for

Dan Brown thrillers as well. Other novelists have also cashed in on the myth: Robert Anton Wilson in his whimsical *Illuminatus! Trilogy* and Umberto Eco in his intellectual bestseller *Foucault's Pendulum.* Both works were written tongue in cheek, with a high sense of irony. With his more lowbrow approach, Brown has brought the Illuminati thoroughly into the mainstream. Like the good Reverend Morse, we live in paranoid times.

In concocting his version, Brown takes even greater leaps than John Robison and Abbé Barruel. The most illustrious Illuminatus in *Angels & Demons*, Galileo, had, in fact, been dead for 134 years when the Bavarian order began. There are other possible connections. During Galileo's lifetime, Alumbrados were skulking around. Like the fictional Illuminati in the novel, they were indeed enemies of the Vatican. But their brand of mystical illumination would hardly have appealed to a scientist.

If I wanted to weave Galileo into a conspiracy theory, I think I would make him a Rosicrucian. In *The Rosicrucian Enlightenment*, the Renaissance scholar Frances Yates speculated that this secret society, similar to the Masons in its grab bag of beliefs, was a precursor to the Royal Society, which was to emerge as the most prestigious scientific organization in the world.

Then I'd connect the Rosicrucians to the Alumbrados and the Alumbrados to the Illuminati. The whole structure is lying there waiting to be twisted like a pretzel into all kinds of fantastic shapes.

When my book, *Architects of Fear: Conspiracy Theories and Paranoia in American Politics,* was published in 1984 it made barely a ripple in the infosphere, selling some three thousand copies before disappearing from the face of the earth. During a call-in radio show in Los Angeles, a member of the John Birch Society (Gary Allen, the guy who wrote *None Dare Call It Conspiracy*) told me I was a purveyor of "accident theory"—the naive belief that sometimes things just happen, that there is a fair amount of randomness in life. After winning a minor literary award, I'd pretty much forgotten about the book until a few years later when it was translated into Japanese.

I suspected something was wrong the moment I saw the cover: The legendary eye in the pyramid looking sternly, ominously, not at all providentially, out over the skyline of Wall Street, with a flurry of American dollars spreading everywhere. On the back was a photograph of a very nerdy Japanese man wearing a beret and large-framed glasses. Who was this person and what had he done to my book?

By then I was living in New York and working for the *New York Times*. Drawing on a colleague's advice, I hired a Japanese music student at Juilliard to translate the translation. The title was now *The World of Illuminati That Exceeds That of the Jews*. The subtitle was *The Power Organization That Rules the World*. On the bottom of the cover were the words "The Top Conspiracy Organization Revealed for the First Time. What Is the Illuminati!? And What About Japan?"

In a new foreword, the man in the beret had put forth his own conspiracy theory, a complex tale in which the Illuminati plotted World War II as part of a plan to subvert his country's economy. "In spite of the author's zealous protests," he wrote, "I am inclined to believe that Illuminati have the power to control the Western society as one great intellectual, economic, and political power." A translator's afterword suggests that my book may actually be Illuminati disinformation—part of a conspiracy to deny the conspiracy.

With some legal help, I was eventually able to get the book removed from the marketplace. I learned that this transmogrified version had sold far more copies than the original American edition. Promoting conspiracy theories turns out to be much more profitable than debunking them, another reason this mania will never go away.

THE FACT-FICTION REVERSAL:
THE ILLUMINATI, THE NEW WORLD ORDER,
AND OTHER CONSPIRACIES

AN INTERVIEW WITH MICHAEL BARKUN

In one of those fascinating inversions of history known only to conspiracy buffs, the Illuminati—which mainstream historians agree was a real society disbanded by the Bavarian government in the 1780s, after barely more than a decade of existence—has been displaced by the far more powerful Illuminati of the imagination. Conspiracy theories involving the Illuminati began appearing within a few decades of the order's dissolution. Since then, the Illuminati have been linked by conspiracists to every major historical event, and to quite a few events that occurred before the society even existed. Occult and esoteric groups claim to be descended from them. Religious leaders decry their global influence. And they have been linked to everything from UFO cover-ups to alien races of the hollow earth.

Why are we so fascinated by the Illuminati and all the rest of the conspiracies that have blossomed in modern times? One compelling reason, speculates Michael Barkun, a professor of political science in the Maxwell School at Syracuse University and an expert on terrorism and conspiracy thinking, is that we live in a time of huge uncertainty—and that conspiracies provide a way of making sense of reality, no matter how skewed. A respected scholar and FBI consultant, he has written extensively about marginalized groups and their cultural and historical roots. What emerges from his book A Culture of

Michael Barkun, author of *A Culture of Conspiracy: Apocalyptic Visions in Contemporary America*, is an expert on conspiracy theories, terrorism, and apocalyptic movements. He has served as a consultant to the FBI.

Conspiracy: Apocalyptic Vision in Contemporary America *is a portrait of an American culture teeming with conspiratorial speculation—a trend that may have disturbing implications for our future.*

⌐⌐⌐

Could you give us a brief outline of what we know historically about the origins and fate of the Illuminati?

The Illuminati was organized in 1776 in the independent kingdom of Bavaria by a professor of canon law, Adam Weishaupt. It was modeled organizationally after Masonic lodges, at a time when secret societies and fraternal orders were exceedingly common in Europe. The general thrust of the Illuminati order was to support a more open, rationalistic style of intellectual discourse. And generally to support less authoritarian and more open political systems. But I've never seen anything like reliable figures on size. There were never more than a few thousand members at its height.

Did the Illuminati infiltrate and control the Freemasons?

Certainly by the second half of the eighteenth century you find a very complex, and still not completely charted, relationship between political opponents of authoritarian governments on the one hand, and the Masonic movement on the other. There does not appear to be any kind of systematic use of the Masonic movement to advance a particular political agenda. But there is evidence that some Masonic lodges in some countries did provide an organizational home for opponents of absolutist monarchies.

Masonry, which grew rapidly in the eighteenth century, provided a body of symbols and a form of organization that lent itself to the needs of those seeking political liberalization. In some cases, Masonic lodges were "hijacked" by politically radical memberships. In others, quasi-Masonic organizations were established. This was a continental phenomenon, evident in France, Great Britain, Switzerland, Italy, and German areas.

There was no Illuminati connection to the Freemasons during Galileo's time because there was no Illuminati at the time.

In terms of the remnants of the historical Illuminati, did their ideas—their secrecy, their notions of organizational structure—persist in the later Mason movement?

Yes, in a way they did. But again, I would emphasize that there were dozens and dozens of organizations like this at roughly the same time. And they all placed a premium on secrecy. They were all trying to avoid being infiltrated by governments. Another, similar organization was the Carbonari, active in southern Italy in the early 1800s. It, too, combined Masonic trappings with an antimonarchical agenda. The heyday of such groups was from roughly

1775 to 1850. Despite their penchant for secrecy, they all went down in defeat.

Did these secret groups have a particular political agenda?

They were certainly hostile to absolutist monarchy. They emphasized the need to abolish traditional political and religious authority—more specifically, that of the Catholic Church and monarchy. And the combination of their intellectual agenda and their political agenda put them at odds with many in the church hierarchy, and with absolutist monarchies. As a result, beginning around the mid-1780s, governments in the areas in which the Illuminati operated began to act to suppress the order. By the late 1780s—roughly, 1787—the Illuminati had effectively been dissolved. So we're talking about an organization whose life span stretched from 1776 to some point in the following decade, maybe thirteen years in all. The geographical distribution of the Illuminati can't be described precisely, but it was certainly in the area now covered principally by Germany and Austria. Their teachings also appeared in other languages, such as French and Italian.

How was the Illuminati suppressed or dissolved?

It was suppressed through government banning, dismissal of members from official positions, and arrests. By the end of the 1780s, the organization had ceased to exist, although some former members undoubtedly migrated to some of the many other secret societies that remained active. There are a lot of people out there in the United States, particularly on the far right politically, who believe that they're still active. But no, the Illuminati ceased to exist in the 1780s.

Do you think different esoteric institutions, or secret societies, see themselves as a continuation of the Illuminati?

Many esoteric institutions create pedigrees for themselves. There are neo-Templar organizations, and there are organizations that claim lineage from ancient Egypt, and so on. These claims are invented without any specific historic evidence.

What can you tell us about the Hassassin, the villain of Angels & Demons?

By "Hassassin" I assume Dan Brown means what is more commonly known as the "Assassins." And I believe that he may have garbled the Arabic, because I've seen it transliterated as "Hashasheen."

The Order of Assassins was a part of Shia Islam that developed in northern Iran, in the eleventh century. It was a branch of Islam that is now known as the Ismaili—the group that's led by the Aga Khan. They are wholly peaceful.

But in their initial period, they had control of a fairly good-sized slice of what's now northern Iran. And they devised, for purposes of proselytizing, a form of terrorism that involved infiltrating individuals into areas that were controlled by their religious enemy. These individuals would then become servants of prominent political or religious leaders considered obstacles to their preaching and serve with great devotion.

At some point—sometimes years after they took the position, and seemingly out of nowhere—they would assassinate their master. Always with a dagger, and always in a public place. The name Hashasheen arose because there were some people who believed that only a person under the influence of hashish could possibly behave in this manner, turning on someone that they had served with such devotion.

There is a whole series of legends about the Assassins. The most common one is that before they left their home territory on their mission they were given hashish, and then taken into a beautiful garden, filled with comely maidens. When they awoke later they were told, You have visited paradise, and after you have completed your mission—which, of course, was in effect a suicide mission—you will have this paradise for eternity. There seems to be absolutely no basis for the hashish story, or the simulation-of-paradise story. The stories filtered west to the Holy Land, where they were picked up by the Crusaders.

The group from which the Assassins came was defeated militarily. Even though the purpose of the assassinations was supposedly to remove opponents of their preaching, it had the effect of increasing political and military opposition, and they were crushed. So there hasn't been an Order of Assassins for many centuries.

Was there any connection between the Assassins and the Illuminati, as Dan Brown suggests?
None. They existed at different points in time, in different areas of the world, in different cultures. The violent Ismaili were defeated probably around the twelfth or thirteenth century.

Besides falsely linking the Illuminati with Galileo, how accurately does Dan Brown portray the group otherwise?
First, a distinction needs to be made between the actual Illuminati and what might be called the myth of the Illuminati.

The myth of the Illuminati doesn't begin until after the actual Illuminati ceased to exist; it was a product of the French Revolution. The claim is that the Illuminati manipulated the French population to destroy the monarchy. And that literature created an alternative history of the French Revolution and also posited the notion of a secret society of enormous power and cunning, whose tentacles could reach across the Atlantic. So there's a period of an Illuminati scare in the United States at the end of the 1700s.

The myth of the Illuminati extends in two directions. We have versions of it that say the Illuminati were not dissolved, that they maintained their existence and their power, and continue on into the present day. That's one version. The other version, which looks more like Dan Brown's, says that they started much earlier than 1776. There is also literature that attempts to read the Illuminati back into earlier periods.

But I must say I've never seen the Galileo connection. Bear in mind that there were no Illuminati during Galileo's time. The other famous people mentioned by Brown—people like Bernini and Milton—couldn't have been in the Illuminati either, because the real, historical Illuminati was not formed until the next century.

As I have said, there is a substantial literature that attempts to link the Illuminati to much earlier secret societies. This literature begins to appear in English in the 1920s and '30s, in the interwar period. There are two English authors, Nesta Webster [*Secret Societies and Subversive Movements*] and Edith Starr Miller [*Occult Theocracy*], who wrote books that tried to make the case that there's a kind of seamless history of evil secret societies from ancient times to the present. That's a version of the Illuminati myth that has become very potent in the English-speaking world. More recent examples of this literature are *The World Order* by Eustace Mullins, who was a protégé of Ezra Pound, and *The New World Order* by evangelist Pat Robertson.

Tell us a little about the latest versions of the conspiracy theory.

The conspiracy literature that's out there now generally goes under the rubric of the *new world order*. And that's become a kind of common conspiracy theory that's accepted both in certain religious circles—principally among some Protestant fundamentalists and ultratraditional Catholics—and in secular circles, particularly on the far right. The right-wing John Birch Society is still selling John Robison's two-hundred-year-old anti-Illuminati book by mail order. There's a leftist version of new world order theory as well. New-world-order conspiracy theory has drawn together a lot of less inclusive conspiracy theories. For example, conspiracy theories about a world Jewish conspiracy. Conspiracy theories about a Jesuit conspiracy. Conspiracy theories about plutocrats and international bankers.

An example of this would be Pat Robertson's book *The New World Order*, which he published in the early 1990s. And it sold very, very widely. In this book, you've got the Trilateral Commission, the Federal Reserve, the Rothschilds and, of course, the Illuminati. So, in effect, the kinds of conspiracy theories that are floating around now have multiple players in them.

One interesting thing is what I call in my book *A Culture of Conspiracy* the *fact-fiction reversal.* You've got people reading works of fiction and saying, well, yes, this uses the conventions of fiction, but it's really intended to communicate a factual message. And to the extent that people read works of fiction with that kind of mind-set, the traditional distinction between fact and fiction begins to break down.

Are the new conspiracy theories modeled on older ones?

Definitely. For example, the Illuminati theories that start out seeking to explain the French Revolution reappear in the twentieth century claiming to explain the Russian Revolution. So they keep getting recycled.

Does Dan Brown add anything new to the earlier conspiratorial template? We hear he's writing a new book set in Washington, DC, that deals with the Freemasons and their history. Any thoughts about that?

Dan Brown's notion of insidious secret societies with activities that span centuries is very much in keeping with the tradition of twentieth-century conspiracist literature. But the Galileo and Roman aspects strike me as somewhat new, as well as his notion of the esoteric meaning of particular locations in Rome. There is now a kind of fringe literature that tries to make these kinds of claims about the street plan of Washington. If you tell me Brown is writing a new book set in Washington, I would not be surprised to see some of these arguments show up.

There's a lot of emphasis in this kind of thinking on the placement of monuments and the alignment of streets. There's also a conspiracy theorist in Britain, David Icke, who's made some of these same claims about European cities, particularly London and Paris. So you've got people out there who are arguing that the spatial placement of streets and buildings channels power in a particular way. These things are associated with the Masons and the Illuminati by various conspiratorial thinkers. It is kind of a quasi-magical notion.

Let's examine some specific claims that Dan Brown makes in Angels & Demons. *Were any members of the Illuminati actually arrested, tortured, and murdered by the church, as Dan Brown claims? Did any part of the Illuminati deliberately develop any sort of terrorist response?*

From my perspective, prior to the creation of the Order of Illuminati by Weishaupt, there were no Illuminati. There certainly were Illuminati who were arrested in the 1780s—but they were arrested not by church authorities, but by governments. As for a terrorist response to oppression, the Illuminati didn't develop one, no. They were viewed as a dangerous organization because of their ideas, but not for any specific violent action.

What about Dan Brown's assertion that the Masons have been infiltrating the government of the United States since its earliest days?

As far as I know, it is reasonably well documented that a number of the Founding Fathers were Masons. I'd be a little more skeptical about the similar claims made about George [H. W.] Bush because by the time you get into the late twentieth century, you're talking about a movement which is in decline in America. Even if a significant number of national political figures were or are Masons, however, I don't think it suggests any conspiracy. I think it suggests a common social background, and a relevant social network.

What conspiracists do is produce circumstantial evidence by indicating, for example, the position of particular individuals in different organizations and governmental hierarchies. So there are claims, for example, that if a particular individual is a member of the Council on Foreign Relations and the Trilateral Commission and so on, that he must therefore be a member of the conspiracy. By policy or self-selection, both the council and the commission have memberships that include many prominent individuals from government, business, and the academy. They have personal and institutional interests they seek to advance. However, neither the prominence of the members nor the fact that those members have interests they pursue supports the conspiracist conclusion that the organizations themselves are instruments of control.

There is a huge conspiracist literature regarding the symbolism of the dollar bill and the Great Seal of the United States. References to this are made in *Angels & Demons*. But there is a government website that has an official explanation for the symbolism [www.state.gov/documents/organization/27807.pdf]. I would guess that there might be some relationship to Masonic symbols, but if there is, it doesn't strike me as sinister. For example, the translation of the motto *Novus Ordo Seclorum* that appears on the dollar bill as "New World Order" is the subject of a lot of debate. I believe that it was nothing more than a fascinating accident that George Bush Sr. started talking about the need for a "new world order" to follow the Cold War period that was ending during his presidency. He did not realize that the phrase was already out there and was linked to the Masons and the Illuminati by conspiracists. As far as I can see, it was simply a very unfortunate choice of words.

How should novus ordo seclorum *be translated?*
I'm not a Latinist, but I see no reason to argue with the official version, which is "new order of the ages." I've also seen it translated the way Dan Brown translates it: "new secular order."

What about accusations of a Masonic conspiracy involved in the death of John Paul I?
I certainly know that the claim has been made. My impression is that more seems to be made of it in ultratraditional Catholic circles than among some other conspiracists. These would be schismatic Catholics who have rejected

Vatican authority, such as the movement that Mel Gibson's father is associated with. For them the notion of a plot inside the Vatican is consistent with their rejection of the Vatican II and post–Vatican II reforms.

Angels & Demons features a conspiracy within a conspiracy. How common is this permutation of conspiracy theory?

Such nested conspiracies are becoming increasingly common. A real explosion in what I call superconspiracies occurred during the 1980s. Two subcultures are particularly supportive of such beliefs. One is Protestant fundamentalism, which became politically activated in the 1980s. The other is the militantly antigovernment right, in the form of militia groups, racist organizations, and others on the political fringe. From a religious standpoint, millennialists find elaborate conspiracy theories to be a convenient way to think about the machinations of the Antichrist. Among political extremists, conspiracy theories give structure to their suspicions about the federal government, the United Nations, Jewish bankers, Masons, and others they distrust.

Positing an evil conspiracy defines the nature of evil in a sufficiently specific way and creates an image of moral order. It allows conspiracists to define themselves and the enemy with certainty in a complex and confusing world.

Could you elaborate on something you mentioned, in A Culture of Conspiracy, *about how these conspiracies have incorporated anti-Semitic, anti-Catholic, and anti-Masonic ideas?*

There is a really immense anti-Masonic literature out there, and it keeps growing. One of the things that surprised me in reading contemporary conspiracist literature is how much of it is either anti-Catholic, anti-Masonic, or both.

Because, as I said before, anything that appears secret, or is poorly understood, becomes a candidate for inclusion in the conspiracy. And the more sweeping the conspiracy theory is, the more it can include. The advantage of a kind of open-ended concept like "the Illuminati" is that you can fill that concept with whatever meaning you want, so that you can make them either anti-Catholic or Catholic. You can include documents like the *Protocols of the Elders of Zion* and say, well, that's part of the Illuminati as well. The Masonic connection is the easiest to make because there were some superficial ties there. But the Illuminati is so vague, and we know so little about them, that you can link them to almost any group and not be afraid that you are going to be contradicted or disapproved of.

You've written that conspiracy theories that have developed in our recent history are uniquely improvisational in character. What do you mean by that?

By that I mean that instead of developing ideas that come solely from a single ideological or religious tradition, they tend to borrow in a quite indiscriminate way. Therefore, you will find belief systems that have elements of religion, fringe science, the occult, and esotericism—all mixed together.

Two factors are at work here. The first is the declining authority that particular religious and political traditions have suffered over the last half-century and their decreased ability to discipline those who use their concepts. The other is the enormous availability of materials that previously might not have been known. In other words, a medium like the Internet makes it possible for conspiracists to draw on ideas that they might not have heard about in an earlier era.

The key point is that explaining how such a conspiratorial organization could sustain itself and remain secret is harder to do than to explain events without recourse to conspiracism. Conspiracists seem to believe that the conspiracy is immune to such factors as accidents, coincidence, ineptitude, disloyalty, or human stupidity—all of which, as we know, have caused the best-laid plans to go awry.

What makes the apocalyptic nature of so many of these conspiracies popular?

I've been wrestling with that for a long time, because we're in a period of unusual apocalyptic ferment—and have been for quite a while. I think part of it stems from a desire to impose some kind of understanding on the world, that is, to make sense of reality. And, of course, conspiracy theories do that, in an extraordinarily economical way, by basically saying that all the evil in the world is attributable to a single source.

Another reason is, I think, a heightened level of anxiety. To the extent that we fear some kind of world-destroying catastrophe, we try to give some expression and understanding to that fear through apocalyptic belief systems.

What fuels the popularity of books like Dan Brown's bestselling Angels & Demons *and* The Da Vinci Code?

This happens to be a time of intense interest in religions, so that religious settings are in tune with mass-market tastes. Other factors that play into this are increasing distrust of institutions, both secular and religious, and the recent fad for "mainstreaming" conspiracism into plot elements in popular culture—in TV series and movies like *The X-Files*, for example. An additional factor is a "leveling" of the media, so that what were once "fringe" ideas now migrate more readily into the mainstream. The Internet has made the barrier between fringe and mainstream more permeable.

Do you see any dangers in conspiracist thinking?

Potentially, yes—although one must be careful here. The vast majority of those exposed to conspiracy theories seem to regard them as fictions. On the other hand, there are some significant potential dangers—for example, further erosion of trust in political, religious, and academic institutions, and the belief that the world is pervaded by invisible enemies. Both of these can endanger our culture's remaining sense of social cohesion and democratic civility.

AN OCCULTIST'S GUIDE TO THE ASSASSINS AND THE ILLUMINATI

AN INTERVIEW WITH JAMES WASSERMAN

Readers of Dan Brown's Angels & Demons *can be forgiven for being haunted by the Hassassin, a hired serial killer, who knocks off one cardinal after another in bizarre and ritualistic fashion. Dan Brown explains that the Hassassin's ancestors were a small, but deadly army of skilled executioners, who terrorized the Middle East from about AD 1090 to 1256, killing fellow Muslims seen as enemies.*

Although Angels & Demons *was published a year before Muslim terrorists struck New York and Washington, DC, on September 11, 2001, some eerie parallels can be drawn between fiction and fact. Like Brown's villain, the Assassins—to use the modern, Anglicized term—always worked undercover, insinuating themselves into the camp of the enemy, and waited for the perfect moment to strike. Trained in remote mountain fortresses in medieval Persia and operating under the spell of charismatic leaders, the Assassins realized that a small group willing to die for its cause could cripple a much more formidable enemy. Unlike modern terrorists, however, the medieval Assassins chose their victims from among rulers and leaders of the existing order.*

James Wasserman is a leading expert on the Assassins. He is author of The Templars and the

A lifelong student of esotericism, James Wasserman is the author of *The Templars and the Assassins: The Militia of Heaven* and *The Slaves Shall Serve: Meditations on Liberty*. He and collaborator Jon Graham are working on translating, editing, and producing an English-language edition of *The Bavarian Illuminati and German Freemasonry* by René Le Forestier.

Assassins: The Militia of Heaven, *and a founder of the modern Ordo Templi Orientis secret society. Wasserman takes a different view of the Muslim group from the one advanced by Brown. According to Wasserman, when the group was being credited with ruthless assassinations, it maintained high ethical standards. Wasserman views Hasan-i Sabbah, the Assassins' founding father, as an "inspired genius," highly spiritual and a "brilliant" organizer. Wasserman also credits the Assassins with providing the "mystical aspirations" for other secret societies—including the Knights Templar and the Masons, which also figure prominently in Brown's fiction. In* Angels & Demons, *Brown insinuates a link, through the Hassassin, between the Assassins and the Illuminati, the secret order directing the murders in that novel and the subject of Wasserman's current research. (Later, in* The Da Vinci Code, *Brown plays with a variation on this theme, connecting the Knights Templar with the mysterious Priory of Sion.) In the following interview, Wasserman takes us on a tour of the strange and esoteric world of the secret societies that have so captivated Dan Brown—and millions of his readers.*

A central character in Angels & Demons *is a hired killer called the "Hassassin," described as a descendant of the Assassins. To what do you credit the current fascination with the Assassins and other secret societies?*

People have always been fascinated with secret societies, however, there are two contributing factors unique to our time. The first is the breakdown of traditional religious belief in modern culture. The social bond that religion provided for much of Western history has crumbled and we are poised on the edge of a new religious understanding. Aleister Crowley, the most influential occultist of the twentieth century, described this period as the dawn of the "New Aeon." Popular culture calls it the Age of Aquarius. Something has changed and people know it. We are casting about for a new sense of meaning. Groups that claim to have either found or preserved that meaning are sought after.

The second factor, specific to the Assassins, is the attacks of September 11, 2001. These provided an explosive example of both the existence of Islamic secret societies and the rekindling of the war of cultures known for a thousand years as the Crusades. Al-Qaeda appears to derive much of its organizational modeling from that of the Assassins. The concept of "sleeper" agents was an Assassin innovation. These are operatives who blend in with their surroundings for what may be years before being activated by a command issued from a distant leadership. Another Assassin-derived practice is the decentralized network of semiautonomous revolutionary centers functioning in concert with an overall directive, but authorized to conceive and execute plans independent of direct supervision.

In your book you describe the Assassins as the "ultimate secret society." What makes them so?

First, the Order of Assassins (properly known as the Nizari Ismaili sect of Islam) had a doctrine—their belief in the true spiritual leadership of Islam. Further, they went well beyond the rigidities of orthodox belief, adapting ideas and practices that were considered heretical by both mainstream Sunni and Shia Islam. They were, therefore, forced to be extremely circumspect. Conversion efforts took place on an individual basis, over time. A growing sense of trust between student and teacher accompanied the progressive unveiling of the inner secrets of the group. If a candidate were found to be unworthy in the early stages, little would have been revealed to compromise the order. As one earned confidence and credibility, deeper doctrines would be unfolded. There was constant interaction as the initiate progressed.

The Assassins succeeded in carving out a territory for themselves in which they could practice and teach their beliefs in an otherwise extremely hostile political environment. They were a true secret society on whose whispered decisions the fate of political rulers and dynasties actually did rest.

Dan Brown describes the Hassassins as brutal killers who celebrated their slayings by using the drug hashish. "These lethal men became known by a single word—Hassassin—literally 'the followers of hashish,'" he writes. Is there any historical basis for either the notion that the name derives from hashish or that the Assassins rewarded themselves by using the drug?

This question is one of history's mysteries. The name Assassin has been etymologically traced to the word *hashish*. Rather than hashish being a reward, however, legend has it that it was used as a recruiting tool. Young men who appeared worthy were said to have been given a potion with the drug (perhaps mixed with opium). After they fell asleep, they would be carried to a garden modeled after Muhammad's descriptions of paradise. Upon awakening, graceful and beautiful young women, skilled in music and the arts of love, attended to their every need. Milk and wine flowed through the garden. Gilded pavilions were decorated with beautifully colored silk tapestries. The garden's landscaping included all manner of exotic fruit, flora, and fauna. After some time spent in the garden, the young men were said to be given the drug again, carried out, and awakened in the presence of the master, the Old Man of the Mountain. Asked to describe their experiences, they would then be handed a golden dagger and assigned a specific target. They were told the master had the power to readmit them to the garden upon the successful completion of their mission. If they died in the process, he would send his angels to return their souls to the garden.

There is no objective historical data to confirm this. Marco Polo popularized the tale in the fourteenth century in the widely read account of his travels. His classic book achieved such extraordinary circulation that it was used as the basis of an Arabic novel, published in 1430, which repeated the story. Modern Ismaili scholars suggest that the term *hashishim* was most probably a pejorative term—like our saying of someone whose behavior is troubling that "he is acting like a drunk," or, "she must be on drugs." In medieval Islam, drug use and intoxication were considered lower-class behavior and scorned.

Brown's Hassassin celebrates after killing by going to brothels and performing sadistic sexual acts. Is there any historical evidence that the Assassins rewarded themselves with this kind of sexual sadism?

No. However, as with any group, there were those who practiced aberrant behavior. For example, the penultimate leader of the Assassin community of Alamut was Muhammad III, also known as Aladdin (ca.1221–1255), a degenerate drunkard, possibly brain damaged, who is said to have sadistically mutilated his homosexual lover. He is not highly regarded, nor does his behavior follow the ascetic example of most Nizari leaders. There is also no suggestion that he conceived this behavior as any type of reward.

Who were the victims of the Assassins and what was the preferred method of execution?

Victims of the Assassins were those who threatened the survival of the community. These included ranking political leaders who directly attacked the Nizaris, or noble advisers who counseled such behavior, or the generals who led such actions. Teachers and religious leaders who preached against the Assassins also fell victim. The preferred method of killing was with the dagger. There was no known use of poison or other "safe" methods of murder. The Assassin *fidai* (faithful) most often met his death at the hands of the guards surrounding his powerful victim.

Can you tell us about Hasan-i Sabbah, the founding father of the Assassins?

Hasan-i Sabbah (ca.1055–1124) was initiated into the Ismaili doctrine regarding the true succession of the prophet Muhammad after a severe illness in his early adulthood. He progressed rapidly through the system and was directed to travel to Egypt to study at the famous university that trained religious missionaries of the Ismaili faith. He was imbued with a deep sense of purpose, a fervent mystical belief, and a charismatic and ascetic personality. After completing his studies, he traveled throughout Persia (modern Iran) as a preacher while seeking to establish a political base for the sect. After further splintering into sects over succession among the Ismailis, Hasan established a

fortress, known as Alamut, in northern Iran, near the Caspian Sea. He became the chief *dai* (leader/teacher) of the Nizari Ismaili sect, which reigned
at Alamut for 166 years.

What were his intentions in forming the Assassins?

His intentions were to formulate a coherent doctrine to explain the succession from the death of Muhammad, to build a community united by spiritual
practices designed to strengthen them as messengers of the Nizari's *imamate*
(his position as the true spiritual successor of the Prophet), and to promote
these teachings by sending forth missionaries to various regions where he believed residents might be amenable to his revolutionary faith.

Referring to the character the Hassassin, Brown writes: "As far back as the eleventh century . . . when the
enemy's crusading armies had first pillaged his land, raping and killing his people . . . His ancestors had
formed a small but deadly army to defend themselves." What role did the Assassins play during the time of
the Crusades?

The characterization of the Assassins as a small but deadly army of executioners has some credibility. However, they were founded before the Crusaders arrived, and lived thousands of miles away from any European
presence. The Crusaders' contact with the Assassins took place with the Syr-
ian branch and is recorded to have first occurred in 1106, eight years after
the Crusaders reached the Holy Land and sixteen years after the founding of
the Assassin order in Persia.

The Assassins were an interesting and independent nexus of power in the
political chaos of the Holy Land. The Crusaders were ostensibly fighting
Sunni Muslims. These same Sunnis despised the Assassins (Nizaris) as
heretics. The Assassins sometimes formed alliances of convenience with the
Crusaders against their Sunni persecutors. At other times, they aligned with
the Sunnis against the common Christian enemy. They also allied themselves
with one or the other side in intra-Muslim rivalries between the Sunni Caliph
in Baghdad and the Shiite caliph in Cairo.

Princeton professor Bernard Lewis has written that for the Assassins "the act of murder was a genuine
religious sacrament." Are there any comparisons to be drawn between the Assassins and modern-day
suicide bombers?

During the military phase of the Nizari Ismaili history, Hasan-i Sabbah and
his successors hand-picked their victims from among the most dangerous and
antagonistic enemies of the community. I also conclude in my book (written
before September 11) that Hasan was a legitimate religious leader who
showed the characteristic respect for life exhibited by those who follow the
spiritual path. In my newest book, *The Slaves Shall Serve,* I contrast this with the

behavior of the modern Islamic terrorist and opine that indiscriminate and wanton murder is not emblematic of the high ethical standards with which I credit the Assassins during their military phase.

Observe that a number of the September 11 killers spent their last nights on earth drinking alcohol at strip clubs. Compare this with Hasan putting one of his sons to death for drinking wine. My take is that the modern Islamic terrorist has borrowed much from the brilliance of Hasan's organizational methodology, while falling short of the spiritual stature of the medieval Assassins.

Are there descendents of the Assassins still living today?

The Assassins were crushed by the Mongol leader, Mangu Khan, in 1256— every man, woman, and child. Stateless and hunted, the remnants of the Nizari escaped northward or integrated themselves with Persian Sufis. A number assimilated into the Shia population. Since there was no longer any political power to protect or project, the Persian Nizaris simply abandoned their practice of assassination. Today, there are several million modern Nizari Ismailis in twenty-five countries who owe their allegiance to the fourth Aga Khan, headquartered in India.

Aga Khan IV is perhaps one of the West's greatest allies and one of the most successful leaders within modern Islam. Under his and his predecessors' leadership, the Nizaris have established mosques, hospitals, businesses, housing, libraries, sports stadiums, schools, and universities (including an international center dedicated to scholarly research in the Ismaili tradition). The modern Nizaris are among the most educated and prosperous of Muslim groups, practicing their faith, maintaining strong community bonds, looking out for each other's interests, and embracing their unique and vibrant history.

Thus, the Nizari use of assassination as a military tool ended nearly seven and a half centuries ago. The Nizari Ismailis today are a recognized modern religion hardly involved in terrorism, assassination, or war.

Is Brown, in your mind, doing an injustice to the descendents of the Assassins through his character the Hassassin, a brutal killer?

In my mind, Dan Brown is a brilliant and imaginative writer who weaves a tantalizing mix of fact and fantasy in his books. Our society needs to become less thin-skinned. Brown's Hassassin has something in common with the medieval Assassin and shares nothing with the modern Nizari Ismaili. However, I would hate to see his creativity burdened with the shackles of political correctness.

Brown also draws a connection between the Assassins and the Illuminati secret society. Do you know of any such connection in history or in occult literature?

At the risk of allowing historical reality to interfere with a good fantasy, the Alamut (or military/assassination) period of Nizari Ismaili history ended in 1256. The Illuminati were founded in 1776.

You have written that there is a historical link between the Assassins and the Knights Templar— who figure so prominently in Dan Brown's newer book, The Da Vinci Code. *Can you explain that link?*

There was a definite historical link between the Assassins and the Templars. I believe Hasan's sect had an esoteric influence on certain members of the Knights Templar and, perhaps, on other Crusaders, who returned to Europe and struck the final death blow against that period of history known as the Dark Ages. I also assert that orders derived from the Templars, such as the seventeenth-century Rosicrucians, the eighteenth-century Masons, and the modern Ordo Templi Orientis, continue to teach and practice elements of the secret wisdom communicated to the West through the Nizari Ismailis.

We have historical evidence that the Assassins and Templars occupied castles within a couple of miles of each other, that they negotiated treaties together, that ransoms and tributes were paid between them, that historical visits to discuss religion are chronicled, and that they allied together against common enemies more than once. We know that they were both structured along the same unique model—that of the monastic warrior (unique in both Islam and Christianity). We know they shared in a similar strict hierarchical discipline. We also know that they both revered courage and honor as their path to spiritual illumination. I state my opinion that the Assassins shared the secret knowledge to which they were privy with chosen Templars.

We can easily imagine that those illuminated knights continued to practice and teach mystical tenets far wide of the mark of orthodox Catholicism. Nor do I find it a great leap of faith to believe that those who learned from the surviving knights continued to teach these doctrines. And that, over time, these individuals and their students evolved into more formalized groups, such as the Rosicrucian and Masonic movements of later centuries.

You write about a "mythical union" between the Assassins and the Templars.

By mythical union, I mean that I cannot sit you down in a secret underground archive somewhere and show you a certificate, signed by Hasan-i Sabbah, recognizing Hughes de Payens, founder of the Knights Templar, as a worthy

OF CONSPIRACIES AND CONSPIRATORS: THE ILLUMINATI ILLUMINATED 147

brother—because such a document does not exist. I can't, or won't, detail every single nuance of similarity I find between the beliefs or structure of the Assassins and the Templars, and their survival in modern occultism. While writing my book, I literally felt the dry desert breezes across my skin. I asked myself where I needed to fill in further details to make my case and where I could count on the intuition of the reader to draw similar conclusions to those I had reached. Simply put, "that's the signpost up ahead," you've entered the realm between reality and imagination. Do the two intertwine? They do in my life. And as I mature, I find my greatest delight in those areas where legitimate historical data becomes the springboard of my imaginative creativity. In other words, I no longer enjoy "speculative facts," the domain perhaps of the very young or the quite deluded.

Returning to the Illuminati, Dan Brown asserts that they were active in early seventeenth-century Rome, and that Galileo and Bernini may have been secret members.

Dan Brown is making use of the Illuminati myth, which will be explored in some depth in my forthcoming book. The connection between spiritual thought and political ambition is very old. The argument can be very persuasive on the surface. Should not the truly wise wield greater power in the affairs of society than either the brute forces of militancy and wealth, or the chaotic potential of individual sovereignty?

The Bavarian Illuminati were the ideal political conspiracy. At this point in my research, I have come to believe that their doctrine was more secular than spiritual. If I am correct, it helps to explain their success. They sought out candidates for initiation who were wealthy and powerful. Unlike the Assassins, for example, who demanded rigorous adherence to the dictates of their faith, the Illuminati were free to recruit more opportunistically.

Do you believe that the interrelation of these groups goes further? For example, that there is a relationship between the historical Illuminati, the Templars, and the Assassins?

No. There was a historical relationship between the Templars and the medieval Assassins. There was no relationship between either group and the Illuminati. They were separated in time by nearly half a millennium. As with much else in this area, however, there is ambiguity and opportunity for speculation. It has been logically supposed that Templar survivors, betrayed by European kings and the pope, nurtured a hatred for both the monarchy and the papacy. Since this position was shared by the historical Illuminati, numerous writers have noted the similarity. Some have suggested that the French Revolution of 1787, which bears much evidence of Illuminati influence, was partly inspired by a desire for retribution for the destruction of the

Templar order some four centuries earlier. However, this is all ahistorical. Dan Brown joins these threads into a rather marvelous fictional tapestry that makes for fun reading, while offering an imaginative suggestion of authenticity.

What do you think of Brown seeming to weave the Illuminati into Masonic history—as a secret society within a secret society?

This is absolutely historical. Weishaupt used the existing Masonic network to spread Illuminati teaching and conduct recruitment efforts. Masonic lodges offered the perfect conditions for these activities. Their proceedings were secret. They attracted men of a philosophical persuasion who were able to think "outside the box" of orthodox Christianity, both Catholic and Protestant. Masonry included the concept of a hierarchy, with progressively revealed secrets attained through time and exertion. Wealthy and aristocratic people flocked to Masonry, as its respectability had been long established. "Illuminized" lodges spread throughout the Masonic movement in Germany, Austria, and France.

What is the thesis of the book you are translating on the Illuminati? Can you tell us about the research on the Illuminati that you have done for your own upcoming book?

Jon Graham, a well-known translator, and I are collaborating on translating, editing, and producing an English language edition (available in spring 2006) of the most accurate, scholarly, and respected work on the Illuminati, *The Bavarian Illuminati and Germany Freemasonry* by René Le Forestier, originally published in 1914. His goal was to explore the Illuminati order and its relation to Freemasonry through the use of original source material. He tried to dispel the myths of both Illuminati supporters and enemies by providing a documentary history. My own book, *The Illuminati in History and Myth*, will present an accurate picture of the historical Illuminati, as well as explore the stream of thought from which the Illuminati emerged, and trace its influence on revolutionary and conspiratorial ideology and organizations through to the present day.

Do you think the Illuminati are still active? Is there any history of activity on their part during the nineteenth and twentieth centuries?

This is a complex question whose answer has sent otherwise sane writers stumbling down the rabbit hole, while providing for others a wellspring of nonsense so ludicrous it draws extraterrestrial life forms into the conspiracy. However, I believe there is a great deal of evidence for the existence of political conspiracies. I intend to discuss this in detail in my book. My goal will be to either leap over the rabbit hole, or, at least bring a parachute so that I may report its geography, fauna, and flora accurately. As I am still some years away from publishing, I would prefer to say here that the history of Western society since the time of the Illuminati (excluding the American Revolution) has demonstrated the existence of an ever more widespread revolutionary ethos, both socially and politically, whose goal appears to be a (generally) benign tyranny of the "expert" and social planner—universal rule by a statist master class straight from the conspiratorial fantasies of the eighteenth-century Adam Weishaupt.

SECRETS OF THE TOMB:
INSIDE AMERICA'S MOST POWERFUL—
AND POLITICALLY CONNECTED—
SECRET SOCIETY

AN INTERVIEW WITH ALEXANDRA ROBBINS

Angels & Demons *trades in shadowy societies whose influence is matched only by their secrecy. Is it possible that organizations like the one Dan Brown imagines continued to exist across the centuries? And, if they did, how did they maintain their structure and goals? How could they keep their members from revealing what they knew?*

For over 150 years America has had its own genuine secret society, replete with an impenetrable headquarters, ties to prominent Americans, and unspoken goals that have fueled the most paranoid conspiracy theories. A powerful network bound together by initiation, ritual, and affinity for power: this is Skull and Bones, Yale's preeminent secret society with a very public reach. Its aims are more mundane than Dan Brown's fictional Illuminati—there is no known plot by them to destroy the Catholic Church, for example. But there is a rumored link: the Yale society was supposedly founded in 1832 as an American chapter of an unidentified German secret society that many believe was the Bavarian Illuminati. While these links are merely speculative, Skull and Bones provides us with a living example of the way in which secrecy and power fascinate us all.

In her book Secrets of the Tomb: Skull and Bones, the Ivy League, and the Hidden Paths of Power, *Alexandra Robbins, journalist, Yale alumna, and herself a member of a kindred secret society in her senior year, probes the mysteries behind America's ruling conspiracy. Using her status*

Alexandra Robbins is an author and lecturer whose books include Pledged: The Secret Life of Sororities and Secrets of the Tomb: Skull and Bones, the Ivy League, and the Hidden Paths of Power.

as an insider, Robbins interviewed more than one hundred of the normally secretive Bonesmen. She describes the origins, growth, and influence that have made them our most beloved and feared secret society and reaches an ironic conclusion—that their power is fueled by our active participation in their myth.

⌒

Can you give us a thumbnail sketch of Skull and Bones and what its influence might be?

Skull and Bones is an organization based at Yale University, founded almost two hundred years ago, that many people believe helps run a secret world government. Members of Skull and Bones have included three presidents, CIA officials, and business tycoons. Skull and Bones has always managed to keep its secrets safe from outsiders, which made this a particularly difficult story to investigate. Incorporated as the Russell Trust Association, Bones has about a four-million-dollar endowment (which is less than people guess), owns a private island on the St. Lawrence River, puts its members through some strange activities, and centers its program around ideas of death, power, and devotion to a goddess.

Skull and Bones's influence is particularly noticeable in the area of public service, although it does no community service. The 2004 election features a Bones versus Bones battle; John Kerry and George W. Bush are both Bonesmen, as was Bush's father.

Skull and Bones has an interesting organizational structure. Tell us about how and why new members are recruited, how their organization is structured at Yale, and how that organization perpetuates and maintains itself.

For decades, Yale seniors, along with throngs of spectators, would gather in a courtyard on a Thursday in April to wait for lines of black-clad seniors to file out of the tombs [the nickname of Skull and Bones's headquarters, a foreboding-looking building also known as the Temple, that is used exclusively by Skull and Bones members and their servants] and tap new candidates on the shoulders. While there were other secret societies besides Skull and Bones at Yale, a Bones tap was considered the highest honor because it meant that a student had truly distinguished himself from the pack at Yale. Tap Day was Yale's pageant of pageants, a public spectacle that left so many men reeling—many in tears and some horizontal because they fainted from anxiety—that some parents refused to send their children to Yale to save them from the possible humiliation of secret society rejection.

Present-day Tap Day, still on a Thursday during the second or third week in April, is more of a private Tap Night. The major societies offer taps on a designated day advertised in advance in an ad in the *Yale Daily News.* The process is handled usually in a junior's room or a decked-out room in a campus building, and the results are no longer announced to the press as they once were. Membership remains as secret as possible for the rest of the year and beyond.

Skull and Bones has historically prepared for "tap" with a somber "pre-tap" presentation. About a week before Tap Night, a Bonesman tells each of the selected fifteen juniors that the society plans to tap him or her. A Bones memo about this presentation instructs the recruiter: "The privacy of the society, which is our greatest strength, should not be compromised in any way. At all costs, we must avoid creating the impression that we are interested in persuading a candidate to accept our offer."

Some Bonesmen classes or *clubs*—as each year's group of Bonesmen are called—tap creatively. In 1975 a junior was supposedly hustled onto a private plane. Midflight, the plane went into a steep dive, at which point the crucial question was posed: "Skull and Bones, accept or reject?"

Sometime after tap, the knights (Bones lingo for the fifteen seniors) deliver to each neophyte a packet that instructs the inductee to be in his or her room between eight and twelve on the following Monday night. That night, again usually between the hours of eight and twelve, traditional Bones protocol decrees that a team of four knights—"a speaker, two shakers, and a guard"—visit the junior. The two shakers stand in front of the speaker as the three of them approach the junior's door. When the door opens, the speaker, still standing behind the shakers, asks in a "firm" voice, "Neophyte [name]?" Once the junior is identified, the shakers grab him by his arms and drag him into a corner of the bathroom. The guard shuts the door and the speaker announces, "At the appointed time tomorrow evening, wearing neither metal, nor sulfur, nor glass, leave the base of Harkness Tower and walk south on High Street. Look neither to the right nor to the left. Pass through the sacred pillars of Hercules and approach the Temple. Take the right Book in your left hand and knock thrice upon the sacred portals. Remember well, but keep silent concerning what you have heard here."

The warning against wearing metal and glass is to protect the junior, who is whirled from room to room throughout the tomb during initiation. Bonesmen are told not to carry sulfur because of a tradition that began before lighters were invented, when knights brought matches into the temple. All of this precedes initiation, which is even more complicated and imaginative than tap events.

The qualifications for a Bones tap are simple: Bones looks for men or women who have distinguished themselves on campus and will likely reflect success and honor back onto the society after their graduation. It's something of a Who's Who of the Yale junior class. Bones has a prestigious roster of alumni and therefore expects new members to follow in those illustrious footsteps. The only exceptions are strong legacies, such as George W. Bush, whose father and grandfather were two of Bones's favorite sons. There have been about ten members of the Bush-Walker family in Bones.

Tell us why Skull and Bones is such a popular focus of conspiracy thinkers. You say that "the great conspiracy surrounding the society is one of half-truths and our own willing complicity." Could you elaborate on this a little? Do you think this holds true for all conspiracies? What about conspiracies where there is no actual organization involved, as with Skull and Bones?

Conspiracy theories construct a matrix beneath a series of events. They create order out of chaos, which is somehow comforting. Perhaps it is more reassuring to believe that there is an institution pulling strings in the shadows than it is to accept that random terrible things can happen for no reason.

Conspiracist thinkers don't *want* secret societies like Skull and Bones to exist. But a powerful, or seemingly powerful, organization like Bones can serve as a tidy, convenient explanation for events that perhaps have no such explanation. Here's an example. I had heard the conspiracy theory that Skull and Bones had dropped the atomic bomb. It sounded far-fetched to me, but I wanted to check it out nonetheless. It turns out that during World War II, the War Department was dominated by Bonesmen. Henry Stimson, a loyal Bonesman who believed that only men of Bones or similar pedigree were men of merit, became FDR's secretary of war in 1940. Stimson hired several Bonesmen, some of whom he essentially put in charge of overseeing the construction and deployment of the atomic bomb. So, did members of Skull and Bones drop the bomb? It seems they were heavily involved. Did Skull and Bones plot from within the bowels of its tomb in New Haven to drop the bomb? That's doubtful. But you can see where the line grows hazy.

The half-truths may hint at why conspiracies are so adaptable for fiction. I would think readers prefer that by the end of a novel, they understand the order and organization behind seemingly random events. That is what conspiracy theories provide.

What separates Skull and Bones from conspiracies of a more speculative variety—such as the Illuminati, the villains in Dan Brown's Angels & Demons, who may or may not exist at all in a modern incarnation—and probably don't?

What sets Skull and Bones apart is primarily its visible success. Skull and Bones may not be operating a secret world government, but it has spawned a number of members who have had a great deal of influence in the world. Bonesmen include both Presidents Bush and President William Howard Taft; Senators Prescott Bush, John Kerry, and John Chafee; McGeorge and William Bundy; Henry Luce and Britton Hadden, the cofounders of Time, Inc.; business leaders W. Averell and Roland Harriman and Percy Rockefeller; and intellectuals and writers like William Buckley and Archibald MacLeish. The list goes on and on.

Skull and Bones's purpose is to spread wealth and power across its network. It seems to be successful. George W. Bush has nominated or appointed a number of Bonesmen to prestigious positions within his administration. William H. Donaldson, his chairman of the Securities and Exchange Commission, Edward McNally, general counsel of the Office of Homeland Security, and Associate Attorney General Robert D. McCallum Jr. are all Bonesmen.

Let's go back to a point you touched upon earlier in the interview. Can you give us some more insight on the relationship that is thought to exist between Skull and Bones and the Illuminati? Are speculations about a connection commonly the province of conspiracy theorists, or is there any historical basis for them?

I am not an expert on the Illuminati, so I can only tell you what I know as it relates to Skull and Bones's history. During the 1832–1833 year at Yale, the secretary of Yale's Phi Beta Kappa chapter was valedictorian William H. Russell, class of 1833. Russell had studied abroad in Germany, where he apparently became acquainted with a German secret society that probably had the skull and crossbones as its logo. When he returned to Yale he was furious to find that Phi Beta Kappa had been stripped of its secrecy in the midst of the anti-Masonic fervor, and so he supposedly decided to create a more powerful society with secrecy intact. This club, the Eulogian Club—which soon changed its name to Skull and Bones—was allegedly the American chapter of the German organization he encountered during his time abroad. The notion that it was an American outgrowth of a European society is clear from an address titled "The Eulogian Club: An Historical Discourse Pronounced before our Venerable Order on the Thirtieth Anniversary of the Foundation of our American Chapter in New Haven July 30th, 1863, Thursday evening." The tomb is full of Germanic artifacts and phrases. And one of the society's traditional songs is sung to the tune of *"Deutschland über alles."* However, I know of no evidence that would specifically support or refute the connection between the Illuminati and Skull and Bones.

What can you tell us about the breadth and depth of the involvement of Skull and Bones in United States history and political culture?

What makes Skull and Bones's roster and influence so staggering is that there are only an estimated eight hundred living members at any one time. And some of those members seem to have relied on Bones for help as much as it relies on them for prestige. George W. Bush is the ultimate example of how an elite, powerful old-boy network can propel a model of mediocrity to the presidency. Beginning with his first job out of college, he seems to have relied on Skull and Bones for money and connections throughout his entire career. Even his Rangers deal, the one venture people believe he achieved alone, had at least one Bonesman involved. As president, Bush seemed to follow a Skull and Bones agenda by appointing Bonesmen to prestigious positions.

Why does Skull and Bones—as well as seemingly many secretive societies—have such a distinctive flavor, including obsessions with death, poetic inspiration, macabre imagery, and arcane ritual?

There are probably a few reasons for that. One is that these societies are based on traditions from other eras. Skull and Bones's program hasn't deviated much since the 1800s. Another could be that the stranger the experience, the more the participants would be expected to bond, because they are part of something so unlike anything that outsiders could envision. This is why I believe Bones has each candidate recite his or her sexual history right off the bat (September of their senior year). By forcing them to share their most intimate experiences with each other, Skull and Bones binds its members together. The year in the Tomb is designed to make fast friends out of the fifteen members, probably so that by the time they graduate, they will be less likely to spill the secrets of Skull and Bones, because to do so would mean betraying their fourteen new best friends. I'd attribute the death motif, arcane ritual, and macabre imagery to this as well. As one Bonesman said to me, he would readily help a fellow member who asked, simply because they had both gone through something so weird.

You yourself are a member of Scroll and Key, a fellow secret society of the Bonesmen at Yale. What did you gain from inclusion in the society?

I was tapped because of my writing skills. Each of the fifteen senior members of Scroll and Key are assigned a specific role; my role involved writing a report every couple of weeks. Scroll and Key is similar to Bones in that it is one of Yale's oldest societies, and it has a prestigious roster of alumni, strange rituals, and a tomb. We were also served multicourse meals to kick off our Thursday and Sunday night meetings, as Bonesmen are.

I gained nothing from my society membership during my time at Yale. I was glad to be a member only because there were a couple people whose friendships I enjoyed. But beyond that, the secret society was a waste of time—with one exception. One reason I was able to get so many Bonesmen to talk to me was because I was a member of a kindred group.

The overall picture you paint of Skull and Bones is rather benign—an unusual networking society despite its reputation as a dark political or social conspiracy. Is there anything about their influence that you find to be of concern?

I don't believe that the people who represent our country, especially the president of the United States, should be allowed to have an allegiance to any secret group. Secrecy overshadows democracy. We need a certain transparency in our government so we can hold elected officials accountable for their actions. I don't think it's a coincidence that the most secretive government in America since the Nixon era is run by a member of the world's most infamous secret society.

"I Didn't Go Looking for the Illuminati; They Came Looking for Me"

An Interview with Robert Anton Wilson

As far as mainstream historians are concerned, the Illuminati existed for little more than a decade at the end of the eighteenth century. Their dissolution by the Bavarian government and the arrest of many of their prominent members ended any significant influence they might have had on world history.

Robert Anton Wilson has done more than any other contemporary individual to resurrect the Illuminati myth. With Robert Shea, he wrote the Illuminatus! Trilogy, a vast, sprawling epic spanning eight hundred pages and twenty thousand years of conspiratorial history, in which Wilson proposed an interlocking superconspiracy among far-flung groups and events—from the fall of Atlantis to the Kennedy assassination. The book, first published three decades ago, became a cult classic and a beacon for the burgeoning counterculture, incorporating an extensive survey of conspiracy literature. Dan Brown undoubtedly read Wilson's books in the course of his research for Angels & Demons. Some elements of the Illuminati, as portrayed by Brown, appear to come right out of the pages of R. A. Wilson.

Although Wilson's flights of fantasy frequently reach absurd heights, his knowledge of real and imagined conspiracy theories and quirky, inventive fictions identify him as an expert on the Illuminati and their persistent existence on the shadowy border between historical fact and paranoid fiction.

Wilson is an intellectual gadfly, whose works, in addition to conspiracy theory and the Illuminati, incorporate science fiction, neurology, the occult, new technology, culture, politics, black magic, and

---

Robert Anton Wilson has worked as a futurist, novelist, playwright, poet, lecturer, and stand-up comic. With Robert Shea, Wilson coauthored the *Illuminatus! Trilogy*

quantum physics. In both his fiction and nonfiction work, Wilson displays a vivid imagination that juxtaposes received ideas of history and science with unlikely countertheories that perplex, challenge, amuse—and utterly madden his critics. Here Wilson shares his interest in all things conspiratorial, his efforts to subvert consensus reality through provocation, and some of the sources that inspired his Illuminati epic.

What spurred your initial interest in the Illuminati?

In a sense, I didn't go looking for the Illuminati; they came looking for me. Back in the 1960s I had a friend named Kerry Thornley. He was accused of complicity in the JFK assassination by New Orleans DA Jim Garrison. The case was built around the fact that Kerry and Oswald served in the same Marine platoon in Japan and later lived within a few blocks of each other in New Orleans. Garrison called that propinquity but Kerry, before he had a particularly bummer trip on LSD, called it coincidence. Considering what it led to, I call it synchronicity.

Thornley had some very slight brushes with a group at UC Berkeley who called themselves the Bavarian Illuminati and had officers with titles like International Jew, International Banker, High Priest of Satan, etcetera—an obvious joke at the expense of right-wing paranoids. A lot of Kerry's friends, including me, decided to make the Bavarian Illuminati a lot more famous and send Garrison on a snark hunt. We all had lots of outlets in publishing. A group called the Black Mass infiltrated the *L.A. Free Press*, claiming to be the Afro-Illuminati. Claims that Chicago mayor Richard Daley was an Illuminati got into *Teenset* magazine, and also the *Spark*, a left-wing Chicago paper. Dozens of similar weird tales appeared hither and yon. *Playboy* mentioned that one of Garrison's investigators named Chapman was seriously investigating the Illuminati. And then Bob Shea and I wrote the *Illuminatus! Trilogy* and nothing and nobody could disentangle reality from satire after that.

Unfortunately, somewhere between 1970 and 1972, Kerry had the bum "cosmic conspiracy trip" which mutated him. He became convinced that he was in fact part of the JFK hit squad—but unknowingly, as a kind of Manchurian candidate. At first, he only believed that both he and Oswald had been brainwashed while in the Marines. Later, it got more elaborate—a lot more elaborate—and involved Nazi flying saucers and all sorts of occult nastiness, including CIA brainwashing and "voices" implanted in Kerry's tooth fillings. Next he decided that all his friends, including me, were either brainwashed robots like himself or CIA "managers," and it became increasingly hard to communicate with him. As Nietzsche said, "When you gaze into the abyss, beware: the abyss will also gaze into you."

I think Garrison eventually agreed with everybody else that Kerry had wigged out. Garrison dropped all charges. Kerry told him to go to hell at their last meeting. If you want more details, see *The Prankster and The Conspiracy: The Story of Kerry Thornley and How He Met Oswald and Inspired the Counterculture* by Adam Gorightly.

How did you go about researching the Illuminati? What led you to begin your initial research?
I had an utterly unscrupulous—or at least undogmatic—attitude. I did not aim to prove a case but to blast open the readers' minds. Every source I found had to pass just one test—did it challenge consensus reality? If so, it got into the novel, whether it seemed plausible or totally nuts to me. In the thirty-nine different theories about the Illuminati in the *Illuminatus! Trilogy*, one may be closer to the truth than the other thirty-eight, but my opinion about that seems no more valid to me than anybody else's. I don't want readers regurgitating my guesses; I want them thinking for themselves.

If your aim was to undermine consensus reality, does this imply that your suggestions are meant to be taken as historical claims, albeit newer or more radical ones? Or does fiction itself, as an alternative myth or epic, undermine consensus reality?
I regard all maps and models as fiction; Darwin, Genesis, Einstein, Joyce all seem good fiction. Of course, some models seem more useful for a time than others. But I don't think anybody, not even me, is clever enough to have created a model that will prove useful at all times and in all circumstances, never needing revision. I call people who think they have such a model *model-theists*, and regard them as custard-heads. Consensus reality—or conventional wisdom—especially needs this kind of skepticism because nobody usually even thinks of challenging it.

Where did this research lead you? What deeper sources did you explore—the sort of books that Dan Brown might also have consulted before writing Angels & Demons*?*
Francis Yates's books, especially *Giordano Bruno and the Hermetic Tradition*, *The World Stage* and *The Rosicrucian Enlightenment*; Aleister Crowley, especially *The Book of Lies*; Baigent, Lincoln & Leigh, *Holy Blood, Holy Grail*; Gérard de Sède, *La Race Fabuleuse*; Michel Lamy, *Jules Verne, Initiate et Initiateur*; Robert Temple, *The Sirius Mystery*.

You make much of esoteric and occult connections to the Illuminati. Do these groups claim them as some sort of pedigree?
Aleister Crowley, prominent occultist and leader of the Ordo Templis Orientalis [the Templar Order of the East, an esoteric organization that combines Masonic initiation with magical and occult ritual], includes the historical Illuminati founder Adam Weishaupt in the 114 saints of Gnosticism in his

Gnostic Catholic Mass. That's a direct link. A few others allegedly involved in the Illuminati pop up in that list of saints, too—Jacques de Molay, Richard Wagner, Ludwig II of Bavaria. Those are indirect links, since allegation does not equal proof. Crowley's magazine, the *Equinox*, had the subtitle *Journal of Scientific Illuminism*. That means whatever you think it means.

The occultist is attracted to organizations like the Illuminati because occult initiation uses experience where churches use dogma. An initiatory order ideally changes your mind at least as often as a sane person changes his underwear.

What do you think about Dan Brown's suggestion that the Illuminati was originally made up of scientists, rationalists and freethinkers, some of whom adopted violence and terrorism?

It seems plausible, but unproven. Variations of it appear in my historical novels, especially *The Widow's Son*. I would place Giordano Bruno [the Italian philosopher, scientist, and heretic who was burned at the stake by the Inquisition in 1600] as the ringleader rather than Galileo, though, because the Inquisition charged him with forming secret societies (note the plural) to oppose the Vatican. You can read more about it in Francis Yates's book on Bruno. Bruno, with one foot in Cabala and the other in science, seems a likely suspect as ringleader of a scientific-occult underworld, much like the drug culture of today.

Additionally, I think Bruno has special interest, because the two most controversial scientists of my lifetime—Dr. Wilhelm Reich and Dr. Timothy Leary, both imprisoned for their books—felt Bruno anticipated their ideas. I strongly suspect Bruno of practicing the same sexual Cabala as Aleister Crowley.

Were members of the Illuminati actually arrested, tortured, and murdered by the church as Dan Brown asserts in Angels & Demons?

Witches, alleged witches, scientists, gays, Jews, and anybody with an opinion suffered at the hands of the Inquisition. I imagine they snagged a few of the Illuminati, too.

Do you think the Illuminati persisted from the eighteenth century into modern times?

Maybe. Some people think I'm one of their leaders. Mae Brussel [a mid-twentieth-century conspiracy theorist and radio personality] accused me of being an Illuminatus in a magazine called *Conspiracy Digest*. I confessed in the next issue and added that David Rockefeller personally pays me in bars of gold. I thought that would improve my credit rating but apparently nobody believed it but Mae. Lyndon Larouche has also called me an Illuminatus, and so does a Christian radio station that I pick up now and then. I've also heard reports of other Christian stations that rant and rave against me regularly.

You trace the existence of the Illuminati in and through virtually every secret society known to conspiracy thinkers, both before and after the historical Illuminati of the late eighteenth century. Are there any historical events that have their stamp on it? What are the Illuminati actually responsible for?

The high price of gas and the fact that you can't get a plumber on weekends anymore.

Angels & Demons *suggests the Illuminati hid themselves inside the Freemasons as a secret society inside a secret society. Is this an accurate view?*

It certainly seems so, in Europe in the eighteenth century. After that, I'm more dubious. John Robison's *Proofs of a Conspiracy* [the book that began the anti-Illuminati hysteria in Europe in 1798] lacks what I recognize as a paranoid style of thinking. He makes sense, even to me, and I don't even sympathize with his Christian-Royalist outlook. Besides, his claim that the Illuminati had taken over a large part of continental Masonry circa 1776 to 1800 seems well accepted by "respectable" sources like Durant's *Rousseau and Revolution*, Solomon's *Beethoven*, and even the *Encyclopaedia Britannica*. I doubt later expansions of Illuminism into Masonry worldwide because all such claims come from weird books with very paranoid odors and lacking even remotely respectable support.

Do you believe the Illuminati were active more than a hundred years before Weishaupt in Bavaria? Were they ever associated with Galileo?

More with Giordano Bruno, Johannes Kepler, and John Dee, I think.

What can you tell us about the breadth and depth of the involvement of Freemasons in United States history, political culture, and official symbolism? What leaps out at you as particularly interesting or remarkable about their presumed or factual involvement?

The Whigs in England, the Jeffersonian Democrats in America, and the Freemasons have all had some influence on one another, but it would take five hundred pages to clarify "who did what and with which and to whom." But I do think the First Amendment almost certainly represents the clearest Masonic influence on US history. Freemasonry in all orders and lodges is committed to opposing superstition and tyranny and promoting religious tolerance. The main intent of the First Amendment is to prevent any religion from stomping on all the others—not a theoretical danger in those days, but one that kept Europe at war in the three hundred years in which Freemasonry and free thought and free markets evolved as parts of the new aeon [a term usually employed to signify a turning point of immense significance in human history, in this case the change from Medieval to Renaissance and Enlightenment culture] which destroyed feudalism and perpetrated that damn constitution.

Dan Brown alludes to but doesn't go very far in explaining the relationship of the Hassassin murderer, his supposed ancestors, and the Illuminati. What do you know about the Hassassin and their origins and fate?

The Hassassin is an Occidental name for what is more properly called the Ismaelian sect of Islam, of which the current head is the Aga Khan. In AD 1092 Hassan i Sabbah was their leader. He invented the *sleeper agent,* a man who would pass as a member of the opposition and really work for Hassan. He made modern men out of his contemporaries, and they didn't like it. Nobody could trust anybody. Usually, they assassinated leaders of groups opposed to the Ismaelians. According to legend, they only struck when the target was about to invade Ismaelian territory. I'd like to believe that; it's both romantic and spooky.

Is there a presumed relationship with the Illuminati?

Both the Illuminati and the Ismaelians, just like Freemasonry, use an initiatory system of orders. The final secret of the top rank of the Ismaelians is said to be "Nothing is true; all is permitted." Hassan's contemporaries didn't like that either. Some say the final secret of the Illuminati of Weishaupt was similar. Crowley stated the same idea as "Do what thou wilt shall be the whole of the Law." The fools stay at their own level; the skeptics rise higher. You can lead a horse's ass to order but you can't make him think.

Is this relationship a historical fact? A common link drawn by conspiracy theorists?

I found it in Draul's *History of Secret Societies,* not a conspiracy book at all. I don't know if it's true or not, but it sounds plausible. The hashish link between Sabbah and Weishaupt is a joke I invented myself. I claimed Weishaupt studied Sabbah and grew his own pot. Later, a guy named Don Jodd made a living on the fundamentalist revival circuit peddling that, and some of my other jokes, as solemn facts. I'm delighted that some people believe it at all, which confirms my low opinion of the intelligence of the American people. The highest orders of mysticism and the highest types of rationalism do not disagree at all. The lower ranks of the Hashishim were probably as superstitious and ignorant as any other gang of Muslims or Christians. But the upper ranks would agree with Buddha and Bertrand Russell: anything capable of being believed is an oversimplification, and therefore nonsense.

You're familiar with the plot of Angels & Demons. *What sort of fictional or conspiratorial sources do you detect in it?*

Immodestly, I see a lot of my own influence. And a lot of the books (allegedly nonfiction) about the Priory of Sion.

Dan Brown identifies his Illuminati with the desire for scientific enlightenment. Yet their reputation becomes conflated with satanism and other forms of occultism because of the church's closed-mindedness. What other themes have the Illuminati been identified with, both factually and fictionally?

When you get into the literature of the Illuminati you find them blamed for anarchism, fascism, Sufism, extraterrestrial manipulations, sea serpents, and even crop circles. The Illuminati conspiracy is the happy hunting grounds of all minds who have lost their balance.

What is it about conspiracy theories that makes them so eminently adaptable for the fictional form?

We live in an age of increasing uncertainty. The greatest writers, like Joyce, use this uncertainty in philosophical ways, and popular authors of spy thrillers use it also. Nobody knows whom they can trust anymore. If you saw the new version of *The Manchurian Candidate*, haven't you wondered yet how many implanted robots exist in your office or your political party, or—gulp!—among your religious leaders?

In your own work, as in much recent conspiracy theory, conspiracies are stackable, like Chinese boxes. Each seems to implicate the other or lead back to each other like a snake eating its tail. What is it about the conspiratorial psychology that makes conspiracies so endlessly daisy-chained?

Suspicion, like trust, grows with experience. The more you suspect, the more you find that should be suspected. Kerry Thornley originally suspected only two of his friends as being robots, but eventually he suspected all of them. Abbé Barruel who was the fountainhead of anti-Illuminist paranoia—originally suspected only the Illuminati, but then suspected the Jews, the English, the bankers, the Arabs, and everybody who wasn't a French Jesuit like himself. He probably suspected some Jesuits, too, by the end of his life.

One of your characters from the Illuminatus! *Trilogy begins to see conspiratorial connections everywhere—in numerology (the law of fives), in history, in literature both high and low, in politics, in folklore, etc. Once you begin to accept the plausibility of a conspiracy, is this sort of free fall inevitable? What can conspiracies tell us about different modes of knowing?*

I suspect a great deal, but believe nothing. After finding the law of fives everywhere, I no longer claim to know anything for certain. This has led me to formulate what I call *maybe logic*, in which I consider ideas not simply true or false, but in degrees of probabilities. If other conspiracy theorists learned this much, they would sound less like paranoids and people would take them more seriously.

Maybe logic is a combination of general semantics, neurolinguistic programming, and Buddhism—all three as methods of bullshit control, not as dogmas. I joined the Flat Earth Society for a year once, just to challenge myself. I didn't learn much from that experiment but it was fun. I just preach that we'd all think and act more sanely if we had to use "maybe" a lot more often. Can you imagine a world in which Jerry Falwell hollers "Maybe Jesus *was* the son of God and maybe he hates gay people as violently as I do." Or every tower in Islam resounds with "There *is* no God except maybe Allah and maybe Muhammad is his prophet"?

What do you think of the overall story line that Dan Brown seems to buy into, connecting seven thousand years of secret knowledge handed down through a succession of secret societies?

The happy live in a happy universe, the sad live in a sad one. Materialists in a material one, spiritualists in a spiritual one. "Facts" adjust to the filing and filtering system of the observer's brain. At seventy-two, I assure you there's a hell of a lot more of what I don't know than there is of what I still think I do know. I suspect Dan Brown has as much sense of humor as me, but chooses to hide the fact. I'd like his books better if the professor came from Miskatonic instead of Harvard.

4: Two Windows on the Same Universe? The Science vs. Religion Discussion

Comprehending the universe: the leap of faith where science begins •
The use and abuse of Einstein's oft-used quotes on religion and science
• The case for the divine hand • The argument for seeing religion as
nothing more than "the mental equivalent of a computer virus" • The
case for mutual recognition if not reconciliation • Why the brain may
be hard-wired for faith

LEONARDO VETRA'S BOOKSHELF

ARNE DE KEIJZER

When Robert Langdon enters Leonardo Vetra's study his eyes are drawn to three books, each available at real-life libraries and bookstores: *The God Particle*, *The Tao of Physics*, and *God: The Evidence*. These choices clearly reflect Vetra's fascination (and, we can suppose, Dan Brown's) with trying to reconcile the conflict whose origins are ascribed to Galileo: religion on the one hand and science on the other. Are they naturally in conflict, or is some kind of interrelationship possible? The books on his shelf seem to promise a reconciliation. Vetra's capsule of antimatter promises the anti-Grail: fission instead of fusion.

Two of these books well reflect the novelist's intent to characterize Vetra as a "religious scientist." In his book *God: The Evidence*, Patrick Glynn, associate director of the George Washington University Institute for Communitarian Policy Studies, argues that the miraculous conditions that have conspired to make the existence of the world possible are irrefutable evidence of God's work. For Glynn, the more science advances, the more proof it discovers about the presence of a creator.

Likewise, Fritjof Capra's work, *The Tao of Physics*, merges science and religion. But here we stray into something of a puzzle. Would Vetra really have gravitated toward Capra's focus on Buddhism, Hinduism, and Taoism? (Although certainly Vittoria Vetra may have had such interest in this given her knowledge of meditation.) Perhaps Langdon failed to spot Capra's later work, *Belonging to the Universe*, which examines Christianity and science specifically—after all, Langdon was rather distracted at the time by a body on the floor.

The work least relevant to this topic on Vetra's shelves is Leon Lederman's *The God Particle*. Lederman, the Nobel Prize–winning physicist, barely gives the coexistence of science and religion much thought. When he does compare the two fields, Lederman concludes, "Physics is not religion. If it were, we'd have a much easier time raising money." Lederman, a brilliant physicist, titled his book to emphasize his belief that questions about cosmological origins are now far more likely to be found through physics than in religious belief. His "God" particle is a play on words.

Presuming Vetra would have additional books on this topic, it is interesting to speculate on which others may have been on his bookshelf. There is a very wide spectrum of opinion available, ranging from those scientists like Steven Weinberg and Richard Dawkins, who absolutely deny the existence of a divine force, to Alan Padgett, a professor of systematic theology, who argues in *Science and the Study of God* that "what science learns from religion is that God is the creator of the world and both rational and good."

Among those who believe in some role for a divine hand is John Polkinghorne, physicist turned priest, who says that "God is party to all that happens but not necessarily the immediate cause of all that happens."

Another shade of opinion in the debate holds that science and religion cannot be meaningful without each other. Greg Easterbrook, who contributes a religion column to Beliefnet.com, sums up this point of view succinctly by quoting Einstein: "Science without religion is lame, religion without science is blind." Another notable voice in this debate is that of Princeton physicist Freeman Dyson. Winner of the 2000 Templeton Prize for Progress in Religion, Dyson believes that "science and religion are two windows that people look through, trying to understand the big universe outside, trying to understand why we are here. The two windows give different views, but they look out at the same universe."

Going a step further in the direction of "separate but equal" are scientists like the late Stephen Jay Gould, who believed science and religion are "two non-overlapping magisteria," echoing Galileo's position that science covers the empirical, while "the net of religion extends over questions of moral meaning and value." The astronomer Neil deGrasse Tyson, whose extended views are included in this chapter, believes that although science will gradually continue to eclipse the creationist point of view espoused by many faiths, to think science will push aside religion is "a gross overstatement of the power or reach of science."

Finally, there are those who might concur with the Nietzschean dictum that "God is dead" and believe twentieth-century science has left religious belief in the realm of the illogical and irrational. Nobel Prize–winning physicist Steven Weinberg sees science as a progression toward the debunking of the myth of God. He maintains that great scientists such as Galileo, Bruno, Newton, Hubble, and Darwin annihilate one religious assertion after another. Quips Weinberg, "Nothing exists except atoms and empty space; everything else is opinion."

More acerbic yet is Richard Dawkins, who is interviewed in this chapter. In one of his sharp-tongued attacks on faith, he challenged religion to either put up or shut up: "Either admit that God is a scientific hypothesis and let him submit to the same judgment as any other scientific hypothesis, or admit that his status is no higher than that of fairies and river sprites."

Perhaps these scientists, although not as bitter as Dan Brown's Maximillian Kohler, share with the fictional director of CERN a deeply held cynicism toward the church and churches of all kinds. At least today scientists like Weinberg and Dawkins would not be subject to the Inquisition.

Finally, there are those who seem to be setting sail for a place beyond the debate. They ask, "Where do we get the need to believe in the first place?" In this chapter Dean Hamer explores the possibility of a "God gene," a biological impulse, strong in some, barely existent in others, that steers us toward some form of spirituality. Hannah de Keijzer explores the intersection of religion and science from the perspective of cognitive science.

We can thank Dan Brown for opening a window into this fascinating realm of "big ideas," letting readers themselves think about where they might fall along this spectrum of opinion—and if they still belong there after reading *Angels & Demons*.

Worshipping in the Church of Einstein, or How I Found Fischbeck's Rule

by George Johnson

As he headed into the last years of his life, Albert Einstein thought he had been given a bad rap. Admittedly he had spoken rather loosely in the past. "I can't believe that God plays dice with the universe," he once exclaimed, expressing his exasperation at the reprehensible randomness of quantum mechanics. And when he had wanted to convey his conviction that the laws of nature, though sometimes obscure, are orderly and understandable by the human mind, he put it like this: "The Lord is subtle but not malicious."

He had never suspected that people would take him so literally, and in such self-serving ways—as a devoutly religious man, a kind of poster boy for a quixotic attempt to heal the rift between science and religion that began when Galileo was forced to recant his belief that the sun, not the earth, sits at the center of the cosmos.

"It was, of course, a lie what you read about my religious convictions, a lie which is being systematically repeated," Einstein complained in a letter written the year before he died. "I do not believe in a personal God and I have never denied this but

George Johnson, the author of *Fire in the Mind: Science, Faith, and the Search for Order*, writes about science for the *New York Times* from Santa Fe, New Mexico, and is winner of the AAAS Science Journalism Award. His seventh book, *Miss Leavitt's Stars*, will be published in the spring of 2005 by Norton.

have expressed it clearly. If something is in me which can be called religious then it is the unbounded admiration for the structure of the world so far as our science can reveal it."

"God" was simply his metaphor for the laws that scientists had been discovering for hundreds of years. And it was the laws that reigned supreme. On the eve of a monumental experiment to test a surprising prediction of his theory of general relativity—that light has mass and can be bent by the gravity of the sun—Einstein irreverently declared, "If it is *not* proven, I pity the Good Lord, for the theory is correct."

That was his bottom line: It was man, not God, who deserved the most profound respect. We live in a universe governed by a deep mathematical order, Einstein maintained, not the whims of a personal creator—and we may just be smart enough to figure some of it out. "I am a deeply religious nonbeliever," he wrote to a friend, adding, "This is a somewhat new kind of religion."

Over the years the Church of Einstein has attracted some illustrious followers. At the end of his surprise bestseller, *A Brief History of Time*, Stephen Hawking, who otherwise doesn't appear to have a religious bone in his body, rhapsodized about science coming to "know the mind of God." What he meant was discovering a set of equations that unite all the forces of nature—pure unadulterated physics. But he, or maybe his editors, suspected that mystical invocations of the Almighty would attract attention and help sell books.

Hoping to match Hawking's royalty statements, other scientists have picked up on the riff, using God not just metaphorically but sometimes, one suspects, a bit facetiously. Leon Lederman, a Nobel laureate at Fermilab, called his own book (a popularization of high-energy physics) *The God Particle*. This was the nickname he coined for the Higgs boson, a hypothetical speck that serves as the missing link in science's long-sought "theory of everything." (Physicists hope to discover it with the new Large Hadron Collider under construction at CERN.) Predicted by the equations, the Higgs would remove one of the last shreds of mystery in science's attempt to explain the universe.

Some of Lederman's readers must have been disappointed when they realized the title was just a joke. What the discovery of the "God particle" would emphatically *not* do is to prove the existence of a supreme being. Rather it would provide the cornerstone for an ambitious theory that seeks to remove the need for such mystical explanations. That is the whole point of science.

Judging from other titles in the popular science genre, God also has his hand in chaos theory (*Does God Play Dice?* by Ian Stewart, a mathematician and science writer) and quantum mechanics (*Sneaking a Look at God's Cards*, by the Italian physicist Giancarlo Ghirardi). A new book called *The God Gene* by geneticist Dean Hamer takes a different tack: explaining scientifically why people are instinctively driven to seek a prime mover—because faith is hard-coded in our genetic software.

A quick sprint through Amazon.com's data base uncovers an ample supply of similar titles: *God's Equation, The God Experiment, The God Hypothesis . . . The Loom of God, The Mind of God, The Fingerprint of God, God and the New Physics . . . God in the Machine, God in the Equation* . . . While some of these writers (not all of them are scientists) put on theological airs only long enough to cook up a catchy title, others genuinely seem to believe that the purpose of science is to find evidence for the existence of a supreme being—the last thing that Einstein intended when he unwittingly set this bandwagon careening down the hill.

The notion that there could be conflicting ways of explaining how the world works struck me at a tender age. As aspiring little scientists, my best friend, Ron Light, and I had already tried to convert aluminum foil into gold with a homemade cyclotron and create life in a test tube by mixing together the chemical ingredients listed in the *World Book Encyclopedia*—carbon from a charcoal briquette, phosphorous from a match tip, hydrogen and oxygen from water. The high point of every week was when our elementary school teacher wheeled in a black-and-white TV set to catch a local public television show hosted by a funny man with a mustache and white lab coat named George Fischbeck. Albuquerque's own Mr. Wizard, Dr. Fischbeck would mix together flasks of strange substances causing spectacular chemical eruptions. Sometimes he would visit our classroom, cracking jokes, teaching us funny handshakes, and proselytizing for science.

Dr. Fischbeck later left us to become a TV weatherman in Los Angeles. But one thing he said has stuck in my mind. He was talking, I think, about cosmology—the big bang, how the universe began—or perhaps it was the theory of evolution, or the eons of time it took to form the Grand Canyon. Anyway, sensing that some of his young viewers might feel a twinge of discomfort, he gently cautioned us not to worry if anything he said seemed to clash with what we learned in Sunday school.

Science and religion, Dr. Fischbeck assured us, holding up an admonishing finger, are two different things. You don't ever put one with the other. "Nooooooo," he said dramatically, rapidly shaking his head to provide some vibrato and wiggling his mustache.

Even then, it seemed a bit of a cop-out. The Bible said the universe, earth and animals and people included, was created in seven days. Science said it started with the big bang and took billions of years. How could both be right? And who or what was really in control—God or the laws of physics? Dr. Fischbeck didn't go into the details: how you could choose to be a deist, believing that God created the laws and then set the universe to run on its own like a giant clock. Or that, as many scientists do, you could compartmentalize, separating what you learned in the lab or at the observatory from what you professed in church—that unless you were a hard-core fundamentalist, believing in the literal truth of the Bible, there didn't have to be any conflict at all.

I'd learned a little about fundamentalists from watching a Saturday night rerun of

Inherit the Wind, Stanley Kramer's fictionalized rendition of the "monkey trial," in which a Tennessee teacher named John T. Scopes was accused of teaching evolution. Spencer Tracy played Scope's lawyer (in real life this had been the great Clarence Darrow) and Frederic March was the attorney for the prosecution. Eating my popcorn, I rooted for Tracy, never imagining that years later these comical creationists would stage a come-back, as "creation scientists" asking for equal time in the classroom. Evolution was "just a theory," right? It was only fair that it be taught side by side with another theory: that everything started when God said, "Let there be light."

Dr. Fischbeck must have been appalled. Science is supposed to be about how the world works. Religion is about ethics and morality—how people should behave. Mix them together and, like baking soda and vinegar, they blow up in your face.

It wasn't always this way. Before Galileo there was just theology, the final word on everything to do with the here and the hereafter. With no perceived conflict between science and religion, it was perfectly natural for Copernicus, the first great promoter of the sun-centered, or heliocentric view, to hold a doctorate in canon law—the law of the church. He did astronomy in his spare time. Kepler, who refined Copernicus's theory into the one accepted today, had originally intended to be a theologian. He be-lieved that his cosmology (with the planets circling the sun on elliptical orbits) was a reflection of the divine, a celebration of God.

Galileo was the one who insisted on pushing the limits. Rome had given him per-mission to write about the sun-centered cosmology, as long as he presented it as noth-ing more than a calculating device—a tool, useful to astrologers, for predicting eclipses and charting the positions of the planets. To the Vatican, it was still Ptolemy's second-century geocentrism, with earth at the focus of the Creator's attention, that seemed more theologically correct. Starting with that assumption, the ancient philosopher had crafted a whirligig universe in which the planets and the sun orbited a stationary earth on complex curlicue paths, a dizzying array of "deferents" and "epicycles"—circles atop circles that could be arbitrarily tuned to revolve at any speed. Adjust everything just so and you could account for any astronomical observation. The structure may have seemed unwieldy, but what of it? God could do anything he wanted. On the fourth day of creation, when he said, "Let there be lights in the heavens," the Great In-terior Decorator was favoring a rococo style.

The church, unlike the blustering prosecutor in *Inherit the Wind,* was actually taking a rather sophisticated philosophical position—that, in the end, both geocentrism and heliocentrism were nothing more than models, mere inventions of the human mind. All one could say for certain was that tiny lights traced paths in the nighttime sky. Most of the lights—the stars—indeed appeared to circle around the earth (which cer-tainly didn't feel as though it were moving). A few others—the planets—wandered along complex trails, sometimes even appearing to reverse course and move the other way. Ptolemy and Galileo were simply accounting for the phenomena using different reference frames. That building these models was possible at all was a wonder to be celebrated. But Man, with his fallible senses and imperfect reason, could hardly expect to discern for himself how the stars and planets *really* moved. To do so one would have to step outside the universe, seeing it from God's privileged point of view.

Galileo gave lip service to the church's equal-time doctrine, agreeing that he would present heliocentrism as though it was just a theory. Then he proceeded to do as he pleased, writing his magnificent *Dialogue Concerning the Two Chief World Systems*, in which three Italian noblemen animatedly argue about astronomy, clearly coming down in favor of the Copernican point of view. It is still a good read—Galileo was the first great popular science writer. But it is impossible to come away from the book feeling that he is presenting his sun-centered model as nothing more than an astronomical calculator, an equal rival, at best, to geocentrism. Presenting it that way would have been the easy way out. But in argument after argument—using everything from rocks dropped from towers and galloping horses to the moonlike phases of Venus and the satellites of Jupiter—he made a compelling case that the earth really moves, and is just one of many objects orbiting the sun.

He didn't get away with it, of course. His half-hearted arguments defending the status quo had, after all, been put in the mouth of Simplicio, who played the role of Galileo's fool. In the eyes of the church, it didn't help matters that geocentrism, with enough fiddling, worked equally well for predicting planetary motions. It also didn't help that Galileo's particular version of a sun-based system was actually no less convoluted than the alternative. Stubbornly insisting that the orbits had to be perfectly circular—that Kepler's idea of ellipses was nonsense—he was forced to use as many epicycles as Ptolemy to make the calculations agree with reality.

Heliocentrism as championed by Galileo didn't have a whole lot going for it. The clinching argument—that an earth-based cosmos doesn't make sense physically—had to wait a generation for Isaac Newton. Astronomers in Galileo's time had only the dimmest notion of what might hold the solar system together. (Kepler toyed with the possibility that it was the attractive pull of sunlight.) Maybe, armed with a theory of gravity, Galileo would have argued his case more forcefully before his inquisitors. How, he might have asked, could something as massive as the sun and stars revolve around the little earth? Instead he recanted and apologized.

Somewhere in my collection of crank scientific literature is a paper, written by a creationist named James Hanson, called "A New Interest in Geocentrism." The centerpiece of his argument is the famous Michelson-Morley experiment of 1887. Using a clever arrangement of mirrors, the scientists sent out two beams of light: one moving in the same direction as the earth, the other at a right angle to its path. They had assumed that the first beam, boosted by the earth's motion, would travel a little faster. To their great surprise, they found that the velocity of both beams was exactly the same, a phenomenon later explained by Einstein's special theory of relativity. Hanson, however, favored a different interpretation: Michelson-Morley proved that the earth is, in fact, standing still, just as one would expect from the Bible. Add in some epicycles and you can get the sun, stars, and planets to circle around us. It's a clever piece of ecclesiastical engineering, but an alien religious fundamentalist could just as readily devise a curlicue universe with Mars at the center, or Halley's Comet, or the moon. Given a set of data, one can arrange it in any number of different ways. There is an infinity of rocks upon which to build.

Other creationists have reworked the equations of nuclear physics so that radioactive dating "proves" that the earth, as in the fundamentalists' bible, is just eight thousand years old—the number you get if you add up the generations (all that begetting and begetting) in the Old Testament. Play a little with electromagnetic field theory and you can change the speed of light, making it so the universe could have been created in seven days. One theory is as good as another. Let a hundred cosmologies bloom, and a hundred geologies contend.

But that would be cheating. A theory, as scientists use the word, is not merely an opinion, but a logically consistent thesis that has been tested and refined and tested again—the best explanation so far of a particular phenomenon. If the Church of Einstein can be said to have a dogma, it would go something like this: that the universe is comprehensible, that it can be explained with precise mathematical laws (the simpler the better), and that the laws prevailing in the vicinity of earth are the same throughout the cosmos—or, if they vary, that they do so because of some other law.

None of that can be proven. It is possible that everything our senses tell us about the world is an illusion, that the reason and logic in which we pride ourselves is as meaningless and arbitrary as the rules of a video game, that the true grand unified theory was conveyed to the authors of the Bible ... or the Koran, or the Rig Veda, or the Egyptian Book of the Dead.

But what a gloomy possibility. With no reason or reward for curiosity, the universe would be a dull, depressing place to live. Oh, well. There is always the afterlife.

In 1999 I was called upon on to participate in a symposium in Cape Town, South Africa, for the Parliament of the World's Religions. I knew I was headed for the right place when I got to the check-in counter for the flight from Miami. There were Hopi Indians with headbands and long braids, black southern Baptists in their Sunday best, African Americans in dashikis, Sikhs in turbans—all crowding onto the eighteen-hour flight, a kind of Noah's Ark of assorted beliefs. Similar scenes were unfolding at airports around the world, as thousands of people converged on Cape Town for this spiritual jamboree.

When I arrived the streets were coursing with Zulus, Hindus, Buddhists, Zoroastrians, Episcopalians, Muslims, Sufis, Catholics ... Except for a small group of fundamentalist Islamic demonstrators (who insisted that the ecumenical gathering was a plot of "the Great Satan"), everyone seemed determined to get along.

The science and religion "dialogue"—I was sheepishly violating Fischbeck's rule—was only a sideshow to the main event, but we gave it our best. There were presentations on "Jainism and Ecology," "Confucian Ethics and the Ecocrisis," "Cosmochemistry and the Origin of Life." And there was a string of talks on cosmology (mine was a fantasy about alien archeologists excavating the ruins of earth and piecing together a curious creation myth, something about a big bang).

Inevitably someone brought up what has become a staple of science and religion conferences—the matter of the "amazing coincidences." It seems that if the speed of light or the charge of the electron or a number from quantum theory called Planck's constant ... if any one of these had been just a tiny bit different, then the laws of physics would not have allowed stars to form, including our own sun. Stars work by cooking together hydrogen and helium—the simple, lightweight elements—into more complex ones, the carbon and phosphorous and so forth that Ron Light and I had mixed together to create life. If there were no stars, there would be no us.

So maybe we are special after all. That was the speaker's argument. If you start with the assumption that God created the universe for the benefit of his creatures and build your science around that, then the universal parameters were obviously fine-tuned to favor the emergence of life. Carefully setting the dials on his creation machine, the supreme being pressed the button and out popped the cosmological ant farm we've come to know and love.

But there is another, chillier interpretation: that it is just dumb, blind luck. Some scientists soften the blow by invoking the anthropic principle: if the universe hadn't turned out this way, then we wouldn't be here to theorize about it. Blessed be the Holy Tautology. (Maybe, as a corollary, some entirely different intelligence, beings of pure energy, or pure number—who knows what might be possible?—would have emerged instead.) A few cosmologists even speculate that the big bang actually resulted in a multitude of different universes, each sealed off from the others and each with a different set of laws. We naturally find ourselves in one of the tiny fraction of universes that support life. The others are fathomless wastelands.

There is no experiment or observation that would favor one of these scenarios over the others. That is too much to ask of science. They are untestable speculations of metaphysics—that which is beyond physics—hardly even qualifying as theories. There will always be some residual mystery.

Once they have traced everything back to the big bang, all scientists can do is stand back in awe. No one can say what preceded it or why it occurred. Even if there was some plausible mathematical hypothesis, science would be left with explaining where mathematics itself came from. In the beginning God said, "Let there be calculus." It is at this point that science bottoms out and you are free to believe what you want to believe. There will always be some residual mystery.

It really is a little weird when you think about it, that the brain—cobbled together by evolution for the purpose of surviving on the third rock from the sun—should be capable of coming up with things like quarks and electrons and quasars and black holes, of understanding a little something about the universe. That is the leap of faith with which science begins.

"We are like a little child entering a huge library," Einstein wrote. "The walls are covered to the ceilings with books in many different tongues. The child knows that someone must have written these books. It does not know who or how. It does not understand the languages in which they are written. But the child notes a definite plan in the arrangement of the books—a mysterious order which it does not comprehend, but only dimly suspects."

The most incomprehensible thing about the universe, as he once put it, is that it is comprehensible at all.

IS THERE A NEED FOR A DIVINE DESIGNER?

BY PAUL DAVIES

One of the main areas of contention in the battle between science and religion is the argument over whether the universe was designed or whether it's just a cosmological quirk of fate. For many scientists, the big bang and Darwinism are enough evidence to quash the theory of a designer universe. But for others, the anthropic principle, which states that the conditions of the universe were set in motion specifically for the creation of man, remains persuasive. Paul Davies, a professor of mathematical physics at the University of Adelaide in Australia, and author of a number of books on the subject, stands somewhere between the two, although he leans toward the side that believes the universe is more than a mere quirk of fate.

In this excerpt from his book The Mind of God, *Professor Davies argues that the laws of physics that have enabled humanity's existence must have been designed. But, in an intellectual puzzle that would have fascinated both Leonardo Vetra and, for that matter, the camerlengo, by whom and for what? Should the designer by perceived as "God"—or at least what religions generally mean by the term God? He seems to lean away from that conclusion.*

The natural world is not just any old concoction of entities and forces, but a marvelously ingenious and unified mathematical scheme. Now, ingenuity and cleverness are undeniably human qualities, yet one cannot help attributing them to nature, too. Is this just another example of our projecting onto nature our own categories of thought, or does it represent a genuinely intrinsic quality of the world?

We have come a long way from Paley's watch. [Paley was an eighteenth-century theologian who developed the analogy that a watchmaker is to a watch as God is to the universe. Just as a watch, with its intelligent design and complexity must have been designed by an intelligent craftsman, so the universe, with its complexity and intricacy must have been made by an intelligent and powerful creator.] The world of particle physics [we know now] is more like a crossword than a clockwork mechanism. Each new discovery is a clue, which finds its solution in some new mathematical linkage. As the discoveries mount up, so more and more cross-links are "filled in," and one begins to see a pattern emerge. At present there remain many blanks on the crossword, but something of its subtlety and consistency can be glimpsed. Unlike mechanisms, which can slowly evolve to more complex or organized forms over time, the "crossword" of particle physics comes ready made. The links do not evolve, they are simply there, in the underlying laws. We must either accept them as truly amazing brute facts, or seek a deeper explanation.

According to Christian tradition, this deeper explanation is that God has designed nature with considerable ingenuity and skill, and that the enterprise of particle physics is uncovering part of this design. If one were to accept that, the next question is, to what purpose has God produced this design? In seeking to answer the question, we need to take into account the many "coincidences" [central to] the anthropic principle and the requirements of biological organisms. The apparent "fine-tuning" of the laws of nature necessary if conscious life is to evolve in the universe then carries the clear implication that God has designed the universe so as to permit such life and consciousness to emerge. It would mean that our own existence in the universe formed a central part of God's plan.

But does design necessarily imply a designer? John Leslie has argued that it doesn't. . . . In his theory of creation the universe exists as a result of "ethical requirement." He writes: "A world existing as a result of an ethical need could be just the same, just as rich in seeming evidence of a designer's touch, whether or not the need depended for its influence on creative acts directed by a benevolent intelligence." In short, a good universe would look designed to us, even if it had not been.

In *The Cosmic Blueprint*, I wrote that the universe looks *as if* it is unfolding according to some plan or blueprint ... [and] that something of *value* emerges as the result of processing according to some ingenious preexisting set of rules. These rules look *as if* they are the product of intelligent design. I do not see how that can be denied.

Whether you wish to believe that they really *have* been so designed, and if so by what sort of being, must remain a matter of personal taste. My own inclination is to suppose that qualities such as ingenuity, economy, beauty, and so on have a genuine transcendent reality—they are not merely the product of human experience—and that these qualities are reflected in the structure of the natural world. Whether such qualities can themselves bring the universe into existence I don't know. If they could, one could conceive of God as merely a mythical personification of such creative qualities, rather than as an independent agent. This would, of course, be unlikely to satisfy anyone who feels he or she has a personal relationship with God. . . .

Through science, we human beings are able to grasp at least some of nature's secrets. We have cracked part of the cosmic code. Why this should be, just why *Homo sapiens* should carry the spark of rationality that provides the key to the universe, is a deep enigma. We, who are children of the universe—animated stardust—can nevertheless reflect on the nature of that same universe, even to the extent of glimpsing the rules on which it runs. How we have become linked into this cosmic dimension is a mystery. Yet the linkage cannot be denied.

What does it mean? What is Man that we might be party to such privilege? I cannot believe that our existence in this universe is a mere quirk of fate, an accident of history, an incidental blip in the great cosmic drama. Our involvement is too intimate. The physical species *Homo* may count for nothing, but the existence of mind in some organism on some planet in the universe is surely a fact of fundamental significance. Through conscious beings the universe has generated self-awareness. This can be no trivial detail, no minor byproduct of mindless, purposeless forces. We are truly meant to be here.

HOLY WARS

BY NEIL DEGRASSE TYSON

Galileo believed the church's domain ought be confined to moral philosophy. Natural philosophy—as science was known then—should be the province of the scientist. Going even further, he believed science could make discoveries about nature that would rule out all other explanations, including the divine. Science would know what God knows, diminishing the need for Him to be seen as the Creator. As Wade Rowland, a scholar of the turning points in the history of science and thought, puts it in his interview in Chapter 2, "The clear implication of this . . . was that as science steadily expanded its knowledge of the world, the domain of moral philosophy would, of necessity, steadily shrink into irrelevance."

Neil deGrasse Tyson, astrophysicist and director of New York City's Hayden Planetarium, is arguably a direct intellectual descendent of Galileo. As Tyson mentions at the start of this compelling essay, the question and answer sessions at the end of his lectures on the big bang and other advances in cosmology inevitably drift to questions about God as the creator and whether a scientist's belief in God supports his or her research—or inevitably thwarts it. The reason behind such questions seems clear to Tyson: our understanding of the laws of physics are far from complete, while the answers religion affords already are. Tyson seems to suggest that, for now, science and religion remain "nonoverlapping magisteria," to invoke Stephen Jay Gould's formulation. Tyson also points out the public's hunger for books by astronomers and physicists who see a way to link God and scientific cosmology, and the generous grants available to those willing to take a God-friendly view of the big bang. Yet he also unabashedly declares that "as they are currently practiced, there is no common ground between science and religion." Tyson the pragmatist believes that religion fills in the blanks where our knowledge of the universe is dim, for example in the areas of love, hate, morals, marriage, and cultures. In that way, Galileo is indeed his intellectual forbearer. But where Galileo believed that scientific progress will eventually do away with the need for religion, Tyson has a more humble view. As he told us, to think science will push aside religion is "a gross overstatement of the power or reach of science." He would find it much more interesting to explore what domains of religion or revealed scriptures might forever remain beyond the realm of science. Perhaps, he suggests, someone might consider publishing an annotated Bible that indicates "all that is safe from the movement of the scientific frontier."

At nearly every public lecture that I give on the universe, I try to reserve adequate time at the end for questions. The succession of subjects is predictable. First, the questions relate directly to the lecture. They next migrate to sexy astrophysical subjects such as black holes, quasars, and the Big Bang. If I have enough time left over to answer all questions, and if the talk is in America, the subject eventually reaches God. Typical questions include "Do scientists believe in God?" "Do you believe in God?" "Do your studies in astrophysics make you more or less religious?"

Publishers have come to learn that there is a lot of money in God, especially when the author is a scientist and when the book title includes a direct juxtaposition of scientific and religious themes. Successful books include Robert Jastrow's *God and the Astronomers*, Leon M. Lederman's *The God Particle*, Frank J. Tipler's *The Physics of Immortality*, and Paul Davies's two works *God and the New Physics* and *The Mind of God*. Each author is either an accomplished physicist or astronomer and, while the books are not strictly religious, they encourage the reader to bring God into conversations about astrophysics. Even Stephen Jay Gould, a Darwinian pit bull and devout agnostic, joined the title parade with his work *Rock of Ages: Science and Religion in the Fullness of Life*. The financial success of these published works indicates that you get bonus dollars from the American public if you are a scientist who openly talks about God. After the publication of *The Physics of Immortality*, which suggested the law of physics might allow you and your soul to exist long after you are gone from this world, Tipler's book tour included many well-paid lectures to Protestant religious groups. This lucrative subindustry has further blossomed in recent years due to efforts made by the wealthy founder of the Templeton investment fund, Sir John Templeton, to find harmony and reconciliation between science and religion. In addition to sponsoring workshops and conferences on the subject, Templeton seeks out widely published religion-friendly scientists to receive an annual award whose cash value exceeds that of the Nobel Prize.

Let there be no doubt that, as they are currently practiced, there is no common ground between science and religion. As was thoroughly documented in the nineteenth-century tome *A History of the Warfare of Science with Theology in Christendom* by the historian and one time president of Cornell University Andrew D. White, history reveals a long and combative relationship between religion and science, depending on who was in control of society at the time. The claims of science rely on experimental verification, while the claims of religions rely on faith. These approaches are irreconcilable approaches to knowing, which ensures an eternity of debate wherever and whenever the two camps meet. Just as in hostage negotiations, it's probably best to keep both sides talking to each other. The schism did not come about for want of earlier attempts to bring the two sides together. Great scientific minds, from Claudius Ptolemy of the second century to Isaac Newton of the seventeenth, invested their formidable intellects in attempts to deduce the nature of the universe from the statements and philosophies contained in religious writings. Indeed, by the time of his death, Newton had penned more words about God and religion than about the laws of physics, all in a futile attempt to use the biblical chronology to understand and predict events in the natural world. Had any of these efforts succeeded, science and religion today might be largely indistinguishable.

The argument is simple. I have yet to see a successful prediction about the physical world that was inferred or extrapolated from the content of any religious document. Indeed, I can make an even stronger statement. Whenever people have used religious documents to make accurate predictions about the physical world they have been famously wrong. By a prediction, I mean a precise statement about the untested behavior of objects or phenomena in the natural world, logged *before* the event takes place. When your model predicts something only after it has happened then you have instead made a *postdiction*. Postdictions are the backbone of most creation myths and, of course, of the Just So stories of Rudyard Kipling, where explanations of everyday phenomena explain what is already known. In the business of science, however, a hundred postdictions are barely worth a single successful prediction.

Topping the list of predictions are the perennial claims about when the world will end, none of which have yet proved true. But other claims and predictions have actually stalled or reversed the progress of science. We find a leading example in the trial of Galileo (which gets my vote for the trial of the millennium) where he showed the universe to be fundamentally different from the dominant views of the Roman Catholic Church. In all fairness to the Inquisition, however, an Earth-centered universe made a lot of sense observationally. With a full complement of epicycles to explain the peculiar motions of the planets against the background stars, the time-honored, Earth-centered model had conflicted with no known observations. This remained true long after Copernicus introduced his Sun-centered model of the universe a century earlier. The Earth-centric model was also aligned with the teachings of the Catholic Church and prevailing interpretations of the Bible, wherein Earth is unambiguously created before the Sun and the Moon as described in the first several verses of Genesis. If you were created first, then you must be in the center of all motion. Where else could you be? Furthermore, the Sun and Moon themselves were also presumed to be smooth orbs. Why would a perfect, omniscient deity create anything else?

All this changed, of course, with the invention of the telescope and Galileo's observations of the heavens. The new optical device revealed aspects of the cosmos that strongly conflicted with people's conceptions of an Earth-centered, blemish-free, divine universe: the Moon's surface was bumpy and rocky; the Sun's surface had spots that moved across its surface; Jupiter had moons of its own that orbited Jupiter and not Earth; and Venus went through phases, just like the Moon. For his radical discoveries, which shook Christendom, Galileo was put on trial, found guilty of heresy, and sentenced to house arrest. This was mild punishment when one considers what happened to the monk Giordano Bruno. A few decades earlier Bruno had been found guilty of heresy and then burned at the stake for suggesting that Earth may not be the only place in the universe that harbors life.

I do not mean to imply that competent scientists, soundly following the scientific method, have not also been famously wrong. They have. Most scientific claims made on the frontier will ultimately be disproved, due primarily to bad or incomplete data. But this scientific method, which allows for expeditions down intellectual dead ends, also promotes ideas, models, and predictive theories, and that can be spectacularly correct. No other enterprise in the history of human thought has been as successful at decoding the ways and means of the universe.

Science is occasionally accused of being a closed-minded or stubborn enterprise. Often people make such accusations when they see scientists swiftly discount astrology, the paranormal, Sasquatch sightings, and other areas of human interest that routinely fail double-blind tests or that possess a dearth of reliable evidence. But this same level of skepticism is also being applied to ordinary scientific claims in the professional research journals. The standards are the same. Look what happened when the Utah chemists B. Stanley Pons and Martin Fleischmann claimed in a press conference to create "cold" nuclear fusion on their laboratory table. Scientists acted swiftly and skeptically. Within days of the announcement it was clear that no one could replicate the cold fusion results that Pons and Fleischmann claimed for their experiment. Their work was summarily dismissed. Similar plot lines unfold almost daily (minus the press conferences) for nearly every new scientific claim. You usually only hear about the ones that could affect the economy.

With scientists exhibiting such strong levels of skepticism, some people may be surprised to learn that scientists heap their largest rewards and praises upon those who do discover flaws in established paradigms. These same rewards also go to those who create new ways to understand the universe. Nearly all famous scientists (pick your favorite one) have been so praised in their own lifetimes. This path to success in one's professional career is antithetical to almost every other human establishment—especially to religion.

None of this is to say that the world does not contain religious scientists. In a recent survey of religious beliefs among math and science professionals, 65 percent of the mathematicians (the highest rate) declared themselves to be religious, as did 22 percent of the physicists and astronomers (the lowest rate). The national average among all scientists was around 40 percent and has remained largely unchanged over the past century. For reference, some surveys show 90 percent of the American public claims to be religious (among the highest in Western society), so either nonreligious people are drawn to science or studying science makes you less religious.

But what of those scientists who are religious? Successful researchers do not get their science from their religious beliefs. On the other hand, the methods of science have little or nothing to contribute to ethics, inspiration, morals, beauty, love, hate, or aesthetics. These are vital elements of civilized life, and are central to the concerns of nearly every religion. What it all means is that for many scientists there is no conflict of interest.

When scientists do talk about God, they typically invoke him at the boundaries of knowledge where we should be most humble and where our sense of wonder is greatest. Examples of this abound. During an era when planetary motions were on the frontier of natural philosophy, Ptolemy couldn't help feeling a religious sense of majesty when he wrote, "When I trace at my pleasure the windings to and fro of the heavenly bodies, I no longer touch the earth with my feet. I stand in the presence of Zeus himself and take my fill of ambrosia." Note that Ptolemy was not weepy about the fact that the element mercury is liquid at room temperature, or that a dropped rock falls straight to the ground. While he could not have fully understood these phenomena either, they were not seen at the time to be on the frontiers of science.

In the thirteenth century, Alfonso the Wise (Alfonso X), the King of Spain who also happened to be an accomplished academician, was frustrated by the complexity of Ptolemy's epicycles. Being less humble than Ptolemy, Alfonso once mused, "Had I been around at the creation, I would have given some useful hints for the better ordering of the universe."

In his 1686 masterpiece, *The Mathematical Principles of Natural Philosophy*, Isaac Newton lamented that his new equations of gravity, which describe the force of attraction between pairs of objects, might not maintain a stable system of orbits for multiple planets. Under this instability, planets would either crash into the Sun or get ejected from the solar system altogether. Worried about the long-term fate of Earth and other planets, Newton invoked the hand of God as a possible restoring force to maintain a long-lived solar system. Over a century later, the French mathematician Pierre Simon de Laplace invented a mathematical approach to gravity, published in his four-volume treatise, *Celestial Mechanics*, which extended the applicability of Newton's equations to complex systems of planets such as ours. Laplace showed that our solar system was stable and did not require the hand of a deity after all. When queried by Napoleon Bonaparte on the absence of any reference to an "author of the universe" in his book, Laplace replied, "I have no need of that hypothesis."

In full agreement with King Alfonso's frustrations with the universe, Albert Einstein noted in a letter to a colleague, "If God created the world, his primary worry was certainly not to make its understanding easy for us." When Einstein could not figure out how or why a deterministic universe could require the probabilistic formalisms of quantum mechanics, he mused, "It is hard to sneak a look at God's cards. But that he would choose to play dice with the world . . . is something that I cannot believe for a single moment." When an experimental result was shown to Einstein that, if correct, would have disproved his new theory of gravity Einstein commented, "The Lord is subtle, but malicious he is not." The Danish physicist Niels Bohr, a contemporary of Einstein, heard one too many of Einstein's God-remarks and declared that Einstein should stop telling God what to do!

Today, you hear the occasional astrophysicist (maybe one in a hundred) invoke God when asked where all our laws of physics come from, or what was around before the Big Bang. As we have come to anticipate, these questions comprise the modern frontier of cosmic discovery and, at the moment, they transcend the answers our available data and theories can supply. Some promising ideas, such as inflationary cosmology and string theory, already exist. These could ultimately give the answers to those questions, thereby pushing back our boundary of awe.

My personal views are entirely pragmatic, and partly resonate with those of Galileo who, during his trial, is credited with saying, "The Bible tells you how to go to heaven, not how the heavens go." Galileo further noted, in a 1615 letter to the Grand Duchess of Tuscany, "In my mind God wrote two books. The first book is the Bible, where humans can find the answers to their questions on values and morals. The second book of God is the book of nature, which allows humans to use observation and experiment to answer our own questions about the universe."

I simply go with what works. And what works is the healthy skepticism embodied in scientific method. Believe me, if the Bible had ever been shown to be a rich source of scientific answers and understanding, we would be mining it daily for cosmic discovery. Yet my vocabulary of scientific inspiration strongly overlaps with that of religious enthusiasts. I, like Ptolemy, am humbled in the presence of our clockwork universe. When I am on the cosmic frontier, and I touch the laws of physics with my pen, or when I look upon the endless sky from a observatory on a mountaintop, I well up with an admiration for its splendor. But I do so knowing and accepting that if I propose a God beyond that horizon, one who graces our valley of collective ignorance, the day will come when our sphere of knowledge will have grown so large that I will have no need of that hypothesis.

RELIGION—THE MENTAL EQUIVALENT OF A COMPUTER VIRUS

AN INTERVIEW WITH RICHARD DAWKINS

The battle between science and religion is central to Angels & Demons, *with the camerlengo trying desperately preserve the primacy of the church with a modern miracle. But to Dr. Richard Dawkins, a professor at Oxford University and one of the most distinguished biologists in the world today, it is science, not religion, which gives us a sense of wonder and awe about life on planet earth. "Science provides the most stupendous sense of wonder at the universe and life, something that eclipses the meager, puny, paltry little sense of wonder that any religion has every managed to muster," he says. Like the humanist Paul Kurtz—or CERN director Maximilian Kohler in the novel—Dawkins is certain that science eventually will explain the reason for our existence. He goes even further, calling religion a mental virus, and that teaching it to children amounts to child abuse.*

TV spiritualists, folk superstitions, the biblical story of creation, and the ascension of Jesus into heaven are all, in Dawkins's view, signs of our tragic vulnerability. "I believe that an orderly universe, one indifferent to human preoccupations, in which everything has an explanation even if we still have a long way to go before we find it, is a more beautiful, more wonderful place than a universe tricked out with capricious, ad hoc magic," Dawkins wrote about spiritual quests in Unweaving the Rainbow: Science, Delusion and the Appetite for Wonder.

Dr. Richard Dawkins, one of the most distinguished biologists in the world today, is the Charles Simonyi Professor of the Public Understanding of Science at the University of Oxford and a leading evolutionist, atheist, and zoologist.

In Angels & Demons, *the central Vatican cardinal, Camerlengo Carlo Ventresca, says that science, while ascendant, is soulless, that it holds nothing sacred, provides no ethics, and burdens us with new powers of destruction. It robs us of wonder. How do you feel about any or all of this?*

The suggestion that science robs us of wonder is utterly preposterous and I hope that someone in the novel says that.

No, no one in the novel does.

It is just diametrically the opposite of the truth. Science provides the most stupendous sense of wonder at the universe and at life, something that eclipses the meager, puny, paltry, little sense of wonder that any religion has ever managed to muster.

Give us an example of the stupendous awe that science generates.

Look at the universe, look at any book by Carl Sagan on the universe, the cosmos. Look at, if you don't mind my saying so, any book by me on the evolution of life. There you get a sense of grandeur, a sense of wonder, and it is enhanced rather than reduced by the fact that we understand it. Understanding is part of the beauty.

In an essay for the Humanist *in 1997 entitled "Is Science a Religion?" you said, "The universe at large couldn't possibly be anything other than indifferent to Christ, his birth, his passion, and his death. Even such momentous news as the origin of life on earth could have traveled only across our little local cluster of galaxies. Yet so ancient was that event on our earthly timescale that, if you span its age with your open arms, the whole of human history, the whole of human culture, would fall in the dust from your fingertip at a single stroke of a nail file."*

The fingernail is a lovely image, and I wish I had thought of it, but I didn't. However, I agree with the idea wholeheartedly.

Within the evolution of life, what would be some examples of the stupendous sense of wonder that science gives you?

Something that gives me awe is the fact that every living creature on this earth, including ourselves, including oak trees, including dragonflies, has come by gradual degrees, by gradual evolution, from an ancestral something like a bacterium. The fact that you can get these enormously complicated creatures like elephants and lions and humans and redwood trees by natural processes, which we fully understand, from exceedingly small beginnings, something like a bacterium, now that's *wonder* . . . and the fact that we understand it is the most beautiful thing of all.

You are saying that our ability to understand evolution gives us awe and is awesome.

Not only is the phenomenon itself worthy of awe, but the fact that we can understand it is, and the fact that the organ with which we understand it, our brain, has itself evolved by the very same principles. Now that's truly wonderful.

What's your reaction to the charge by the camerlengo in Angels & Demons *that science has no ethics?*

Ethics? Now that's a different matter. Science, it is true, cannot give you any ethics. Religion can't either. Because if we based our ethics on religion, we would still be stoning adulteresses to death. What has happened is that we have moved away from those bad old times that religion gave us, the Old Testament, the book of Leviticus, Deuteronomy, and so on. We've moved away from that and we've moved away from it by a kind of liberal critique, a sort of sitting down together to work out the kind of world we want to live in. That's going on all the time, in the form of democratic discussions, in the form of legal case law, in the form of moral philosophers writing books and giving lectures.

So now we live in a world where we don't stone adulteresses to death, we don't have the death penalty (except in your country), we don't have cannibalism, we don't have slavery. There are all kinds of things that have now gone because of this sort of liberal consensus. And that has come about not through religion, but through a consensus of people of good will getting together to discuss it.

We have moved away from the ethics of religion, not toward an ethics of science, but toward, as I say, this liberal consensus. And the methods of thinking, the methods of reasoning which have led to that are somewhat like the reasoning methods of science. If you look at the way moral philosophers reason, it is a kind of scientific reasoning, although it is not science itself.

It sounds as though you view the ethics of religion as punitive and somewhat dangerous.

I am not necessarily talking about modern religious people. Of course not. But modern religious people get their ethics not from religion but from the same liberal consensus that I get my ethics from. To the extent that modern people do base their ethics on religion, those ethics are bad because they include things like resistance to stem cell research.

Are you in favor of stem cell research?

Of course I am. There is absolutely no ethical objection that I can see to it.

I guess as an atheist you are not concerned with the fetus, or the soul of a fetus.

I am concerned with the fetus. But I am no more concerned with a human fetus than I am with a cow fetus, and much less than I am concerned with an adult cow. And I am certainly not concerned with souls. It is simply muddled to elevate a human fetus over, say, an adult cow. So anyone who is not a vegetarian who objects to stem cell research on the grounds that it hurts human fetuses is being illogical.

Overall, then, what's your view of religion? You've written, "Faith, being belief that isn't based on evidence, is the principal vice of any religion." It seems your view comes down to the idea that if religion weren't so dangerous, it's still rubbish and tragic.

I think it's tragic because it's such a waste of a good mind. That's what I really feel about it. The world is such a wonderful place. And the gift of understanding is so wonderful. But to fill poor unfortunate children's minds with medieval rubbish that gets in the way of true understanding is genuinely sad. And I feel truly sorry for children who are brought up with this kind of religious upbringing.

How would it get in the way?

By filling the child's mind with false alternatives to what we now know to be the truth. 50 percent of American voters are said to believe literally in Adam and Eve. And that the world was created in six days less than ten thousand years ago. Now, that's not only false, it's tragically false because it is filling up children's minds not just with falsehoods but ludicrous falsehoods that get in the way of the wonder of true understanding.

And the Catholic Church? Does that come in for special ire?

Well, the Catholic Church is not against evolution. The pope has come out in favor of evolution. So none of what I just said applies to the Catholic Church. Presumably that 50 percent of American voters who believe that the world came into existence less than ten thousand years ago are not Catholic. I don't know what they are. I suppose Protestant. But no, the Catholic Church is comparatively sound on evolution.

Do you feel the Catholic Church has been a patron of science or has benefited science at all?

They do have occasional conferences on science. But no, I wouldn't say the church has made any great positive contribution to science.

Has the church, on the other hand, been doing what the camerlengo says in Angels & Demons*: "Since the days of Galileo, the church has tried to slow the relentless march of science, sometimes with misguided means, but always with benevolent intention."*

I don't know about the benevolent intention but, yes, I think it's true.

Angels & Demons *talks about a new physics as a surer path to God than religion, meaning that quantum physics has radical theological implications and has reopened old questions about God's activity in the universe. The CERN scientist Leonardo Vetra who is murdered believes that by studying subatomic forces, signs of the earth's origin may be found that may match with the Bible's account of its creation.*

There are scientists who call themselves religious. But if you ask them very carefully what they believe, it turns out not to be a belief in anything supernatural. Or they talk about Einstein. Einstein did speak in the language of religion, but it's perfectly clear that he didn't believe in any designer or intelligent creator.

I believe there is something deeply mysterious at the center of the universe. At present there is an awful lot we don't understand. Meanwhile, this is deeply mysterious and that, too, is sort of wonderful.

What is the mystery?

The mystery is, where do the laws of physics come from? Are there other universes that have other laws and constants different from those of the universe we live in? These sorts of questions. Physics is trying to answer them . . . but that's leagues away from saying therefore the universe must be created by a higher being.

Are these physicists the ones who feel the urge to marry science and religion—like Vetra in Angels & Demons, *who explodes energy in a particle accelerator and creates matter and antimatter in an effort to vindicate Genesis as an account of earth's beginnings?*

I think if the physicists did that, they would not think of it in that way. There are certainly physicists trying to understand how the universe came into existence. But I bet it has nothing to do with religion. If anything were to come out of that experiment, it would be a million times grander than religion.

Will physics ever get to the bottom of the singularity?

I hope so. As to whether I think so, I don't know.

Will science find a gene for religious faith? Even the late Francis Crick said that belief must have a biological explanation because it is almost universal in humans.

There has to be a biological explanation for anything universal. What you could say is that there has to be a biological explanation for the kind of brain that under certain circumstances has religion, but it doesn't have to be religion.

For example, it could be a tendency in child brains to believe whatever they are told by adults because that is a good thing for survival. So Darwinian natural selection would tend to build into child brains whatever adults tell them. So child brains are vulnerable to the mental equivalent of a mental virus. It could be that is what religion is—the mental equivalent of a computer virus.

You use the idea of a virus now instead of memes for the replicable cultural beliefs you talked about in The Selfish Gene?
Computer virus is another way of expressing the same idea.

So faith can have a genetic component?
I am saying there is a genetic tendency in child brains to be gullible because it means they survive better. Religion is a manifestation of that genetically mediated vulnerability, and it replicates itself through the mental equivalent of a computer virus. The brain is set up to be vulnerable to infection by mind viruses.

You are using virus in the sense of replicable?
Yes.

In your 1997 Humanist *essay, you gave persuasive evidence that religion is a delusion. Are you truly convinced there is no sense in which religion is a boon?*
Well, I think it is perfectly possible for a belief in a falsehood to be psychologically comforting. If someone is afraid of death, or if someone is bereaved and missing a loved one, then I can easily imagine that a psychiatrist might prescribe religion, as they would a drug, to comfort someone in distress. I wouldn't wish to deprive people of religion if it is comforting to them, but as a scientist I am concerned with what is true. There can be psychological benefits in a falsehood, but as a scientist I wouldn't want to avail myself of that.

Do you think science can provide comfort?
It provides huge uplift. I love being alive. I feel privileged to be in the world. I love to open my eyes and look around. I call that comfort. So yes. And I just used the analogy of science as a drug. I wouldn't wish to deprive a mental patient of a drug that consoled him. In that sense, science can give the same sort of comfort as religion.

And in fact religion involves some harmful activities?

Yes. For example, opposition to all sorts of reproductive technologies—stem cells is one, in vitro fertilization, birth control—just about any advance of reproductive technologies is opposed by the Catholic Church when it first comes out.

To sum up, religion is a delusion, but also dangerous and can have tragic consequences.

Yes.

And also can bring about death. You often talk of Muslim suicide bombers.

To be really effective in causing death, you need weapons. A truly lethal combination would be suicide bombers equipped with an atomic weapon. I have no doubt that they would use them if they could get their hands on them.

Is it possible to hold a passionate conviction in evolution, as you do, and also to be religious?

I believe I am very spiritual in the sense of the wonder I was talking about earlier. It's deeper than the sort of spirituality that appeals to cheap supernaturalism.

Do you think science will ever discover evidence to substantiate Christian dogmas like transubstantiation or the ascension?

No, of course not. Where would the body of Christ go if it ascended? No one believes that heaven is up there, so how could it ascend?

None of these dogmas will be proven?

I can't say that until you name them. Because there may be some things you can name in the Bible that are unexceptionable. The idea that once upon a time there was nothing and the universe came into existence, that's in the Bible, and that is what modern physics now believes. But it is not interesting or impressive that the Bible said something similar. It's a kind of random fact that the Bible happens to get partly right. Above all, the Bible attributes the creation of the world to a supernatural intelligence, which is very different from what physicists say.

Why do you think there is something, to quote you, "deeply mysterious at the center of the universe?"

Natural selection is a sufficient explanation for life, but not for the universe, because it came into being long before life. I think it is something that physicists will one day solve. The mysterious entity is that which we don't yet know.

Patrick Glynn, in his book God: The Evidence, *says you're as dogmatic in your belief in evolution as the born-again Christian is in his belief in Jesus Christ.*

That's so stupid. The difference is that dogmatic belief in evolution is based on evidence. There's massive, great, crashing evidence, whereas the evidence for born-again belief is zilch.

Do you still hold to the idea that we are "survival machines" as you said in The Selfish Gene*?*

I think that is a helpful phrase. Yes.

I am puzzled by this line in the book, "We, alone on earth, can rebel against the tyranny of the selfish replicators [genes]." What does that mean?

We have big brains which were given to us by natural selection, but the big brains are so big that they are capable of rebelling. We know we do rebel because we use birth control, which is something a selfish gene would not have bred into the brain because it stops them from replicating. Clearly, we do rebel whenever we spend time doing something other than working to survive and reproduce. So the time I spend writing a book is not time well spent.

From the point of view of the gene.

Yes. Of course it is time very well spent from other points of view.

In the future, what do you think the relationship between science and religion will be?

I have no idea. I am not a crystal ball gazer.

From all that you've said, it sounds like you expect it'll be conflict.

I suspect it probably is. It looks so different in America than here in England. What you see on this side of the Atlantic is religion dying. The United States seems to be a country of religious maniacs led by a religious maniac. And when I look at the future in America, I have great pessimism.

Why?

America is without a doubt the leading scientific nation in the world, and what is so bewildering is the religious mania that has gripped America. If you look at the elite of American scientists, which really means the elite of the world, those elected to the American Academy of Sciences, more than 90 percent of them are atheists.

You contrast that to Senators and zero percent claim to be atheists. That can't be true, because they are drawn from the same type of people. The irresistible conclusion is that they are lying. What is so sad is that they have to lie to be elected. In America, it seems that you don't get votes if you happen to be an atheist. They would rather vote for any other category than an atheist.

You must get very tired of these science-religion clash questions, but you seem to be saying it won't ever end.

I don't know about that. It is not looking good in America because religion is somehow so powerful there. But religion is not powerful in western Europe. It is in the Middle East. You have to go to Iran to find a country where religion is as powerful as it is in America.

THE GOD GENE

AN INTERVIEW WITH DEAN HAMER

Dr. Dean Hamer is no stranger to controversy. A leading geneticist and chief of the Gene Structure and Regulation Section at the National Cancer Institute in Bethesda, Maryland, he has discovered, over the course of the last decade, the existence of genes for anxiety, thrill seeking, gay sexuality, and now spirituality—all once assumed impossible to prove scientifically. In the process, Hamer is challenging our views of personality and what can and cannot be changed in human behavior.

Hamer believes spirituality is innate, serving in human evolution to keep us optimistic in the face of obstacles. But as he makes clear, his recent discovery of the so-called God gene, the VMAT2, does not mean that religion is also innate. Unlike physicist Leonardo Vetra in Angels & Demons, *Hamer feels no need to reconcile religion and science. Religion, he argues, is taught by culture and reinforced by bureaucracies. As two fundamentally opposed belief systems, science and religion will always clash, and in Hamer's view—religion will lose.*

In one area, however, Hamer's research has proven that science actually supports religion. While some physicists, like the fictional Vetra, long to prove the story in Genesis that earth was created out of nothing in one moment in time, geneticists have studied blood samples of Jews living in many parts of the world today and found that they share a common genetic marker. This demonstrates that, as a chosen

---

Dr. Dean Hamer, one of America's leading geneticists, has written about the so-called gay gene and God gene, and has turned conventional thinking about human personality on its head, demonstrating how behavioral traits are hardwired into our genes.

people, they obeyed God's edict to keep themselves separate and not intermarry. What's more, the marker can be dated to three thousand years ago, the time of the exodus from Egypt—thereby validating the Old Testament.

What is the background to your new book, The God Gene: How Faith is Hardwired into Our Genes? *How does it relate to your work?*

We were working on personality traits like anxiety and smoking for the National Cancer Institute. We use this psychological questionnaire called TCI, Temperament and Character Inventory, a 240-question true-false quiz that has as one of its components questions about a person's capacity for self-transcendence. It is supposed to measure spirituality. At first I thought this was some odd added-on thing. But the more work we did, the more groups we gave the TCI to, the more genes we looked at, and the more work about genetics done by others, like twin studies, that we tested, the more it became clear to me that there is something about spirituality that can be measured or studied.

Is this the first gene found for an abstraction like faith?

It certainly is among the first. There are definite genes identified now for language ability, which is kind of abstract and certainly specifically human. And, of course, many genes are involved in cognition, like mental retardation. There are also various genes for aspects of personality like anxiety and depression. This is as far out a trait as anyone in genetics has looked at.

Like any original research, afterward you say, why didn't someone else do this work before? It seems easy, obvious, to examine groups of highly spiritual people to see if they share a unique gene.

Either they never thought of it or it's completely wrong!

Can you summarize the implications of your findings?

We found that there's a critical distinction between spirituality and religion. Most people think of them as one thing. But the new research we did shows that they are fundamentally different, and they are different also in their origin. Spirituality is an innate part of human beings and it's something that people are born with and it's intrinsic to the way the human brain works and develops. We think we have understood a little bit of how that works. We expect we will eventually understand all of it.

Do other God genes exist besides the one you have identified?

Undoubtedly others will be found. Because spirituality, like any human behavior, is clearly very complex.

How do you think religious people will respond to your discovery of a God gene?

What I've found out already is that people have very deeply held beliefs about religion, probably more so than about anything else in life. I hope some realize now that you can be scientific about religion or spirituality without being a religion basher.

What do you think the Catholic Church in particular, which views questions like this with unease, will say about your book?

I'm not sure. I am not the first person who's argued that there is a biological component to spirituality. There have been quite a few who have argued that. One interpretation is that our findings show that spirituality is not some sort of accident; it's actually programmed into our brains. Some scientists will be very fascinated by that. I have talked about it to some priests, and they are not so excited about it. They have a more traditional view—that religion came down to us from God.

What do you think scientists will say?

When I mentioned I was even thinking about studying this, most of my colleagues raised their eyebrows pretty high. My boss even said I should work on this after I retire. Most scientists will accept that there is something biological about anxiety—they will accept that because they can see that in animals. They will accept that less about spirituality because it's more abstract. It's harder to measure, it's not immediately obvious evolutionarily. And scientists have their own prejudices: religion is mostly viewed as a separate part of life.

Angels & Demons *posits a profound chasm between science and religion. First, do you accept the characterization of it as a "profound chasm"? And second, where do you stand on this persistent debate?*

I think the key point for me is that there has been this long-standing conflict between science and religion, but not between science and spirituality. Religion often tries to interpolate itself into areas of natural science and tries to explain where the universe came from and how life arose. These are truly religious beliefs. They are purely cultural; they are not anything innate. They are taught by priests and parents, and reinforced by inquisitions.

Science is in conflict with religion because religions have a different way of figuring things out, and that conflict doesn't surprise me at all. It's a conflict that continues on to this very day, particularly in the United States, where you still have people believing in creationism instead of evolution. Religion and science are just two different cultural systems. They are different realms.

Some scientists, including Einstein, believe that there is indeed some kind of connection between the two.
For Einstein the big connection was that he recognized that science wasn't a purely rational area of human behavior. It's really intuitive. It's jumping to things and believing—very much the way spirituality behaves.

You mean the process of scientific inquiry is spiritual?
Yes, it's not a matter of proving that things are not as they seem or that there's a connection between everything. It's a matter of feelings. Einstein was very sensitive to the fact that the scientific process is intuitive—that's where he proved himself spiritual and scientific, not religious and scientific.

Are you yourself religious? And if not, do you feel a connection to some form of spirituality?
I am a typical scientist, a rationalist. I am one of those people who is spiritual but not interested in organized religion. In other words, I am a believer in the power of spirituality, not in a particular God. I'm a Zen Buddhist. I try to follow it a little bit. I feel better when I do. It's not that Zen Buddhists don't believe in some form of God. It is just that we don't believe it's critical.

One of your points in The God Gene *is that this specific genetic and biochemical mechanism that makes for spirituality is the same whether you are a Mormon or a Catholic or a Zen Buddhist.*
Yes. It's always remarkable how similar people's spiritual experiences are, no matter whether they are praying in a Zen Buddhist monastery or a church. What I mean is how they describe it, how they see the world, how they feel transformed afterward. If you read Saul's description of how he saw God on the road to Damascus and changed his name to Paul, it is remarkably similar to Mohammed's description of his dream states.

A really good example is Jesus' recounting of the time when the devil tempted him in the red desert. It sounds just like what Buddha reported in his time of wandering. That's because the way that the brain reacts is very similar [in all religious experiences], no matter whether you believe it's listening to God or to Buddha or any other higher power.

And what is that brain reaction?
That mechanism is a change in consciousness that's mediated by chemicals called monoamines. These are brain chemicals that are involved in how the brain processes information and links it to our sense of what's real, and how we perceive the world. If you change that, the whole world looks different. More important, it feels different, and that to me is the hallmark of spiritual experience. People see the world in a different light. If you think about it, if you alter how you see yourself in the world, that changes everything.

You know the idea that brain chemistry creates spirituality will make people reduce your discovery to more dopamine equals more religion.

They will say that, but it's not that simple. Religion is not a drug. It's just that the way the brain undergoes spiritual experience is somewhat similar to the way it experiences a drug. That is, both involve brain chemistry. So it's not surprising that you can partially mimic that by using drugs.

The fact of the matter is that most early religions used drugs. If you look today at hunter-gatherer societies, they almost all use drugs—Amazonian Indians, Eskimos, and other indigenous people way up in the Arctic Ocean, people all throughout South and Central America where drug use is very common, Papua New Guinea. People who can't know anything about what others in the world are doing because of their isolation.

Getting back to Angels & Demons, *are there any Leonardo Vetras at work today trying to smash energy in a particle accelerator to, in effect, recreate the big bang and thereby vindicate Genesis?*

Certainly there are a lot of people trying to understand the very early origins of the universe. What it really boils down to is not the mechanics of the big bang, or how did the universe start, or what does that tell us about a God or not, but why was there a big bang in the first place. That's the spiritual question. Why is there a universe? Why is there matter at all? If you believe in the big bang, there was zilch before it. Nada. No one has the exact answer.

Or, if you believe in God and a creator, that is the moment in which God would have been at work.

Back to your discovery. Do you think you have found in the God gene the means to reconcile science and religion?

I think so—yes, but only partially. It reconciles them in the sense that you don't have to be nonscientific to believe in spirituality. There are a lot of scientists who say that if you are going to believe in spirituality, you can't be scientific about it. That's a matter of taste. And there are lots of spiritual and religious people who say that if you have faith, you just have it, it's not science.

I'm saying you can look at it both ways without being nonspiritual. I think actually they are connected.

Your book said about half the people in the world have the God gene.

Yes, 50 percent may have a bit more than the other 50 percent. The point, though, is that everyone has some of it. Five percent of people have sickle cell disease, but really everyone has hemoglobin and can use oxygen in their blood. It's the same as spirituality. Everyone has the VMAT2 gene and everyone has the brain machinery to handle monoamines and to create consciousness; and so everyone has all of the necessary components to be spiritual. For some people, about 50 percent, it's easier than for others. They might be more spiritual on average.

So what's the evolutionary advantage of the God gene?
My argument is that in the evolution of humans it's a good thing to have a belief in faith. It helps a little with health. It may also add to longevity. And it makes us optimistic. Probably the main thing, however, is that it gives us a rationale to go on living, instead of saying, oh we are going to die, why bother?

The renowned biologist E. O. Wilson says religion helped improve our chances of survival.
Well . . . maybe [skeptically]. Arguing for genes that help the whole society is always tricky. Genes help the individual. But a really cool thing that scientists like me can do is to study biblical history and Bible stories through genetics. Indeed, it turns out that the Bible story about the exodus of the Jews from Egypt is correct, as far as we can tell about them from genetics. Because the Jews diverged from that part of the world around the time of Jesus. We found by collecting blood and testing for twelve Y-chromosome markers that Cohanim Jews [a special priesthood] around the world had a distinctive genetic signature. Even black South Africans who were Jews, way down at the end of Africa, who were very isolated, they still kept that injunction—to pass the priesthood only to their sons.

Here science, in the form of DNA analysis, conclusively proves that a part of the Bible is historically accurate. Science reinforces religion?
Yes.

In your opinion, is the Catholic Church headed for fewer or more clashes with science in the future?
It doesn't like abortion, stem cells, homosexuality, individual liberties—they have quite a few prejudices. Science and religion are not done clashing. As long as religion stays religion, rooted in cultural ideas that are not necessarily right and are reinforced by bureaucracy, it will continue to clash with science and it will continue to lose.

Why hasn't the church reached out to science and found a means of reconciliation?
They make sporadic attempts to do so but only on condition that the science not contradict their cultural beliefs. The Catholic Church in particular continues to drag its feet in all regards. The Eastern religions don't have that conflict at all.

You seem to direct a lot of your criticism—even anger—at the Catholic Church.
I am outraged by every type of organized religion. I don't see them as having

anything to do with spirituality. Spirituality would be very hard to change in people.

How do you put the argument between the church and Galileo in this context?

They were fighting, but it wasn't about spirituality. My suspicion is that Galileo probably had more spirituality than the pope. The guy who originally developed the TCI psychological test that we use was Abraham Maslow. His big claim to fame—and the thing he was proudest of, he used to tell people—was that when he gave the test, the people who scored the lowest were priests. He said they were not really spiritual. They were something else. They were authoritarian. And that characterizes the relationship between the church and Galileo.

So to think this through: your findings would be that Urban VIII and Galileo both had the God gene, but one upheld the church and one upheld science, and so we are back where we started.

Yes.

Cognitive Science Takes On Religion: A New Approach to an Age-Old Question

by Hannah de Keijzer

Over the centuries, the metaphorical warfare between science and religion has been waged on two major battlefields. One is in the heavens, where the fighting is over questions of cosmology and whether or not there is a divine design behind this awe-inspiring universe. The other battlefield is on earth, where there are clashes over questions of evolutionary biology and human creation.

Recently, science has begun sending unusual spies into religion's camp: cognitive scientists. Sidestepping the established debates almost completely, these men and women are working to find out what makes the customary enemy tick. Some work with an eye towards debunking religion, and some with an eye towards proving the existence of God. No matter their personal orientation, they are all asking the question, "Why does our brain choose to believe in the first place?" They make use not only of traditional psychology and history, but also of recent work into the properties and evolution of the human brain. They look into the mind's inferential systems and attempt to discover what goes on subconsciously, behind our daily awareness, at the mechanistic level.

Work in cognitive science is a continual process of theorizing, investigating, ex-

Hannah de Keijzer pursues her interests in cognitive science, religion, and dance at Swarthmore College.

perimenting, and discovering—as yet, we know remarkably little about the human brain. There is also little to no consensus on what is encompassed by the term "religion." Practically every theorist has tried to answer this philosophical/theological/definitional question in a different way.

The French sociologist and philosopher Emile Durkheim (1858–1917) saw it this way: "Religion is a unified system of beliefs and practices relative to *sacred things* . . . things set apart and forbidden." He envisioned religion and religious activities as a kind of social glue, reinforcing a sense of community identity and increasing chances of survival. Sigmund Freud (1856–1939) went the opposite direction: he drew a direct parallel between neurosis and the activities of religious people, saying, "Religion would thus be the universal obsessional neurosis of humanity."

Steward Guthrie, a contemporary scholar at Fordham University, believes the "common denominator of religions [is] seeing more organization in things and events than these things and events really have." Peter Berger, a widely quoted expert in the field who teaches at Boston University's School of Theology, believes religion to be the epitome of "man's self-examination, of his infusion of reality with his own meaning . . . Religion is the audacious attempt to conceive of the entire universe as being humanly significant."

While there is clearly no accord on the meaning of "religion," the will to "believe" seems universally wired in the brain, regardless of culture. So why and how *does* the brain believe?

Pascal Boyer, who studies the acquisition, use and transmission of cultural knowledge, believes supernatural concepts (common across the globe and, he claims, the basis for all spiritual or religious beliefs) perpetuate because such concepts violate certain aspects of our cognitive filing system. We create categories in our minds to help us classify the world around us, but certain things just don't fit. These not-quite-categorizable concepts—ghosts, for example—stick out in our minds, and hence are more likely to be remembered and shared with others, creating a foundation for a larger belief system.

Even if such a "cognitive filing system" exists, where might it be located in the brain? Answering this question requires inviting religion into the laboratory. As is to be expected, just as there isn't much consensus over what constitutes religion, there isn't much consensus over what its neural substrates might be. Patrick McNamara, a behavioral neuroscientist at Boston University, believes we can plausibly localize many components of religious practices in the frontal lobes—the hypothesized neurological site of emotions, integral to religious experiences and belief. Because religion is often thought to involve the human cognitive system for detecting (and probably over-ascribing) intentionality in others, McNamara believes scientists should work with autistic children, who do not detect intentionality in the normal way. Are they capable of understanding religious ideas? Is their impaired ability a complete obstacle to religious belief, or can belief persist, indicating a different (or perhaps additional) cognitive grounding?

Others believe that we should turn to epileptics to get our clues to neural substrates, examining the sites of brain disorders that cause experiences similar to normal religious ones. Preliminarily, the researchers Jeffrey Savre and John Rabin believe the "primary substrate for the religious experience is the limbic system," where many epileptic seizures are focused.

Of course "altered" brain states are not just characteristics of neurological problems: they also apply to the meditation of Buddhist monks and the prayers of Franciscan nuns. Dr. Andrew Newberg, Director of Clinical Nuclear Medicine at the University of Pennsylvania, has used neuroimaging to study the neurophysiological architecture of meditation, a sensation, he contends, caused by the blockage of blood flow to crucial areas of the brain.

Altered brain states can also be induced by psychedelic drugs, used for centuries to stimulate religious experience. Some scientists believe experiments with drug-induced religious experiences might yield valuable information about cognition and the neuroscience of religion. Scientists do not imply the drug itself is responsible for the altered state. As Matthew Alper, author of The "God" Part of the Brain, insists, "no drug can elicit a response to which we are not physiologically predisposed. Drugs can only enhance or suppress those capacities we already possess."

We are, in some sense, back where we started: It is clear that there is an enormous range of theories about the cognitive and neurological bases of religion. Is there a common thread or theme?

One plausible way of making order out of this chaos is to conceive of religion as an "emergent" or "self-organizing" system. (Self-organization refers to spontaneous ordering tendencies sometimes observed in certain classes of complex systems, both artificial and natural.) Why is this a plausible model? Despite much of the work of the neuroscientists, there is little evidence as yet that "religion" itself is a phenomenon whose substrates we can pinpoint in the brain. Brain regions whose functioning appears to be crucial to the spiritual experience have been identified, but there are too many contributing factors to claim one area or another as specifically and/or entirely responsible. There is no single religion "module," but rather different cognitive aspects working in tandem to create something unintended. A similar example is music: it is highly unlikely that humans developed with a specific and 'proper' module for music, but much more likely that we have several modules which can adapt and combine so as to enable us to create and enjoy music. Thus on both the cognitive and cultural levels (intertwined as they are), the model of the emergent system suggests that religion—an obviously complex and rich phenomenon—can arise from simple structures, abilities, and processes.

Religious experience and cognition are almost daunting in their complexity. Many crucial pieces of the puzzle have not even been touched upon here: emotion, love and war, the sexual experience (in the normal, non-Freudian sense), language, symbols, dreams ... the list is endless. A very important question seems as yet unaddressed (perhaps as yet unaddressable): why do religious experiences—qualitatively different as they can be from normal life—feel so *real*, even when they are induced by epilepsy or drugs? Will we ever be able to discover what it is about the brain that makes religion possible? And if we do, what will it mean for religion itself?

ADAM VS. ATOM

BY JOSH WOLFE

The argument is made in Angels & Demons *(largely through the soliloquies of the camerlengo), that the Vatican is or should be opposed to a variety of new scientific and technological breakthroughs in which man is "playing God." Nanotechnology—the science of manipulating matter at an extremely small scale—is one of the most obvious and compelling of those new technologies where man is "usurping" God's role in a variety of powerful ways. Among many applications, nanotechnology is integrally related to the creation of antimatter, which, of course, lies at the heart of the* Angels & Demons *plot.*

Josh Wolfe is a cofounder and managing partner of Lux Capital, a venture capital firm that focuses on investments in nanotechnology. He is also one of the most articulate and visible commentators on nanotechnology, as author of the acclaimed Nanotech Report *and editor of the Forbes publication the* Forbes/Wolfe Nanotech Report. *We asked Wolfe to reflect on nanotechnology, antimatter, and the theme of the conflict between science and religion reflected in* Angels & Demons. *Among the many fascinating ideas in the piece that follows, Wolfe goes well beyond even Dan Brown's search for hidden meanings and messages in the work of artists from the past. He suggests the possibility of what we have dubbed the "Michelangelo code," which may lie hidden in the Renaissance master's famous (and iconic)* Creation of Adam, *painted on the ceiling of the Sistine Chapel.*

Perhaps, Wolfe argues, drawing on a variety of papers and Web arguments by scientists, neurologists,

Josh Wolfe is a venture investor in nanotechnology and edits the *Forbes/Wolfe Nanotech Report.* He is also a columnist for *Forbes.*

and others, the depiction of God in Michelangelo's masterpiece is really a depiction of the human brain as seen from the perspective known in medicine as the sagittal cross section. In other words, maybe Michelangelo was trying to tell us, even from the hallowed grounds of the Vatican's most sacred chamber, that mankind's concept of God is not an external scientific reality, but is constructed inside the human brain.

If *Angels & Demons* had a prologue, it might read something like this:

"A devoutly religious man—with deep reverence for God and a strong belief in the power of faith—sits in a small room hunched over an old wooden table gripping a pen tightly. With a mere scribble of his signature, a man of his stature and power can shift billions of dollars and move stock markets. Maybe he doesn't fully realize what he is about to do. Behind him hovers a young hotshot physicist from MIT and a Nobel Prize–winning chemist. Both try to suppress their excitement over what this will mean for them and their scientific brethren. Pen to the paper, the man signs over nearly $4 billion for a brand new realm of science—a field that has already taken the scientific community by storm and has activists around the world protesting and calling for immediate bans. The field: nanotechnology—controlling matter at the atomic scale. *Man playing god.*"

This isn't fiction. The man was President George W. Bush, the room the Oval Office of the White House—and I was fortunate enough to be standing behind him as he signed into law the $3.6 billion Nanotech R&D Act on December 3, 2003.

THE PROMISE AND PERILS OF NANOTECHNOLOGY

Angles & Demons was published the same year the National Nanotechnology Initiative began. The book makes a passing mention of nanotechnology—an area of research conducted at CERN and presumed by the novel to be condemned by the Vatican (although in fact the Vatican has made no denunciation of nanotechnology).

Nanotechnology has benefited from bipartisan support in DC—largely because of its predicted impact in health care (treating cancer without side effects and discovering and delivering new drugs with pinpoint precision); electronics (computers the size of a sugar cube that could contain the entire Library of Congress); and energy (cheap and flexible solar cells that could reduce our suckling dependence on foreign oil).

Nanotechnology is technology created at the scale of atoms and molecules. And at that ultra-small-size regime, classical Newtonian physics, which governs our daily lives, gives way to quantum physics—where matter starts to act in unexpected ways. Interestingly, while most religious imagery and symbols are often based on balance and order (perhaps a function of the human brain's pattern-seeking tendencies and the universal impulse to find beauty in symmetrical objects like flowers and faces), quantum physics is based upon asymmetry, probability, uncertainty, electron clouds, and tunable matter.

Our material world is of course made up of atoms—which are far too small to see with the naked eye. Even the best microscope can't see that small. But about twenty years ago, a tool was invented that lets us not only observe individual atoms, but also tinker with them. We can nudge them about, create patterns, and even get them to self-assemble into complex arrangements. The holy grail of nanotechnology is literally to grow objects from the atomic scale up. The economic implications of this kind of atomic-level control are profound when you remember that the only difference between the graphite in a pencil and the diamond in a brilliantly sparkling engagement ring is the way the carbon atoms in both objects are arranged. That's it.

In the history of the world, economic growth has come only from making new combinations of a fixed set of resources. The iron oxide (aka rust) that was once used to store data via cave paintings has now been repurposed as the substrate for magnetic memory disks. Silicon, which came from sand, was primarily used for glass and later repurposed for computation. Who would have ever looked at a window and thought that its composition could be reformulated to create a Pentium computer chip? The overall trend is toward more economic value per unit of raw material. Consider that four atoms off the periodic table of elements can combine in 94 million ways and, kept in proportions of less than ten atoms, with 3,500 different sets, could yield 330 billion recipes. The point is this: man has only begun to experiment with the enormous unrealized combinations of atoms to create new matter and new materials we've never seen before.

The properties of matter can be tuned with precision by changing the size and composition of molecules in combinations and configurations that aren't found in nature. That's not to say the natural world will become irrelevant—quite the contrary. Some of the most exciting developments in nanotechnology will be derived from an engineer who's already invested billions of years in research and development— Mother Nature.

Scientists at one private nanotech company are genetically engineering bacteria and viruses so as to program them to manufacture complex semiconductor devices cheaply and safely—in other words, using biology to make electronics equipment the same way that we make beer, cheese, and wine! Another nanotech company has reverse engineered the sticky feet of a gecko lizard to create a thinner and stronger synthetic version that allows a 150-pound person to climb a wall like Spider-Man.

RELIGION AND NANOTECHNOLOGY

I often display a painting during my speeches on nanotech, not for religious significance, but to make an analogy—an inverted Tower of Babel. It depicts hordes of people building up toward the sky, all speaking different languages. In nanotechnology, researchers who previously spoke distinct scientific languages are now communicating at the boundaries of their disciplines: biologists are collaborating with electrical engineers and chemists with computer scientists. There's a scientific renaissance—a consilience of knowledge.

Nanotechnology has widely been recognized as the new version of the Cold War's international space race. And this fierce competition has created a metaphorical poker game where each country's ante raises the stakes for technological and economic dominance in the twenty-first century. In this poker game, the American lead is by no means guaranteed.

It's a bit discomforting to think that if nanotech, which Bush has fully supported, was ever framed as "playing God" (i.e., manipulating matter in ways not previously done), it would be anathema to his belief system and he'd have vetoed the nanotech bill on the spot.

SCIENCE IS CUMULATIVE, RELIGION IS STATIC

The money appropriated, of course, goes to scientists. It funds their discoveries which, in turn, serve as the foundation for other scientists to build on. Science is cumulative. And here lies one great tension between religion and science: religious creeds are static. Their foundation fixed, sacred relics preserved with high fidelity and passed down through the minds of their carriers from generation to generation over the centuries.

The funny thing about science is that you could teach Newton or Aristotle or Copernicus or any of the ancient gurus a lesson. Any one of them might've been smarter than any of us, but we happen to know more than they did about the world and how everything in it works. Science advances cumulatively and, since we live later, even the nonscientists among us know much more about a lot of things than the great scientists of past epochs. It's that simple. Sure, Aristotle could walk into a philosophy discussion and hold his own. But in a modern-day science class, he'd be lost. Here are some basic things we all know that he'd be shocked by: the earth orbits the sun and—despite the Illuminati's symbols—there are more than four elements and none of them are earth, water, fire, or air. Forget about explaining electricity, magnetism, lasers, transistors, microprocessors, solar cells, quantum physics, or carbon nanotubes!

CAN SCIENCE AND RELIGION PEACEFULLY COEXIST?

I've witnessed a culture of politeness with staunch advocates of science and religion tiptoeing around one another to avoid a great clash. To suggest that your belief is right and another's wrong is considered arrogance of the highest order—yet it is that arrogance and that dogmatism that have driven all scientific and technological progress and, ironically, also launched nearly all of mankind's wars. So let's have at it: the armies of empiricism at the fortress of faith.

The peaceful coexistence of science and religion is an illusion. They are incompatible and mutually exclusive. The scientific method is antithetical to religious doctrine and even nontheistic mysticism. Science rests upon testable hypotheses, repeatable results, empirical evidence, reason, experimentation, skepticism, and challenging established beliefs and conventional wisdoms. Religion rests upon the unquestioning faith of its believers. Religious narratives contain beliefs about the creation of the universe, the creation of man, and concepts like afterlife or reincarnation. Science asserts itself not in value-laden beliefs but in factual understandings of the world and the mechanisms and phenomena by which it operates, stripped of any theological significance. And it lives by this creed: *nullius in verba*, "take no one's word for it."

But whether science and religion can peacefully coexist in the long term, pseudo-science and religion definitely can. Many people unfortunately twist the complexity of nanotechnology or quantum physics into a spiritual hodgepodge of energy fields and what could muster as New Age science. They try to use uncertainty principles to explain things that are uncertain and suggest that our own brains or the mind of God or the universe are really a giant quantum computer. The truth is that we tend to see what we believe rather than believe what we see.

It's been suggested that religion exists to explain the unexplainable. As humans, we feel cognitive dissonance in the absence of explanations. And part of the lure of spirituality and religion is that they appear to fill in the blanks in the questions that science has yet to answer.

THE PURSUIT OF NOBLE TRUTHS

Many religious critics feel that science strips away the beauty and mystery of life. But many scientists I know feel there is something greater than themselves. That something is truth.

Science-fiction author William Gibson once said the future is here, it's just unevenly distributed. I believe the same holds for truth. Everyone may be searching for that elusive answer, perhaps for happiness, fulfillment, living a richer life, or attaining greater knowledge. The quest to understand provokes the curiosity that leads to the pursuit of truth.

Scientific truth tells us who we are, where we've been, and where we're going. Myths and mysticism are ultimately subjugated and submit to empirical reality. Modern miracles are really found in modern medicine: insulin injections, pacemakers, MRIs, X-rays, transplant surgeries, and pharmaceuticals.

Nanotech and related scientific development have all the markings and social power of a belief system or surrogate form of religion. Some proponents suggest nanotechnology could lead to much longer life spans, if not outright immortality. But this is a slippery slope from where the technology really is today. From magnetism to radio waves and electric shocks—technology has always had its fair share of soothsayers selling faith that some new invention will cure people's illness. In the absence of evidence, the scientific community has always been quick to demand proof and discredit devious charlatans. The Vatican, of course, took 350 years to settle up with Galileo.

Science by its very nature is open and strengthened by the scrutiny of the public. But the integrity and usefulness of science is threatened whenever it is attacked on ideological grounds. Thomas Jefferson said, "We are not afraid to follow truth wherever it may lead, nor to tolerate any error so long as reason is left free to combat it."

DOES SCIENCE NEED RELIGION FOR MORAL GUIDANCE?

Many critics of science caricature the pursuit of advancements by invoking images of mad scientists, ignorant or aloof to the impact these advancements will have. So singularly focused on achievement while dwelling in the realm of value-free problem solving, scientists lack a moral compass to guide them in considering the societal implications of their work. *Dr. Frankenstein.*

There's an irony here: it seems that which is poorly understood is either feared or revered. Critics of nanotechnology demand proof that its effects will be benign. But all technology and human progress has trade-offs. Gasoline is flammable and highly toxic, airplanes and cars cause numerous deaths, CD players have trace amounts of arsenic, and fire, one of man's greatest discoveries, has scorched millions dead.

Our modern analog existence has been defined by wars fought over polarized and intransigent beliefs. With these binary outcomes it almost makes sense to view the logic of human destiny as digital.

SCIENCE OPENS DOORS TO MORE QUESTIONS

The beauty of science is that we are always left with more questions. Try this: compare Michelangelo's *Creation of Adam* emblazoned upon the ceiling of the Sistine Chapel to any image of the midsagittal cross section of the brain. Could Michelangelo have played the ultimate insider's prank on the church? Historians have always interpreted the artwork as the defining depiction of man made in God's image. Could it have been the other way around? Could Michelangelo really have been sending a secret message to suggest that God was constructed in the mind of man? Take a look at this website for a graphical comparison and judge for yourself: http://psych-www.colorado. edu/users/spencer/psyc2012/michelangelo.html.

For the many scientists who believe in God, science provides explanations and answers to "how," but religion provides meaning, a sense of purpose, and answers "why." Other scientists are so zealous in their antireligiosity and worship of pure science that they unintentionally come across as dogmatically religious.

Einstein, in his iconic credibility, is often misreported to have believed in God. In his own words, "It was, of course, a lie what you read about my religious convictions, a lie which is being systematically repeated ... If something is in me which can be called religious then it is the unbounded admiration for the structure of the world so far as our science can reveal it." Amen.

5: ROBERT LANGDON'S ROME: ART AND ARCHITECTURE

Bernini, the sculptor who helped create the Eternal City • Secrets and symbols of Vatican art and architecture • The real truth behind the Secret Vatican Library • The ritual use of astrology, magic, alchemy, and other occult practices in the Vatican • What the sharp-eyed Harvard symbology professor got right—and wrong—on his tour of Rome • A guided tour of the nonfiction Rome

A BERNINI EXPERT REFLECTS ON DAN BROWN'S USE OF THE BAROQUE MASTER

BY TOD MARDER

After reading Angels & Demons *and deciding that our editorial team was going to develop a guidebook to help readers better understand and think about the novel, the very first book we bought to begin our own quest was Tod Marder's* Bernini and the Art of Architecture. *This magnificent survey brought Bernini and his works to life in a whole new way. By looking at the photographs and reading Marder's commentary, you could put yourself into the very scenes Dan Brown described in the novel. You could immediately see the problems with Brown's inaccuracies. But you could also see the visceral power of Bernini's body of work and the fascinating questions thrown up by the baroque era, which straddled the Renaissance and the Enlightenment, the ancient world and the modern world, the fading era of religious cosmology and the future of scientific cosmology.*

To understand Bernini, you have, as well, to understand Rome, the Counter-Reformation, the politics of the Vatican, and the baroque era. Tod Marder is a world-class expert on Bernini, but he is also, of necessity, an expert on all these other issues as well. Here, and in another piece in this chapter, he talks

---

Tod Marder is Chair of the Department of Art History at Rutgers The State University of New Jersey, and a Fellow of the American Academy in Rome. He recommends these works for further reading: Laurie Nussdorfer, *Civic Politics in the Rome of Urban VIII*; Charles Avery, *Bernini: Genius of the Roman Baroque*; Howard Hibbard, *Bernini*; and T. A. Marder, *Bernini and the Art of Architecture*.

about his personal experiences over the years doing research in the Vatican Library and Secret Archives. Professor Marder shares a lifetime of insights into Bernini and his art, as well as about the Vatican, Rome, and baroque culture. He also hints at some new discoveries and new scholarship on Bernini. Here, then, is one of the best tour guides possible to the world of baroque Rome that lies at the epicenter of Angels & Demons.

Plenty of recent fiction claims to be based on art history. But is it? Do these mysteries, novels, and stories have a firm grounding in art historical fact? It's a fair question if only because claims made to the contrary or in support of scrupulous research seem to have an effect on readers. Indeed, more people have posed questions to me about Dan Brown's *Angels & Demons* than any fictional writing in recent years. These reactions tell me that a lot of people bought and read *Angels & Demons* and that, happily, my friends still remember me as a Bernini specialist. Their questions also tell me that readers had problems deciding what was true to life in this particular narrative and what was simply invented. With a statement in the preamble of *Angels & Demons* claiming that all places, objects, and historical personalities in the novel have a factual basis, the reader is meant to believe the information in the story. In many cases this is misplaced trust.

In the end, the best reason for reconsidering a work of fiction set in a historical context is that in some cases—and this is one—the historical and topographical realities of people, cities, and events end up being at least as interesting to many people as the fictionalized versions are. Can the use of poetic license to alter well-established facts and information be justified only when the result is more entertaining, more revelatory, more deeply provocative and compelling than the realities? This is an argument professional historians would like to make, I suspect, because their lives and livelihoods depend on it. So here are a few facts, themes, and interpretations that readers of *Angels & Demons* might like to have clarified.

THE VACANT SEE

Let's start by taking the fundamental setting of the story, the interregnum that occurs when a pope dies and preparations are made to elect a papal successor. The moment has an official designation—the Vacant See—and usually lasts a month or two. During this time arrangements are made to gather the College of Cardinals to elect the new pontiff. Historically, the Vacant See was an aberrant moment, one fraught with changes and challenges of power that would serve any thriller writer well. In the seventeenth century the passage of power was less smooth and less controlled at the Vatican than in modern times; indeed, it was most often characterized by thinly sanctioned lawlessness and revenge particularly directed against the family and forces of the deceased pope.

In 1644, when Urban VIII Barberini died (in *Angels & Demons* he is a patron of the artist Gianlorenzo Bernini), he and his family were publicly mocked for their taxes on bread, their pursuit of a vain war, and their personal enrichment while in office—criticisms comparable in most ways, with adjustments for context, to recent American presidencies. The cardinal's nephew Francesco immediately became the target of pent-up hostilities and was teased as the "cardinal of the half ounce," referring to the newly shrunken size of legal bread loaves and to his new impotence in matters of governance. On Urban's unfinished tomb it was suggested that an inscription be dedicated to the pope who "fattened the bees (the Barberini family symbol) and flayed the flock." Bernini had been contacted, it was said in jest, to carve a crucifixion to be set in the apse of St. Peter's between the tombs of the two "thieves" Urban VIII and Paul III Farnese, as their tombs do in fact flank the apse of the basilica.

Another interesting feature of the seventeenth-century background for the Vacant See included the freeing of all prisoners in city jails during the interregnum, leaving intact only the jails of the most hardened criminals at the Castle of Sant'Angelo. Imagine if one among the Illuminati had been jailed and freed under these circumstances, only to serve the ends of murder and chaos!

During the Vacant See, the crowds and civic officials usually moved more quickly than the church, the one to extract revenge and the other to reassert control over the city once the pope had died. An angry mob, it was reported, had turned an effigy of Urban VIII into dust within forty-five minutes of his death on the morning of July 29, 1644. On the same day, by tradition, patrician Romans met in the palaces of Michelangelo's Capitoline Hill to elect forty officials from their number to keep order in the city. Edicts were passed and enforced with a rigor unusual for the papacy but entirely workable for the officials of the various quarters of the city, who kept their guard units patrolling the neighborhood turf. Firearms were banned, as was the wearing of costumes or disguises. Gambling was forbidden, and the presence of all overnight lodgers had to be reported each day to the authorities. Barbers and surgeons were required to report the names of anyone treated for serious wounds.

At the Vatican, the *camerlengo* (cardinal chamberlain) headed a four-cardinal executive committee that set the organization of a conclave into motion and took whatever steps it could muster to retain power over church dominions. It generally took ten days after a pope's death for the cardinals to convene at the Vatican to elect a successor. Centuries-old protocol dictated this interval in part to allow for the obsequies of the deceased pope. Once these rites were observed and completed, there were rules that encouraged the cardinals to make a concerted effort to find the appropriate successor. The cardinals had a mandate to vote formally twice a day until the process was successfully completed. In earlier centuries the cardinals were restricted to one-course meals at lunch and dinner if they didn't produce an election after the first three days of the conclave. After five days, they were to be limited to bread, wine, and water. But these restrictions were so frequently reiterated and then relaxed over time that they were probably largely ignored.

In the aftermath of Urban VIII's rule, the voting went on through the month of August into mid-September 1644 before any candidate received the necessary majority. The victor was very much a compromise candidate, a Roman-born cleric whose family was considered arriviste, with barely a century's residence in the city. Aspiring but ungenerous, known as "Monsignor No-Go," and guided and bank-rolled by his avaricious sister-in-law, Donna Olimpia Maidalchini (she was called "the Dominatrix"), Innocent X Pamphili became the patron of Bernini's great Four Rivers Fountain on Piazza Navona, scene of the last planned murder in *Angels & Demons.*

In the early 1400s, to prevent the infiltration of political influences, the cardinals had met to elect a pope in Roman churches closed to the outside world. By the middle of the fifteenth century, the process was transferred to the Vatican forever in order to benefit from a setting that could be secured under lock and key—conclave (*con clave*) literally means "with key." The keeping of the keys was entrusted by tradition to the patrician Savelli family, whose members had been granted exclusive rights as Vatican marshals to lock and unlock the doors leading to the cardinals' meeting place. Indeed, the principal entrance to the secured space for the elections in the Vatican Palace was and still is called the Cortile del Maresciallo (Courtyard of the Marshal).

By contrast, responsibility for control over the turn boxes that permitted food and other supplies to be passed to the cardinals during the course of a conclave was given to the cleric who served as the governor of the Borgo, the "Burg" or neighborhood that immediately surrounds the Vatican Palace and St. Peter's Basilica. (The area around the Vatican is still referred to as the Borgo.) The *rote* (turn boxes) were common features in Roman Renaissance palaces, where the women's quarters were separate from the men's and female contact with the rest of the palace was always severely limited. At the Vatican they had the analogous function of slowing the flow of information from entering or leaving the assembly of cardinals. Attempts to breach security were fairly frequent, if we can infer from the historical records. In one instance a worker was jailed for having bored a hole in an exterior wall permitting Cardinal Francesco Barberini to smuggle notes and news in and out of the hall. All wine had to pass through the turn boxes in clear glass receptacles, and whole chickens were cut in half to reduce the possibilities for smuggling.

Cardinals and their servants actually resided in temporary cells located along the perimeters of the meeting spaces. These cells, constructed of wooden frames and hanging drapery, formed a kind of indoor tent city erected for the duration of a conclave. This community embraced between thirty and sixty cardinals, the number varying with both the full size of the college at any given time and the number of those who could participate. In the sixteenth and seventeenth centuries the cells were set up in the Sistine Chapel; later they also were built in the adjoining Sala Regia and Sala Ducale, which were the main reception halls of the palace. The votes were usually held in the nearby Pauline Chapel (Cappella Paolina), and only transferred to the Sistine

Chapel during the conclave for Urban VIII Barberini. The Sistine Chapel then became the preferred polling place into the modern era.

Typically, the conclave opened when cardinals assembled to be read their instructions, to participate in a Mass, and to make their first vote. The chalice used in the celebration of the Mass became the receptacle for the ballots. After each vote the ballots were counted. When there was no winner, the ballots were burned with damp straw that emitted a black smoke seen by crowds of onlookers in St. Peter's Piazza, some sixty feet below and to the south of the main palace. When a candidate received the required majority, the ballots were burned with dry straw, producing a white smoke, followed by the appearance of a cardinal to announce *"Papa habemus . . ."* with the name taken by the new pope. And with that achieved, the work of the Sacred College of Cardinals for the moment was done.

THE ARRANGEMENT OF THE VATICAN PALACE

The Vatican Palace and hence the library and archives housed in it owe their existence to the presence of the basilica that commemorates the burial site of St. Peter. According to some accounts Peter was martyred on the Janiculum Hill, where Bramante's Tempietto commemorates the spot. Others believe it was elsewhere. Whether Peter's is truly the body lying in the crypt directly under the dome of the basilica is debated, although the archaeological evidence is now reasonably certain that it is a tomb of the same era. And the same evidence points to the tomb belonging to a deceased man of the appropriate age named Peter.

Owing to the presence of this relic and the shrine and cult that grew on the burial site, the popes came to reside at the Vatican as a matter of convenience and defense. The Cathedral of Rome was and is still located at St. John the Lateran, fully across town, on flat land at the far edge of the walled city. Thus, although St. Peter's boasts a ceremonial *cathedra petri* (throne of Peter) in its apse, the basilica is not a cathedral (as Dan Brown erroneously refers to it in *Angels & Demons*). As ceremonials were elaborated and feast days at the tomb required ever-increasing participation of the pope and his court, a palace grew there to house the needs of the papacy and its papal court.

It is ironic that the Vatican Palace, whose ceremonies must have affected the shape and size of so many other palaces throughout history, is itself a highly irregular building, defying all notions of symmetry and cohesiveness of design. This is but one obstacle to knowing it well. Another is the fact that it simultaneously serves as a huge museum, a site of religious observances, and a working governmental center. As a result, public access is limited to museum areas, and even specialists are not allowed in many rooms of the working palace. Even among Renaissance art historians, the various floor levels, connecting corridors, and staircases are not as commonly known as one might expect from the keen interest everyone takes in the frescoes and architecture of the individual spaces.

This much can be gleaned from a plan of the Vatican in the Touring Club Italiano guidebook to Rome. The Via della Fondamenta skirts the northwestern flank of St. Peter's Basilica. It is not "directly up a hill from the Gate of Santa Ana" (Porta Sant'Anna, presumably) and there are no archives there, secret or otherwise, despite Robert Langdon's finding them there in the novel. The Via della Fondamenta *does* lead to the entrance of the Cortile della Sentinella (Courtyard of the Sentinel), which is in turn connected to the Cortile Borgia. But the routes necessary to arrive at these locations are so unusually circuitous that no one would want to place our hero striding "powerfully" along them to find the real location of the archives.

Both the Cortile della Sentinella and the Cortile Borgia border on the location of the Sistine Chapel, or at least its substructural foundations. The Sistine Chapel is a rectangular space whose main axis runs parallel to that of St. Peter's. A visitor approaching the palace from Bernini's Piazza would recognize the Sistina from the exterior by its peaked roofline, but little else reveals its location on the main ceremonial level of the papal state rooms, which stand some sixty feet above the piazza level.

The main route of approach to the major rooms of reception, worship, and presentation at the Vatican Palace is along a straight staircase reached from the north side of the piazza. The piazza is bordered by an enclosed corridor on the north—visitors can just turn to the right to see it—and this leads directly to Bernini's famous Scala Regia. For the average visitor, this walk can only be made on a map—the entrance to the corridor on the north (right) side of the piazza is protected by Swiss Guards who let only official visitors through their doors. The official visitor climbs to the summit of the Scala Regia to arrive at a huge hall of reception. Entering and turning to the left, he or she would be able to enter the Sistine Chapel.

All this is to say that when the fictional camerlengo Carlo Ventresca arrived at the top of the Scala Regia (Royal Staircase), he may have felt "as though he were standing on the precipice of his life" (p.185), but there would have been no chatter from the activity of cardinals in the Sistine Chapel below. The Sistine Chapel is also at the top of the stairs. Lucky are the museum visitors who, when viewing the Sistine ceiling frescoes by Michelangelo, are occasionally permitted to exit by way of the Scala Regia next door, and, as a means of crowd control, to descend to the piazza, thus experiencing Bernini's famous entrance to the palace, but in reverse.

A CLARIFICATION OF BERNINI'S MONUMENTS

Bernini is the focus artist for the story told in *Angels & Demons*. His works provide the location and backdrop for four terrible murders, and the implication is that he was a member of the Illuminati brotherhood in the seventeenth century, a close friend of Galileo in this regard, and an opponent of the teachings of the Catholic Church. If these notions were all true, baroque art historians would be grateful for the endless opportunities each of these themes would offer for intriguing research, teaching, and discussion. In historical fact, however, Bernini had nothing to do with any group called the Illuminati. That Bernini was more than fleetingly acquainted with Galileo is very likely, although their exact relationship remains conjectural. As for Bernini's opposition to church teachings, not a shred of evidence exists. Indeed, there is much information from the seventeenth century to the contrary.

At this point, we must turn to the Bernini monuments themselves. The rush to reach the first murder scene initially takes the protagonist Robert Langdon to the Pantheon. A misreading of his cues then corrected, Langdon hurries on to the Chigi Chapel in the church of Santa Maria del Popolo. The church stands at the northeast (not southeast, p. 259) corner of Piazza del Popolo, the urban space located just inside the city walls to welcome all visitors to Rome from the north. The church was built in the 1470s as part of an effort to populate the far reaches of the inhabited city. In the 1620s an impecunious descendent of the influential Chigi family, Monsignor Fabio Chigi, returned to rehabilitate a funerary chapel that had been founded a century earlier to honor his wealthy forebears. To have the artist's brilliant reputation reflect upon his own taste and heritage, Monsignor Fabio hoped to dust off the components of the chapel that had been initially designed in the Renaissance and decorated by the great Raphael himself. To help in this effort, Fabio hired the young Bernini.

Little was done for decades, until the monsignor-turned-cardinal became Pope Alexander VII in 1655 and asked Bernini to finish the decoration. So far as I know, the Chigi Chapel has never been known as the Cappella della Terra (Chapel of the Land, or Earth), as it is cast in *Angels & Demons* in order to represent one of the four Illuminati elements (earth, wind, fire, water). However, a Cappella della Terra Santa (Chapel of the Holy Land) is located in the Pantheon. It may be that this was the author's source of the name invented for the Chigi Chapel.

For the record, Santa Maria del Popolo is a church, not a cathedral (pp. 264, 266), that is, it is not governed by a bishop. In my experience, descriptions nearly always refer to the first, second, or third chapels on the right or left of a church from the vantage of an entering visitor. The Chigi Chapel is second on the left upon entering, just as Vittoria has it and despite Harvard art historian Langdon's momentary confusion (p. 266). And when Langdon's "trained eye" looks up to the dome to see astronomical imagery and the zodiac that plays a role in the narrative, he should have been thinking less about Galileo or Bernini in the seventeenth century than about Raphael's original designs of the sixteenth century, for that is when the dome was decorated. Likewise, the pyramids that are the Chigi tombs on the sides of the chapel are Raphael's design. The medallions with portraits of the Chigi forebears are Bernini's design, as is the skeleton depicted as though rising from the flat pavement in colored marbles. This is a burial chapel, and Bernini's skeleton appears to rise from the crypt in response to both the aforementioned zodiac and, especially, to the outstretched arms of a beckoning God the Father depicted by Raphael at the apex of the dome. The meaning of the skeleton made explicit in the inscription here—MORS AD CAELOS (death to heaven)—shows how Bernini related his work to Raphael's.

The use of pyramids as Christian images ("What are pyramids doing inside a Christian Chapel?" Langdon exclaims on p. 268) is common. In ancient Egypt the pyramid signified burial and insured a happy afterlife. The image was borrowed first by the ancient Romans and later during the Renaissance to denote the themes of death and salvation that are central to Christian belief. So perhaps this *is* a good place for a cardinal's murder. In truth, under the skeleton "manhole cover" in the center of the chapel is a crypt that has a surprise in it—another pyramid, underground, that was presumably Raphael's work. The redundant imagery, which was only relatively recently discovered, probably served as a subterranean ossuary, or housing for bones, to accompany the purely symbolic function of the pyramid-tombs in the chapel.

Much of this information contradicts the idea that Bernini could have invented the imagery of the Chigi Chapel, much less a path of illumination that traverses the city of Rome. In finishing the chapel decoration, for example, he carved two major figures in marble for two of the empty niches in the space, a figure of Daniel and a depiction of Habakkuk and the angel. The first is on the back left of the chapel and the second is diagonally opposite, flanking the right of the altar. As the great Bernini scholar Rudolf Wittkower explained, the image of Daniel in the lion's den is a symbol of salvation and so, too, is Habakkuk and the angel. In the midst of bringing food to laborers in the field, the story goes, Habakkuk was miraculously diverted by an angel to Daniel's den. Habakkuk points to his original goal, while the angel points instead to Daniel. The story that relates the two Old Testament prophets is recounted in a unique version of the Greek Septuagint text of the book of Daniel that was part of the Chigi Library. Neither Langdon nor his creator allude to this richness of meaning, either out of ignorance or perhaps because of the unwelcome implication of the pope's own role (rather than Bernini's) in creating the imagery of this supposedly antipapal chapel.

Whether by design or coincidence, in pointing to Daniel, Habakkuk's guiding angel also points in the actual direction of the Vatican. This is the sign that propels both Langdon and the narrative back to St. Peter's Square. There the intrepid art historian and his companion discover at the foot of the central obelisk a flat stone which shows a representation of the "West Ponente," the west wind, in relief. The stone relief is purported to be a work of Bernini with a secret message mixing astronomy, geometry, and directional symbolism. In truth, Bernini's pavement patterns for the piazza were never executed. As a result, many proposals were generated over time. To the best of my knowledge the West Ponente engraving was made and set in place in 1818 by the papal astronomer Filippo Luigi Gilii, who wished to use the Vatican obelisk as a sundial and thus laid out the pavement north of the spire with a meridian. Gilii also inscribed the lengths of the principal churches of Christendom on the floor pavement of St. Peter's, a device that visitors see and admire far more often than the complicated time and directional indicators on the piazza.

"Death to Heaven," Chigi Chapel, Santa Maria del Popolo.

The site of the third murder is the church of Santa Maria della Vittoria, where Bernini's most famous work, the *Ecstasy of St. Teresa*, is located. It is emphatically not true that the original location of the St. Teresa was "inside the Vatican" (p. 336). Nor is it true that the group of the ecstatic saint in the company of her angel was "too sexually explicit for the Vatican" (p. 337). Nor is it therefore true that the sculpture had been banished by Pope Urban VIII to an "obscure chapel" across town on the suggestion of the artist (p. 337). Urban VIII died in 1644; the *Ecstasy of St. Teresa* was begun in 1646. Finally, it cannot be true that an art historian from Harvard or anywhere else could have only a "vague familiarity with the statue," which is one of the most popular works of art in nearly every introductory college course.

The *Ecstasy of St. Teresa* was commissioned by a retired cardinal from Venice, Federico Cornaro, in 1647, during the reign of Pope Innocent X, to commemorate the famous Spanish nun. A mystic whose claims of visions were corroborated through extensive investigations, Theresa became a heroine of the Discalced Carmelites and their nunnery in Rome. According to her autobiography, she was frequently subject to visions of angels, Jesus, and the soul of God himself, experiences she claimed were a mixture of sweetness and pain so intense "that one cannot possibly wish it to cease." Bernini depicted her in the presence of an angel who gently lifts her garments to plunge a fiery arrow into her heart. The reclining swooning saint is rendered both powerless and ecstatic, her head rolled back, eyes blank, and mouth open to utter an imaginary moan of rapture and surrender.

Whether the St. Teresa is depicted "in the throes of a toe-curling orgasm" (p. 337) or a completely religious experience is a matter of considerable debate, but most undergraduates (not to mention adults) never forget this impressionable image. One eighteenth-century critic made himself famous for declaring that "if this is divine love, I know it well." Yet there is some serious question about Bernini's motives: was he trying hard to capture the fervor of the saint's autobiography, or was he rather using recognizable carnal reactions to elicit the nature of deeply religious experience? Perhaps it is fitting to cast one of the most visceral encounters in the Langdon narrative here, where faith and fervor intersect. Certainly this was the right spot to stage the abduction of the female protagonist Vittoria for the carnal appetite of the murderer.

The final stop on the Bernini tour of Rome in *Angels & Demons* is Piazza Navona, the huge open space that has evolved over the millennia, maintaining the original shape of the ancient stadium of Emperor Domitian. Dominating the space and facing the twin-towered church of St. Agnes, Bernini built his most commanding civic monument, the Fontana dei Quattro Fiumi (Fountain of the Four Rivers, 1647–1651), which does indeed feature personifications of the Danube, Nile, Ganges, and Rio della Plata—representing the four continents of seventeenth-century Catholicism. Of Langdon's dramatic frolics in the basin here there is little to say, apart from the fact that—owing to its position at the end of the Acqua Vergine aqueduct—the basin

The West Ponente—one of many winds depicted in inlaid tile work in St. Peter's Square.

is rather shallow, its water show has not often "sizzled" (p. 408) nor is it ever "thundering" (p. 411) in my experience. On the contrary, it is the inscrutable symbolism of natural images that is most outstanding for both casual spectator and scholar alike.

The Four Rivers Fountain is composed of a jagged pile of travertine carved to look like it came untouched from the depths of the earth. Accompanying the personifications of the rivers is a palm tree, a lion, a serpent, a fish, an unidentified sea monster, and an armadillo. Above this rocky base sits an obelisk brought here on the express order of Pope Innocent X Pamphili from an ancient circus on the outskirts of Rome. The obelisk is capped by a metal dove, an emblem of the Pamphili family, as most art historians know. Not Langdon, however, who mistakes it for a pigeon casually alighting on the apex, that is, until he throws a fistful of coins at it, a throw that might challenge the pitcher of any farm team in the country. It is then revealed as a bronze dove, a permanent part of the ensemble.

Despite years of attempts, no one has ever deciphered the meaning of these elements at the fountain. The closest we have come to understanding them is to recall Bernini's link with a Jesuit polymath named Athanasius Kircher. As Europe's leading Egyptologist, Kircher was asked by the pope to interpret the ancient hieroglyphs carved on the obelisk. This he did, calling on as much scientific knowledge as he could muster but relying also on an overly imaginative concept of the world as a theater of images. In Kircher's view the eternal truth of God's omniscience was revealed in the most obscure ways. Cabalistic in the extreme, Kircher claimed to be purposefully obscuring the real meaning of the obelisk, lest he deprive some other erudite soul of the enlightenment that comes from personal decipherment. Kircher wrote a book about the Pamphili Obelisk, as it was called. On the title page appears a little cherub with his forefinger raised to his lips to signal silence—if you know the secrets herein, he seems to say, keep them to yourself. I point out this little sidelight of the fountain's history because it might have easily played into the scheme of the Illuminati plot. As a scientist, Galileo was certainly in touch with Kircher, although it is hard to imagine their having much in common.

Finally, there is the notion that the text of Galileo's 1639 *Diagramma* described a cross inscribed over the map of Rome that purposefully linked four of Bernini's creations in a way that the artist would have intended. The origin of this idea obviously derives from well-known propaganda of the sixteenth century, in which the relocation of the ancient obelisks during the Renaissance era was claimed, quite incorrectly, to form a cross. It is equally unlikely that a meaningful path of enlightenment have been realized by Bernini in commissions that dated from the 1650s (in the first two cases) and the late 1640s to early 1650s (in the other two). The chronological sequence and the circumstances of the individual commissions argues against our seeing a relationship among these works in any but the most generalized way. For how and when could one have followed a path of enlightenment set up by these monuments? The obelisks

Bernini's Fountain of the Four Rivers with Obelisk, Piazza Navona.

that link so much of Roman topography were largely the work of the sixteenth-century Pope Sixtus V (1585–1590); and the spire over the Four Rivers Fountain was ordered by Innocent X (1644–1655).

A FINAL WORD: BERNINI AND GALILEO?

Galileo's artistic go-to man in *Angels & Demons* is identified as Bernini. This would be an odd choice, historically speaking, on two counts. First, as Langdon asserts (p. 282), Bernini was "the" papal artist par excellence and would have had no reason to challenge the teachings or the authority of the church. Second, Galileo (1564–1642) had no known contact with Bernini. On the first count, we may rest secure in the knowledge of Bernini's orthodoxy—no amount of crisscrossing Rome with imaginary axes can compensate for the evidence of a life that threw off enough documentary information to sink a papal galleon. On the second count, some interesting ambiguity exists.

In the older art historical literature there is no mention or evidence of any relationship between Bernini and Galileo, even though Galileo was an accomplished artist and theorist. As a draughtsman, geometer, and perspectivalist, Galileo had once petitioned the Academy of Design in Florence for a position as an instructor (he didn't get it). Yet historians of art and science are convinced that his ability to decode the significance of light and shadow was paramount in his discovery of the contours of the moon as a series of mountains and valleys. It was also important to his understanding of the line between the dark and light sides of the moon, enabling him to calculate the approximate size of the moon and later to postulate a solar system for which he was famously persecuted.

Galileo wrote a letter in 1612 that has become a seminal text in the old dispute pitting the superiority of painting against that of sculpture. Very recently this letter has been directly and convincingly linked to the first works of papal sculpture produced in Rome by Bernini's father, Pietro, who had been summoned to the city for this purpose. According to this interpretation, Pietro had self-consciously shaped his sculptures to participate in this old argument. Bernini's father and all of his paternal forebears were Florentine, and it is likely that he knew the Florentine Galileo, too. If this is true, the young prodigy Bernini would also have known the great scientist.

Since one of Galileo's early supporters was Urban VIII Barberini, who was Bernini's most faithful and active patron, there is another reason to suppose that the two men were acquainted with each other. Eventually Urban VIII turned against Galileo, who ended his days under house arrest in Florence. But there is no reason to suppose that Bernini expressed any official or personal solidarity with the scientist or his science. Their common interest was art and art theory, which is a far cry from a secret cult devoted to overthrowing the papacy.

In the end, then, we may conclude that Dan Brown's Author's Note—which claims that "references to all works of art, tombs, tunnels, and architecture in Rome are entirely factual (as are their exact locations)"—is where the fiction begins. The reader is left to track Dan Brown's code for what is true and factual in the book and what is merely the author's invention. Perhaps this is acceptable in such a robust romp around Rome, where even the Harvard art historian Langdon treats the art as a trivial pursuit.

BERNINI AND HIS ANGELS

AN INTERVIEW WITH MARK S. WEIL

It is obvious why Dan Brown named Angels & Demons *as he did. Angels—specifically, the angels of Gianlorenzo Bernini, the great baroque sculptor—are at the epicenter of the novel. As Professor Mark S. Weil of Washington University in St. Louis points out, angels were used historically to represent messengers of God who bring the good news of salvation to earth. What better plot device than to use Bernini's angels as markers not to salvation, but as the Illuminati's hidden messengers, laying out the path to the destruction of the Catholic Church?*

And who better to deconstruct Dan Brown's artifice than Weil, a renowned authority on Bernini? Weil wrote his dissertation on Bernini's decoration of the Ponte Sant'Angelo, the Bridge of Angels that Robert Langdon crosses on his way to the Castel Sant'Angelo in search of the Illuminati lair. That led to The History and Decoration of the Ponte S. Angelo, *published in 1974. Weil has also written about the Cornaro Chapel, located in the Church of Santa Maria della Vittoria, where Robert Langdon finds Bernini's* Ectstasy of St. Teresa, *the third altar of science and the one representing fire.*

Was Bernini one of those gifted artists who seem destined, almost from birth, to be a painter or sculptor?
Gianlorenzo Bernini (1598–1680) was educated from childhood to be a

---

Mark S. Weil is a leading expert on the art of Gianlorenzo Bernini. He goes to Rome each year for several months to conduct research at the Vatican Library and Archives.

sculptor and an artist. He was a child prodigy and was continuously lauded for his ability to create strikingly naturalistic, emotionally dramatic works of art. Bernini's early work includes sculptures of large nude men and women drawn from ancient myths. Two of these are *Pluto and Proserpina* (1621–1622) and *Apollo and Daphne* (1622–1625), both now in the Galleria Borghese in Rome. He also produced a wonderfully dramatic statue of David (1623) in the act of preparing to slay Goliath, which is also in the Galleria Borghese. The objects were and continue to be admired as tour de force representations of dramatic moments in marble, not as works that teach allegorical, moral, or religious lessons.

What was Bernini like as a person? Was he as religious as art historians would have us believe?

Bernini was very interested in stage design, and was very good at what is known today as special effects. He wrote and produced works that were "machine plays" full of dramatic events that seemed to be happening in real time on the stage. In the 1630s his play about the inundation of the Tiber River caused the audience to panic because the water from the flooded river appeared to be flowing off the stage.

As a young adult Bernini was pretty wild, and he married late. According to a letter written in 1638 by his mother to Cardinal Francesco Barberini, papal nephew and vice chancellor of the church, Bernini was seen chasing his brother with a sword through the streets of Rome, and even through the basilica of Santa Maria Maggiore, because he caught him talking to his mistress. Bernini's mother urged Barberini and Pope Urban VIII to take matters into their hands and find a suitable woman for her forty-year-old son. They did so, forcing him into marriage in 1639. He then settled down with his wife and had ten children. It was at this time that Bernini became very religious and got involved with the Society of Jesus (the Jesuits).

Is there any evidence to support the idea, as Dan Brown suggests in Angels & Demons, *that Bernini and Galileo were friends and members of a secret society?*

There is no evidence to support the idea that either belonged to any secret society. Nor is there evidence that they were friends or colleagues. Galileo Galilei (1564–1642) was more than a generation older than Bernini and was far better educated. They may have known one another because both were associated with the papal court and lived in Rome, which by modern standards was a small city.

Later in his life, Bernini became deeply religious and associated himself with the Jesuits' most important lay congregation, the Congregation of Nobles dedicated to the Assumed Virgin (Congregazione dei Nobili dell'Assunta). With the exception of a few years in the 1640s when he was out of favor, Bernini remained the most powerful artist in Rome until the end of his life. Like all artists, he would have been provided with programs for each design he made and no design would have been executed without papal approval. He had no reason to join an antichurch secret society.

Why was Bernini, as Dan Brown describes him, considered the "Vatican Wonder Boy"?

The leaders of the Catholic Church wanted art that could represent its doctrines and stimulate piety. Bernini's works of art did this and the church loved him for it. He had the ability to follow the orthodox Catholic doctrines written in the religious programs.

Another reason why he had such close ties to many of the popes who commissioned his work was because they were artists themselves. Cardinal Maffeo Barberini (Pope Urban VIII) was a poet who had written some short verses that were placed beneath Bernini's pieces of classical sculpture from the Borghese Collection in Rome. And Cardinal Giulio Rospigliosi (Pope Clement IX) was a playwright for whom Bernini designed stage sets. When Barberini became Pope Urban VIII in 1623, he made Bernini the papal artist and put him to work creating pieces to decorate St. Peter's Basilica and other religious sites. Urban probably chose Bernini because of his ability to create dramatic works of art that immediately attracted the attention of viewers. Between 1624 and 1678 Bernini was responsible for most of the sculpture and interior and exterior decoration of St. Peter's Basilica, all of which was designed to enhance the papacy and the doctrines of the Catholic Church.

Why are angels so pervasive as a motif in baroque art—so pervasive that Dan Brown uses them in the title of his novel? What do they represent?

If you look at the history of early Christian art, angels are constantly used to represent messengers of God who bring the good news of salvation to earth. They bring the divine message of victory over death. Hence, angels usually are given the form of the winged victories found in ancient sculpture. If you look at altars and church decorations throughout Christianity, angels are used abundantly for that purpose.

Did Bernini use angels in that way—as divine messengers?

His angels that decorate the Baldacchino (1624–1633), the great bronze structure marking the location of the high altar of the basilica of St. Peter, serve as intermediaries between God and man. Baldachin and altar are placed directly over the tomb of St. Peter. Angels also decorate Bernini's Cathedral Petri (Throne of St. Peter) in the principal apse of the liturgical east end of the basilica. This is a colossal monument, partially covered in gold, that represents the throne of St. Peter, the first pope, and, through him, the unbroken line of popes.

Similarly, an angel appears on the crown of the Castel Sant'Angelo.

Bernini decorated the Ponte Sant'Angelo (1667–1672), the Angel Bridge that links the papal fortress and the Vatican. Angels figure prominently on the castle and the bridge because of a miracle that took place in AD 590, the year that Gregory the Great was elected pope. Rome had been struck by a deadly plague the year before. In order to save the people from the plague, Pope Gregory organized a procession from Santa Maria Maggiore to St. Peter's. As the procession approached the bridge, the crowd witnessed a vision of the archangel Michael floating atop the fortress, sheathing his sword as a sign that the plague had ended.

The bridge is decorated with ten statues of angels marking it as the beginning of the road leading from Rome to the Vatican and, hence, to salvation. The Catholic Church considers itself the one true church and the Catholic hierarchy, the pope, and those appointed by him, are the arbiters of salvation. Catholic iconography insists that there is one true church, one specific road to salvation, and this is the road through the Vatican—symbolized by the bridge.

What about Bernini's angel in the Chigi Chapel, where the first cardinal is murdered in Angels & Demons?

The angel used in *Angels & Demons* as a marker helping to lead the Illuminati to their destination—that is, the angel accompanying Habakkuk in the Chigi Chapel in Santa Maria del'Popolo—serves as a messenger of God. The major portion of Bernini's decoration of the Chigi Chapel (1655–1657) was the carving of two statues representing the story of the salvation of Daniel when he was cast in the lion's den. Daniel is shown in a niche to the left of the entrance, kneeling in prayer with a very domesticated lion reclining beside him. The statue of Habakkuk is placed across the chapel from Daniel, in a niche to the right of the altar. The story, which is part of the tale of Bel and the Dragon that is appended to the book of Daniel in the Catholic Bible, tells us that when Daniel had been in the lion's den for thirty-two days, God sent an angel to Habakkuk, whom he found with a basket of food. The angel picked up Habakkuk by the beard and carried him, basket and all, to Daniel. Habakkuk gave the basket of food to Daniel, who thanked God for his salvation. In the Chigi Chapel, the angel grabs Habakkuk by the beard and points to Daniel.

What about the use of pagan symbols in the Chigi Chapel? Why are there stars and the twelve signs of the zodiac on a domed cupola in this chapel?

In Christian religion and iconography, ancient forms are often adapted and reused. As far as the zodiac material is concerned, its symbolism dates back to the Ptolemaic way of seeing the universe as earth centered. It was believed that the universe was made up of concentric spheres; the stars were in fixed positions and God controlled the heavens. The pyramids date back to the Raphael period; Bernini decorated them during the seventeenth century by carving marble portraits on them of members of the Chigi family.

What is the meaning of the image of the human skeleton with wings that Robert Langdon finds on the floor of the Chigi Chapel?

Dead bodies were normally interred in crypts beneath the churches. The image of skeletons coming to life from beneath the floor has to do with the resurrection of the flesh.

Did Bernini create a special kind of angel for the Ecstasy of St. Teresa *in the Cornaro Chapel, where the third murder takes place?*

Yes, this angel is a seraphim, a very elevated angel and a very special messenger of God. The *Ecstasy of St. Teresa* (who lived from 1515 to 1582), in the Cornaro Chapel in the church of Santa Maria della Vittoria, is part of an illustration representing the pain and pleasure felt by the saint during her most famous vision. Bernini worked on it from 1645 to 1652. St. Theresa described that vision in her autobiography in terms that have always been recognized as being related to sexual ecstasy. Bernini represented the experience in the manner that St. Teresa described it. Teresa of Avila became a saint during the sixteenth century because she was one of the great reformers of the church.

Does Dan Brown play fast and loose with his art facts in Angels & Demons? *Or is he, for the most part, accurate?*

Dan Brown manipulates and distorts facts of history, geography, buildings, and works of art to move his story along. For instance, Brown says that originally the *Ecstasy of St. Teresa* was intended for the inside of the Vatican but was rejected because of its sexual explicitness. The book implies that Bernini suggested moving this masterpiece to some obscure location to hide it. The truth is that the *Ecstasy of St. Teresa* was intended for the Cornaro Chapel and had nothing to do with the Vatican. Federico Cornaro was a cardinal from Venice and his palace was very close to the site of Santa Maria della Vittoria, which was the church that he supported and sponsored as a cardinal; he was buried there. He commissioned a mortuary chapel both as a tribute to himself and to the Cornaros as a religious family, one that provided cardinals for the Catholic Church.

Did Bernini work on the Castel Sant'Angelo?

No. Bernini had nothing to do with the castle, nor the sword-wielding bronze angel that sits atop it. The Castel Sant'Angelo was dedicated in AD 139 as the tomb of the emperor Hadrian. It was fortified as a strong point in the defenses of Rome in the fifth or sixth century and was slowly converted into the massive papal fortress we see today. Pope Nicholas III, who was elected pope in 1277, first built the *passetto*. This "corridor" led from the Vatican Palace to the Castel Sant'Angelo a safe passage that popes and their entourage could use to escape to the fortress if the Vatican came under attack. Pope Alexander VI rebuilt the *passetto* in 1493. It was used by Pope Clement VII to escape to the fortress during the sack of Rome by the forces of the Holy Roman emperor Charles V in 1527. Throughout most of the history of the papacy, the Castel Sant'Angelo housed the papal treasury, prisons for high-profile offenders, and papal apartments. With the unification of Italy under a secular government in 1870, the castle became the property of the state. It is presently a national museum—one of the most popular tourist attractions in Rome.

Is it true, as Dan Brown writes, that Il Passetto was where less pious popes met their mistresses?
That idea strikes me as being untrue simply because it wouldn't have been necessary. Furthermore, it couldn't have been a very comfortable passageway.

Why do you think the writer chose the Fountain of Four Rivers as the last marker in the supposed Illuminati path?
Simply to move the story along. The Fountain of the Four Rivers (1648–1651) is useful to the plot because it is a fountain with a large basin in which someone could be drowned. In fact, it is a rather secular monument celebrating the papacy of Innocent X Pamphili, who had built a large palace for his family on the Piazza Navona, the square in the center of which the fountain is placed. The Piazza Navona has often been called the living room of Rome. It is a great gathering place where festivals and entertainments were held during the seventeenth century. Superficially, there is church iconography on the fountain. The four continents—Europe, Asia, Africa, and America—are represented by river gods. These rest on what Bernini carved to look like a rock formation, which in gardening we tend to call a rockery. The rockery represents the world and, in turn, supports an obelisk that may be said to represent the ancient world. And on top of that are a small orb and a dove, which is the emblem both of the Pamphili family and the Holy Spirit. Hence, the dove may be said to symbolize the domination of the church over both the world and antiquity.

THE MAGICAL AND MYTHICAL IN BERNINI'S SCULPTURE

AN INTERVIEW WITH GEORGE LECHNER

Where would Angels & Demons *be without Gianlorenzo Bernini, the master sculptor and artist whose myriad works, found throughout Rome, are the quintessence of the Italian baroque era, which broadly spanned the seventeenth and eighteenth centuries? In the novel, Dan Brown makes great use of Bernini's sculpture—including the* Ecstasy of St. Teresa, *which scholars of the period have called a touchstone of baroque art; his famed* Four Rivers Fountain; *his iconic colonnade and Baldacchino for St. Peter's; and even some of his heretofore not quite as prominent works, such as the* Angel *and* Habakkuk *in the Chigi Chapel. Novelist Brown also weaves his plot around the contention that Bernini secretly harbored antichurch feelings and was the secret artistic master of the Illuminati.*

George Lechner is an adjunct professor of Italian art and culture at the University of Hartford and a specialist on the religious iconography of Roman art—a real-life Robert Langdon, so to speak. While Lechner disagrees with Langdon's premise that Bernini was a secret member of the Illuminati and that his work was infused with Illuminati myths and symbolism, he observes in our interview that Angels & Demons *could have alluded to even darker mysteries and more occult secrets than it does. The picture Lechner paints of Renaissance Rome and of the baroque period that followed is one filled with magic, astrology, pagan symbols, and the influence of the ancient Jewish mystical tradition known as the Cabala.*

George Lechner, an adjunct professor at the University of Hartford, is a specialist in the astrological symbolism and talismanic magic of Roman Renaissance and baroque art.

One pope, Urban VIII, kept his own private astrologer, Tomasso Campanella, who practiced talismanic magic in the pope's private chambers to ward off evil.

Lechner is especially intrigued by the way the deeply religious Christian society of the Italian Renaissance came to grips with its pagan past. He first became acquainted with occult lore when he took a course in baroque allegory—the expression of religious concepts through symbols and art—at Bryn Mawr College, where he earned a master's degree in art history. While there, he was given an assignment to research the symbolic content of an Andrea Sacchi fresco that was commissioned by Urban VIII for his palace ceiling. It was in the course of researching the fresco in Rome at the Bibliotheca Hertziana, the American Academy, and the Vatican Library that he discovered that it was a star map containing many mystical and astrological themes, and that, beneath this ceiling, the pope practiced astrology and magic.

⌒

What is your personal response to the architecture and monuments in Rome? Are they filled with hidden symbols, as Dan Brown claims?

Much of the artwork during Bernini's time was created for a populace that was still largely illiterate. Sculpture served as a type of visual language, a kind of "readable" art for the public to see and understand, which is a tradition that dates back to before the Renaissance.

Many of the public pieces of art in *Angels & Demons* were perfectly well understood in their own time period. Indeed, they were designed to be didactic in nature. We may not know why the angel accompanying Habakkuk in the Chigi Chapel is pointing one way and Habakkuk is pointing in the opposite direction. Those who knew the Bible, however, understood that the angel is pointing toward the figure of Daniel (represented in a niche to the left), and directs the prophet to rescue him from the lion's den. Habakkuk wants no part of this and points the other way. The seventeenth-century viewer knew who would win this argument: the angel will grab Habakkuk by the hair and fly him over to the lion's den.

Brown's use of symbolism is very interesting and enjoyable. His idea that there is, even in these public monuments, a further level of hidden symbolism that only the initiated members of the Illuminati can comprehend is a very intriguing aspect of the book. Brown's points may not be literally true of the Illuminati or baroque Rome, but he raises the intriguing idea that familiar works hold important secret meanings and contain clues to those meanings that are hidden in plain sight. This is why Rome can be a conspirator's dream.

Brown makes full use of this formula in his next book, *The Da Vinci Code*, where the secret society is not the Illuminati but the Priory of Sion. Instead of hidden Illuminati messages in Bernini's Chigi Chapel decorations or the *Ecstasy of St. Teresa* in Santa Maria della Vittoria, there are said to be hidden Priory messages in Leonardo's *Mona Lisa*, *Madonna of the Rocks*, and, of course, the *Last Supper*.

Was there ever a time in history when a controversial group like the Illuminati ever existed? And, if so, how radical was it?

The only Illuminati that would fit in Dan Brown's time frame—the early seventeenth century—would be the so-called Alumbrados ("Enlightened Ones") or Spanish Illuminati. These Illuminati were an extension of the sixteenth-century Spanish mystical tradition, and they sought direct and personal contact with God through visions and religious ecstasy. Ignatius of Loyola (1491–1556) the founder of the Jesuits, was influenced by the Alumbrados in the writing of his *Spiritual Exercises*, which, among other things, advocated the use of the senses as a means of comprehending Christ's passion and the punishment for sin. Ignatius was briefly imprisoned and censured by the Inquisition in 1527 for his connections with these Illuminati. Other important Spanish mystics such as St. Teresa of Avila and St. John of the Cross were investigated for heresy around the same time.

The Inquisition feared that the popular Alumbrados were influenced by Luther's teachings, and had sought to bypass traditional Catholic practices and doctrines (such as the sacraments) in favor of direct mystical communion with God. It is interesting to note that Bernini's statue, the *Ecstasy of St. Teresa* which forms such a dramatic part of *Angels & Demons*, is actually a fascinating example in visual form of such a mystical relationship with God.

However, it is quite clear that the mystical spirituality of the Alumbrados, Ignatius, and St. Teresa has much more in common with Counter-Reformation ideas of religious reform than the avowedly secular, pro-science, and highly political anti-Catholic Illuminati that Dan Brown presents in his book. The similarity between the Illuminati of *Angels & Demons* and the Alumbrados of history is merely in name. True, the Spanish Illuminati were investigated and persecuted by the Inquisition, but for different reasons. First, there was the concern that the leaders of the Alumbrados were "converted" Jews, also known as *conversos*. In many ways the more punitive character of the Inquisition in Spain was an extension of long-standing, and institutionalized anti-Semitic persecution in that country. Many of the Jews in Spain were forcibly converted, and the concern was that these *conversos* would use the Alumbrados as a means of secretly undermining Catholic authority and furthering an underground return to their true Jewish faith.

Second, a significant number of the Alumbrados were charismatic women such as Isabel de la Cruz and Maria de Cazalla, and their desire for an increased role in the affairs of the church was seen as an additional threat. The very idea that mystical experience could be shared equally by men and women was also seen as an unacceptable elevation of women's status in the church. This prejudice was so strong that, even after St. Teresa of Avila's death and her eventual canonization, a number of her written works were still kept on the "forbidden" list of the Index of Prohibited Books—all because of her supposed connection to the Alumbrados.

In the late 1700s there was a second group called the Illuminati, the Bavarian Illuminati, which were founded by Adam Weishaupt (1748–1811). A former Jesuit and a Freemason, Weishaupt and his Illuminati sought freedom from church control over intellectual and scientific matters as well as greater equality for women. Its members included the great German poet Goethe. However, while the society was anticlerical and favored rational and scientific thinking as a counterpoint to religious doctrine, it was not anti-Christian or atheistic in nature; and it certainly had no plans for the destruction of the institutional Catholic Church as promulgated by the fictional Illuminati in Brown's book. In any event, Bernini and Galileo lived in the earlier part of the seventeenth century—approximately a century and a half before the founding and brief rise of the Bavarian Illuminati.

Do you think Bernini could have been a member of an antichurch secret society?

It is very difficult to believe that Bernini could have been a member of any secret society. His life is very thoroughly documented. He was closely associated with the Jesuits, and he attended Mass every day at the nearby Jesuit church in Rome, Il Gesù, which is still there today, close to Bernini's famous fountain in the Piazza Navona. Bernini was also a *cavaliere*, or "knight," and supported the popular religious reform movement of the Congregation of the Oratory, founded by St. Philip Neri (1515–1595), which, with the Jesuits, was one of the great religious reform movements in Rome in the late sixteenth century. The Orations, as they were known, were quite democratic in approach, in that it encouraged lay people of faith to preach publicly and become more involved in the devotional activities of the Catholic Church.

Bernini's daily devotional reading was Thomas à Kempis's mystical *Imitation of Christ*, and his bedroom was adorned with his painting of Christ looking down and shedding his blood over the earth. He was friends with important church officials, such as Cardinal Scipione Borghese, his early patron, as well as the French cardinal, Mazarin. He was very close to Pope Urban VIII, who took care of him and visited him every day when he was seriously ill. These friendships were sincere and affectionate. It is hard to believe that Bernini would so completely betray his religion and his friends as to become a member of a society dedicated to the destruction of the Catholic Church.

Do you think that the Bernini sculptures that serve as the markers in the novel along Dan Brown's so-called Path of Illumination, were intentionally designed to represent the four elements of early science—earth, air, fire, and water?

No. First of all, the sculptures included in Brown's book were done over a good number of years, so it's difficult to see any kind of plan or Illuminati map involved in their making. Also, Bernini was commissioned by the pope or private patrons to produce these works, so he didn't get to pick or choose their location. For example, the only reason why Bernini completed the *Ecstasy of St. Teresa* in the church of Santa Maria della Vittoria, which features prominently in the book, was because it was specifically commissioned for that church in 1647 by Cardinal Federico Cornaro. Cornaro was a member of the powerful Cornaro family in Venice, and he was Patriarch of Venice from 1632 to 1644. He was friends with Urban VIII and was made a cardinal in 1626. He moved to Rome in 1644 and commissioned the *St. Teresa* three years later.

Bernini's design shows the cardinal and members of his family witnessing St. Teresa's ecstatic mystical experience as recounted in her own writings. This inclusion of patrons in the artwork itself is actually a very traditional device in both northern and southern European art. It emphasizes the Christian tradition of "witnessing" and makes a direct statement of faith and devotion. The floor design over the lower tombs by Bernini also includes his images of praying skeletons. The contemporary viewer of the sculpture thus completes the connections between past and present, living and dead, all of whom bear witness to God's dramatic mystical presence.

The frequently emphasized sensuality of the piece is entirely in keeping with Teresa's own account of this experience. Indeed, if this spiritual rapture was also as profoundly manifested in a physical sense as she describes, it would be difficult to imagine how she could have been presented differently by the artist. Brown says that Urban VIII disapproved of the statue's sensuality. This was not possible, because he died in 1644 and Bernini began working on the statue and its attendant architectural adornments in 1647.

Dan Brown makes a dramatic point of Bernini carving pyramids—supposedly pagan symbols—in the Chigi Chapel. Would this have been highly unconventional?

No. Bernini's carving of pyramids was not as unusual as it sounds. One of the most popular ancient monuments in Rome was, and continues to be, the pyramid of Caius Cestus. It should be remembered that ancient Rome was an imperial power and that Egypt was part of the Roman Empire. Ancient Romans were as fascinated by the wonders of Egypt as we are today. The use of pyramids in designs like the adornments for the Chigi Chapel, as well as the numerous obelisks found in the city of Rome, are good examples of this.

Also, during the time of the Renaissance, it was believed that Egypt was the source of the original philosophical wisdom before the ancient Greeks.

This wisdom, which was thought to foretell the coming of Christianity, survived in the form of writings called the Hermetic texts, which were studied by the important Renaissance priest, philosopher, and magician, Marsilio Ficino [1433–1499], and later by the philosopher Giordano Bruno, among others. The discovery the Hermetic texts was deemed so important that, in 1463, Cosimo de' Medici had Ficino stop work on his translations of a cache of Plato manuscripts to translate the Hermetic writings first. The fact that the Hermetic texts dealt not only with philosophy and theology, but also with astrology and magic, made these occult studies more acceptable to later intellectuals and theologians.

The philosophy of Hermeticism was proven at a much later date to be part of the Gnostic writings of the early Christian era. But for some artists and thinkers of the Renaissance and later baroque eras, Hermetic thought and its Egyptian connection were seen as being of supreme religious and philosophical value.

How did the Renaissance belief in Hermeticism play into the use of astrology and magic during the 1600s?

Ficino believed that the supposed ancient Egyptian Hermetic texts contained powerful formulae for attracting the helpful influences of the stars and planets, as well as magical rites for warding off demons and harmful astral phenomena such as eclipses. This type of white magic was a "natural" magic based on the use of appropriate colors, herbs, flowers, gems, and other stones. Astrologically themed paintings with favorable zodiac charts would also be used to attract the positive energy from the sun and the beneficent planets Venus, and Jupiter.

The sun was also important as a symbol of God—the "light of the world" in traditional Christian thought. Traditionally, Christian churches had their altars facing the east. Thus the priest, in elevating the host during the Mass, would symbolically mimic Christ's resurrection as well as the symbolic rising of the sun. The importance of the sun in ancient Egyptian spiritual practices was not lost on Ficino. He advocated the use of golden, sun-colored priestly robes, and the use of fragrances and "celestial music" to create the proper atmosphere for these solarian rites.

The natural magic of Ficino lives on today in Wicca practice and in the traditions of green, or nature-based witchcraft. In both cases spells are cast using astrological information as well as the appropriate herbs, stones, gems, and other natural substances intended to attract good influences and repel those that are seen as evil.

What about the Cabala?

Interestingly, the ritual use of astrology and angels is also found in the Renaissance revival of the Cabala. Cabala can be used as an aid to mystical spiritual contemplation. In its traditional form, it can also become a type of magic that employs the power of the Hebrew language and the invocation of holy angels to work miracles. The philosopher and magician Pico della Mirandola (1463–1494), whose work *Oration on the Dignity of Man* is the classic humanistic text par excellence, sought to discover the roots of Christian belief in the esoteric writings of Cabala. Pico learned Hebrew with the help of his learned Jewish friends Elia del Medigo and Flavius Mithridates to further study the Cabala. One of the great theological controversies Pico wrestled with was whether or not Jesus' healing power as presented in the Gospels was due to his use of Cabalistic spells and magic (Pico decided not).

In both the secret processes of the Hermetic rites and the mysticism of the Cabala we see the importance of the angels. Both also made use of talismans and protective magic in carefully defined rituals. The use of red string tied around the wrist to protect against the evil eye is an example of the use of talismans among some contemporary practitioners of Cabala.

Did the popes of the period practice what we would think of as magic?

Yes, they did. One of the rituals was astrology, which the Dominican priest, magician, and philosopher Tomasso Campanella (1568–1639) practiced to protect Pope Urban VIII from harm. Campanella viewed his magic as a physical rather than psychological process. He sealed one of the pope's rooms in the Palazzo Barberini against the contamination of an eclipse going on outside. He sprinkled the pope's chamber with aromatic substances such as rose vinegar, and cypress; rosemary, laurel, and myrtle were burned. The room was hung with white silk cloths and decorated with branches. Next, two candles and five torches were lit—representing the sun, moon, and planets. These were situated in beneficial aspects to one another to form a balance against the harmful aspect of the real heavens. Jovial and venereal music was played to attract the good influences of Jupiter and Venus and to dispel the bad influences of Saturn and Mars. In this same vein, stones, plants, colors, and odors associated with Jupiter and Venus were used to draw beneficial powers from these two planets.

This ceremony was performed under a ceiling fresco, which echoed these magical elements. It had been painted by Andrea Sacchi, a friend of Bernini. The ceiling shows, as part of an allegory of divine wisdom, a symbolic star chart emphasizing Urban's birth date and his accession to the papacy, as well as a scene symbolically representing the sun, one of Urban's personal symbols. It is portrayed as the center of the known universe—the first representation in art of the heliocentric system. All of this sun symbolism was deemed necessary to protect the pope from the perceived harm of eclipses. (Urban VIII's fear of demonic magic was so great that in 1631 he ordered the severest punishment for anyone who used astrological magic against his person. In 1634, the nobleman Giacinto Centini was beheaded, and two of his accomplices were hanged and then burned for practicing black magic in prophesying Urban's death.)

The value of astrology in this religious context seems unsettling until we realize that according to the writings of the great theologian St. Thomas Aquinas, the stars were not physical bodies of heat and light, but rather the visual evidence of angels. These "angelic intelligences" were thought to be visible manifestations of God's will.

Campanella was also an avowed heliocentrist who wrote *Defense of Galileo* (*Apologia pro Galileo*) in 1622. Campanella also wrote a utopian novel, *The City of the Sun*, which was first published in 1623. Along with Sir Thomas More's *Utopia*, published in 1516, and Francis Bacon's *Neew Atlantis* (1626) it was one of the great utopian writings. In it, Campanella developed the notion of a new city-state, led by a philosopher-priest-king, and guided by Hermetic magical principles. He attempted unsuccessfully to interest the papacy in his ideas. Shortly before his death in 1639, he finally found favor with Cardinal Richelieu and the French monarchy. One of Campanella's last poems celebrated the birth of the future King Louis XIV. He was the first to call him the "Sun King."

Do you think it is possible that Bernini, who designed Pope Urban VIII's tomb, knew Tomasso Campanella, the heliocentrist?

It's very possible, because Bernini was a very close friend of Urban VIII. Bernini may have even been influenced by the astrological nature of Sacchi's ceiling when he represented the zodiac, planets, and stars on the domed cupola that Robert Langdon sees in the Chigi Chapel, described by Dan Brown this way: "The domed cupola shone with a field of illuminated stars and the seven astronomical planets. Below that, the twelve signs of the zodiac—pagan, earthly symbols rooted in astronomy."

How were the ancient religious teachings and pagan symbols synthesized with the later ones of Christianity, specifically those related to the sun?

Bernini's huge bronze Baldacchino in the crossing of St. Peter's is covered with images of the sun, bees, and swags of laurel leaves. Many viewers of the seventeenth century would have understood these three images to be the three symbols most frequently related to Pope Urban VIII (whose papacy extended from 1623 to 1644). These images also represent the sun. The bees make the pure beeswax used to fashion church candles. When lit, they create a second type of sun from their light. The laurel leaves are sacred to the ancient sun god Apollo, and the image of the sun itself is an image found in many of the buildings associated with Urban VIII, including his residence, the Palazzo Barberini.

The twisting columns of the Baldacchino would have been understood as a reference to the twisting "Solomonic columns" of Solomon's temple in Jerusalem and presented as a way of linking up the great Jewish temple of the Old Testament with the new center of Christendom in Urban VIII's Rome.

In both Angels & Demons *and the subsequent* Da Vinci Code, *Dan Brown claims that the image of the Great Seal on the back side of the US dollar bill—the eye inside the triangle that sits atop a pyramid—represents Illuminati symbolism. Is that true?*

As is the case with many symbols, the image of the eye and pyramid is open to several, and often more benign, interpretations. In traditional Christian symbolism, the all-seeing eye within the triangle is a symbol of divine providence. The incomplete pyramid is the symbol of human endeavor, and the eye above the pyramid represents the concept that divine aid is needed and welcomed in all human tasks. It is true that the pyramid with the all-seeing eye of God is a Masonic symbol. But it is not true that it is therefore an Illuminati symbol.

Clearly, you feel that Bernini was not scheming against the Catholic Church, or a member of a subversive secret society, or encrypting his sculptures with hidden messages. But do you think that, beneath it all, he might have been attuned to a mysticism on which the official church might have looked askance?

Yes. I wouldn't be surprised if Bernini was influenced by Spanish mysticism because he was born in Naples, which had been controlled by Spain. As a devout Catholic he would quite naturally have been familiar with Spanish Illuminist ideas of religious reform. This is what may have then attracted him to the daily practice of the Alumbrados-inspired Jesuit form of mystical and strongly sense-oriented spiritual devotion and prayer. This idea of intense, personal, and very private communion with God was considered quite radical by the many enemies of the Jesuits. Were many of the aspects of the Church's teachings and ritual necessary when one could experience God even more personally and directly?

THE SECRETS OF THE VATICAN LIBRARY

Robert Langdon, as scholar and Harvard Professor, had collected nothing but rejection letters when he had tried to fulfill one of his "life's dreams" and gain access to the Archivio Vaticano. Langdon muses that no other non-Catholic American scholar had been allowed access either. Only the most desperate situation allowed him that access now, twice entering archives so secret not even the Swiss Guard could follow him. Once inside, things quickly turn most unscholarly: he and Vittoria purloin a priceless piece of manuscript, he fights for air—and his life—as someone cuts the power that generates the air circulators, and plays dominoes with massive bookshelves to escape through a pile of shattered glass. Phew.

It would not seem difficult for the reader of the novel to separate fact from fiction in this part of Dan Brown's tale; restricted access certainly seems logical, while daring-do is the sine qua non of good fiction. In reality, however, there is more fiction here than meets the eye, as our two experts explain.

IT ISN'T SO SECRET AFTER ALL

BY MICHAEL HERRERA

When Michael Herrera was doing graduate work on Christianity during the time of the Roman Empire, he often came across references to the Secret Vatican Archives. Those three words, Secret Vatican

Michael Herrera is a freelance writer who spent several years pursuing a PhD in early Christianity. He now works as public relations specialist in the high-tech industry.

Archives, *conjured up images of medieval vaults filled with ancient scrolls; dusty, leather-bound manuscripts containing original works by the Greek and Roman masters; long-lost biblical scriptures; records of papal scandals; and every other historical document that a naïve, first-year graduate student of ancient history could imagine. It was not hard to imagine the Secret Archives as some sort of historical black hole where information went in, never to surface again. He resigned himself to the notion that he would never know the truth about its contents.*

Then Dan Brown came along. Years after Herrera's career path took him far away from campus libraries and academia and into the world of high tech, he picked up a copy of Angels & Demons *and eagerly absorbed the tale of Robert Langdon's experiences inside the Secret Vatican Archives. He could easily draw parallels to his own notions about restricted access to hidden documents. It seemed perfectly plausible that the archives contained a document written by Galileo that the Vatican had suppressed throughout the centuries.*

Herrera himself had seen the Swiss Guard standing watch outside unmarked buildings, the roped-off hallways that led to parts unknown inside the Vatican Museum, and the crypts underneath St. Peter's—which undoubtedly held their own secrets. Therefore, it wasn't difficult to imagine that what lay beyond the guards, locked doors, or velvet ropes was indeed a secret manuscript written by Galileo, stashed away inside a hermetically sealed glass vault.

As it turned out, a closer investigation revealed that not only did the glass vaults not exist, but the Secret Vatican Archives are not so secret after all. But let us allow Mr. Herrera to tell his own story.

Dan Brown sprinkles just enough facts about the Secret Vatican Archives into *Angels & Demons* to leave the reader with the impression that one of the world's great archival collections is also one of its most inaccessible. Even if one were granted access, the book suggests that there are documents within special rooms upon which no visitor may cast their eyes: Galileo's *Diagramma*, for example. What other treasures of Western civilization might be hidden from view in the archives?

The Secret Vatican Archives traces its lineage to the earliest days of Christianity and the church's persecution by the Romans, through the Middle Ages and the Renaissance to the present day. Along the way, the church tried its best to keep its archives out of harm's way, but in many cases documents were inevitably lost, selectively destroyed, or fell victim to the ravages of nature.

The archives as we know them today were created when Pope Innocent III undertook the first systematic collection of official church papers in the late twelfth century. With the invention of the printing press around 1450, the Vatican's collection multiplied until it was destroyed during the sack of Rome by the Holy Roman emperor Charles V in 1527. In the early 1600s, Pope Paul V assembled church records and other materials from around Christendom and separated the collection into the Vatican Library and the Secret Vatican Archives.

Throughout the turbulent first several centuries of existence, the archives' most important items were moved frequently from one hiding place to another in hopes of safeguarding them from attack or theft. For a time, the popes even stored their most precious records inside Castel Sant'Angelo, the historic Roman fortress which Dan Brown uses as the meeting place for the church's sworn enemy, the Illuminati.

Around 1810, shortly after annexing the Papal States and arresting the pope, Napoleon Bonaparte hauled off the archives to Paris. When Napoleon abdicated his throne a few years later, the pope wanted his papers returned, but many of the documents never made it back to Rome. Quite a few were burned as refuse along the way or, in one case, sold to Parisian merchants for wrapping paper.

Today the Vatican Archives actually consist of a number of different archives, but the one referred to in *Angels & Demons* is "L'Archivio Segreto Vaticano," or the Secret Vatican Archives. It contains approximately fifty miles of shelves, which hold an estimated sixty thousand items (the number is probably much higher because many of the items contain numerous individual records) and more than six hundred indices to help navigate the collection.

The Secret Archives were off limits to all but the most vetted visitors until the end of the nineteenth century. Individuals found leaking documents—or even setting foot inside the building—were harshly punished, excommunicated, or both. This policy began to change under Pope Leo XIII (1878–1903), who made the contents available to qualified academics as part of a public relations campaign designed to placate the flood of antipapal sentiment set off by Giuseppe Garibaldi in the mid–nineteenth century. He and his revolutionaries felt that the Vatican and the church stood in the way of Italy's future prosperity. Leo III hoped that by opening up the archives researchers would discover just how much the church had contributed to preserving society during the darkest periods of Western civilization.

Since that time, the Vatican has gradually made available more and more documents as fragile historical papers are preserved (even washing them is part of the process) and then catalogued. Most materials dating up to 1922 are available for study. But not everything: the private papers of the popes, for example. According to Vatican archivist Cardinal Jorge Meija, "Many archival documents are kept secret—by the Vatican as by other governments and institutions—because their publication could harm the reputations of living people, families, or institutions; or because the administration of the current government requires this discretion; or finally because of respect for what we now call *privacy rights*, which pertain to those who have died, as well as those who are still alive."

Periodically, due to public pressure, controversy, or perhaps because the materials are no longer considered confidential, the Vatican will release a collection that had been previously considered off limits. For instance, in reaction to extreme pressure by groups demanding the church account for its alleged dealings concerning Nazi Germany and the Holocaust, beginning in the late 1990s, the Vatican released certain documents relating to the years prior to and during World War II, providing a window into what scholars have said was, at best, a hands-off policy by the church toward Hitler's actions during that time.

A different type of recent public pressure prompted the Vatican to supply a tool that it hopes will forever wash away the perception of total secrecy: the Vatican joined the cyber age. The result is the Secret Vatican Archives' official website (www.vatican. va/library_archives/vat_secret_archives/)—a treasure trove of information about the archives that might have saved Langdon and his partner, Vittoria Vetra, precious time in their search for Galileo's so-called *Diagramma*. They would have learned critical pieces of information like hours of operation, bibliographies of the contents and— for those who don't have the verbal commitment from the acting pope, as Langdon and Vetra did—the criteria to gain access to study in the archives.

In order to use the archives all applicants must satisfy the condition which states, "The Archives are open to qualified scholars from institutions of higher education pursuing academic research." Just being a "qualified scholar" does not guarantee access, however. Technically, the pope approves all applicants, but the prefect of the archives actually reviews and decides who makes the cut. The competition is stiff. Even Professor Robert Langdon, esteemed Harvard symbologist, received several rejection notices. (It's worth mentioning that nowhere does the Vatican state or imply that it denies access to "non-Catholic, American scholars" as Langdon implies on page 192.)

During the twenty-four-hour period of the novel, of course, Langdon had a rather unorthodox request—to visit after business hours—and high authority to back him. A request which under normal circumstance is rarely granted. Despite his professed reverence for the collection, he proceeded to abuse nearly every one of the archives' rules. As with any collection of rare books, removing materials from the premises is strictly forbidden. Strictly speaking, when he removed the Vatican's copy of Galileo's *Diagramma*, he was stealing. For ordinary mortals not in such a hurry, and not looking for a highly valued, fragile manuscript, a copy could have been provided by a member of the archives' staff—at the cost of about fifty cents.

The entire collection employs a variety of indices, cross-referencing lists, and other cataloging tools professional archivists call *finding aids* to help researchers identify what they would like to review. Luckily, Langdon knew what he was looking for and didn't need many finding aids other than his intuition. Ordinarily, researchers must fill out a written request to review a specific item or items (only three allowed per day) and once approved, they must wait for a staff member to go and retrieve it off the shelf. Browsing is forbidden and, as Brown correctly points out, a Vatican staff member must accompany visitors at all times—the exception in this case clearly being the threat of the Vatican's imminent destruction by a secret society.

Once he found what he was looking for, Langdon's efforts to respect the physical condition of the documents as he sifted through them basically hit the mark, according to archiving and conservation experts. The tools he employed to review the *Diagramma* are not unlike those used by experts today. For example, white gloves are generally on hand in most rare books collections. When Langdon talks about the *Diagramma*'s "permanence rating" to describe its durability, his description is not that far from the Society of American Archivists' glossary listing for *permanence*, which it defines as "the inherent stability of material that allows it to resist degradation over time." Granted, Brown applies a bit of poetic license to describe Langdon's use of the tools, but his descriptions of the tools and their uses have their basis in fact.

Brown could have been more generous in his description of the archives' interior, however. When he enters the building and is confronted by what looks like a "darkened airline hangar," a disappointed Langdon's preconceived notions of "dusty bookshelves, piled high with tattered volumes" quickly evaporate into thin air. It's too bad Langdon was in such a hurry. Had he more time to explore, he would have seen the ornately decorated reading rooms in the older section of the building, adorned wall to wall (and ceiling) with beautiful frescoes and intricately inlaid hardwood cabinets packed with leather-bound books.

One thing researchers will not see inside the archives is hermetically sealed glass vaults. These vaults, which Brown compares to large, free-standing racquetball courts, add to the suspense of a pivotal scene in the book—one nearly becomes Langdon's coffin. This projects a dramatic visual for the reader, but they do not exist. Moreover, some professional archivists maintain that the need for hermetically sealed glass vaults would be overkill, because heating, ventilation, and air-conditioning and fire suppression systems are typically more than adequate for storing ancient documents. In the case of the Secret Vatican Archives the vaults that contain its most valuable contents actually resemble a modern bank vault lined with safety deposit boxes.

What about the archives' collection of materials related to the real hero of *Angels & Demons*, Galileo Galilei? Today the Vatican's collection of documents concerning the trial of Galileo consists of a single volume of hand-written records. Originally, the records, along with two other volumes, were stored in the archives of the Congregation of the Doctrine of the Faith (formerly known as the "Sacred Congregation of the Universal Inquisition"). The two additional volumes have been lost to history, leaving scholars to wonder if they ended up as wrapping paper in a Parisian butcher shop or at the bottom of a river on the path to Rome (after Napoleon's defeat). The Vatican considers the Galileo documents one of its crown jewels, so ordinarily it does not permit one to view the original documents. Digital copies of the original materials are available to scholars, however.

Then we come to the *Diagramma*. It is highly unlikely, if not impossible, that such a document would ever be on display, simply for the reason that there is not a shred of evidence that it ever existed. It's unfortunate, because if Galileo *had* written it and the Vatican somehow possessed a copy, it probably would be publicly displayed. The need to suppress it became moot in 1992 when the church publicly admitted that it had wrongly condemned Galileo more than three centuries earlier—a fact left out, perhaps conveniently, by the novelist.

Dan Brown paints a picture that leaves the reader believing that the Vatican does all it can to see to it that the Secret Vatican Archives are just that—secret. Yet, today, the word *secret* exists, one suspects, only to perpetuate an old image of a time past when the Secret Vatican Archives were also the *private* Vatican Archives. Once the Vatican posted the bibliographies and indices of its collections on the Internet for the whole world to see, any romantic notion of vaults piled high with hidden manuscripts vanished forever. Nowadays, the Secret Vatican Archives of *Angels & Demons* is but fodder for novelists.

Yet one cannot help but wonder. Considering the controversy and scandal permeating its history, it seems probable, even likely, that the church has more skeletons in its closet that it would prefer not to disclose. Should such documents exist, they might never see the light of day—unless doing so might prove beneficial to the church in its ongoing public relations campaign to demonstrate openness. In 2003 a researcher working in the archives of the Vatican's Congregation for the Doctrine of the Faith discovered a letter written in 1633 from one high-ranking Vatican official to another expressing the pope's wish that the trial against Galileo take place as soon as possible, out of concern for the astronomer's failing health. The Vatican wasted no time in using the letter as leverage to support its claim that the church's treatment of Galileo was not as harsh as history records.

What other documents have yet to be uncovered that might affect the way history looks at the Vatican's checkered past? Perhaps a *Diagramma*-like document still lurks in the stacks, wedged between two ordinary, inconsequential papers, just waiting to be discovered—or at least speculated about by fiction writers, historians, conspiracy theorists, and Dan Brown.

A SCHOLAR VISITS THE VATICAN LIBRARY

BY TOD MARDER

In Angels & Demons, *Dan Brown makes it seem as if entry to the Vatican's "secret" archives and library is nearly impossible. Poor Robert Langdon, the fictional Harvard professor—the Vatican authorities have not seen fit to grant his requests for access. And when he does finally get in (only under the emergency of the kidnapping of the cardinals and the antimatter threat), Langdon must navigate through the world's highest-tech document storage vaults to find some of the deepest, darkest secrets of all time.*

Tod Marder, a professor of art history at Rutgers University, has used the Vatican Library for years, often for his work on Bernini, on whom he is one of the world's foremost experts.

*Tod Marder, a professor of art history at Rutgers University and a real-life expert on Gianlorenzo
Bernini, paints a much more prosaic picture of research at the Vatican. It turns out that it is
comparatively easy for real scholars to gain access. There are no hermetically sealed climate-controlled
vaults, and probably no secret documents that the world has never seen. Here's Professor Marder's report
on his numerous visits over the years to the Vatican archives.*

Much of the detective work of the fictional art historian Robert Langdon in *Angels &
Demons* takes place in the Papal Secret Archives of the Vatican, a site with a name that
creates far more mystique than the institution deserves or is accorded by those who actually use it. To gain access is a slightly cumbersome project for a researcher, but it is
not difficult or unduly restrictive. Most art historians use the repositories of the
archives and the library together, although they are separate administrative entities
with separate protocols and staffs of functionaries that report to their own prefects.
The resources are not open to the general public or those with a casual interest in their
materials. But for those with an interest in working there and who are qualified, one
need only refer to the website at www.vatican.va/library_archives/vat_library.

To gain access, prospective readers generally present evidence of an advanced degree or qualification and letters of recommendation from an established institution
like a university, a museum, or a learned society; they must also have a passport for
purposes of identification. You enter the grounds of the Vatican through St. Anne's
Gate (Porta Sant'Anna), just as Robert Langdon does, and there you are immediately
intercepted by pairs of Swiss Guards still dressed in the colorful garb designed by
Michelangelo. To get past them you need to mutter something about needing a reader's
card (*tessera*) and then you wave your qualifying papers. A second line of iron gates
comes next, manned by even taller and more imposing forces wearing modern dark
blue uniforms that constitute the Vatican police. To them you must reiterate your mission and display your papers, which they now scrutinize carefully—especially the
passport—before letting you proceed.

As a scholar, my own feeling about this process is one of sympathy, respect, and
gratitude. On a hot summer day when literally hundreds of tourists are passing
through the Porta Sant'Anna every few minutes, the job of these men is to permit legitimate scholars with serious purposes to enter the grounds, while the eager tourists
have to be kept out and redirected either toward the piazza and the basilica of St. Peter's or toward the entrances to the Vatican museums. It isn't an easy task to wave some
arrivals into the grounds and shoo others politely away. The potential for confrontation is enormous and always avoided in the most effective ways.

Once the serious scholar is past the Vatican police, there is a long walk past a
branch of the Vatican Post Office on the right and the steps to the infamous bank on
the left, up to an imposing sixteenth-century portal. This gateway, with its huge stones
and an inscription to Julius II (recalling the era of Michelangelo, Raphael, and Bra-

mante), leads into the lower zone of the Cortile del Belvedere, where another blue-uniformed Vatican police sentry checks exactly the same papers before permitting you to move on and turn right.

Before the visitor there now lies a long, straight wing that cuts laterally across and encloses the lower half of Bramante's Cortile. The doors to the archive and the library appear before you, occupying opposite ends of this wing. At the closer end, to the right, is the library, in whose lobby you formally present your papers to the librarian in charge of access.

For someone with the necessary credentials, a legitimate need, and the appropriate recommendations, there is little problem getting a reader's card, although there may be a forty-minute wait for the processing to be completed. Passport-size pictures are needed, one copy entered into a file and the other mounted on a reader's card. (For many years, the accession office preferred the picture brought on the first visit. Thus, well into my forties, I used the photo I had presented as a beginning graduate student which was, as it happened, my yearbook picture from high school. My colleagues and I had lots of fun comparing these relics through the years until the policy suddenly changed, and we had to present ourselves in a more realistic way.)

Once finished checking in at the library, the user can scurry to the other end of the building and repeat the process for the officials at the archive. From there you simply take an elevator or climb the stairs to the main floor of these collections and begin work. An open, brick-paved veranda on the back of the building links the library and archive. Beyond it, in a huge niche that dates to the original design of the Belvedere Courtyard (1503), is a small café serving espresso, cappucchino, and sweet rolls in the morning, and light sandwiches around noon. The café makes it possible to extend the hours of a visit and to work with an intensity uncompromised by hunger, thirst, or a lack of caffeine.

Anyone with Robert Langdon's credentials as an art historian from Harvard would have no trouble gaining access to archival materials in the Vatican. Nothing of legitimate historical interest (that I am aware of) is off-limits for scholars. This is true regardless of the official position of the church in matters of theology, politics, or science. For example, the church officially acknowledged the heliocentric organization of outer space only in the 1990s, saying, in effect, that Galileo was right. Yet modern historians of science have been allowed free access to the holdings of the Vatican Library and the Papal Secret Archives for decades.

The collections are indexed and the procedure is to fill out a request form for each item, based on the Vatican's unique call-number system. Books are organized and shelved mainly by the collection that they came from—Cardinal Chigi's collections bear the locator "Chigiana," and Cardinal Rossi's donations are labelled "Rossiana." There is no gathering by topic, as falsely suggested in *Angels & Demons*, and certainly no Galileo Room that I am aware of.

To order books users are required to fill out request forms. Employees then take these forms into the bowels of the building to fetch the materials. On a day when li-

brary attendance is light, the books and articles and manuscripts appear in fifteen minutes. More often the wait is a half hour. On a crowded day at midmorning, however,
you can wait an hour for materials to arrive. The materials are shelved conventionally,
as is obvious by the way the bindings have aged. Vaults are not the rule, and climate
control is only just beginning to be employed. Given the healthy physical appearance
of the employees, whether functionaries or supervisors who deal directly with the
books and manuscripts, adequate ventilation in the stacks is not a problem despite the
exciting sequences Robert Langdon endures in *Angels & Demons.* Certainly no one appears to suffer the effects of lack of oxygen as Langdon did.

In truth, the worst physical obstacle to research in the Vatican Library and the Papal Secret Archive is that facing a visitor of any Italian collection in the scorching heat
of a Roman summer—the lack of air conditioning. Until quite recently it was required that men wear suit or sport coats in these facilities and that women wear dresses
below the knee and have their shoulders covered. The newcomer was recognized when,
in the heat of the day, he put the jacket over the back of his chair, only to be admon-
ished by a functionary that the jacket had to be worn at all times. Lately, these rules
have been relaxed. Jeans are permitted. Jackets can be shed. Short skirts are tolerated,
up to a point. But conservative dress is still the norm, and conservative standards are
enforced.

Readers of *Angels & Demons* may be tempted to envision the resources of the Vatican Library and the Papal Secret Archives as akin to a Mormon repository protected
so securely against any natural or man-made calamity that it is almost impossible to
use. Yet this is not the case. To the outsider it may seem odd that these holdings are
kept largely without climate control, that readers are allowed to turn pages of rare materials without the white gloves required by so many American libraries with less richly
endowed collections, and that the elaborate book holders designed to preserve bindings are nowhere to be seen. The real wonder of this (and of many other European
archives) is that the materials are so well kept and have survived so completely. And ac-
cessibly.

Bernini's Symbology and Angels & Demons

by Diane Apostolos-Cappadona

Prior to the rise of Dan Brown's fiction, most people had never heard of "symbology" as an academic endeavor. Indeed, one would be hard pressed to identify any real-world academics who refer to themselves as symbologists. It wouldn't surprise us, though, if Dan Brown someday decided to use the profits from his novels to endow a Robert Langdon chair in symbology at Harvard.

Diane Apostolos-Cappadona comes about as close to a real-life symbologist as one can find in the real world of academia. In the following commentary, she addresses the mismatch between her vision of Bernini—an artist she studied in depth during her undergraduate years—and Robert Langdon's very different vision of the same artist.

The summer I spent between college graduation and the beginning of graduate school was made magical by a lengthy six-week stay in Rome, where I looked with great excitement at the many churches and works of religious art that I had studied so carefully as an erstwhile student of Christian iconography. My artist hero was none other

---

Diane Apostolos-Cappadona is Adjunct Professor of Religious Art and Cultural History in the Center for Muslim-Christian Understanding and Adjunct Professor of Art and Culture in the Liberal Studies Program of Georgetown University. She is a widely published cultural historian specializing in religious art.

than Gianlorenzo Bernini, *the* baroque sculptor and architect, who had captured my attention with the ways in which he refashioned Christian iconography (the visual language of signs and symbols), both in the new art style of his times known as "baroque" and that revival of Catholicism named historically as the Counter-Reformation.

I spent many days walking the same paths that Bernini had trod from his home to the different sites—churches, palazzos, and piazzas—where his works were created or installed. What could have been more astounding than to walk into the Basilica Church of St. Peter for the first time at exactly the right time of day as the intersecting rays of the sun crisscrossed his magnificent Baldacchino and illuminated the Cathedra Petri so that it floated in midair within the frame of the Baldacchino's twisted monumental bronze columns—just as Professor Leite, my first professor of Christian art and symbolism, had described Bernini's plan? Only, perhaps, to be in the Cornaro Chapel at dusk as the candlelight infused Bernini's magnificent *Ecstasy of St. Teresa* with an aura of ethereality that only added to my reading of her mystical visions. Sun-filled afternoons visiting Bernini fountains were matched by late-morning visits to his many churches. Then there were those daily early-morning and dusk pilgrimages to the Piazza San Pietro, conveniently located near the convent-pensione where I lived.

My graduate studies took a dramatic turn when I fell hopelessly in love a second time—with the nineteenth-century Romantics. I left Gianlorenzo Bernini and baroque art in my undergraduate past, but somehow I always returned. Rome and Bernini are intertwined in both my study of religious art and my own history, so much so that I can't imagine the one without the other. As Pope Urban VIII said to the young artist, "You were made for Rome and Rome for you."

I have spent these years after graduate school engaged in research, studying, and lecturing on how to read religious signs and symbols. Perhaps, according to Dan Brown's categories, I am a professional symbologist, or at least as close to that description of coordinating signs, symbols, texts, and interpretative analyses as exists in contemporary academia.

Given my background in Rome, my study of Bernini, and my years engaged in other aspects of "symbology," you can imagine my sense of excitement, if not delight, when I learned that Dan Brown's *Angels & Demons* took place in Rome and that the secret code that solved the mystery revolved around Bernini's works. I anticipated my imaginative journey with Harvard professor of art history and religious iconology Robert Langdon on those Roman streets so familiar to me and inside those churches and museums so well known from my regular visits. I was intrigued by the idea of the coding of those symbolically complex sculptures that I had studied both in classes and at first hand. I eagerly opened the text and was immediately immersed in the initial action of murder and conspiracy.

Without doubt, *Angels & Demons* was a well-crafted page turner, so well crafted, in fact, that I didn't realize that I was past page 200 before I came upon the first reference to Bernini. However, as I read Brown's discussion of the "secret codes" of the Illumi-

Bernini's Baldacchino in St. Peter's Basilica.

nati encoded within religious art, and then proceeded to the description of the murder of the first of the four kidnapped cardinals in the Church of Santa Maria del Popolo, an ominous chill ran through me as I thought, "Oh, no, Brown's *Illuminati artist is going to be Bernini!*" In the Author's Note he had been careful to advise readers that "references to all works of art, tombs, tunnels, or architecture in Rome are entirely factual (as is their exact locations). They can still be seen today." I cautioned myself that this was a work of fiction, a thriller in fact, so that the author is to be granted artistic license. I sped along in the text. As the description of Bernini's sculptures in the Chigi Chapel unfolded, however, I gritted my teeth and said aloud, "This is not my Bernini you are writing about!"

BRIEF BIOGRAPHY OF GIANLORENZO BERNINI

Gianlorenzo Bernini was born on December 7, 1598, in Naples to a Florentine sculptor father, Pietro, and a Neapolitan mother, Angelica Galante. When Bernini was seven years old, his father received the commission to design the tomb of the then Pope Paul V. This required that the family move to Rome, a Rome in the midst of restoration following the Reformation. It was the Rome in which Gianlorenzo would make his home—with only one brief six-month excursion to France—until his death on November 28, 1680. A child prodigy, Bernini carved a marble head at age eight apparently so cleverly that his artistic gift was acknowledged by Maffeo Cardinal Barberini (the future Pope Urban VIII and the very same pope who would first befriend and then later clash with Galileo). Thereafter, Cardinal Barberini oversaw the young sculptor's education. Bernini astounded the then Pope Paul V with his ability to draw heads, particularly one of St. Paul, so that the pope is reported to have exclaimed, "This child will be the Michelangelo of his age." Bernini lived under the rule of eight popes, many of whom were his patrons and friends, and his works can be seen today in some fifty locations—churches, fountains, private homes, museums, and piazzas—throughout Rome.

He married the youthful Caterina Tezio, then twenty-two to his forty-one years, in 1639. The Bernini family came to include their eleven children and provided the sculptor with supportive companionship and happiness until Caterina's death in 1673. As best as can be determined, Bernini was a devout Roman Catholic, attending daily Mass and partaking regularly of the Eucharist. Partial to Jesuit spirituality, the sculptor practiced the spiritual exercises initiated by St. Ignatius of Loyola (ca. 1491–1556) and eventually became a member of a Jesuit group devoted to the Blessed Sacrament. Thereafter, Bernini attended daily Mass at Sant'Andrea delle Fratte and completed his daily labors with a kneeling meditation before the sacrament in Il Gesú, the church of the Jesuits in Rome. His Ignatian practices emphasized the individual development of visual images as both an initiation to and a mode of meditation. Such an emphasis on the effectiveness of the visual enhanced Bernini's natural tendency toward visual drama and emotive engagement. That famed convert to Catholicism, Queen Christina of Sweden, befriended Bernini and visited his studio often to view his works in progress and to discuss matters related to art and spirituality.

By 1680 Bernini's health had deteriorated significantly so that, after several days' illness and a slowly escalating paralysis, he received the pope's Benediction early on the morning of November 28 and died soon thereafter. The Basilica Church of Santa Maria Maggiore was so overloaded with public mourners that the funeral was delayed for a day.

BERNINI AND THE BAROQUE ERA

The style of art, whether painting, sculpture, or architecture, associated with both northern and southern Europe during the cultural, economic, and religious revolution known as the Reformation and the Counter-Reformation is identified as baroque (from the Portuguese *barocco*, meaning "irregularly shaped pearl"). As much a reaction against the artistic ideals of beauty, balance, and harmony found in Renaissance art, baroque art was characterized as dramatic and theatrical both in its visual presentation and in its selected themes. To garner such descriptors, baroque artists, including Caravaggio and Rembrandt, employed off-center compositions, darkened or muddy colors, and a theatrical spotlighting called *chiaroscuro* in Italy or tenebrism in the North. Italian baroque art was a form of a popular and visual defense of the Roman Catholic teachings, especially those questioned by the reformers. This new emphasis on visual signs and symbols, oftentimes identified as a complex iconography, provided visual references for the decrees of the Council of Trent (1545–1563), which defined formally what it meant to be Roman Catholic.

Although not the originator of Italian baroque art, Bernini was its greatest exponent. He perfected the sculptural concept of a single frontal viewpoint bringing all aspects of his image into clear focus, sharp lines, and realistic perspective *if* you stood on exactly the right spot and looked from the correct angle. However, if you stood away from that spot when you looked at Bernini's sculpture, what you saw was fuzzy in form, unclear in line, and distorted in perspective. Thus the art of Bernini, like that of other Italian baroque artists, was predicated upon a worldview that assimilated the religious values of "the Church." Either you were a member and saved, or else outside the boundaries and your soul was among the lost.

This was the Bernini I knew and loved. The world in which he lived was one in which art and religion were so intensely connected that it was impossible to distinguish one from the other. It was a world made even more dramatic by the split of the church into what we know today as Protestantism and Roman Catholicism—a world in which the public declaration of one's religious faith was required, as it defined an individual's social identity. However, such a public declaration included the potential dangers of imprisonment or death, as wars initiated by these new religious identities were waged throughout Europe for the next two centuries. National boundaries included the reality of religious boundaries. European environments where Catholics lived and worked were distinct from those in which Protestants lived and worked; the twain did not meet comfortably, if at all. Against this backdrop, Bernini was the artist par excellence who defined visually what it meant to be Roman Catholic.

My Bernini was that exuberant ten-year-old who, when the famed painter Annibale Carracci's mentioned that the Basilica Church of St. Peter needed to be redesigned to signal the restored glory of the Church of Rome, is said to have replied, "If only I could be the one!" No Illuminatus, he, nor a conspirator of any kind against either the institution or the hierarchy of the Church of Rome.

Many of Bernini's churches, monuments, piazzas, or fountains incorporate the magnificent Egyptian obelisks that varied Roman emperors had brought to the Imperial City. Bernini did not relocate these obelisks, however, as Professor Langdon seems to think, nor did Bernini use these obelisks and other symbols to create a secret architectural monument pattern on the map of Rome leading to the Illuminati's "secret" lair, as suggested in *Angels & Demons*. Indeed, the movers and shakers of obelisk relocations were Pope Sixtus V and his innovative engineer Domenico Fontana. During the late 1580s (at least ten years before Bernini was born), Pope Sixtus V resited and/or moved the obelisks throughout Rome. He capped each with a cross as a stunning visual sign of both the spiritual aegis of Christianity triumphant over paganism and its further expansion throughout the world, thereby signaling the restoration and glorification of the church during the Counter-Reformation.

Bernini is, however, responsible for the sculptures found at the four locations identified in *Angels & Demons* as the sites of the grisly, methodical—and utterly fictional—murders of the four cardinals who Dan Brown identifies by the term *preferiti*, the leading candidates for election as the new pope. So we now turn our attention to a discussion of the specific Bernini sculptures that are so important both as symbolic backdrops and as clues for the conspiratorial murders of four cardinals.

THE SITE OF THE FIRST MURDER, OR WHY DANIEL AND HABAKKUK ARE IN THE CHIGI CHAPEL

Robert Langdon's search for the first missing cardinal, Ebner of Frankfurt, takes him first to the Pantheon and from there to the church of Santa Maria del Popolo. In a desperate search to locate and save the kidnapped cardinal, Langdon and his companion, Vittoria Vetra, seek out the Chigi Chapel. There they uncover there the identity of the alleged Illuminati artist whose works hold the keys to the locations of both the other potential murders and the infamous "Church of the Illuminati" in Rome.

The great piazza we know today as the Piazza del Popolo is a nineteenth-century design, although the central Obelisk of Pharaoh Ramses II was relocated from the Circus Maximus by Pope Sixtus V. The Church of Santa Maria del Popolo was commissioned in 1472 by order of Pope Sixtus IV, who dedicated the first side chapel on the right to his family, the della Rovere. More often than not, art history students and tourists come to Santa Maria del Popolo to see Caravaggio's masterworks, the *Conversion of St. Paul* (1601) and the *Crucifixion of St. Peter* (1601) located in the Cerasi Chapel to the left of the altar. However, for readers of *Angels & Demons* attention is given over to the Chigi Chapel located second on the left as one enters the church. The initial commission for this mortuary chapel for the famed banking family was given by Agostino Chigi to Raphael, who designed the octagonal space with a central altar flanked by four large niches and pyramidal tombs. When Fabio Cardinal Chigi (soon to be Pope Alexander VII) accepted family responsibility for this ancestral chapel in 1655, he asked Bernini to refurbish the chapel with an eye to filling the two empty niches, resurfacing the pyramid tombs with bronze and marble medallions, and providing a marble inlay floor.

In keeping with the function of the Chigi Chapel as a family mortuary, Bernini took his cues from Lucas Holstensius, then Vatican librarian, who selected the theme of Bel and the Dragon from the Greek book of Daniel, a copy of which belonged to the Chigi family. This story is accepted as part of the Vulgate—St. Jerome's fourth-century Latin translation of the Bible—that was declared canon at the Council of Trent. In this text, the prophet Habakkuk sets out to deliver food promised to the field laborers when he is stopped by an angel, and redirected to deliver this food to Daniel, then trapped in the lion's den. Bernini depicted a stunned Habakkuk gesturing toward the famished laborers as the angel points to the new target, who Bernini presented kneeling in prayer diagonally across the Chigi Chapel.

From the beginnings of Christianity, Daniel in the lions' den signified the Christian soul in peril of death and in need of salvation, while Habakkuk's angelic transport of a basket filled with bread echoed the Early Christian interest in the miraculous meal of bread and wine delivered by the priest-king Melchisedek to Abraham in the desert. In his mastery of baroque swirling garments and dramatic gestures, Bernini has transformed the Chigi Chapel into a stunning and energized setting for this scriptural story, not as directional guide on the path of the Illuminati.

THE SITE OF THE SECOND MURDER, OR WHY BERNINI'S "LITTLE" PLAQUE IS IMPORTANT

Departing on their effort to foil the murder of the second kidnapped *preferiti*, Cardinal Lamassé of Paris, Langdon, and Vetra are led to a little known and rarely discussed work of Bernini's located in the Piazza San Pietro in Vatican City. In 1655 Fabio Cardinal Chigi became Pope Alexander VII. One of his first acts as pope was to name Bernini as "our own architect," resulting in the commission to redesign the "piazza of piazzas," Piazza San Pietro, in 1656. The absolute center of this public space is the giant eighty-foot obelisk that Pope Sixtus V had moved in December 1585. Readers of

Bernini's Habakkuk and the Angel, Chigi Chapel, Santa Maria del Popolo.

Angels & Demons find their attention directed to the marble disks placed near the piazza's fountains. One of these is central to more than the grisly second murder and the directional code for the alleged path of the Illuminati—it is the silent witness of Bernini's fundamental baroque personality.

Bernini's challenge was to transform this spectacular oval into a space that filled pilgrims with awe and wonder, yet projected spiritual intimacy. Bernini reshaped the oval into an ellipse replete with a series of illusions including the internal space-gathering progression from fountain to obelisk to fountain. Then he encircled his ellipse with a four-rowed colonnade of 284 columns topped with ninety colossal statues of saints. The two circular arcs of the colonnade imitated two outstretched arms in a visual *concetto* (conceit) of Mother Church enfolding protectively and lovingly all those present. This understanding of Bernini's *concetto* envisions the adage of the Early Church Father Cyprian of Carthage that "he who does not have the church for his mother, cannot have God for his father." Thus, Bernini connected Early Christianity and the contemporary Church of Rome, for which there was no salvation outside of the church.

During Bernini's lifetime, the crowded neighborhood known as the Borgo prevented the existence of the spectacular open path we see today as we cross the famed Ponte San Angelo, turn to our left, and look down the Via della Conciliazione toward St. Peter's Basilica. We can only imagine the drama and effect experienced by a pilgrim in Bernini's time when, after wandering first the narrow and crowded streets of the Borgo, she found herself in the vast open space encompassed by the protective arms of the monumental columns, watched over by the colossal statues, and drawn to the central space shared by the obelisk and fountains, toward the steps into the great basilica.

When I stand upon this marble disk now made infamous by the murder of Cardinal Lamassé, I remember that the baroque origin and thereby Bernini's purpose for this disk was specific to the art and religious values of baroque Rome. Such markers, whether depicted as a star, a cross, or an angel, are found in all major churches with baroque ceilings. As I enter such a church and walk around it, or through it, and look up to see the baroque ceiling, I see swirling and fuzzy forms in a mode akin to that early-morning glance into the mirror without my glasses on. However, when I stand on the marker, the fuzzy disorder comes into clear focus just as Bernini's four-rowed colonnade becomes a clear, singular row of columns. It is a visual metaphor for Counter-Reformation theology that espouses a theological one-point perspective— one is either saved in the arms of Mother Church, or damned outside her arms— which parallels the one-point perspective of baroque art.

THE SITE OF THE THIRD MURDER, OR WHY THIS WOMAN FLOATS IN THE AIR

According to *Angels & Demons*, the site of the third murder (Cardinal Guidera of Barcelona) is the Church of Santa Maria della Vittoria, located "on Piazza Barberini."

Bernini's masterful colonnade leading to the Basilica, St. Peter's Square, Vatican City.

Further, readers are told by Brown incorrectly that this piazza was once the site of an obelisk, replaced in the late twentieth century by Bernini's Triton Fountain. This description is problematic to say the least. The church with its famed Bernini sculpture of the *Ecstasy of St. Teresa* is actually located on Via XX Settembre, two extralong and curving blocks from Piazza Barberini. Moreover, Bernini created his Triton Fountain (1642–1643) as a civic monument to the Barberini pope who had recognized him as a child prodigy, attended to his education, and patronized him as a mature sculptor. His visual praise of Urban VIII included the family crest with the famed Barberini bees and a triton with an upraised conch shell that sounded the pope's praises like a trumpet. Bernini designed this fountain for the location it has always occupied. The discrepancies between the story recounted in *Angels & Demons* on the one hand, and history and facts on the other, again caused me to ask myself, "Is this my Bernini or Langdon's Bernini whose works are being shuffled about like playing cards during a game of solitaire?"

Once inside Santa Maria della Vittoria, readers of *Angels & Demons* encounter one of Bernini's most famous works, his exceptional sculpture of the *Ecstasy of St. Teresa.* that is located in the left transept Cornaro Chapel. From the interconnections between art, iconography, and theology, this image of one of the Counter-Reformations most important figures is crucial to my understanding of Bernini. Pope Gregory X had only canonized Teresa of Avila in October 1622. Given his religious devotion, Bernini must have experienced her as a living saint. Teresa of Avila had both the aura of historicity and contemporary reality for Bernini. She founded a reformed order of nuns, the Discalced Carmelites, established sixteen monasteries in Spain, and wrote several significant texts on Catholic spirituality. Santa Maria della Vittoria is the church of the Discalced Carmelites in Rome. Bernini selected the image of one of her mystical visions, so central to both her autobiography and the cult of her sainthood, as an appropriate subject for the Cornaro mortuary chapel.

In *Angels & Demons*, Langdon describes this sculpture as originally a Vatican commission rejected by Pope Urban VIII, as the sculptor had anticipated. However, historical documentation confirms that Bernini received a private commission from the Venetian Frederico Cardinal Cornaro (1579–1653) soon after he acquired the patronage of the left transept chapel in 1647. Late-twentieth-century discoveries of documentation from Cardinal Cornaro's ledgers include an unusually large payment of 12,089 scudi to Bernini for a sculpture of St. Teresa to grace the chapel altar. Clearly, then, this statue was created for the specific space which it has always occupied. Further, Pope Urban VIII died in 1644 so he couldn't have commissioned, seen, evaluated, or rejected the *Ecstasy of St. Teresa*, which was not commissioned until 1647 nor completed until 1652.

Bernini's artistic challenge was to transform the experiences of a singular female saint, lost in wordlessness as she momentarily but totally experienced God's love, into a vision in marble. Once the baroque style of art faded into the background as other cultural and artistic styles emerged, Bernini's imaging of St. Teresa became a topic of constant criticism for having what became perceived as a lascivious and sexual nature. A visiting president of France commented that this sculpture belonged in a bedroom, not in a church. However, to see or describe this marble impression of feminine softness and mystical swoon as merely sexual is to do a serious injustice to Bernini, St. Teresa, and Catholic spirituality.

Every world religion includes a tradition of mysticism. Generically, a mystic can be characterized as seeking an immediate and total immersion in the sacred, the holy, the divine. Whether male or female, clergy or laity, mystics describe the mystical encounter in terms replete with sexual metaphors or innuendoes. For Bernini's understanding of Teresa of Avila, her use of such metaphors was directly related to the levels of love identified in baroque spirituality. The highest level of human love is that between two lovers as each gives himself completely to the other. However, this is merely a glimpse of what God's love is like. As a mystic graced with the gift of momentary glimpses of God's love, St. Teresa's swoon is a total surrender of mind, body, and soul to God, as evidenced by the benevolence on the angel's face and the yearning on St. Teresa's face. Bernini's image parallels her descriptions even to "the entire body contracts and neither arm nor foot can be moved." St. Teresa's autobiographical description, like Bernini's sculpture, is not the "toe-curling orgasm" Dan Brown describes in his postmodern vulgarization of the spiritual and physical power of mystical union.

One last game between my Bernini and Langdon's Bernini occurred in the discussion of the third murder. To affirm my visual and geographic memory, I looked carefully at a detailed map of Rome and color photographs of Bernini's sculpture. As I had remembered, the angel holds the golden arrow that the female mystic so carefully described: "In his hands I saw a great golden spear, and at the iron tip there appeared to be a point of fire. This he plunged into my heart several times so that it penetrated to my entrails. When he pulled it out I felt that he took them with it, and left me utterly consumed by the great love of God."

Remembering Bernini's use of that famed baroque one-point perspective, I positioned myself on the right spot to see the angle of the golden arrow in the angel's right hand. As I did so, I noted that its target is St. Teresa's upper body. Coordinating the location of the Cornaro Chapel inside the Church of Santa Maria della Vittoria with the church's geographic placement, readers of *Angels & Demons* may be disappointed to learn that this golden arrow points toward the saint's heart and if its target is extended beyond her, then it is directionally east—away from, not toward, either Piazza Navona or the Vatican. In other words, the real arrow points in the opposite direction from the way Robert Langdon thinks it points as a clue to the next murder. Langdon's reading of the works created by his Bernini remind me that the so-called "innocent eye" does not exist.

Bernini's Ecstasy of St. Teresa, Santa Maria della Vittoria.

THE SITE OF THE FOURTH MURDER, OR WHY THE DOVE COUNTS

The murder of the fourth and last remaining of Brown's *preferiti*, Cardinal Baggia of Milan, takes place in one of Rome's most popular tourist centers, the famed Piazza Navona, which has been an *isola pedonale* (pedestrian zone) in the heart of Rome since its original first-century design for foot races by the emperor Domitian. Located in front of the Church of St. Agnes in Agony, this piazza also incorporated the adjacent Palazzo Pamphili, family home of Pope Innocent X who commissioned the Fountain of the Four Rivers (1648–1651). As with other significant commissions, Bernini would integrate the papal family crest within the symbolism of this new monumental fountain.

Building upon the Classical Greek and Roman idea of the four rivers of the earth, and the medieval Christian concept of the four rivers of Paradise, Bernini conceived this commission as a tribute to both the Pamphili family and to the glorification of the church after the Reformation. However, Bernini's *concetto* is more direct than that at Piazza San Pietro. This obelisk is crowned with a golden globe topped by a dove with an olive branch in its mouth. This motif is a visual affirmation of Christian (read Catholic) evangelization to all corners of the world, illustrated in Bernini's careful facial depictions upon the four languid bodies representing the classical river gods of the Nile, Danube, Plate, and Ganges. The image of the dove holding the olive branch has a multitude of meanings or references, as suggested by Robert Langdon. But Bernini's meaning is specific—the Pamphili family crest contained a dove with an olive branch.

A CONCLUDING POSTSCRIPT, OR WHOSE BERNINI IS IT ANYWAY?

Bernini and his works retain a special place in both my continuing work in religious symbolism, and, yes, also in my heart. Although I was engaged by the mystery and thriller aspects of *Angels & Demons*, I confess that I found Langdon's discussion of religious symbols and Bernini's works particularly disconcerting. There may be the proverbial "fourteen ways to view a blackbird" but as I have suggested in this essay, the truth claim asserted in the Author's Note is worrisome. I am trained as a cultural historian, so this truth-claim business represents a meaningful principle for me. Wouldn't we find Robert Langdon just as engaging a sleuth without that questionable assertion? I could then, of course, easily forgive him his art and symbology mistakes, and he could ignore my questions.

Curiously, Professor Langdon omits any discussion of other Bernini works replete with the pagan and Christian symbolism he should find terribly interesting. Some significant examples include the Baldacchino (1624–1633) and the Cathedra Petri (1657–1666). The former signifies the triumphant canopy that shelters the pontifical altar and marks the tomb of St. Peter. The latter is the visual sign uniting the central teachings about Peter's role, especially the dogmas of Apostolic Succession and the

Primacy of Peter. To convey the singularity and importance of Peter, Bernini visually unites scripture, theology, and liturgy. Yet Langdon remains silent even as he rushes past both monuments inside St. Peter's Basilica.

I wonder if readers, especially nonspecialists, would find enlightening the inclusion of illustrations of all the significant works of art and locations mentioned in *Angels & Demons*? After all, Professor Langdon describes from his own perspective such well-known Bernini works as the *Ecstasy of St. Teresa* and the Fountain of the Four Rivers, and even so obscure a work as the marker incised with the "west wind." Perhaps the classic adage that a picture speaks a thousand words is not simply true but integral to any story so dependent upon art and symbology. Whatever am I going to do? A long weekend in Rome, perhaps, revisiting those oh so familiar pathways, churches, and Bernini works is a most sensible beginning.

Rome: City of Angels and Demonic Imaginings

by David Downie

In many ways, it is the city of Rome that is the protagonist of Angels & Demons, even more so than Galileo, Bernini, Robert Langdon, Vittoria Vetra, or the camerlengo. Considering the large part the city plays in the story, we asked David Downie—a Europe-based freelance writer who commented on touring Paris in the footsteps of The Da Vinci Code *for our previous book,* Secrets of the Code—*to write a report for our readers on visiting Rome in the wake of* Angels & Demons.

Dan Brown's *Angels & Demons* plays itself out almost entirely in Rome, a city the author describes as "a labyrinth—an indecipherable maze of ancient roadways winding around buildings, fountains, and crumbling ruins." Spoilsports quip that *maze* and *labyrinth* mean the same thing, roadways often wind around buildings and fountains, and ruins by their nature have crumbled. Never mind. The charm of Brown's prose, and even that of Rome itself, is that it often defies comprehension.

Readers acquainted with the Italian capital appear delighted and bemused in equal measure to discover the book's surreal cityscape and to follow in the footsteps of Har-

David Downie is a Europe-based freelance writer, editor, and translator. His topics are European culture, travel, and food.

vard "symbologist" Robert Langdon and the other Etch A Sketch characters that populate it, all of them reliably American in outlook and speech, no matter what their supposed nationality is according to the novel.

Rome provides Brown with a backdrop of antiquity and intrigue that even he can't fully misrepresent. The city's ruins, churches, fountains, squares, ancient roadways, and even the Castel Sant'Angelo, soaked in blood, attract tens of millions of tourists a year. Alongside the standard tourist routes, Brown has invented an alternative way to see some of the Eternal City's lesser-known sites, including what Brown calls "cruciforms," "funeraries," "sore thumbs," "runaway trains," and a variety of items, such as sculptures of angels, that he describes as "mammoth."

Of mixed nationality and creed, curious *Angels & Demons* aficionados carrying tattered copies of the book seek out spots explored on the run (but at impressive length) by the indefatigably professorial Langdon and his ostensibly Italian sidekick, Vittoria Vetra. Most editions of the book incorporate a handy city map.

Unfortunately, a variety of mistakes are included: Sant'Agnese in Agone is placed by Brown on the wrong side of Piazza Navona and called "Saint Agnes in Agony." The experience of Agnes, a young Christian virgin who was brutally martyred by the Romans, might be interpreted as a state of emotional agony, but that is not the origin of "Agone" in the church's name. *Agone* actually means athletic competition and refers to the games held on the site in Emperor Domitian's Circus Agonalis. Moreover, the church of Santa Maria della Vittoria, where one of the murders takes place in the novel, isn't on Piazza Barberini, where Brown sets it. Instead, it's a quarter of a mile away on Via XX Settembre. These and other deviations from cartographic reality make the treasure hunt all the more thrilling. To demand accuracy from a writer of Brown's talent may be unrealistic.

As with *The Da Vinci Code*, in a note prefacing the *Angels & Demons* text, Brown demonstrates that he's not content to write fiction. He proclaims, "References to all works of art, tombs, tunnels, and architecture in Rome are entirely factual as are their exact locations. They can still be seen today." An ungrammatical riddle worthy of Madison Avenue lawyers, as written, it is the "references" that are "factual" and may "still be seen today." That might explain why artworks, buildings, and historical events sometimes refuse to conform to Brown's evocations.

The action starts and peaks at the Vatican, but the best place to pick up Robert Langdon's scent is the Pantheon. Above its cyclopean colonnade even shortsighted art historians and "symbologists" can spot the ancient inscription: *M. AGRIPPA L. F. COS. TERTIUM FECIT* (Marcus Agrippa, son of Lucius, Consul for the third time, built this). Agrippa was possibly history's greatest patron of waterworks. In the single year 33 BC he splashed out for the construction of an aqueduct, five hundred fountains, and seven hundred basins for central Rome. However, the Pantheon that visitors see today was rebuilt entirely by Emperor Hadrian from AD 120 to 125. It stands over Agrippa's Baths. As Langdon points out, medieval soldiers of God, who wrecked so many other "pagan" monuments, spared the Pantheon because it had been Christianized: the Byzantine Emperor Phocas gave it to Pope Boniface IV in AD 608.

Brown gets the early history and first Latin inscription about right (he leaves out the "son of Lucius"). For reasons related to scansion, however, he persists in having Langdon call Raffaello Sanzio, alias Raphael, "Santi." This is in the style of "the influential English poet" John Milton, the perpetrator of the verses written along the edges of a leaf in Galileo's *Diagramma*—the key to the rusty Illuminati lock. If one interprets works of literature to be works of art, then Brown's statement swearing to the truth of all such references is even more of a whopper, since no nonfiction expert on Galileo believes he wrote a final book called the *Diagramma* that would be lying around in the Vatican's secret archives waiting for Robert Langdon to find and use as a guide to where the next serial murder will happen.

Brown has some unusual ideas about when Raphael was supposedly entombed at the Pantheon in an "ornate funerary" (presumably a funerary monument). The correct date for the first entombment is April 8, 1520, two days after Raphael's death. In 1833 the original tomb was opened to make sure Raphael's remains were still in it; they were then transferred to the "ornate funerary" now on display. To set right the record that is confused by the novel, the Pantheon's ancient sculptures were removed long before the nineteenth century and the Pantheon's dramatic oculus has never been known as a "demon's hole"—or the obscene-sounding literal translation of it into Italian provided by Brown. Though it wreaks havoc on the plot, an 8:00 p.m. Pantheon murder is inconvenient: the church closes at 7:30 p.m. There are no huckster guides like the novel's cicerone anymore—they went out with the novels of E. M. Forster. Information officers from the Ministry of Culture provide free of charge the kind of info Langdon needs to get to square two—Santa Maria del Popolo.

To cover the mile-plus between the Pantheon and Piazza del Popolo in the one minute Brown allots, Langdon and his posse of Keystone Cops in Swiss Guard getup would need not taxis and police cars but space planes. Not even Brown can drive up Via della Scrofa and Via di Ripetta, enter Piazza Augusto Imperatore, and come out at Piazza del Popolo. The streets are one-way in the wrong direction, and there's a traffic barrier in Via Tomacelli.

It would be interesting to know how journalist Gunther Glick hid his fully equipped BBC van "in the shadows" of one of Rome's least shadowy, liveliest squares, which has no parking places. And anyone other than Brown who's spotted "literati" at Caffè Rosati in the last forty years should step forward.

The narrator can't seem to decide whether Santa Maria del Popolo is an eleventh-century "stone aerie" or a "misplaced battleship," its interior "a murky cave" or "a half-finished subway station." Reality is less confused. The church is a Renaissance structure built atop the Romanesque foundations of a former convent. It's wedged between the square and Rome's ancient city walls. Alas, there's nothing mysterious about entering it from either the side or the main door. And the front stairs are not, as Brown calls them, *un ventaglio* (a welcoming, curved fan) but rather form *una scalinata stondata* (a slightly rounded bracket shape).

The Chigi Chapel exists and boasts a burial chamber beneath it. There are indeed two pyramids, though Raphael designed them, not Bernini. Bernini added the marble cladding.

[Editor's note: Pyramids are not at all unusual or exotic in Rome, any more than the Egyptian obelisks found near many churches and monuments. Romans of two thousand years ago were fascinated by Egyptian history and culture and considered Rome's conquest of Egypt one of the great achievements of the empire. The fascination with Egypt is abiding—after all, modern Americans and Europeans still feel it. In the Renaissance and especially the Baroque era, the Vatican used its Egyptian treasures in the redecoration and glorification of the city. Obelisks, with crosses atop them, were not secretly set up by Illuminati architects, but openly placed by Catholic authorities in front of many churches, including Santa Maria del Popolo and St. Peter's itself, in order to highlight these monuments and make it easy for pilgrims to find them.]

The medallions on the pyramids in the Chigi Chapel are not gold, as Brown claims. However, the angel in Bernini's *Habakkuk and the Angel* does seem to point somewhere, as Brown suggests, perhaps even in the general direction of St. Peter's. Until recently, few glanced at this sculpture, preferring the art treasures the church is best known for: Caravaggio's sublime canvases, *Conversion of St. Paul* and *Crucifixion of St. Peter*. With the popularity of *Angels & Demons*, however, tourist multitudes now besiege *Habakkuk*. Some crawl through prodigious dust (restoration work continues), trying to peer into the "demon's hole" for traces of a dead cardinal branded with the Illuminati "ambigram" of earth. Unfortunately, a round marble cover thwarts them. Other acolytes have been spotted jumping up and down on the staircase leading to the Pincio overlook east of the church, desperate to find a sight line to the next square in Dan Brown's murder mystery—St. Peter's.

In the center of Bernini's Piazza San Pietro rises an obelisk brought to Rome during the reign of Caligula or Nero (learned opinions vary) and moved to its present position in 1585 by Domenico Fontana. Ranged around it are objects designed by Brown's alleged master Illuminatus, Bernini. A set of marble rounds marks the signs of the zodiac and a white marble circle with a black stone disk marks the focal point of the square. From it visitors may view a trick perspective of the colonnade. It appears to have one row of columns instead of four. Diabolical!

Having laid aside another dead cardinal (this one perforated), Langdon only has eyes for one of the sixteen carved marble slabs marking a compass of the winds that buffet Rome, specifically *ponente*, the westerly referred to as God's Breath (because it seems to issue from the basilica).

In the novel the westerly blows long-winded Langdon and his stick-figure lady love back across Rome along a "cruciform" to Illuminati square four—Piazza Barberini and Santa Maria della Vittoria. The trouble is the fictional church happens to be in the wrong place. While Brown would have us believe that Bernini's Triton Fountain was set up in Piazza Barberini recently, replacing an obelisk (the Illuminati symbol), it's discouraging to report that the Triton has been spouting merrily in the same spot since at least 1643. There is no record of an obelisk ever having been there, even before 1643. And since this is the wrong piazza for Santa Maria della Vittoria's location, the erroneous references cancel each other out.

Skew the cruciform and hike a few hundred yards to the corner of Via XX Settembre and Largo Santa Susanna; there may be found the movable church often encircled, nowadays, by gawping readers and foot fetishists eager to see Bernini's rendition of St. Teresa "in the throes of a toe-curling orgasm."

In this church, Langdon watches a branded cardinal (suspended from votive-lamp cables) roast over flaming pews. Our hero spends precious minutes trapped under an overturned sarcophagus while the evil Hassassin drags Vittoria away, King Kong style, for later ravishing. With a nod to Disney, Mickey saves the day [Langdon uses the alarm on his Mickey Mouse watch to alert a passerby; see p. 396].

Some readers admit to bitter disappointment upon discovering that the church's sarcophagi are mounted high on walls (they cannot possibly be turned over), and that the pews have not been burned recently. They did burn, however, in an 1833 fire that also destroyed the church's former treasure, a picture of the Madonna of Victory. As to Teresa, where Langdon sees "some sort of pornographic still life" featuring a bruiser angel about to plunge a flaming phallic spear into the moaning saint, others with perhaps less toe-curling imaginations see what is technically a cherub holding an iron-tipped gold dart.

Spear or dart, it points, in Brown's mind, to Piazza Navona and the differently agonizing St. Agnes. Luckily, her church is spared Langdon's attentions, perhaps because it was built by the great architect Francesco Borromini, Bernini's chief rival in the seventeenth century. This time the obelisk rises over Bernini's Four Rivers Fountain, centerpiece of the Piazza Navona, which is one of Europe's liveliest public spaces, especially in the evening. On this April night, however, the Hassassin finds the usually crowded square conveniently empty (the narrator even observes that Robert Langdon finds the piazza "deserted"), drives a van to the fountain's edge, and rolls a chain-bound cardinal into the water—yet another conundrum. The iron banister and twenty-eight bollards that keep people and vehicles more than four feet away from the basin are notorious perches for pickup artists. Also puzzling is how Langdon slips on coins (that must be the Trevi Fountain Brown is thinking of), breathes from an air hose (wrong fountain again), shoots a gun, wrestles the villain, and scales the fountain unnoticed when, in fact, on a spring evening he would be surrounded by café clients, caricature artists, and musicians, not to mention police squads on round-the-clock duty.

The fountain's sculptures do not represent "Old Europe" as Brown claims. They represent four continents and four rivers: Europe/the Danube (the horse); Africa/the

Nile (the lion); Asia/the Ganges (the palm and serpent); and the Americas/the Rio de la Plata (the armadillo). An interesting dilemma for Dan Brown's theory of pyramids = Illuminati symbols = Bernini is that when commissioned to build this stupendous fountain, one facet of which was to represent Egypt and the Nile, Bernini chose not to place any pyramids in the design. Furthermore, any art historian-"symbologist" unaware that Pope Innocent X commissioned the fountain and had his family symbol, the dove, set atop the obelisk, might want to invest in a guidebook or hire a cicerone. In any event, the dove atop the statue, which Langdon thinks is a pagan symbol, is said to be pointing to Castel Sant'Angelo, the next stop on the murder mystery tour.

Imagine an Italian pulp fiction author describing a popular museum like the Smithsonian as a labyrinthine Illuminati lodge linked to the White House and you get a sense of how Italians might read Dan Brown. Hadrian's Mausoleum, completed in AD 139, atop which Gregory the Great spotted an angel in AD 590, was later reconfigured as a fortress and became known as Castel Sant'Angelo, for Gregory's vision. It was linked to the Vatican by an elevated passageway (called Il Passetto), expanded and embellished by various popes, and transformed into a national museum in 1925. It indeed has an ancient spiral ramp, oil reservoirs and silos, dungeons and secret tunnels. It's also open almost in its entirety to the public, is thronged year round, does not have a functioning drawbridge, and has a panoramic café and electric lighting (sorry, no torches). The bastions are pentagonal, not the park, which was built by Mussolini in the 1930s. The dungeons where the kidnapped cardinals of *Angels & Demons* were presumably kept are on the visitor's tour, and so too (at least some of the time) is the interior corridor of Il Passetto, which debouches next to the Vatican's colonnade.

The less said the better about Brown's perceptions of the Sistine Chapel and its frescoes. Many inspired and cogent works have been written about the Vatican, its art and architecture, history and dilemmas, and one can only hope *Angels & Demons* readers will eventually turn to them. Regarding the seemingly off-limits grottoes, archeological excavations, and putative tomb of St. Peter beneath the basilica, as well as much of Vatican City and its gardens, they, too, are accessible either during regular visiting hours or by written request.

The so-called Confessio (beneath the papal altar and Bernini's Baldacchino) is at crypt level, reached by two curving flights of steps. Straight below the altar is the gilt grillwork that covers the Niche of the Pallia, which, if Vatican historians are to be trusted, holds St. Peter's Shrine. This is where the camerlengo disappears, having lifted off the heavy grille, and this is where rubbernecking readers now congregate, thrillers in hand. The frantic to and fro of Brown's characters in the crypt makes it sound as if the underground access route to St. Peter's tomb stretches for miles. Happily it doesn't, otherwise the book might have run to an even more daunting length.

The Confessio is horseshoe-shaped and surrounded by a balustrade topped by gilt oil lamps lit in perpetuity. A favorite topic of debate among Brown acolytes appears to center around the exact number of lamps (officially ninety-five but the count varies daily) and whether the fuel contained in one of them—harmless liquefied beeswax and not Brown's napalmlike fluid—could actually burn to ash a human being bent on self-immolation. With luck we'll never know.

"LET ANGELS GUIDE YOU ON YOUR LOFTY QUEST"

BY SUSAN SANDERS

> From Santi's earthly tomb with demon's hole,
> 'Cross Rome the mystic elements unfold.
> The path of light is laid, the sacred test,
> Let angels guide you on your lofty quest.
> —John Milton

Much time and energy have been devoted to the discussion of Dan Brown's bestselling novel *Angels & Demons*. Both lovers and critics of the book have posed questions concerning the historical accuracy of the seventeenth-century events recounted in the thriller and have wondered about the contemporary issues discussed in the book, from papal conclaves to antimatter to the secrets of the Vatican Library. Yet that which the book accomplishes is much more than the sum of its accuracies, inaccuracies, and bestselling status. In *Angels & Demons*, Brown opens a door into the historical past that engages the imagination and stimulates the intellect. In the fictionalized world of *Angels & Demons* (as in Brown's other popular novel, *The Da Vinci Code*), history plays a major part. Its starring role compels many travelers to visit Rome and trace their own path " 'cross Rome" to see "the mystic elements unfold."

Susan Sanders is the executive director of the Institute for Design and Culture, a non-profit group dedicated to educating travelers about Rome's history, art, and architecture.

For those who live in the Eternal City, tourists are a normal part of daily life. In antiquity, visitors came to Rome to experience the city that ruled the Western world. Since that time, tourism has been vital to the city's economic well-being. Rome has hosted a long parade of visitors, ranging from religious pilgrims to Romantic poets to contemporary cruise-ship travelers. All are eager to see one of the world's most beautiful and historic cities.

The vast majority of these tourists allow traditional guidebooks to lead them on their "lofty quest" for Rome's art, history, and culture. However, the publication of *Angels & Demons* has brought forth a new type of tourist—one who doesn't sport the traditional *Fodor's* or *Rick Steves'*, but instead totes a worn copy of *Angels & Demons* as their guidebook. They make their way around Rome by referring to the book's map, found in the opening pages, just after the Author's Note, in which Brown claims that the "references to all works of art, tombs, tunnels, and architecture in Rome are entirely factual (as are their exact locations). They can still be seen today."

Despite this claim, *Angels & Demons* is more fiction than fact. As the thrilling plot unfolds, the two main characters, symbologist Robert Langdon and physicist Vittoria Vetra, race back and forth " 'cross Rome" in an attempt to apprehend the Hassassin before he commits another crime. The locations they visit *are* real and in Brown's book these four history- and art-filled sites become "Altars of Science"—sets for the gruesome and graphic murders of the four *preferiti* (the cardinals likely to be elected pope). Langdon and Vittoria race through the city trying to stop the murders and decode the clues that will lead them to the next one.

The greatest value of *Angels & Demons* may be found in the fact that it offers a welcome alternative from the Europe-off-the-Beaten-Path and Back-Door-Budget guidebooks that have dominated tourism for the past decades. Brown's book, and the tourism it has sparked, loosely resembles the travel practices of eighteenth- and nineteenth-century patrons of the Grand Tour, who came to Rome with the intention of seeing first hand the sites about which they had studied and read. Most *Angels & Demons* tourists recognize that the book is fictional and therefore imparts very little factual information about Rome's history, art, or architecture. Like their early modern counterparts, however, they are seeking to illustrate a riveting narrative. This time, it's not the rise and fall of the Roman Empire, but the baroque world of Bernini and the Counter-Reformation, of the Piazza San Pietro and the Piazza Navona, of a seventeenth-century secret society, and a great deal of papal intrigue.

Unlike tourists posing for photos in front of the Trevi Fountain or the Colosseum and then checking the site off their list of must-sees, tourists with *Angels & Demons* in hand engage in a more complex and interactive form of sightseeing. In following the path of the lead characters though Rome, *Angels & Demons* tourists experience the complexities of the Eternal City as they make their way from one murder site to the next. In following the path laid out in the book, their goals are twofold: first, they want to see and experience the locations featured in the book; second, they want to learn more about the sites than can be learned from the descriptions in the book.

Though *Angels & Demons*, travelers may stay in Rome no longer than those who are following the prescriptions of a standard guidebook, they are more engaged with the city and achieve a broader view of Rome's complexities. For example, the first murder takes place in a memorial chapel built for the richest man of the Renaissance, Agostino Chigi, in the church of Santa Maria del Popolo. The Chigi Chapel was initially designed by Raphael, the "wonder boy" of Renaissance painting, and it was completed by the prodigious talent of the baroque era, Gianlorenzo Bernini. Though it is an exquisitely beautiful chapel and it features a very complex and interesting iconographical program, it is unlikely that this chapel would be featured on any top ten list of sites a tourist should see. Those tourists who would venture into the Chigi Chapel might well find themselves daunted by the complex symbols and images featured within it. From references to the Old and New Testaments to the astrological symbols associated with the planets, and from associations with the Pantheon to references to the ancient Roman emperor Augustus, most casual visitors to this chapel find it mute or largely unintelligible.

Of course, Brown's book is a thriller and the action must speed along, so most of the details of the Chigi Chapel are passed over when it becomes the setting of the first murder. Yet Brown introduces his readers to the concept of family memorial chapels and their importance in the culture of sixteenth- and seventeenth-century Rome. And, because the lead characters of the book resolve a small piece of the mystery by undertaking an in-depth examination of some of the chapel's iconographic elements, *Angels & Demons* tourists are inclined to do a similarly careful examination of the chapel's imagery and to consider its meaning and function in relative depth. Brown's text, therefore, provides its readers with a way of entering into a complex artistic site and a means of reaching at least a partial understanding of its aesthetic and cultural significance.

Not only does *Angels & Demons* provide a dramatic medium by which the modern tourist can achieve his or her own understanding of a select group of Rome's complex monuments, the book also introduces the reader-tourist to one of the great sculptors and architects of the seventeenth century, Bernini. In the popular mind, Bernini is often overshadowed by his Renaissance predecessor in the field of sculpture, Michelangelo. Yet Bernini was the foremost proponent of the baroque style in Rome. He was a man of virtually unlimited artistic talent, and he was a charming individual whose savvy understanding of the papal court through which he circulated afforded him commissions from the highest-ranking clergy and nobles in Rome.

All four murders in *Angels & Demons* are staged in churches, piazzas, or fountains designed by Bernini. As Brown portrays the artist, he was a member of the secret society of the Illuminati. This bit of invention within Bernini's biography does not detract from the awe and wonder felt by many tourists when, thanks to their on-site investigation of *Angels & Demons*, they discover the incomparable wonders of Bernini's work, often for the first time. Certainly *Angels & Demons* tourists, while standing in front of Bernini's *St. Teresa in Ecstasy* in the Cornaro Chapel in the church of Santa Maria della Vittoria, are curious to know if Bernini did participate in the Illuminati. But that question quickly fades from the mind and is replaced by other, more important inquiries: "How could one actually depict St. Teresa's moment of ecstasy in cold, hard marble?" and "How can a figure made of stone appear to be weightless, floating, and consumed with fiery passion?" Without a doubt, *Angels & Demons* has won this seventeenth-century artist a host of new, devoted fans that long to know more about his life and work.

Dan Brown has sparked a new kind of interest in Rome. *Angels & Demons* tourists come to the city to explore the "mystic elements," using his thrilling narrative as guide. Their "lofty quest" leads them to discover much more than the identity and affiliations of a murderer bent on correcting the Catholic Church's opinions on scientific advancements. By setting *Angels & Demons* in Rome, Brown has stimulated the intellectual curiosity of a large number of Rome's visitors and has provided them with a map by which to explore some of the city's greatest artistic treasures.

6: THE SCIENCE AND TECHNOLOGY OF *ANGELS & DEMONS*

The world's top CSI unit investigates the murder and mayhem of Angels & Demons • *What your ophthalmologist may not know about a ripped-out eyeball; will it pass the retina scan identification test?* • *If birds fly, then why, oh why, can't Robert Langdon?* • *What science has learned about cosmology since the days of Galileo* • *Antimatter: science fission* • *Untangling entanglement*

DEATH COMES TO THE CARDINALS: A FORENSICS EXPERT ON MURDER, MAYHEM, AND SURVIVAL

AN INTERVIEW WITH CYRIL H. WECHT

Death plays a major role in Angels & Demons, *and it comes in fairly gruesome forms, from drowning to punctured lungs to—most graphic of all—the cutting out of scientist Leonardo Vetra's eyeball before his neck is broken and his head twisted completely around. Vivid as the deaths are, how accurate is each? Renowned Allegheny County coroner and forensic expert Cyril H. Wecht gives high marks to Brown for the accuracy of most of the deaths and near escapes over the course of* Angels & Demons' *twenty-four-hour killing spree. He faults only two crucial scenes: Langdon's simulated drowning in the fountain of the Piazza Navona at the hands of the Hassassin and, later, his fall through the Roman night from the helicopter, holding on to a two-by-four-yard windshield tarp as the energy waves from the exploding antimatter hit him. Although answered succinctly, his conclusion on the question of whether a "dead" eye can still be used to fool a retina scanner is the same as the more detailed analysis of this problem elsewhere in this chapter.*

Over his long career, Dr. Wecht has performed fifteen thousand autopsies and been called in on another thirty-five thousand cases of suspicious death here and abroad. He has written over 475 professional publications and is the editor of thirty-five books.

One of America's leading forensic experts, Cyril H. Wecht is coroner of Allegheny County in Pittsburgh, Pennsylvania, and chairman of the advisory board of the Cyril H. Wecht Institute of Forensic Science and Law at Duquesne University School of Law.

In Angels & Demons, *scientist Leonardo Vetra's eye is cut out before his death so that it can be used to verify identity in a retinal scan. Is an eye cut out of the skull of a victim in this way "alive" enough to be used like this?*

When the eye is cut out and obviously deprived of vascular supply, degenerative changes would begin to occur quickly. The retina would be quite sensitive to the lack of arterial supply of oxygen. In my opinion it would not remain "alive" enough to function as a key for retina scans. I don't believe that anybody has ever done this kind of research, however, with the possible exception, perhaps, of some of our "spook agencies."

Retinal scanning analyzes the layer of blood vessels at the back of the eye. Scanning involves using a low-intensity light source and an optical coupler, and can read the patterns at a great level of accuracy. It requires the user to remove his glasses, place his eye close to the device, and focus on a certain point. The user looks through a small opening in the device at a small green light. This process takes about ten to fifteen seconds total.

There is no known way to replicate a retina, and a retina from a dead person would deteriorate too fast to be useful, so no extra precautions have been taken with retinal scans to be sure the user is a living human being.

Is it possible to twist a victim's head 180 degrees so the head looks behind him, which the Hassassin supposedly does to Leonardo Vetra?

Twisting the head—no. Remember, the head remains upright because of the vertebral column, the bony vertebrae as well as the muscles, tendons, and ligaments. You couldn't have a lot of soft-tissue damage and still have the head remain stable. You'd be twisting the various bundles of muscles that are present on the neck laterally, anteriorly, posteriorly. That, in my opinion, would be absolutely impossible. I don't mean it would be twisted off, but it would plop down.

The body is lying on the floor. Could it happen in that position?

Well, if it were lying on the floor, that would make a difference. But I've never seen a head turned 180 degrees. I've seen heads markedly twisted and torn to the side and so on, but not 180 degrees.

In Angels & Demons, *four cardinals are attacked and branded, but die by other means. Would a person die of burns, shock, or a heart attack from being branded with a red-hot ambigram-headed poker on the chest?*

If someone has a very bad heart condition, any kind of stress, including being burned, could precipitate cardiac arrhythmia, abnormal beating of the heart, and death due to what is generically referred to as a heart attack. But absent somebody who has a severe heart disease with severely compromised coronary arteries, being branded is no different than being severely burned.

People don't just die because they're burnt. Many recover, some even with burns of over 50 percent of the body. They recover and then live for days or weeks or months.

In the prologue to Angels & Demons, *Leonard Vetra is described as "drifting toward unconsciousness" after he's branded. Is it going to cause so much pain that the victim becomes unconscious?*
Some people could become unconscious. Others would not. When you talk about consciousness, there is no way to predict that. Some people faint easily and readily. Some people can't stand any kind of pain. There are great variables which are quite unpredictable.

That's interesting, because of the four victims who are branded, some last a lot longer than others. And then one, the bad guy, Cardinal Carlo Ventresca, runs around, jumps in a helicopter and leads everyone on a chase through the catacombs after having been branded.
You could do that. You could have a severe burn and remain conscious. If you could withstand pain and you have a strong enough desire, motivation, and so on, you could remain conscious and continue to think, move, and be functional. That's why people who get burned keep fighting their way out of a burning house or a flaming car—they want to survive, right? They've got more severe burns than being branded on the chest.

Consciousness is a very, very variable factor. There's no way to predict that. Some people just look at blood and they faint. Other people can withstand tremendous pain and not pass out. But what I'm saying is you are not going to die from being branded on the chest.

In the novel, the pope is poisoned with Heparin, a powerful anticoagulant that he takes for his thrombophlebitis. Is that plausible? And would a person's oral mucous bleed so much after taking Heparin that his or her tongue would turn black?
Well, it wouldn't be referred to as "poisoning" in its broadest sense.

Why?
You can talk about it that way, but it's not truly a toxic reaction. Heparin is an anticoagulant administered intravenously to people who have to be anticoagulated quickly, who have a blood clot. The answer is it could certainly cause a lot of bleeding, but as far as turning the tongue black, there's no reason why the tongue would turn black as a result of any direct effect on the tongue muscle.

Now, bleeding could cause hemorrhage underneath the skin. The blood could then coat the tongue and as it dries, it becomes a dark, reddish brown color; after a while it gets caked and somebody might say it is black. Careful here.

Dan Brown says clearly that the pope has a "tongue black as death" when his sarcophagus is opened.
The blood cakes, it dries, it becomes oxidized. Instead of being red, it starts to assume a darker color and somebody might say, "Well, it's blackened."

Another strange forensic point here on the subject of Heparin. The Vatican doesn't discover this crime because papal law states that popes cannot be autopsied. Do you happen to know if that's true?
I don't know specifically about the pope. I've done autopsies on nuns and priests over the years and I've worked in Catholic hospitals. It's not against their religion. But I can't tell you about the pope. I guess perhaps they don't want to desecrate the body; he's considered to be the vicar of Christ on earth.

In one of the climactic moments of the book, Robert Langdon survives a fall from a helicopter while it's exploding above Rome by using a two-by-four-yard windshield tarp as a parachute. Is that possible?
In my opinion it is extremely unlikely that that could be done. Not unless you had very special winds. Also, it would vary greatly as to where the fall occurs.

Even if you did survive, is that enough to prevent your landing without breaking most of your bones?'
I'd say no, if the person is going to be landing on a hard surface. If the person lands on a very soft surface, if the fall is not from a very great height, if the tarp does catch the wind in such a way as to slow things down dramatically, I can't say it's impossible to land in such a way as to not break bones. But I think it would be highly unlikely.

Langdon is described as landing in the river, in which the water is "raging," "frothy and air-filled," and "three times softer than standing water." Is it true that moving water might soften the fall?
It's a matter, so to speak, of the density of the water. Raging, foamy water contains a lot of air. Hence, it would be much softer than a flat, nonfoamy water surface.

What's the largest fall from which you have ever known anyone to survive—a fall of a thousand feet or a mile or two without a parachute?
It wasn't a case of mine, but a long time ago I remember a stewardess fell from a plane in Yugoslavia, I think it was, into a snow bank and survived [a fall of] thousands of feet.

In Angels & Demons, *the helicopter is supposedly a couple of miles above the earth. Could a person survive a fall of that height?*
A couple of miles? Well, that I have grave doubts about. If it's a couple of miles up, you are talking over ten thousand feet. And here I do not believe you would likely survive. And I don't believe you would land without breaking your bones.

My other question regarding a fall from, say, five thousand to ten thousand feet is, can you remain lucid?
You could remain lucid. Don't forget that people parachute and they remain conscious.

Is it likely that some kind of protective mechanism would kick in? In the novel, Langdon maneuvers himself over the Tiber by jerking the tarp, and you are led to believe he has enough presence of mind to improve his chances and save himself.
There again, it's a subjective thing.

A question about blood. Later in the novel, in an important scene in which the camerlengo brands himself and the guards shoot both Maximilian Kohler and Captain Rocher, Rocher falls on the tile floor face-first. Brown writes that he "slid lifeless through his own blood." Can you slide through blood like that?
The answer is that it's possible. Blood is very slippery. An adult man has about five to six liters of blood depending on his size, about 5,000 to 6,000 cc's. You could loose 20 to 25 percent without becoming unconscious. So if you lost 1,000 cc's of blood, which equals a quart, could you then slip and slide in that blood? Sure you could. Particularly if it's on a smooth surface. If the blood is absorbed by earth, or absorbed by cracks and crevices, no. But if you've got a smooth floor of wood or tile, you could certainly slip and slide in your own blood.

There is a scene in the book in which the hero is pressed under water in the Piazza Navona fountain in Rome by the Hassassin. And he stays under a fair bit because he is a swimmer and can hold his breath. Then he fakes death by imitating rigor for five seconds, a second longer than the Hassassin believes rigor lasts, and, finally, he sinks. Wouldn't the body, if it were dead, float up to the surface of the fountain instead?
You don't float up right away. When you are dead, the body goes down toward the bottom. It doesn't float up until gases begin to form when the body undergoes decomposition. Sometimes bodies remain under water for very long periods of time.

How long can someone stay under water holding his breath?
People can hold their breath if they are accomplished swimmers, especially if they do it with some conscious awareness and planning, for two minutes or more. Pearl divers can hold their breath for three to four minutes. They train themselves. Their lungs have expanded and they breathe heavily and deeply to build up the reserve volume of their lungs.

Could a person imitate rigor? Is that possible?
First of all, you don't go into rigor just because you are dead. You don't go into rigor spontaneously.

There is no such thing?

You aren't going to go into rigor just because you drown. And you are not going to drown in six seconds. Even if you become unconscious, and that would take fifteen to thirty seconds depending upon your state of health and other factors, and then you do become unconscious; you are not dead. You only develop rigor mortis after you die.

Rigor mortis, by definition, is a process of death. And rigor mortis doesn't usually set in for a minimum of an hour, usually two hours.

In another death scene, there is a cardinal who dies because the Hassassin punctures his lungs on either side of his chest. There are two small holes underneath the breast bone, and when Langdon gives him CPR, the punctures spray blood "into the air like blowholes on a whale, and hit him in the face."

You can inject needles or make stab wounds with something like an ice pick that would go in and perforate the lungs and cause the air to escape as the lungs collapse. That's a condition called pneumothorax—air in the chest cavity—the result of the collapsing of the lungs or a portion of them collapsing.

So something sharp, like a stiletto or an ice pick, could puncture the lungs and you could get some bleeding. And if they were larger stab wounds, then you could have more blood expressed. And the larger stab wounds would also cause more damage to the lungs.

So yes, you could have perforating stab wounds into the lungs, causing the lungs to collapse, producing pneumothorax. This person can't breath in, doesn't get good respiratory activity. And it's possible that when you have the chest compressed for purposes of resuscitation, some blood could be pushed out through those stab wounds.

Another question that concerns breathing. Robert Langdon is in the Vatican's Secret Archives at one point, which are hermetic, and which I take it don't have a lot of oxygen. Here's the description: "Langdon prepared his body for the physical shock that always accompanied the first few seconds in a hermetic vault. Entering a sealed archive was like going from sea level to twenty thousand feet in an instant. Nausea and light-headedness are not uncommon."

So he fights a gag reflex and relaxes his chest while his pulmonary capillaries dilate. The tightness passes and he's gratified that his fifty laps of swimming a day are good for something. Is that all correct?

You can relax your chest by breathing more slowly. I think maybe what he is saying is that Langdon breathes in deeply in preparation for this and gets in more oxygen.

At one point, somebody tries to kill Langdon by turning off the reoxygenation system. Is that plausible?

Obviously, if you have something that is hermetically sealed, and somebody mechanically obstructs the oxygen supply, you're going to be deprived of oxygen. That's, to a greater degree, what happens when you go up to a high altitude. It's the diminution of oxygen in the atmosphere that affects you. So what he is describing is correct. If you were to analogize it, from zero to twenty thousand feet very quickly, that's what he's describing.

And if somebody cuts off air in some way and the person is deprived of oxygen, they could become sick, including becoming nauseated. That's true.

Could it kill you after a while?

If it were dramatic enough, it would kill you because of the deprivation of oxygen. Anytime you are deprived of oxygen, you might be asphyxiated.

And the converse, the description of what happens after he figures out how to escape—he is outside breathing in fresh air that "feels like a drug and the purple spots in his vision fade"—is that correct? The purple spots?

I can't tell you the color. You might have some spots in your eyes and as they begin to clear up, then everything improves, so that's possible. Sure.

A final question, this one about the cardinal burnt to death suspended above a pyre of burning pews in a church. Would that be a quick death?

The answer is no. I can't tell you how fast this death would occur, but I will tell you this: a person will not die immediately. There is going to be a tremendous amount of pain and suffering. You are going to die of dehydration and shock. The body loses water, and you are going to die of shock associated with electrolyte imbalance as fluid is being lost and your electrolytes, like sodium and potassium, go out of whack. How fast depends on the intensity of the fire.

In the old days, both Catholics and Protestants had three methods of burning at the stake. In Nordic countries, the victim was tied to a ladder and, in fact, the law required they be strangled before being burned because of the tremendous amount of pain and so on. Burning at the stake began to fall out of favor in the eighteenth century because it was not considered a humane punishment.

EYEBALL TO EYEBALL: THE USE OF BIOMETRICS IN *ANGELS & DEMONS*

BY JAMES CARLISLE AND JENNIFER CARLISLE

Like any good writer of this genre, Dan Brown has provided enough mayhem in his twenty-four-hour day to keep crime labs, coroners, and investigators very busy. A drugged pope, horrifying deaths by branding iron, midair explosions, and, most gruesome of all, the murder of Leonardo Vetra by the hassassin, who rips out one Vetra's eyes to to gain access to the highly secret lab and steal a canister of antimatter.

This act, pivotal to the book's plot, is based on a single striking assumption, that a "dead" eyeball can trick an optical scanner into believing that it's still attached to the original owner, allowing a criminal access to an otherwise secure room or building. Can that be true? To find out, we turned to Dr. James Carlisle and (appropriately paralleling the two Vetras) his daughter Jennifer Carlisle, who are expert in biometrics, the science of recognizing a person based on a physiological or behavioral characteristic. The biometrics industry is developing an extensive array of personal identity verification technology to scan faces, fingerprints, hand geometry, handwriting, voices, veins, irises, and—most relevant to Angels & Demons *—retinas.*

The Carlisles have provided a sampling of references to the reader who wishes to dig deeper into biometrics. A preview of the newest retinal-scanning products from Retica Systems, complete with a

James Carlisle is a managing partner of Greystone Capital Advisors, a scientist, and a serial entrepreneur. Jennifer Carlisle is also an expert in biometrics, international security, and economics and has her own company, Anzen Research.

fascinating video can be found on the Web at www.retinaltech.com/technology.html. For a tutorial on biometric identification technologies and an exhaustive compendium of biometrics in the movies, visit the French site perso.wanadoo.fr/fingerchip/biometrics/movies.htm. Some of the most advanced research in the field is conducted by Ultrafast and NanoScale Optics Group at the University of California San Diego; kfir.ucsd.edu/Research/Eye/eye.shtml. A leading expert in biometrics, Ravi Das, has published a helpful tutorial paper at www.technologyexecutivesclub.com/retinalrecognition2.htm.

 The following essay, done in the style of a briefing paper, left us wondering whether to cringe or laugh at the outrageous details of the travails of poor Leonardo Vetra's eyeball.

Retinal scanning is an exact science, offering an extremely secure means of verifying the identity of a person. Dr. Leonardo Vetra selected this technology for the access control system to protect both his underground laboratory and the sublaboratory in which the antimatter samples were stored. The biometric access control system had been trained to recognize only two people, Dr. Vetra and his daughter, Vittoria. At the time Dr. Vetra was murdered and branded with the Illuminati ambigram, the assassin removed one of Dr. Vetra's eyeballs. The detached eyeball was taken from Dr. Vetra's apartment to the secret laboratory, where it was used first to unlock the doors to the main laboratory and subsequently to gain access to the subbasement hazardous materials lab.

QUESTIONS

This scenario is horrific to say the least. But is it plausible? Did Dan Brown stretch the facts of science and physiology to achieve a dramatic effect? Can a disembodied eyeball be used to open a door protected by a retinal scanner? Wouldn't blood drain out of the eyeball and wouldn't the retina detach, thus rendering it unreadable by the scanner? Could steps have been taken at the time the eye was detached to preserve the retina's scanability? Could a detached eyeball be properly aligned in the scanner to permit accurate recognition? Why was this particular biometric technology chosen by Dr. Vetra (i.e., by Dan Brown) over other options? If the lab held such potentially devastating material, why not use multiple biometric identification methods? Is this scenario any more far-fetched than use of eye-scanning biometrics in other books and movies?

BACKGROUND

Experts seem to be divided on whether a disembodied eyeball would retain its characteristic morphology of blood vessels sufficiently to match a "retinal signature" stored in a biometric scanner. Biometrics manufacturers insist that this is impossible. Ophthalmologists, pathologists, and government security experts interviewed specifically for this analysis were more sanguine, although no one admits to actually having tested this scenario. Film directors and special effects consultants not only believe that retinal scanners can be fooled, they have incorporated such deception into several movies in recent years.

To appreciate these differences in opinion, it is helpful to consider how this biometric identification technique works. Retinal identification technology is based on the fact that no two persons have the same retinal vasculature pattern. In 1935 Dr. Carleton Simon and Dr. Isadore Goldstein, while studying eye disease, made a startling discovery: every eye has its own totally unique pattern of blood vessels. Even identical twins have different patterns. Unlike fingerprints and facial recognition, the retinal patterns do not change over the life of a person, unless they get cataracts.

The retina, a thin layer of nerve tissue (one-fiftieth of an inch) on the back of the eye, senses light and transmits impulses through the optic nerve to the brain—the equivalent of film or the digital imaging chip in a camera. Blood vessels used for biometric identification are located along the neural retina, the outermost of the retina's four cell layers.

The overall recognition process took about ten to fifteen seconds at the time *Angels & Demons* was written. Today's technology takes under three seconds to verify a retinal signature. Retinal-scanning devices read through the pupil, which requires the user to situate his or her eye within half an inch of the capture device and to hold still while the reader ascertains the patterns. The user looks at a rotating green light as the patterns of the retina are measured at over four hundred points. By comparison, a fingerprint may only provide thirty to forty distinctive points (minutia) to be used in the enrollment, template creation, and verification process. Retinal scanning has the highest level of accuracy in comparison to all other biometrics.

Retinal scanning has been used almost exclusively in high-end security applications for controlling access to areas or rooms in military installations and power plants that are considered high-risk security areas.

Dr. Vetra most likely installed the EyeDentify ICAM 2001 in his labs. This was the most accurate biometric identification system available at the time of this story. None of the experts interviewed at the NSA, CIA, and DoD knew of any other retinal-scanning product available prior to 2001. The reliability of the EyeDentify scanners was 100 percent. The installation manual claims that, in over five hundred field trials, no false acceptance has ever been reported.

While Dan Brown did select the best access control technology, his Dr. Vetra failed to utilize the full security capability of the product. Brown writes (on page 64) that "Vittoria stepped up to the device and carefully aligned her right eye with a protruding lens that looked like a telescope. Then she pressed a button." The ICAM 2001 does have a short protruding lens, but it also has a keypad for entering a personal identification number plus a card reader. Had Dr. Vetra left the ICAM in the "Verify Mode," he might literally be alive today, since it is unlikely that any amount of torture would have forced him to surrender his personal identification code and the eyeball would have been useless without it. However, in the "Recognition Mode" no personal ID number is required.

Surprisingly, in 2004 there are no commercial (i.e., nonclassified) retinal-scanning products on the market. In commercial applications, such as airport, building, and data center security, there has been strong user resistance to retinal scanners. Less intrusive, albeit also less reliable, iris scanners and facial recognition have replaced them in the marketplace.

But the demand for the ultimate biometric identifier is driving new retinal scanner breakthroughs. The Ultrafast and NanoScale Optics Group, which is conducting research at UC San Diego, is using microscopic MEMS mirrors to greatly reduce the size and cost of retinal scanners. [MEMS is the acronym for Micro-Electro-Mechanical Systems, referring to the integration of mechanical elements, sensors, actuators, and electronics on a silicon substrate through microfabrication technology.]

In the future, retinal scanning could be used to verify the identity of pilots, automobile drivers, even PC users. Of course, the most significant and to some the most terrifying application of biometrics and retinal scanning in particular is the "National Identity Card." With falling prices and post-9/11 fears, this is ever closer to becoming a reality. For such an application, 100% accuracy is of paramount importance and the risk of tricking the verification systems of great concern.

Retica Systems, a manufacturer, is launching a new line of retinal-scanning products in 2005, which will work faster and cost far less than the EyeDentify products. Employing a small, handheld scanner, Retica uses a patented aspheric lens array that can capture a retinal image at distances as great as a meter from the user's eye. Unlike prior retinal scanners, Retica's product can scan through glasses, contact lenses, and even cataracts. Dr. David Muller, CEO of Retica, assured me that there is no way any retinal scanner could be fooled by using the eyeball of a dead person.

ANALYSIS

Senior technologists in the US Department of Defense and some doctors disagree. They argue that, while it is plausible for a detached eyeball to be used with a retinal scanner to verify the holder's identity, the killer would have to know what he was doing, as one small slip would render the eyeball useless.

If the eyes were gouged out with fingers or with an instrument such as ice tongs, then the optic nerve would be severed, blood would quickly drain out, and the vessels would collapse. This would substantially reduce the contrast of the vascular pattern against the white background. However, medical experts insist that the blood vessels would still be visible to a retinal scanner even after death, even if the blood drained from the eye, as some residue would be left.

The primary problem with Dan Brown's scenario is that, with an older person, the retina would detach soon after the heart stopped beating. The retina is held to the back of the eye wall by a combination of forces, including an active metabolic process that begins to break down after death. The retina spontaneously detaches a few hours after death. A retinal detachment would destroy the normal architecture of the blood vessels and certainly disrupt a biometric scan.

To appreciate how easily damage may be caused by detachment, think of the retina as a thin piece of tissue paper lining the inside of a sink filled with water. When the water is disturbed, the tissue will detach from the surface of the sink. In a very young person, the vitreous gel is almost solid and might preserve the retinal architecture longer than in an older person. Dr. Vetra was old enough that the assassin would have had to bring the eye to the lab within minutes after the murder.

The best way to preserve the retinal pattern after death is to cut the eyeball surgically, a process called *enucleation*. There are four muscles to be cut, after which the optic nerve must be carefully sliced. In the book, there is no evidence that the assassin had any surgical training or took special care in removing the eyeball. (Kohler does refer to the act as one of "surgical" removal, but Langdon only uses words such as "tattered," "random mutilation," "defacement" [p. 48]. If this had been done, then preservation of the retinal pattern might be possible. Blood would drain from the veins, but detachment would be delayed.

Medically, there should not have been pools of blood next to the two retinal scanners in Dr. Vetra's labs. The actual volume of blood inside the eyeball is minute, so most of the blood would come from the eye socket. There would have been a small pool of blood (several tablespoons) next to the body, as the eye socket would bleed a lot if the eye were cut out while the person was still alive. It would ooze very little (less than a teaspoon) if cut out after death. When eyes are enucleated postmortem, they don't bleed much. As soon as the heart stops, the blood almost immediately drains from the retinal veins back into the body. One way to explain the blood on the floor near the retinal scanners is that it may have come from the eye socket at the time of enucleation and been captured in the container used to transport the eyeball. Rather than draining out of the eyeball, it may have been used to cradle or protect the eyeball within the transport container.

One other problem with doing a postmortem scan would be focusing the eyes on the light source inside the scanner. While less important in the newest generation of retinal scanners, it was necessary to focus the eye for several seconds when using the ICAM 2001, the scanner in use at the time the book was written. The assassin could have positioned the eye manually and hoped for the best, trying different positions until a successful scan was achieved.

Venturing far into the realm of conjecture, it might be possible to photograph the living retina of someone and then paste the photograph into a plastic sphere to simulate an eye. Doctors use a little white rubber synthetic eyeball to teach residents how to examine the retina. It has fake blood vessels painted on the inside and the optics of the lens and cornea are designed to simulate the real thing. The image could be printed onto the inside of a white ball, using orthographic projection software for spherical adjustment. Although this has apparently never been done, such a photograph might fool a scanner.

Alternatively, the image could be printed on a flat piece of paper and placed a specific distance in front of the scanner lens. Retinal scanners are not stereoscopic, so they generate a flat image.

The use of photographs and synthetic eyeballs has two drawbacks. First, biometric vendors deny its feasibility. Second, it is not nearly as gory and disgusting as the scenario in Dan Brown's story. The assassin is meant to be ruthless and brutal, not clever and educated.

RETINAL SCANNING IN THE MOVIES

However loose with the science and technology of biometric identification Dan Brown may have been, he was not as wild as some highly respected film directors. For example, in *Minority Report*, the futuristic movie directed in 2002 by Stephen Spielberg, the character played by Tom Cruise undergoes a voluntary enucleation, having his own eyeballs replaced with those of a stranger, in order to escape detection by the "Eyedentiscan" retinal scanners which are abundantly located throughout the city.

Spielberg stretches science in many ways. For example, Cruise keeps his eyeballs (which mark him as a fugitive) in a plastic bag for later use to open doors to top-secret government facilities. They still work after several weeks, when his wife uses one of his eyeballs to break into the prison where Cruise is being held. All of the doctors I spoke with insist that it is impossible that the blood vessels in the retina would retain their structure and not detach or be distorted over such a long period. Since Cruise's character is a young man, his retina might not have detached for a few hours after the operation, but he has to wait many hours for his transplanted eyes to heal. When Cruise drops the plastic bag and chases his eyeball as it bounces down a long hallway, the retina would certainly detach and render a retinal scan impossible. But *Minority Report* gets kudos for anticipating the next generation of products, in the near future, when portable, handheld retinal scanners will work through eyeglasses and surveillance scanners will work at a considerable distance, to track people and to direct personalized ads to them while they walk about.

Many films have shown retinal scanning realistically. In *Star Trek II: The Wrath of Kahn* (1982), retinal recognition is used to open the Genesis Project file. In the James Bond film *Never Say Never Again* (1983) an eyeball replacement is used to access a nuclear weapon. In *Demolition Man* (1993) the warden accesses the cryojail through retinal scan identification, but then Wesley Snipes removes the warden's eyeball and uses it to escape. This scenario is similar to the one in *Angels & Demons*, but the time between detachment and use in the scanner was so short that, according to several doctors I spoke with, it probably would work. In the James Bond film *GoldenEye* (1995), a retinal scan is used to access MI6 offices.

Presumably the CIA should know how to use biometric identification. In the 1996 movie *Mission: Impossible*, Tom Cruise and friends break into a computer room at the CIA's Langley Headquarters which is protected, not only by retinal scan, voice-print, six-digit code, and an electric key card, but also by voice, temperature, and pressure gauges within the deserted room. Cruise bypasses all these devices, avoiding a laser beam grid installed in the ceiling vent by a system of mirrors, and the pressure-sensitive alarm system built into the floor by the use of a harness system.

Entrapment (1999) contains the most unrealistic means of faking a retinal scan, but since it is done by Catherine Zeta-Jones, who cares? When the chairman of a bank is maced on the street, he goes to an eye doctor for an exam. They do a retinal scan and from that record Catherine captures a fake image of his retina into a portable machine which projects this digital image into the retinal scanner. This is absurd. The image they show at the doctor's office is an analog graph, not even a photograph which might have been printed into an eyeball. Even if the ophthalmologist had captured the digital signature representing the vasculature of the retina in the exact format used to train the retinal scanner, there is no way to input that signature through the lens of the scanner at the door.

In *Bad Company* (2002) the director dispenses with the lens altogether. The CIA encodes Chris Rock's retina in the bomb code that protects a nuclear suitcase bomb. The terrorists capture Rock and somehow scan his eye using only the screen of the laptop—not a retinal scanning lens in sight. The plot, if you can call it that, requires that Rock be looking at the computer screen while they are scanning his retina, so he can memorize a long sequence of numbers.

In comparison with these film directors, Dan Brown's use of retinal scanning biometrics is not so far-fetched. Nevertheless, it is intriguing that there was no consensus among the experts interviewed for this chapter about the feasibility of using an enucleated eyeball. Almost all other biometric identification techniques are susceptible to forgeries and trickery. Fingers and hands can be cut off, fingerprints can be molded onto fake fingers, an iris can be copied onto a contact lens, voiceprints and signatures can be copied, but no two retinas are alike and the challenge in tricking a retinal scanner is enormous.

THE EYE THEME

The choice of retinal scanning as the biometric protection for the laboratory fits nicely within Dan Brown's recurring theme of eyes. Langdon lectures Vittoria about the origin of the Great Seal on the US dollar bill. He states that the "all-seeing eye" above the pyramid is a well-known Illuminati symbol called the Shining Delta. The eye signifies the Illuminati's "all-seeing" infiltration of government and community, floating

above a pyramid. How appropriate then that an eye should open the door to a source
of unimaginable energy and destruction.

As Maxmilian Kohler, director of CERN tells our Harvard professor early in the
book, "Mr. Langdon, believe me, that missing eye does indeed serve a higher purpose . . .
a much higher purpose."

THE TECHNOLOGY TOYS OF
ANGELS & DEMONS

BY DAVID A. SHUGARTS

From Jules Verne to Ian Fleming, from Tom Clancy to Michael Crichton, popular authors have woven technology into their novels by closely studying the science of their times, and then projecting the techno trends into the near or distant future. A thread that ties all these authors together is a foundation of scientific accuracy. Their dirigibles are reliably tethered.

Dan Brown is not always that kind of writer. While there are occasional flirtations with true technology, most of the scientific references and assertions in *Angels & Demons* are blithely disconnected from fact. Science-wise, the book is more like an untethered, hot air balloon. *A&D* introduces concepts such as the sizable production of antimatter in the famed Large Hadron Collider (LHC), the hypersonic transportation of people in an "X-33 prototype," a bunch of minor technical marvels and weapons, and a spectacular antimatter explosion just after the hero jumps out of a helicopter. This commentary surveys the science and technology introduced in *Angels & Demons* to figure out just where Dan Brown is talking about something real and of interest, and where he is using sci-tech simply to sound cool while moving his plot forward.

David A. Shugarts is a journalist of more than thirty years' experience. He has written extensively on aviation and technology-related subjects.

INSIDE CERN

CERN is a real world-class research facility based in Switzerland, just as Dan Brown says.

During the early days before eleven original member European countries founded the formal organization, they had formed a provisional group, the Conseil Européene pour la Recherche Nucléaire (CERN). Headquartered in Geneva, CERN has grown to twenty member countries, all from Europe, along with some eight "observer" countries, such as India and Japan. The United States joined as an observer in 1997.

Tim Berners-Lee, a British scientist at CERN in the early 1990s, is, in fact, widely considered to be the key individual who helped the World Wide Web come into being, just as Dan Brown notes in *Angels & Demons*.

Dan Brown, finishing up his research on *Angels & Demons* sometime before its publication date in the year 2000, would have learned by digging that the Large Hadron Collider, his centerpiece antimatter production machine, had not yet been built. It is still not completed. The current hoped-for completion date is 2007.

In fact, the construction of the big ring of the LHC relied on dismantling the previous giant machine, the Large Electron-Positron collider (usually called LEP for short), because the big 27-kilometer tunnel will be re-used. But the LEP was still going strong until late in 2000, searching for hints of the elusive Higgs particle.

In *Angels & Demons*, Dan Brown has Vittoria Vetra describe the method that her father used to (recently, it is assumed) "recreate the big bang." It relies on accelerating particles in two streams going in opposite directions around a ring.

It appears that Dan Brown was hoping to make this seem like a revelation of a deep secret, but, in fact, this description loosely applies to practically all the circular colliders that have ever been built, for about seventy-five years now. It is no secret at all. The basic idea of the circular acceleration of particles was a 1929 invention of Ernest O. Lawrence, a Berkeley professor.

Getting particles to collide at high energy is complex. In the CERN equipment this requires various stages of generating, accelerating, and passing the particle stream on to the next acceleration device. Eventually, particles collide and in turn produce other particles, or energy, or both. The next step, detecting exactly what happened, becomes a huge challenge all by itself. It requires cutting-edge techniques to detect the tiny amounts of matter and energy (and antimatter) produced, and this process often gobbles up huge computing resources.

Due to budget constraints, CERN itself is somewhat preoccupied with building and operating the hugely expensive LEP and LHC, the machines that achieve the collisions. So the detection end of the operation has been handed over to a wide range of scientific organizations, universities, and corporations. Teams of scientists arrive from all over the world, set up their equipment, and begin gathering data from collisions. Sometimes the results are seen quickly, and other times it requires long months and years of data analysis to learn answers.

Scientific teams are often 300 or 500 strong—and sometimes as many as 1,700. The atmosphere is very international, with "broken English" said to be the semi-official language. At any given time, there may be 3,000 to 5,000 scientists and technicians working at CERN. According to various loose estimates, in a given year around half of the world's 13,000 particle physicists have some connection with CERN.

CERN was originally founded as somewhat of a reaction to the drain of physicists lured to the United States, where some major laboratories dominated the field of particle physics, most notably the Brookhaven National Laboratory in Long Island, New York, and later, Fermilab, near Chicago. The race to build ever-more-powerful colliders—and thus atttract the best scientists—was a contest until the United States failed to pay the ante about twenty years ago.

In the 1970s Brookhaven was building a large collider but had run into some problems. CERN then surged ahead, discovering the boson particle in 1983 and getting ready to build the LEP. This led the United States to make plans for "bigger and better research facilities." CERN's big ring for the next-generation LEP would be 27 kilometers in diameter, located 100 meters below the surface at Geneva, and it was built by 1989. American scientists set out to build the mother of all colliders, the "Superconducting Super Collider," a vast 87-kilometer underground ring. This facility was $2 billion along in a $10 billion construction program at Waxahachie, Texas, when a belt-tightening Congress pulled the plug in 1993. Most tales of CERN and its world-class rivalries rely on the story of the competition between Europeans and Americans building giant colliders, rather than CERN versus the Vatican.

By becoming a CERN observer country in 1997 and sending about $500 million across the pond—not to mention large teams of American scientists—the United States has more or less conceded the race to the Europeans, although some world-class work continues to be done at Brookhaven and Fermilab. For instance, Fermilab, since 1985, has been creating antiprotons—over 2.3 nanograms to date, more than any other facility in the world. But if a scientific team wants to use the biggest collider, it must travel to CERN.

CANISTERS OF ANTIMATTER

The scientists Vetra, father and daughter, in their clandestine lab at CERN, manage to manufacture what would have to be called phenomenal quantities of antimattter. They then store the antimatter in canisters with "airtight nanocomposite shells." This is pseudo-techno-babble. Nothing specific is to be gained from "nanocomposite" shells. In both *Angels & Demons* as well as *The Da Vinci Code*, Dan Brown adds the prefix *nano* (presumably a gratuitous allusion to nanotechnology) to technical words in a way to make them sound cooler or more leading edge. Vittoria's basic "gimmick" is to suspend the antimattter between two electromagnets. The only known attempt to build a "portable" antimatter container was an experiment at Pennsylvania State University that produced a unit that couldn't be carried under a Hassassin's arm. The container weighed about 130 pounds, was about 39 inches tall and 13 inches in diameter. While it is true that strong magnets were part of the "gimmick" of suspending the anit-protons, the technique was also dependent on a charge of liquid helium and liquid nitrogen.

VATICAN WEAPONS

Dan Brown has the Swiss Guards—the defenders of Vatican security—armed with "the traditional 'Vatican long sword'—an eight-foot spear with a razor-sharp scythe." He is mistaken; these long ceremonial weapons are called halberds.

When the Swiss Guards sally forth into Rome, they drive in four unmarked "Alfa Romeo 155 T-Sparks." The Alfa Romeo 155 began production in 1992, but a splash was made with the 1995 model and the "T-Spark" engine, as it came to be nicknamed. The Twin Spark (Cuore Sportivo) engine was a 2.0-liter, 16-valve engine with two spark plugs per cylinder. It yields 90 percent of its torque within the first 2,000 rpm.

The Swiss Guards of *Angels & Demons* are armed with "Cherchi-Pardini semi-automatics, local-radius nerve gas canisters, and long-range stun guns." In fact, while Pardini pistols are prized as Olympic competition target pistols, they would never be used as a police sidearm. We do not know the reason why Dan Brown glued the word *Cherchi* on the name. The pistols actually used by the Swiss Guards are SIG 9 mm, well suited to security forces and known as the sidearm of the US Navy SEALS, among many others.

There is no such thing as a "local-radius nerve gas canister" and nothing like this is in use by police forces. The "long-range stun gun" is a contradiction in terms. The most famous of "stun guns" is the Taser, which has a range of about twenty-one feet. There are some tentative concepts for longer-range electric shock weapons of the same general type, but the power requirement alone would dictate a vehicle-mounted gun, not a handheld weapon.

VAULTED SECRETS

Vittoria and Langdon visit the Vatican Secret Archives. Langdon describes the special atmosphere of the "hermetic vault." It has a "partial vacuum" in order to reduce the oxygen level, he says. It has only 8 percent humidity. It is "like going from sea level to 20,000 feet in an instant" when one steps inside. "Nausea and light-headedness were not uncommon."

Libraries that have archives for rare books are lucky when they have rooms with temperature and humidity control. They do not have hermetically sealed vaults.

To the degree Dan Brown wants us to believe the fiction that the Vatican keeps its prized antique documents in hermetically sealed vaults, there are some inherent contradictions in his description. First and foremost, if the goal is to reduce the oxygen content of a space, setting up a vacuum is a poor way to do it. The composition of air does not change, so oxygen is still about 21 percent of the mixture. But if we take Langdon's 20,000 feet literally, this means an air pressure of about 6.75 pounds per square inch (psi) inside the chamber, and 14.7 psi outside. This pressure differential of about 8.0 psi is enormous. Engineering an enclosure for this, with sealed doors allowing access for people, would be prohibitively expensive and would be rejected as unfeasible. Above all, nobody would design it with large glass walls. (Ever wonder why an airliner's windows are so small?)

In addition, no one would ask a human being to step from sea-level pressure to 20,000 feet through a doorway. When the military trains pilots in an altitude chamber, they decrease the pressure steadily. The most pronounced symptoms of hypoxia would not be nausea and light-headedness, but, rather, a dull headache and euphoria (a feeling of well-being that can become giddiness), along with slowed reactions and impaired thinking.

But it isn't hard to reduce oxygen in a room, without a pressure differential. Just fill the place with nitrogen! For instance, millions of bushels of apples are kept under storage in controlled atmosphere (CA) systems that create a cool, low-humidity, high-nitrogen environment, which can stop an apple from ripening for up to one year. Oxygen is held to about 2.5 percent. Human beings don't enter the CA storage areas until the rooms are flushed with normal air.

GEE, BUCK, IT'S A SPACEPLANE!

In *Angels & Demons*, Dan Brown poses a kind of "spaceplane" that he claims is an "X-33 prototype" but then he begins to throw around specifications that don't jibe, and references to actual aircraft concepts that don't belong together. Here are the passages from *Angels & Demons* where Professor Langdon first encounters the "X-33" aircraft:

> The craft before them was enormous. It was vaguely reminiscent of the space shuttle except that the top had been shaved off, leaving it perfectly flat. Parked there on the runway, it resembled a colossal wedge. Langdon's first impression was that he must be dreaming. The vehicle looked as airworthy as a Buick. The wings were practically nonexistent—just two stubby fins on the rear of the fuselage. A pair of dorsal guiders rose out of the aft section. The rest of the plane was hull—about 200 feet from front to back—no windows, nothing but hull.
>
> "Two hundred fifty thousand kilos fully fueled," the pilot offered, like a father bragging about his newborn. "Runs on slush hydrogen. The shell's a titanium matrix with silicon carbide fibers. She packs a 20:1 thrust/weight ratio; most jets run at 7:1. The director must be in one helluva a hurry to see you. He doesn't usually send the big boy."

For the record, the real X-33 never flew, although it was at least 75 percent built when the funding spigot was turned off in 2001 after large cost overruns. Also, it was never intended to have humans aboard at all, and it was designed to take off vertically, but land on a runway.

Dan Brown's description is a recognizable portrait of the X-33 through a layman's eyes, although the terminology is imprecise (for example, the "dorsal guiders" are properly called vertical stabilizers and rudders). However, the size of the aircraft is greatly overstated. The actual X-33 was to be only 69 feet long (not 200) and it would weigh about 130,000 kilograms fully fueled (not 250,000). The construction of "a titanium matrix with silicon carbide fibers" is just a string of nonsensical techie-sounding words. But a very interesting actual feature of the X-33 was the much-improved heat shielding system that would incorporate metallics into the surface tiles.

The prime contractor was not Boeing, but Lockheed Martin's Skunk Works and, if the X-33 had been successful, it would have blossomed into the full-scale "Venture-Star™" program. It was really the pursuit of one of the Holy Grail concepts of space-flight, the Single Stage to Orbit. The X-33 itself, however, was only intended to reach an altitude of about 60 miles or 317,000 feet. It would have taken a follow-upon program to create an aircraft for true orbital missions.

One of the niftiest parts of the X-33 was to be the Rocketdyne "Linear Aerospike" engines, a completely novel liquid-fueled rocket engine design with slot-shaped exhausts, reminiscent of the Millennium Falcon in *Star Wars*. Rocketdyne achieved successful test-stand firings of these engines, which not only produced their rated thrust, but also provided directional control of the blast vector to assist in steering.

But the airframe was behind schedule. It was basically a "lifting body" shape that would house an aluminum liquid-oxygen tank in the forward body, and two composite liquid-hydrogen tanks aft of that, ahead of the engines. The oxygen tank had been tested and accepted, and thermal tile production was chugging along in good shape. Then the hydrogen tanks failed their tests. The project, which had blown through about $912 million of allotted NASA money plus about $200 million from Lock-heed Martin, was cancelled when it looked as though it would cost a lot more.

When the fictional X-33 pilot tells Langdon that "she packs a 20:1 thrust/ weight ratio; most jets run at 7:1," Dan Brown gets to glue a merely unbelievable fantasy onto an erroneous "factoid." Neither the 20:1 nor the 7:1 ratio is at all plausible. There has never been a jet aircraft with a thrust-to-weight ratio of 7:1 and it would be illogical to build such a machine, even for a jet fighter. No conceivable aircraft—even a rocket—would have a thrust-to-weight ratio of 20:1. Merely reaching slightly greater than a 1:1 ratio allows an aircraft or rocket to take off vertically and/or climb straight up. The Space Shuttle, for instance, weighs about 4.5 million pounds and its engines can develop about 7.3 million pounds of thrust at liftoff, yielding a ratio of about 1.6:1. This is fantastic performance. Ratios of 2:1 or 3:1 would produce an aircraft with revolutionary performance. Ratios higher than that would make little sense, because the airframe would need to withstand unbelievable acceleration forces.

As designed, the X-33 (had it been built) would have had a takeoff weight of 285,000 pounds and a takeoff thrust of 410,000 pounds, giving it a ratio of about 1.4:1. It would have ascended vertically, with excellent acceleration.

The real X-33's Aerospike engines would have been nifty enough for any futuristic novel, but Dan Brown decided to change horses and refer to the X-33's propulsion as "HEDM." Upon landing in Geneva, the pilot is "yelling over the roar of the X-33's misted-fuel HEDM engines winding down behind them."

High-Energy Density Matter (HEDM) engines would never be "winding down" behind them. Unlike a jet engine with its turbine blades, nothing spins in an HEDM engine. It's like a big tube that blasts fire. The engine would be either lit, or unlit. The high-density materials in question would be additives, such as particles of carbon, aluminum, or boron, added to the liquid oxygen-hydrogen fuel.

Langdon's pilot also says, " 'In five years, all you'll see are these babies— HSCT's—High Speed Civil Transports.'

" 'This one's a protoype of the Boeing X-33 . . . but there are dozens of others— the National Aero Space Plane, the Russians have Scramjet, the Brits have HOTOL. The future's here, it's just taking some time to get to the public sector. You can kiss conventional jets good-bye.' "

The pilot's list of aircraft is a strange one. None of these aircraft was intended to transport passengers in flights between points on earth. Most have never been built. There is no likelihood that anything like these conceptual aircraft will be built in the next ten to fifteen years. HSCT's essentially died after the Concorde retired in 2003.

RARE AIRS

For those of us who tend to check the math and science in what they read in *Angels & Demons*, Dan Brown reaches some flabbergasting heights of inaccuracy in *Angels & Demons*. On landing in Geneva, the pilot learns that Langdon feels slightly queasy:

"The pilot nodded. 'Altitude sickness. We were at sixty thousand feet. You're thirty percent lighter up there.' "

Dan Brown needs the Exeter physics department to review his work. You're not 30 percent lighter at that altitude, you're not 3 percent lighter, not even 1 percent lighter.

The force of gravity between two objects varies with the square of the distance between the two centers of mass—in this case, the center of your body versus the center of the earth. When you climb to 60,000 feet, it is true that this distance gets larger. So gravity is less—by about half a percent. That's a loss of about a pound for a two-hundred-pound man (not sixty pounds, as Dan Brown would have us believe).

Says the pilot, "Lucky we only did a puddle jump. If we'd gone to Tokyo I'd have taken her all the way up—a hundred miles. Now that'll get your insides rolling."

Dan Brown is confused about cabin altitude versus actual altitude. Luckily for his passengers, the concepts are not the same. In cabin aircraft, the "altitude" inside only rises to about 8,000 feet and then levels off, even when the outside altitude is 30,000 or 60,000 feet, or higher.

Typically, the cabin pressure, or "altitude" is held at a tolerable level by pumping in lots of outside air, using spare pressure produced by the intake of the jet engines. In spacecraft such as the Space Shuttle, the cabin pressure is provided by stored air under pressure. Since "altitude" is irrelevant, the system is engineered so that the astronauts actually enjoy sea-level cabin pressure and normal oxygen levels—better than airline passengers get.

Maybe Dan Brown is talking about motion sickness "rolling your insides." But practical experience shows that there is very little turbulence at the higher altitudes. Aircraft such as the Concorde, which regularly flew at about 59,000 feet during decades of service, typically had butter-smooth flights in cruise because there is almost zero turbulence at these flight levels. In fact, on page 16, Brown does depict high-altitude flight. Langdon describes the flight as "fairly typical—occasional minor turbulence, a few presssure changes as they'd climbed, but nothing at all to suggest they had been hurtling through space at the mind-numbing speed of 11,000 miles per hour."

TAKEOFF VERSUS BLASTOFF

By calling attention to a fictitious hypersonic transport, Dan Brown possibly could get us to focus on the genuine shortcomings of our national spaceflight program. The idea of flying into space in a winged aircraft is quite old in science fiction, and it is certainly fifty years old in science fact. Right from the start, the test pilots and the budding aerospace community were looking for a way to *fly* into space. As told in *The Right Stuff*, by Tom Wolfe, at the very dawn of the US space program in the 1950s, scientists who felt it was expedient to lob "space capsules" into orbit—with occupants such as dogs, chimps, and hapless humans—were opposed by practically everyone else in the aerospace community and the public at large, who wanted to see something more like "flight" under control by "astronauts."

Billions of dollars and decades later, we got the Space Shuttle, an imperfect vehicle for many reasons, but a "spaceplane" nonetheless, at least in the sense that it can be piloted back to earth. Today, the United States is in the unadmirable position of having cancelled all new piloted flight space programs, in favor of upgrading the Space Shuttle. The grim fact is that only five Shuttles were ever brought to launch readiness, and two of them were destroyed in accidents. Two of the three remaining orbiters are scheduled for overhaul. The Shuttle program originally was supposed to allow weekly flights into orbit, but clearly it will never achieve that goal.

Encouraging developments from private industry, including the spectacular achievements of Burt Rutan and his SpaceShipOne in winning the X Prize competition in 2004, show that it is possible to reach for space under the banner of private enterprise.

However, if we desire the speed, convenience, and scientific and technological break-throughs Dan Brown points at with his fictitious X-33, we need some major political, business, and technological changes in our space and aviation culture.

CHUTING STAR

Toward the end of *Angels & Demons*, with the antimatter canister ticking, the camer-lengo and Langdon have about three minutes to get to a safe altitude in the helicopter. Langdon is thinking in terms of the altitudes that planes fly at, about four or five miles. But this is immaterial: helicopters are limited to a maximum rate of climb of about 2,500 feet per minute; this gives them at best about 7,500 feet of altitude at the top.

When the camerlengo jumps, Langdon follows him with thirty-two seconds left to go. If he free-falls, he can probably make it clear of the blast, but if he deploys the makeshift parachute described in the story right away, he would probably not be able to get clear of the blast. This is not in the book, but let's give him the benefit of the doubt. Langdon carries a lesson from early in the novel, where an obese woman gets help from a small parachute in the CERN vertical wind tunnel. He is told that a square yard of parachute will slow a person's fall by 20 percent. (In actual practice, people who run vertical wind tunnels do not equip their customers with parachutes. It's just not done. But okay, this is a fictional plot device that provides crucial knowl-edge to Langdon that he will use later.)

When Langdon is forced to jump, there is no parachute for him, so he uses the helicopter's windshield cover, said to be two yards by four yards. (By Langdon's math, he should get a 160 percent speed reduction, right?) By our calculations, Langdon would get an excellent benefit from an eight-square-yard chute, but, of course, this as-sumes that the bungee cords don't slip off or break, and that the chute doesn't collapse into a streaming bundle.

In fact, among the many millions of successful jumps and some thousands of fa-tal ones, a surprising number of people whose chutes have failed to open at all have survived the fall.

A person's free-fall from any given altitude will, in a few seconds, reach a velocity that is dependent on their weight and the amount of drag they pose. This is the per-son's terminal velocity. It can be changed dramatically by changing shape, the shape which creates the slowest velocity being with arms and legs fully extended. This shape results in a velocity of about 110 to 125 mph—give or take a little for various indi-viduals.

So, the bottom line is that Langdon may get a velocity drop from about 120 mph to about 50 or 60 mph using his makeshift 'chute. But this velocity still is quite suffi-cient to kill him under almost all circumstances. Parachute accident survivors tend to be those who fell into water, mud, or marshes—no doubt why Dan Brown has Langdon fall conveniently right into the Tiber River, which, because it is raging after a storm, is said to cushion his fall even further. However, most of those survivors who do fall into water end up drowning. But in Langdon's case, he has the Tiber Hospital close at hand.

BOOM-BOOM!

The antimatter explosion in the helicopter over Rome, Dan Brown tell us, is a 5-kiloton blast that consumes everything within a half-mile radius. A rapid expansion of anti-matter particles, meeting up with air molecules, creates particle annihilations that yield massive amounts of energy. A flash, a boom, then everything is just plain normal again in the Roman sky.

Well, that's just not likely. A blast of the stated magnitude would create a pressure wave that would knock down buildings within a certain radius, blow out all the windows within a much larger radius, and leave everyone who saw it either temporarily or permanently blinded. Furthermore, while this blast can be considered nonnuclear, the energy release would probably emit very large and disruptive electrical fields, if not other types of radiation.

The description of the camerlengo's helicopter evacuation draws on some extreme and anomalous real-life incidents. True, helicopters have reached 20,000-foot-plus altitudes in extreme circumstances, such as Mt. Everest rescue missions. Yes, people have survived falls without parachutes by grabbing onto tarps or other bits of cloth. But the combination of circumstances presented in *Angels & Demons* and the multiplier effect of each extreme aspect, make this climactic scene completely unrealistic. Langdon—and the camerlengo—must survive because of Dan Brown's secret belief in divine intervention (by the god of novelists whose plots have run amok), not his confidence in Galileo, the laws of falling bodies, or the other scientific principles of physics.

SCIENCE AS AN EVOLVING NARRATIVE: FROM GALILEO TO THE BIG BANG

AN INTERVIEW WITH MARCELO GLEISER

Cosmology has come a long way since Galileo made his own telescope and first aimed it at the stars. Scientists now understand the history of the universe from the time it was a cosmic soup of quarks, electrons, and photons, to the time the first stars and galaxies were formed. We now know why stars shine and how the solar system was formed. But bewildering questions about the origin of the universe are still at the red-hot center of the great debate between science and religion.

Enter Dan Brown and Angels & Demons. Starting with Galileo's clash with the church and ending with a modern-day war between physicists and the Vatican, the tussle between science and religion oozes from almost every page of Brown's thriller. Marcelo Gleiser, a professor of natural philosophy at Dartmouth College, covers the same territory over a longer historical span in his highly acclaimed The Dancing Universe: From Creation Myths to the Big Bang *(to be reprinted February 2005 by University Press of New England). Only, Gleiser sticks to the facts.*

Brazilian-born Gleiser could easily replace the Harvard symbologist Robert Langdon as the hero of a Brown novel. Among his many intellectual credentials, Gleiser is an award-winning physicist, a researcher in cosmology, a lecturer on science, religion, and society, and a former fellow at Fermilab, the country's foremost high-energy physics laboratory. You get the sense that what took Langdon—with the help of the ever-so-attractive physicist Vittoria Vetra—569 pages to sort out, Gleiser could have resolved in a nanosecond.

Marcelo Gleiser is a professor of natural philosophy at Dartmouth College and the recipient of a Presidential Faculty Fellows Award, one of only fifteen scientists to be so honored.

In an earlier interview in this book, Gleiser expounded on the issues revolving around Galileo's battle with the church. Here, he discusses how we got from Galileo to the big bang.

After Galileo, what is the next major step in the evolution of our understanding of the universe?

Without a doubt, Isaac Newton was the next great name after Galileo and Johannes Kepler. As an added coincidence, Newton was born the same year Galileo died, as if the Italian was passing the baton to the Englishman. I mention Kepler because without him it is hard to understand the magnitude of Newton's achievements. By the time Newton entered the scene, in the mid-1600s, physics was going through a very confusing stage. Galileo had revealed new wonders about the night sky, all of them pointing away from the prevailing Aristotelian view that the celestial objects were made of perfect and unchanging ether, the fifth substance. (The other four substances— earth, air, fire, and water—of course, are featured prominently in *Angels & Demons.*) Also, Galileo's discoveries of the four largest moons of Jupiter proved that the earth was not that special. If moons could orbit another planet, why was it so obvious that the earth was the center of the cosmos?

Furthermore, Galileo had developed a physics of projectile motion, that is, an explanation as to how things fall under earth's gravitational pull. Here is where the famous story of Galileo and the Tower of Pisa comes in. According to his first biographer, Galileo did drop different objects from the tower, showing they landed practically at the same time. Aristotle had said heavier objects fall faster. But Galileo showed that gravity attracted all objects the same way, irrespective of their mass. Nevertheless, in spite of all his earthly forwardness, Galileo was still a conservative when it came to the causes of planetary motion and the shapes of their orbits. He thought planets moved around the sun in circles due to a form of circular inertia, without any forces pushing them. His celestial physics was nothing to write home about.

At about the same time, Kepler was unveiling the three laws of planetary motion, the most famous being the one stating that planetary orbits are elliptical in shape with the sun sitting in one of the foci. (An ellipse is an elongated circle, like the number 0, with two "centers" called foci.) Kepler understood that there was a force emanating from the sun, which was somehow responsible for driving the planets, but he fell short of actually obtaining its mathematical expression. On the other hand, Kepler was not too concerned with motions close to earth's surface.

So, when Newton came into the scene, the physics of objects near earth and the physics of celestial objects were completely disjointed. What Newton did was unify the two physics, showing that the same force that caused things to fall on earth made planets and comets race around the sun. This is Newton's famous theory of universal gravitation. Together with his three laws of motion, this theory is the cornerstone of classical physics, the physics that describes most phenomena in our everyday life.

God took a back seat during the eighteenth-century Enlightenment period, as science became more efficient at explaining natural phenomenon. Was God's diminished role generally accepted by scientists of the era?

There was clearly a split between the "theists" and the "deists," although the theist view became increasingly old-fashioned. The theists were those that, like Newton, believed in God's constant presence in the cosmos, fixing things here and there as needed. For example, Newton believed that God was responsible for keeping matter in balance in an infinite universe. Otherwise, gravity would tend to make planets and stars bundle up together into huge concentrations of mass. From a theological viewpoint, if God were not a presence it would be hard to believe in miracles. The deists, like Benjamin Franklin, didn't believe in miracles or God's interference. God was the creator of the world and the rules driving it; science was the tool that unveiled those rules. The more scientists learned about nature, the harder it became to believe in supernatural forces and beings. The Romantic movement of the early nineteenth century [typified by the poet Lord Byron, the artist Delacroix, the composer Chopin, and others] sought to fill, to some extent, the spiritual void left in science's wake.

Can you describe the major elements of the expansion that took place in physics during the end of the nineteenth century?

By the end of the nineteenth century, physics was dominated by the so-called three pillars: mechanics and gravitation, as described by Newton and then refined by many others; electromagnetism, which unified electric and magnetic phenomena and showed that light was nothing more than electromagnetic waves propagating in space; and thermodynamics, which described heat and its properties in terms of macroscopic concepts such as temperature and pressure. Famous physicists such as Lord Kelvin stated that physics was practically finished. The work was mostly done. All that was left was filling in the details here and there. The confidence inspired by the success of science squeezed God into an even tighter corner, especially when one adds Darwin's theory of evolution, which questioned the other face of creation, the development of life on earth, as told in the Bible's genesis story.

But all was not well. A series of laboratory experiments exposed the limitations of the three pillars: light seemed to propagate in empty space, contradicting accepted knowledge that waves "waved" on a material medium, like sound waves in air; spectra from heated substances only glowed at specific colors or frequencies, as if each chemical element had its own fingerprint; no one understood the deceptively simple question as to why hot bodies glowed red and, when hotter still, glowed blue; Mercury's orbit had an anomalous precession that Newtonian gravitation couldn't explain properly. These discoveries pointed toward new physics beyond the classical horizon: by 1920 the theory of relativity and the quantum nature of atoms and of light had shaken away any conviction that physics was even close to being "finished." The humbling lesson had been learned: Nature is much smarter than we are, and we will always be scrambling to catch up.

Did all this new science signify the end of deism? Not necessarily. As long as there are open questions in science, there will always be room for filling our ignorance with belief. This may or not be the proper approach, but it is a choice that one has. Personally, I prefer to think that science's most important lesson is that it's okay *not* to have all the answers, to live in doubt. In fact, not just okay but absolutely necessary. Without ignorance, knowledge cannot leap forward.

During the early part of the twentieth century, astronomy was the leading example of big science. What did astronomers of that period add to our understanding of the universe?

There were many things, but perhaps two stand out, both attributed to Edwin Hubble. In 1924 Hubble resolved a question that had plagued astronomers for a long time: was the Milky Way the only galaxy in the cosmos or were there other galaxies just like it? Astronomers could see nebulae and gas clouds, but they didn't know if they were outside or inside our galaxy. The difficulty was to measure their distances, a great challenge in astronomy. To determine how far an object is, an astronomer must find what is called a *standard candle*, that is, a source of light with known luminosity shining within that object. This way, he or she can compare the amount of light put out by the standard candle with a similar one nearby and use the fact that its luminosity drops with the square of the distance to estimate the distance to the faraway object. Hubble did just that. He identified a type of star called a Cepheid variable in the distant nebulae, and established that they were outside the boundary of the Milky Way. That is, our galaxy is just one of billions spread across the visible universe.

Hubble's other great discovery came in 1929. Using a similar technique to measure distances, he also measured the frequency of the light emitted by distant galaxies. When he analyzed his results, he noticed that most distant galaxies had frequencies pushed toward the red end of the spectrum, as if their light waves were being stretched like the bellows of an accordion. He knew of a similar effect with sound waves called the Doppler effect: when a sound wave approaches us, its pitch goes up; when it goes away, its pitch decreases. Just think of a siren approaching you on the road, or the horn of an eighteen-wheeler on an interstate. Hubble concluded that the galaxies were moving away from us with speeds that increased in proportion to their distance. Although he didn't like it, his discovery pointed to the expansion of the universe, a major landmark of twentieth-century cosmology.

To what extent did Einstein's theory of relativity help lay the groundwork for our present understanding of the universe?

The two landmark developments of the early twentieth century, Einstein's theory of relativity and quantum mechanics, form the foundation of our modern understanding of the cosmos. On the one hand, relativity taught us that gravity could be interpreted as the curvature of space, that massive objects bend space around them. As time is intrinsically bundled up with space in what is called *spacetime*, the flow of time is also affected by gravity: the stronger the gravitational pull, the slower the passage of time. One extreme example of this is a black hole, an object with such enormous gravity that nothing can escape its pull, not even light. We now know that our galaxy, and probably most others, has a giant black hole nested in its center with a mass millions of times larger than the sun; the extreme effects of general relativity are a reality.

And the second landmark development—quantum mechanics?

The world of the very small, the quantum world of atoms and elementary particles such as electrons and protons, has shown how weird nature can be. Although relativity was mostly the product of Einstein's mind, quantum mechanics emerged out of the efforts of many people, Max Planck, Niels Bohr, Erwin Schrödinger, Werner Heisenberg, Paul Dirac, and others. They struggled to make sense of the bizarre behavior of matter at submicroscopic distances, a behavior that has its own rules, very different from the ones we are used to. For example, let's consider the electron, that negatively charged component of atoms. It's not a little ball. We don't know what it is, really. All we can say is that it may behave as a ball or it may behave as a wave, according to how we decide to observe it in the lab. We also can't say for sure where it's going to be at a given time; we can only give the probability it will be here or there. Oh yes, it can also go across barriers as a ghost would across a wall. With all that, you may think that quantum mechanics is a mess and that we are hopeless at trying to understand the world of the very small. Not at all. Every piece of digital equipment surrounding you right now, computers, laser scanners, cell phones, DVDs, etc., exists as a by-product of the quantum revolution. The same is true of nuclear power and nuclear energy, of biochemistry, of genetic engineering.

What properties of the universe do we now clearly understand?

We now can reproduce the history of the universe from fractions of a second after the "bang," when the universe was a cosmic soup of electrons, photons, and quarks (the particles that make up protons and neutrons) all the way to the formation of the first stars and galaxies. We know the universe is just a bit short of 14 billion years old, that its geometry is flat, that it is expanding like the surface of a rubber balloon. We understand how stars shine and that they forge all chemical elements found in the universe (with the exception of the lightest ones, hydrogen, helium, and lithium). When Carl Sagan said we are stardust he wasn't kidding. We know how the solar system formed and how the earth was born some 4.6 billion years ago. We have found more than 120 planets orbiting other stars, as we strive to understand how unique, or not, we are.

How accurate is Brown's treatment of antimatter in Angels & Demons. *That is, how he describes its creation, the way it is stored, and its explosive properties compared with the actual experimental work going on at places like CERN and Fermilab, where you were formerly a fellow?*

The key scientific idea behind *Angels & Demons* is the creation of a blob of antimatter particles kept in suspension by magnetic fields inside a special container, which is an almost perfect vacuum. This device can work as a bomb, as Brown suggested: antimatter must be kept in complete isolation from matter. It turns out that when matter and antimatter meet or, more technically, collide, they mutually disintegrate into energy, carried away by little bundles of highly energetic electromagnetic radiation called photons. This is the most beautiful expression of the famous $E = mc^2$ formula, which states that energy and matter are interconvertible. In practice, this means that not only do matter and antimatter turn into radiation upon contact, but also that radiation may spontaneously create pairs of matter and antimatter particles. Every particle of matter, say, an electron or a proton, has an antiparticle counterpart with pretty much the same properties but with opposite electric charge. The positron, the antiparticle of the electron, has positive charge. Antiprotons are negatively charged.

Although we cannot currently make the amount of antimatter used for the devastating ends in the book, antimatter is nothing mysterious or science-fiction-like. It is made every day in high-energy laboratories such as the European CERN or the American Fermilab, among others. The idea of keeping the antimatter in suspension by magnetic field traps is also current; the process was invented over twenty years ago at CERN. In fact, CERN has produced bundles of antiprotons and even antihydrogen atoms, made of antiprotons and positrons zipping around them.

What about the plausibility of connecting antimatter and the big bang, as Brown seems to do? Does any connection exist?

That's where things get a bit more far-fetched and implausible—when Brown suggests that production of antimatter in the laboratory has something to do with the big bang. The "experiment" that created a mini big bang consisted of two colliding beams of highly energetic particles. New particles were created from the collision, including antimatter particles. Vittoria Vetra, Leonardo Vetra's daughter and his collaborator in the experiment, said, "My father created a universe . . . from nothing at all." Not really. All that happens when two beams collide—and, of course, they are not "nothing"—is the conversion of their mass and energy of motion into matter, according to the $E=mc^2$ relation that I mentioned earlier. This is done routinely at particle accelerators. If anything, the real-life process of creating antimatter suggests the opposite of the big bang. Assume for fun that incredibly high densities could be achieved in such collisions. The probable result would be a mini black hole, in a sense the opposite of a mini big bang.

This is not to say that the research at CERN, Fermilab, and other high-energy laboratories doesn't teach us things about the big bang. It does, and much of what we know about the earliest moments of cosmic history comes from the machines at these labs. We actually say that they reproduce the conditions of the universe at fractions of a second *after* the "bang." I imagine this is where Dan Brown took his cue from, a perfectly reasonable fictional device. But we don't recreate the bang itself. Cosmogenesis remains outside the realm of experimentation. Until we have a better understanding of the quantum properties of gravity, we are bound to stay stuck on this question.

Will we ever be able to explain the big bang scientifically?

I don't see why not, at least in part. As models become more sophisticated, they may be able to explain how the universe emerged out of nothing and evolved to be what we see today. We may be able to find the *one* explanation that is consistent with observations. But is that model *the* final answer? I'm afraid we won't be able to tell. It may be the accepted answer of its time, just as Dante's spherical static cosmos was for the fourteenth century. Until we have total knowledge of the universe we will not be sure that our answer is final. And since we will *never* have this knowledge, our answer will never be final. As long as we keep asking and measuring, the story will keep changing. Science is a work in progress. We will add our verses to the grand narrative, and others will surely follow. Another page will be turned in the Book of Nature. But it will not be the last.

What are the next steps in expanding our knowledge? What will scientists be contemplating in 2025, 2050?
Despite all we've learned about the cosmos, we still know very little. Three questions lie at the forefront of research, questions that were once the exclusive province of religion and that I call jointly "the problem of the three origins": the origin of the universe, the origin of life, and the origin of mind. These three questions will dominate much of twenty-first-century science.

To understand the origin of the universe we must first marry the two great theories of the twentieth century, general relativity and quantum mechanics; as we go back in time, the whole universe starts to behave as a subatomic particle, rendering the usual treatment based on Einstein's relativity useless. For over forty years physicists have been trying to construct a quantum theory of gravity. We still don't have it, although there are candidates, the most promising being superstring theory, the idea that the fundamental entities of matter are not particles but one-dimensional wiggling things one trillionth of a trillionth the size of an atom.

The origin of life has also eluded us, although we now understand some of the basic biochemistry involved. The nagging question remains of how to identify the point at which an organic molecule becomes complex enough to begin replicating and feeding from its environment. That is, at what point the inanimate becomes animated. We still cannot create life in the laboratory. In fact, we can't even define it. If we think about life we must address the issue of extraterrestrial life. Are there other living beings in the cosmos? Probably yes. The sheer number of stars and planets makes it hard to believe we are that special. Hopefully, we will soon be able to probe the atmospheres of extrasolar planets to search for signs of life-related chemistry, such as water and ozone. Are there other intelligent beings in the cosmos? That's a much more complicated question.

If our history is any indication, the development of intelligent life is the result of a series of random planetary and cosmic cataclysms. There may be many evolutionary pathways to intelligence, but we certainly don't know what they are. Certainly, intelligence is not a sure consequence of evolution. Just think that the dinosaurs were here for 150 million years before an asteroid wiped them out 65 million years ago. We are the newcomers on the planetary scene, the kids on the block. Many life-supporting planets may not be there yet, or may *never* develop the conditions for intelligent life to prevail. We will have to wait and see.

Finally, the human brain—the most complex system we can identify in the cosmos. Can the brain understand itself? Can thinking explain how we think? Can we pinpoint where and what is the "I" that makes us who we are, the seat of the self? Cognitive neuroscience is a fascinating and fast-developing field of research, based on new imaging techniques such as MRIs and PET scans (all derived from quantum mechanics) that can show neurons and clusters of neurons firing in unison as the brain responds to a stimulus. Whether it will or will not give us an answer to the question of mind is something we have to wait and see. I am confident.

These three questions of origins, together with genetic engineering, will keep scientists busy for a long time. Of one thing we can be sure: as we inch forward toward answers, new questions will emerge, questions that we can't even anticipate at this point. And as we answer these questions we will revise our definitions of the cosmos and of who we are. Science is an evolving narrative.

A DAY WITHOUT YESTERDAY: GEORGES LEMAÎTRE AND THE BIG BANG

by Mark Midbon

Standing in her father's study, and trying to explain his work, Vittoria Vetra acquaints Robert Langdon with the big bang: "When the Catholic Church first proposed the Big Bang Theory in 1927 . . ." (p. 69). Langdon interrupts, doubtful this could have been the church's idea. "Of course," answers Vittoria. "Proposed by a Catholic monk, George Lemaître, in 1927."

Readers who have a passing acquaintance with the theory that the universe was born in a huge explosion and has been expanding ever since may think this is another one of Dan Brown's artful fictions, agreeing with Robert Langdon's protestation that the idea of the big bang was first proposed by the American physicist Edwin Hubble. But here Dan Brown stands on solid historical ground. It was indeed Georges Lemaître who first came up with the idea that the origins of the universe were like a burst of fireworks.

Lemaître was both monk and scientist, but kept a firewall between them (in that way , Vittoria's statement that the church first proposed the idea is inaccurate). Unlike the case of Galileo, however, the Vatican has never taken a stand against the big bang theory. Lemaître's story is a fascinating one, and is told here by computer programmer and writer Mark Midbon.

" 'A Day Without Yesterday': Georges Lemaître & the Big Bang," Commonweal (March 24, 2000): 18–19. Copyright © 2000 Commonweal. Used with permission. Mark Midbon is a senior programmer and analyst at the University of Wisconsin. He has also written about the priest-geologist Pierre Teilhard de Chardin.

In the winter of 1998, two separate teams of astronomers in Berkeley, California, made a similar, startling discovery. They were both observing supernovae—exploding stars visible over great distances—to see how fast the universe is expanding. In accordance with prevailing scientific wisdom, the astronomers expected to find the rate of expansion to be decreasing, Instead they found it to be increasing—a discovery which has since "shaken astronomy to its core" (*Astronomy*, October 1999).

This discovery would have come as no surprise to Georges Lemaître (1894–1966), a Belgian mathematician and Catholic priest who developed the theory of the big bang. Lemaître described the beginning of the universe as a burst of fireworks, comparing galaxies to the burning embers spreading out in a growing sphere from the center of the burst. He believed this burst of fireworks was the beginning of time, taking place on "a day without yesterday."

After decades of struggle, other scientists came to accept the big bang as fact. But while most scientists—including the mathematician Stephen Hawking—predicted that gravity would eventually slow down the expansion of the universe and make the universe fall back toward its center, Lemaître believed that the universe would keep expanding. He argued that the big bang was a unique event, while other scientists believed that the universe would shrink to the point of another big bang, and so on. The observations made in Berkeley supported Lemaître's contention that the big bang was in fact "a day without yesterday."

When Georges Lemaître was born in Charleroi, Belgium, most scientists thought that the universe was infinite in age and constant in its general appearance. The work of Isaac Newton and James C. Maxwell suggested an eternal universe. When Albert Einstein first published his theory of relativity in 1916, it seemed to confirm that the universe had gone on forever, stable and unchanging.

Lemaître began his own scientific career at the College of Engineering in Louvain in 1913. He was forced to leave after a year, however, to serve in the Belgian artillery during World War I. When the war was over, he entered Maison Saint-Rombaut, a seminary of the Archdiocese of Malines, where, in his leisure time, he read mathematics and science. After his ordination in 1923, Lemaître studied math and science at Cambridge University where one of his professors, Arthur Eddington, was the director of the observatory.

For his research at Cambridge, Lemaître reviewed the general theory of relativity. As with Einstein's calculations ten years earlier, Lemaître's calculations showed that the universe had to be either shrinking or expanding. But while Einstein imagined an unknown force—a cosmological constant—which kept the world stable, Lemaître decided that the universe was expanding. He came to this conclusion after observing the reddish glow, known as a red shift, surrounding objects outside of our galaxy. If interpreted as a Doppler effect, this shift in color meant that the galaxies were moving away from us. Lemaître published his calculations and his reasoning in *Annales de la Société Scientifique de Bruxelles* in 1927. Few people took notice. That same year he talked with Einstein in Brussels but the latter, unimpressed, said, "Your calculations are correct, but your grasp of physics is abominable."

It was Einstein's own grasp of physics, however, that soon came under fire. In 1929 Edwin Hubble's systematic observations of other galaxies confirmed the red shift. In England the Royal Astronomical Society gathered to consider this seeming contradiction between visual observation and the theory of relativity. Sir Arthur Eddington volunteered to work out a solution. When Lemaître read of these proceedings, he sent Eddington a copy of his 1927 paper. The British astronomer realized that Lemaître had bridged the gap between observation and theory. At Eddington's suggestion, the Royal Astronomical Society published an English translation of Lemaître's paper in its Monthly Notices of March 1931.

Most scientists who read Lemaître's paper accepted that the universe was expanding, at least in the present era, but they resisted the implication that the universe had a beginning. They were used to the idea that time had gone on forever. It seemed illogical that infinite millions of years had passed before the universe came into existence. Eddington himself wrote in the English journal *Nature* that the notion of a beginning of the world was "repugnant."

The Belgian priest responded to Eddington with a letter published in *Nature* on May 9, 1931. Lemaître suggested that the world had a definite beginning in which all its matter and energy were concentrated at one point:

> *If the world has begun with a single quantum, the notions of space and time would altogether fail to have any meaning at the beginning; they would only begin to have a sensible meaning when the original quantum had been divided into a sufficient number of quanta. If this suggestion is correct, the beginning of the world happened a little before the beginning of space and time.*

In January 1933, both Lemaître and Einstein traveled to California for a series of seminars. After the Belgian detailed his theory, Einstein stood up, applauded, and said, "This is the most beautiful and satisfactory explanation of creation to which I have ever listened." Duncan Aikman covered these seminars for the *New York Times Magazine*. An article about Lemaître appeared on February 19, 1933, and featured a large photo of Einstein and Lemaître standing side by side. The caption read, "They have a profound respect and admiration for each other."

For his work, Lemaître was inducted as a member of the Royal Academy of Belgium. An international commission awarded him the Francqui Prize. The archbishop of Malines, Cardinal Josef Van Roey, made Lemaître a canon of the cathedral in 1935. The next year Pope Pius XI inducted Lemaître into the Pontifical Academy of Science.

Despite this high praise, there were some problems with Lemaître's theory. For one, Lemaître's calculated rate of expansion did not work out. If the universe was expanding at a steady rate, the time it had taken to cover its radius was too short to allow for the formation of the stars and planets. Lemaître solved this problem by expropriating Einstein's cosmological constant. Where Einstein had used it in an attempt to keep the universe at a steady size, Lemaître used it to speed up the expansion of the universe over time.

Einstein did not take kindly to Lemaître's use of the cosmological constant. He regarded the constant as the worst mistake of his career, and he was upset by Lemaître's use of his supergalactic fudge factor.

After Arthur Eddington died in 1944, Cambridge University became a center of opposition to Lemaître's theory of the big bang. In fact, it was Fred Hoyle, an astronomer at Cambridge, who sarcastically coined the term *big bang*. Hoyle and others favored an approach to the history of the universe known as the steady state, in which hydrogen atoms were continuously created and gradually coalesced into gas clouds, which then formed stars.

But in 1964 there was a significant breakthrough that confirmed some of Lemaître's theories. Workers at Bell Laboratories in New Jersey were tinkering with a radio telescope when they discovered a frustrating kind of microwave interference. It was equally strong whether they pointed their telescope at the center of the galaxy or in the opposite direction. What was more, it always had the same wavelength and it always conveyed the same source temperature. This accidental discovery required the passage of several months for its importance to sink in. Eventually, it won Arno Penzias the Nobel Prize in physics. This microwave interference came to be recognized as cosmic background radiation, a remnant of the big bang. Lemaître received the good news while recovering from a heart attack in the Hospital Saint-Pierre at the University of Louvain. He died in Louvain in 1966, at the age of seventy-one.

After his death, a consensus built in favor of Lemaître's burst of fireworks. But doubts did persist: Did this event really happen on a day without yesterday? Perhaps gravity could provide an alternative explanation. Some theorized that gravity would slow down the expansion of the universe and make it fall back toward its center, where there would be a big crunch and another big bang. The big bang, therefore, was not a unique event which marked the beginning of time but only part of an infinite sequence of big bangs and big crunches.

When word of the 1998 Berkeley discovery that the universe is expanding at an increasing rate first reached Stephen Hawking, he said it was too preliminary to be taken seriously. Later, he changed his mind. "I have now had more time to consider the observations, and they look quite good," he told *Astronomy* magazine (October 1999). "This led me to reconsider my theoretical prejudices."

Hawking was actually being modest. In the face of the scientific turmoil caused by the supernovae results, he adapted very quickly. But the phrase "theoretical prejudices" makes one think of the attitudes that hampered scientists seventy years ago. It took a mathematician who also happened to be a Catholic priest to look at the evidence with an open mind and create a model that worked.

Is there a paradox in this situation? Lemaître did not think so. Duncan Aikman of the *New York Times* spotlighted Lemaître's view in 1933: " 'There is no conflict between religion and science,' Lemaître has been telling audiences over and over again in this country. . . . His view is interesting and important not because he is a Catholic priest, not because he is one of the leading mathematical physicists of our time, but because he is both."

ANTIMATTER MATTERS

BY STEPHAN HERRERA

Anyone who has read Angels & Demons *has no doubt wondered if antimatter is real and if it could be used as a weapon to create the threat of mass destruction, as it is in the novel. We turned to a leading science writer, Stephan Herrera, to help our readers understand what antimatter is and isn't and what the current state of research into its development and production is. Herrera is the life sciences editor at MIT's* Technology Review *and is the author of the forthcoming book* Closer to God: The Fantastic Voyage of Nanotechnology.

It is certainly true that good science fiction has its roots in good science. Almost lost within the *Angels & Demons* murder mystery and love story is a clever piece of science fiction writing. Dan Brown uses his artistic license to posit an alternative vision of the future of antimatter—a vision quite different from the one scientists at places like CERN and NASA are talking about. It is a vision born of good intentions that somehow goes terribly astray.

Quite understandably, for novelistic treatment, Brown fills in the blanks surround-

Stephan Herrera has written about life sciences and nanotechnology for the *Economist*, *Nature*, and MIT's *Technology Review*, and many other publications. His book, *Closer to God: The Fantastic Voyage of Nanotechnology*, will be published in the fall of 2005 by Random House.

ing the creation, storage, and transport of antimatter with convenient plot devices that make antimatter seem altogether more dangerous than it really is. But give him credit for raising awareness about antimatter and posing, albeit in a fictional construct, some compelling real-world questions, such as What happens when "intellectual miracles" like antimatter arrive in this world with no intellectual instructions attached? And are such discoveries, in and of themselves, "perilous"? What if, contrary to the assurances of well-meaning scientists, antimatter falls into the wrong hands? These questions do not have easy answers.

Some critics of controversial science and technology believe that new developments should be quarantined until their myriad risks and unintended consequences can be identified, and safeguards put in place to deal with those consequences. Unfortunately, we can't possibly know all the answers about things like antimatter, stem cells, nanotechnology, or genetic engineering until we get the questions right. And we can't get the questions right until our scientists are allowed to experiment. Like everything, there will be risks involved. But there could also be enormous rewards.

Antimatter just might be the "energy source of tomorrow." As *Angels & Demons* heroine Vittoria Vetra explains to Robert Langdon early in the story, commercial-grade antimatter might prove itself "a thousand times more powerful than nuclear energy." She also promises that it can be "one hundred percent efficient. No byproducts. No radiation. No pollution. A few grams could power a major city for a week."

As Dr. George Schmidt, chief of propulsion research and technology at NASA's Marshall facility, puts it, "Antimatter has tremendous energy density. Matter-antimatter annihilation—the complete conversion of matter into energy—releases the most energy per unit mass of any known reaction in physics." The website for NASA's Marshall Space Flight Center in Huntsville, Alabama, declares with some conviction that "traveling to the stars will require ultra-high-energy propulsion systems. The mutual annihilation of antimatter and matter packs the highest energy density of any reaction known in physics—perhaps just the energy source needed to trek to the stars. . . . Technology development activities now under way . . . could loft an antimatter-powered starship into the realm of reality before the close of the twenty-first century."

Here at the opening of the twenty-first century, however, the first real-world applications of antimatter will likely be more prosaic: a research tool, maybe an element working in tandem with a fusion-fuel system in hybrid rocket fuel. We are so early on in the life cycle of antimatter development that it is impossible to know with any confidence whether, or if, antimatter has the benefits NASA and others hope for. It could be that scientific work with antimatter "only" provides pure knowledge about the origins of our universe—although that in itself is obviously no small matter.

Of course, it is also possible that someday antimatter might also be turned into a deadly weapon. The important thing to understand is that, contrary to the fears that *Angels & Demons* might stimulate in the imagination, many years separate us from the time when those risks might actually confront us. Indeed, it is hard to fathom why anybody would want to bother. An atomic bomb, which has plenty of destructive capabilities, can be constructed much more easily. And, as should be abundantly clear by now, fissile material, and scientists who know what to do with it, can unfortunately be bought on the black market. More to the point, to build the equivalent of a 10-megaton hydrogen bomb, it would take 125 kilograms of antimatter and a team of antimatter specialists with experience weaponizing this stuff. Nothing even close to these ingredients can be bought anywhere at present because neither exists, and that small detail likely won't change anytime this century, if ever. And this is the just the tip of the iceberg of reasons why scientists working in the field of antimatter do not believe it is likely to become the next weapon of mass destruction. Moreover, unless scientists continue their experiments with antimatter and learn how to control it, they will not be able to offer solutions for dealing with it should antimatter fall into the wrong hands.

THE HISTORY OF ANTIMATTER

Anybody who has ever watched *Star Trek* knows that antimatter fueled the warp drive that powered the starship *Enterprise* on its five-year mission to "seek out new life and new civilizations, to boldly go where no man has gone before." Less well known is the fact that scientists have long mused about the mysteries of antimatter. In 1928 British physicist Paul A. M. Dirac used Einstein's special theory of relativity to formulate his theory on the motion of electrons close to the speed of light in electric and magnetic fields. Dirac's formula predicted that the electron must have an *antiparticle*, a particle having the same mass as the electron, but a positive electrical charge (the opposite of a normal electron's negative charge). Then, in 1932, Carl Anderson observed this new particle and dubbed it the *positron*. For all practical purposes, this was the first known example of antimatter. In 1955 the *antiproton* was produced at the recently decommissioned Bevatron accelerator at the Lawrence Berkeley National Laboratory.

At the real-life CERN (Conseil Européen de Recherche Nucléaire) in Geneva, physicists in recent years have gone much further. And, contrary to what one reads in *Angels & Demons*, their work has been anything but secret. Indeed, on January 4, 1996, CERN announced that scientists in its labs had created nine antihydrogen atoms for the first time, moving at 90% of the speed of light. Then in 2002, CERN researchers working on the ATHENA experiment announced the production of more than 50,000 slow-moving antihydrogen atoms produced in so-called Penning traps. These atoms of antimatter only survived for a few tenths of a millionth of a second before being annihilated as they came into contact with ordinary matter, but their mere existence is seen by physicists around the world as *proof of concept*, meaning that forms of antimatter can be created by the hand of man.

CERN and other facilities where experiments with antimatter are taking place (such as Fermilab and Brookhaven in the United States) have each gone to great lengths to assure the public that no one is rushing in recklessly to develop antimatter. Both note on their websites that scientists believe that the true nature of antimatter is one of the top ten mysteries of the universe. As CERN physicist Rolf Landua explains, "Once it became clear that any transformation of energy into mass produces equal amounts of particles and antiparticles, it was obvious that during the big bang, equal amounts of matter and antimatter must have formed. But observations show that our universe nowadays consists of only matter (if you neglect secondary antiparticles produced in collisions in cosmic ray events, or through radioactive decay). So, where did all the antimatter go?" Perhaps it was for good reasons that antimatter disappeared outright in the nanoseconds following the big bang. Perhaps we weren't meant to have antimatter on earth.

WORST-CASE SCENARIOS

There are some obvious downsides to antimatter, just as Dan Brown explains at the beginning of *Angels & Demons*. As he says on his "Fact" page that precedes Chapter 1, "Antimatter is highly unstable. It ignites when it comes in contact with absolutely anything . . . even air. A single gram of antimatter contains the energy of a 20-kiloton nuclear bomb—the size of the bomb dropped on Hiroshima." Adding to those facts, Dan Brown says on his website (www.danbrown.com), ". . . . Antimatter releases energy with 100% efficiency (nuclear fission is 1.5% efficient). Antimatter is 100,000 times more powerful than rocket fuel. But until recently antimatter has been created only in very small amounts (a few atoms at a time). But CERN has now broken ground on its new Antiproton Decelerator—an advanced antimatter production facility that promises to create antimatter in much larger quantities."

It is not irrational to fret about the potential downside of antimatter. Just because the CERN and NASA websites reveal nothing about antimatter's potential as a weapon doesn't mean they (or ill-intentioned governments, armies, intelligence agencies, or other forces) aren't thinking about or planning for the full range of possibilities. Though, in fairness, CERN's website does calculate how much antimatter would be needed to produce the equivalent of an atomic bomb.

ARE WE THERE YET?

Although it might seem otherwise after reading *Angels & Demons* (or reading about computer hard drives being spirited out of Los Alamos National Laboratory in New Mexico, for that matter), it certainly wouldn't be easy to make off with a canister of antimatter. The stuff scarcely sticks around long enough to be stored, let alone stolen.

Moreover, far from the handy-sized canister that the Hassassin steals from Leonardo Vetra's lab in *Angels & Demons*, scientists are still working on the task of shrinking storage canisters down to a manageable size. Antiprotons, for example, according to Dr. Gerald Smith of Pennsylvania State University, can be obtained in modest quantities from high-energy accelerators like those at CERN. A magnetic canister called a Penning trap keeps antiprotons cold and quiet by means of liquid nitrogen and helium and a stable magnetic field. (CERN is using Penning traps to store antiprotons, which are then recombined with positrons inside the trap to make antihydrogen.) As noted on the NASA website Smith and his colleagues are working on a Penning trap that will be both lightweight and robust. The inside of the canister will contain a cloud of liquid nitrogen and helium to keep afloat about a trillion (less than a nanogram) antiprotons. When completed, it will weigh about 100 kg (220 lbs). While not impossible to steal, something that size won't be easy to pocket.

And nobody is going to have a lot of the stuff floating around in Penning traps anytime soon. In addition to CERN's old and new "atom-smashers," Fermilab will soon be producing more antimatter, too, probably somewhere in the neighborhood of 1.5–15 nanograms a year. This is no small task. To produce even this infinitesimally small amount, it will take 80 giga-electron volts. Using today's technology, antimatter consumes 10 billion times more energy to make it than it yields. Dramatically more stable storage and transport technologies are decades away.

Many in the particle physics community believe there is virtually no chance of ever producing more than micrograms of antimatter. At present, scientists at CERN believe it would take many millions of CERNs to make even a gram of antimatter and more money than all the government treasuries combined. Gram for gram, antimatter is the most expensive substance on earth. To produce a single gram of antimatter using today's technology would require an expenditure of more than $100 quadrillion say CERN scientists. Yes, the cost of creating antimatter will come down over time, but science is still far too early in the process for anyone to benefit from meaningful cost-reduction curves.

NICE ANTIMATTER

The physicists at CERN are not sure whether to love or hate *Angels & Demons*. On the one hand, Dan Brown has publicized their hard-to-understand work and even publicized CERN itself—a showcase of advanced technology that bolsters European claims to continuing leadership in fields of scientific inquiry that have otherwise moved largely to America. But on the other hand, Dan Brown oversimplifies the scientific issues involved with antimatter, massively distorting the complexities of producing, storing, and then transporting a quarter gram of antimatter from Geneva to the Vatican nearly seven hundred kilometers away. Let's give Dan Brown his due. He gets the most important point about this stuff right. Antimatter is the most powerful and volatile substance ever created by the hand of man—and that is enough to give us all pause.

Untangling Dan Brown's Entanglement Theory

An Interview with Amir D. Aczel

Scientists are no longer tortured and executed for making discoveries that shatter established views of the cosmos. But if they were, then scientist and antimatter expert Leonardo Vetra, the Hassassin's first victim in Angels & Demons, *would be the perfect target. Vetra inhabits the frontiers of physics, a world of ideas so complex that even scientists have trouble fully comprehending them. Both entanglement and antimatter, two phenomena discovered in the twentieth century and studied in huge particle accelerators at scientific research centers like CERN in Switzerland, hold profound philosophical implications for our understanding of the universe—as well as, in the case of antimatter, terrifying power.*

In his book Entanglement, *Amir Aczel, a mathematician and author of other well-received books on science, including the bestselling* Fermat's Last Theorem, *presents the dramatic history of entanglement theory and the intense conflicts that it brought about between scientists such as Niels Bohr and Albert Einstein. Entanglement and antimatter are found in the subatomic world of quantum mechanics where the "cause and effect" logic of everyday life breaks down. What is known about antimatter is that it annihilates matter, creating pure energy. Scientists have only been able to isolate particles of antimatter for brief periods of time, but they know that its power is staggering. The awe-inspiring explosion of antimatter in* Angels & Demons *high above Vatican City is only too realistic.*

Mathematician Amir D. Aczel is the author of nine nonfiction books about science, including *Entanglement: The Greatest Mystery in Physics* and the bestselling *Fermat's Last Theorem*.

Entanglement theory, which describes an unusual relationship between two subatomic particles, is especially bizarre. Einstein thought it was so threatening to established notions of life that he refused to accept it. As Aczel notes in the introduction to entanglement, "No longer do we speak about 'here or there' in the quantum world; we speak about 'here and there.'" Entangled particles can be located on opposite ends of the earth from one another, and yet an action performed on one particle is reflected in the other. Some scientists believe that entanglement is only explainable by the existence of another dimension—an idea that upends conventional views of reality as dramatically as did Copernicus's discovery that the world is not, after all, at the center of the universe.

In Angels & Demons, *Leonardo Vetra is a scientist-priest working at CERN, who is using a particle collider to study antimatter. He believes antimatter holds clues to the origin of the universe. What does the study of antimatter have to do with the origin of the universe?*

There is a cosmological theory that says that when the universe was created, there was matter and antimatter. But because of an asymmetry, there was a lot more matter than antimatter; the equal amounts that were there annihilated each other, and what remained was matter. When matter meets antimatter, they annihilate each other and just energy comes out. So by chance (or divine decree, if you will), the universe has a predominance of matter. Antimatter is very rare because as soon as it meets matter it explodes into energy.

At one point in Angels & Demons, *Maximilian Kohler, the fictional director of CERN, asserts that recent discoveries in particle physics are providing answers to the origin of the universe as well as answering questions about the "forces that bind us all." And although no explicit connection is drawn between antimatter and entanglement theory in the book, Leonardo Vetra's work involves the study of both phenomena. Is there an actual connection between the study of antimatter and entanglement theory?*

Entanglement is a very dramatic phenomenon in physics, in which you have two entities and when something happens to one of them, the same thing happens to the other. It is a fascinating and completely unexpected phenomenon in nature. Einstein thought that entanglement was insane, impossible. He called it "spooky action at a distance," since, in a way, it seemed to violate the *spirit* of his own theories of relativity. To the best of my knowledge, the relationship between entanglement and antimatter is only the fact that the first known source of entanglement was a matter-antimatter source. It is a tangential kind of relationship.

The first experiment on entanglement was done in 1949 at Columbia University by Chien-Shiung Wu [a professor of physics at Columbia who was also known as "Madame Wu"]—and she didn't study entanglement. She studied positronium, an artificial element comprised of an electron and a positron that exists for only a fraction of a second before the electron and positron annihilate each other. When they do, the two high-energy photons (gamma rays, which are one type of radioactivity) that come out of this annihilation are entangled. Madame Wu and her colleague I. Shaknov didn't know that the photons were entangled when they did the experiment, and that wasn't the purpose of their study. But years later, in the 1970s, scientists looked at the experiment's results, and they realized that this was probably the first example of entanglement. In the 1970s and 1980s, two groups, one in the United States and one in France, proved that entanglement is a real phenomenon by using visible light, rather than the high-energy photons of the 1949 experiments.

Is there someone at CERN like Leonardo Vetra who is working on both entanglement theory and the study of antimatter?

Now where did Dan Brown get the idea of entanglement and the collider? I suspect that he might have read about John Bell. Bell was working at CERN—he is in my book *Entanglement*. The connection between the two things is that John Bell worked at CERN and was an expert on particle accelerators. But at night, or at home on weekends, he worked on entanglement. In fact, as I say in *Entanglement*, Abner Shimony of Boston University read John Bell's theorem, which was published in an obscure physics journal, and got the idea that entanglement could actually be produced in a laboratory. He worked on this idea with his doctoral student Michael Horne.

Meanwhile, at Columbia University, a doctoral student in physics named John Clauser had exactly the same idea as Professor Shimony in Boston—at about the same time. Physicists who do entanglement research will tell you that this kind of *human entanglement* happens to them all the time! The three scientists got together and, instead of the two competing against the third, they collaborated on studying entanglement. They were the first people whose work—other than the "hidden" Wu-Shaknov results, which were understood to contain an entanglement element only decades after the fact—actually produced entanglement, based on John Bell's theoretical work at CERN a decade earlier. The actual experiments were done by John Clauser and Stuart Freedman at the University of California at Berkeley in 1972 (Clauser had gone there as a postdoctoral fellow; Freedman was his graduate assistant). That is the connection that I am guessing exists between entanglement and CERN—the fact that John Bell worked there in the early 1960s, and that there he wrote an enormously important (yet obscure) paper that allowed Abner Shimony to see the way from Einstein's original "spooky action at a distance" theoretical idea of entanglement right into actual experimentation at Berkeley proving that—"spooky" or not—entanglement does exist.

Is there any connection between entanglement theory and Einstein's theory of general relativity?

Entanglement is a phenomenon that comes out of the laws of quantum mechanics. And the relationship between quantum mechanics and general relativity is not yet well understood.

The issue here is an extremely deep one. The theories of Einstein—special relativity and general relativity—manifest themselves in the realm of the very large or the very fast. If you are in the vicinity of a very massive object such as a black hole, then space is *curved* in a very strong way; and your time slows down and even "stops" (as seen by someone from outside). Einstein's breakthrough in general relativity shows that space itself curves around massive objects. Space is even curved around the earth, but the curvature here, because the earth is nowhere nearly as massive as a black hole, is not large and we don't feel it. Another thing: when you go very fast, your time slows down—that is special relativity. And according to special relativity, nothing can go faster than light. So the laws of physics for the very fast and the very large form the theory of special relativity and general relativity, and that is where Einstein rules.

The genius of Einstein is, of course, that he could mathematically derive these theories without the ability to go so fast (nearing the speed of light) or travel to the vicinity of a black hole to actually "see" how things work there. Einstein proved with the special relativity theory that if you travel very fast, your time will actually slow down! This is not an illusion; it really happens. This was a very unintuitive result. When jet airplanes became available in the 1960s and 1970s, experiments with atomic clocks actually proved Einstein right when one clock flew on a jet and the other stayed on the ground. The flying clock was a fraction of a second (a very, very small fraction) slower than the ground-based clock. But the first and most dramatic demonstration of Einstein's relativity came in 1919 when Arthur Eddington went to Principe Island in the middle of the Atlantic Ocean and photographed the sun during a total solar eclipse. His photographic plates revealed that starlight was bent around the sun—proving Einstein's general relativity claim that space itself bends around a massive object.

Now, Einstein never liked the quantum theory for a number of reasons. For one thing, he didn't like the probabilistic nature of the quantum theory. He said in an attack against the nascent quantum theory in the 1920s: "I shall never believe that God plays dice with the universe." The dice here are the probabilities of quantum mechanics. Einstein was so smart that he figured out that if you *really* took the quantum theory literally, then, in the extreme, there could be a very weird phenomenon: entanglement. Since such a phenomenon, by Einstein's reasoning, couldn't happen in the real world, quantum theory had to be "incomplete," as he called it. Einstein wrote up this attack on quantum mechanics in a now famous paper coauthored with two assistants (Podolsky and Rosen) in 1935. Then John Bell at CERN took Einstein at his word and translated his theory, paving the way to checking whether entanglement is a real phenomenon. Shimony and Horne and Clauser designed the experiment, Clauser and Freedman experimented and proved it, and others who followed in the 1990s and 2000 made it all real. Einstein was right: entanglement does exist; and he was—in a sense—wrong: for quantum theory does work!

Is there any way to reconcile the laws of Einstein's theory of general relativity with quantum mechanics?

There are theories that people are working on now called quantum gravity. So you have quantum theory and the greater theory of gravity, which is Einstein's general theory of relativity. Quantum gravity is a set of theories designed to wed the two theories—quantum mechanics and general relativity—together.

So would that be a general unified theory?

Absolutely. That is what this theory would be, the holy grail of all of physics. They think that string theory would bring us that unification, but the truth is that they haven't done it yet. String theory is a very complex, mathematically-based theory in physics. Its basic tenet is that particles are really tiny vibrating strings. And it holds that nature has other dimensions than the three dimensions of space, or the four dimensions of *space* + *time* that Einstein had used. String theory assumes up to ten or more dimensions, the remaining six or more (after counting *space* + *time* = *4*) being "very small" and "hidden"— whatever that means. It should be pointed out that—wouldn't you have guessed it?—Einstein himself had laid down the very rudimentary foundations of this immensely complex theory.

Are they actually trying to establish a unified theory at CERN?

They cannot, because you need too much energy to do that. It would require something like the total amount of energy in our galaxy. But they are doing something very interesting now at CERN. They are looking for the very elusive *Higgs particle* [a type of particle believed to have appeared shortly after the big bang, which physicists theorize was the creation of our universe]. It is not necessarily a quantum gravity theory or a string theory; it is somewhere in that netherworld of particles that haven't been discovered. But to discover the Higgs particle you need a lot of energy.

Leonardo Vetra uses the collider or particle accelerator to discover particles that are identified as the building blocks of the universe. Is this actually the method that scientists use to discover particles such as the Higgs particle?

Yes. It's in particle accelerators that they discover things about the universe. Particles and antiparticles come out there. Scientists can create a "soup" of particles that mimic what happened some time after the big bang, when, as cosmologists put it, the universe consisted of a "primordial soup" of particles and energy.

Vetra's work with particle accelerators is referred to in Angels & Demons *as "re-creating the big bang." Is it actually possible to re-create the big bang?*

It's not possible to create a "soup" of particles of the dimensions of the early universe—that's for sure. But recently, they've been able to create this plasma that may resemble the primordial soup. After the big bang there existed a soup of particles of all kinds with very high energies, and the universe was opaque. You couldn't see through it, because light wasn't released yet—the universe was just too dense. This was something that happened in the first period after the big bang—the universe was opaque for a few hundred thousand years. Then light was finally "released." At any rate, when you smash these particles against each other with enormous energy in an accelerator such as the one at CERN, they can create something that people think may resemble what the universe was like right after the big bang.

This type of work is going on at particle accelerators in the United States, at Fermilab near Chicago, and in Europe. The Europeans are going ahead with a new, larger accelerator at CERN, which is expected to answer many physics questions. Will it help solve the quantum theory of everything? That is questionable—I don't think so.

But there is speculation that the Higgs particle might be discovered. The Higgs particle was in a sense important in theories about the early universe. It might help explain how *inflation* worked—which is something that happened after the big bang. When the universe first exploded with the big bang, it expanded at an exponential rate, which means that it was expanding faster than light. That seems like a paradox but it really isn't. Nothing can beat a ray of light. But the whole universe was expanding faster than the rate at which light propagates, so that is how you solve that paradox. But, at any rate, inflation is explainable in part by this Higgs particle. Inflation theory solves a lot of riddles about the birth of our universe. It is an ingenious cosmological theory that really came out of the study of particles! A theory of the entire huge universe based on things learned about tiny particles. This theory was developed in 1980 by the physicist Alan Guth of MIT. And twenty-five years later, virtually all physicists and cosmologists and astronomers believe that Guth's theory is right on the money.

Leonardo Vetra's daughter, Vittoria Vetra, is a bio-entanglement physicist who is studying the interconnectivity of life. Does entanglement theory prove that we are all somehow interconnected, that the molecules in one body are connected with those in another body, that there is a single force connecting us all?

I don't think so. You have to make a distinction between what is physics and what is not physics, what is science, and what is not science. Entanglement doesn't happen that easily. Entanglement is a process that is (a) hard to create, (b) hard to maintain, and (c) hard to detect.

But does entanglement indicate some kind of interconnection? What do these phenomena do to our notion of spatial separation?

When two particles are entangled, space or separation or distance have no meaning to them. In some metaphysical sense or physical sense that we haven't discovered, they are in the same place, even though one is here and one is in Paris. When one jumps, the other one jumps in exactly the same way—as if they were touching one another! It could be that there is a dimension that we don't see along which they are actually touching; maybe that's what string theory will prove someday—at least theoretically.

Here's the most amazing example of entanglement I know: if you send a photon (or an electron) into an experimental apparatus that you build, and you send in another one in such a way that you cannot tell by looking at your experimental apparatus from the outside which photon is which, then they become entangled! Isn't that the freakiest thing that you have ever heard in your life? If you know that the photon that you let go to the right is photon A and the one that went to the left is photon B, they won't entangle. But if you send them in in such a way that you cannot tell which one is which, then they are entangled. And in fact Anton Zeilinger [a prominent Viennese scientist who did pioneering work on three-particle entanglement as well as entanglement swapping] creates entanglement by sending photons into an apparatus that jumbles them up, so to speak, so he cannot tell which is which. And then they are entangled.

Does entanglement occur in nature? Occur naturally, that is?

Positronium is natural, where you have a positron and an electron going around each other. But you have to create the experiment in a laboratory, because a positron and an electron don't just happen to go around each other. Otherwise we would be dead from the radiation that is produced. It is something that you do in a radiation laboratory.

What type of laboratory experiment produces entanglement?

People really don't want to work with positronium because, first of all, you cannot see those photons. You cannot measure them with polarization, the way you do with visible light. Also, it is radioactive, so it is much more complicated to work with positronium. You probably have to wear lead shielding and all of that. So people work with visible light (and often, nowadays, laser light, for greater precision) instead. With positronium, it's the direction of the high-energy photons that is correlated (entangled). With visible light, you measure the entanglement as a correlation between the polarization direction of two entangled photons. With electrons, it's the spin direction that is entangled (correlated). People like to do these experiments best with visible laser light.

On the wall of his study, Leonardo Vetra has a poster of Einstein and his famous quote reading, "God doesn't play dice with the universe." Vetra, like Einstein, apparently believes that his study of physics will reveal God's natural laws. Does entanglement actually hold implications for theology, or the idea that there is some divine order to the universe?

The relationship between science and religion is obviously a very old one. Einstein thought that God was the god of physics. What he meant by "I shall never believe that God plays dice with the universe" was a very specific thing, and that is that quantum theory cannot be real. He also said, "Subtle is the Lord, but malicious he is not," implying that God's laws of physics are hard to discover, but not hidden in a vicious way (and Einstein, of all people, would know that best). This is actually my favorite Einstein quote.

Quantum theory is intrinsically probabilistic; you have probability theory everywhere in quantum mechanics, at least in the way humans interpret the quantum world. So by saying that God doesn't play dice with the universe, Einstein is taking out the element of probability. It really is a statement about determinism versus the stochastic nature of the universe: is the universe stochastic, meaning probabilistic, or is it deterministic? Einstein died believing that quantum theory was not real, because it was stochastic. He said that entanglement couldn't happen. He believed in what he called local realism—whatever happens here happens here, and whatever happens there, happens there.

We now know that entanglement does happen, and that the world therefore, at least in our interpretation of the quantum, is probabilistic. But it is still a rare thing; and to say that we are all connected, who knows? We haven't been able to prove it through physics.

So are notions of causality shattered by entanglement theory?

Yes. All of quantum mechanics shatters causality. In the quantum world there is causality, but it is different from the way we usually view it.

Does entanglement pose any threats to the Catholic Church?

Well, I don't see threats to it at all. God created the universe. And whether he plays dice or not, he is still God. In one of my books I say, "God does play dice, it seems; but he always knows the outcome."

In any case, entanglement, quantum theory, and relativity don't have much to do directly with institutional religion. Einstein had his debates with his own God because he thought his theory was right and that God had better acknowledge that he was right by making the experiments come out right. That's when he said, "Subtle is the Lord, but malicious he is not." But Einstein failed in terms of entanglement and quantum theory, because no human brain, at least until now, has been able to explain both theories together.

In the novel, Vittoria Vetra asserts that "one of the fundamental laws of physics states that matter cannot be created out of nothing." She maintains that this law challenges the notion that God created the universe. Is that true?

I don't think that anyone knows the answer to that. What does it mean from nothing? Cosmologists and physicists will tell you that our universe was a fraction of the size of a proton when it exploded in the big bang. I don't see the difference between that and reading the book of Genesis. God said, "Let there be light," and the earth and the waters above and the waters below and so on and so forth. And the big bang was a creation of this tremendously huge universe that has a radius from what we can tell right now of something like 13.7 billion light-years, and it began from something that was smaller than a proton. Isn't that "matter out of nothing"?

One of the big plot devices in this novel involves someone making away with a vial containing a quarter of a gram of antimatter and threatening to blow up the Vatican with it. Is that possible?

I'll give you an example of the energy produced when matter hits antimatter. We cannot travel to the stars right now, because it would take something like eight thousand years to reach the nearest star (Alpha Centauri, seen from our Southern Hemisphere, which is 4.25 light-years away from earth) if you went at the fastest speed a modern spacecraft could achieve. Scientists are talking about creating engines that use antimatter, having something suspended in a magnetic field in a vacuum aboard ship, and in a very controlled way letting some of it escape to another location in the engine, where it meets normal matter. It annihilates the normal matter, producing tremendous energy. You are creating positronium there (and, yes, incidentally, entangled photons, as we know). And that would propel the ship faster than we could ever have imagined in the past.

Getting back to the novel, I am not an expert on this, but by my calculations a quarter of a gram of antimatter will certainly endanger the Vatican, since it packs the energy of a small nuclear bomb. With ten grams (the equivalent of a teaspoonful) of antimatter, you would have enough energy to destroy the entire city of Rome. So a single gram of antimatter (a tenth of a teaspoonful) would be enough to destroy Vatican City, which is in the center of Rome.

7: *Angels & Demons*, Dan Brown, and the Art of Fictionalizing "Fact"

Explaining the fascinating plot details of the novel • Why Dan Brown may want to do more fact checking the next time around • The art and skill behind the creation of the ambigrams of death • The demons in the novelist's writing style • What happens when rational philosophy meets irrational fiction

THE PLOT HOLES AND INTRIGUING DETAILS OF *ANGELS & DEMONS*

by David A. Shugarts

One of the most talked about features of our prior book, Secrets of the Code, *was a page-by-page analysis of* The Da Vinci Code *prepared by veteran investigative reporter David Shugarts. We asked Shugarts to do the same thing for* Secrets of Angels & Demons—*analyze the plot flaws (digging up the same information Dan Brown may have looked at in the course of researching his novel), highlight the intriguing details that sometimes get passed over too quickly in the story, and review Dan Brown's factual claims about everything from antimatter to Galileo. What follows is only a small selection from Shugarts's findings. If you want to know more, visit our website at www.secretsofthecode.com and look for an announcement about how and when the full dossier of these plots holes and intriguing details will be made available. Readers who find this kind of close textual analysis of interest will also want to read the two pieces by Shugarts that follow in this chapter—one on the character names in* Angels & Demons *and the other on the tech toys of* Angels & Demons *(for example, the X-33 aircraft, the high-flying papal helicopter, and antimatter.) Note: As elsewhere in this book, the page numbers listed below refer to the standard US editions of Dan Brown's* Angels & Demons *available in 2004.*

David A. Shugarts is a journalist of more than thirty years' experience. His skill as an investigative reporter led him to be the first to uncover and write about the plot flaws and intriguing details of Dan Brown's *The Da Vinci Code,* which he presented in *Secrets of the Code.*

Page ix: CERN "recently succeeded in producing the first particles of antimatter." Is this accurate?

No. The first known antimatter particle, the positron, was detected in 1932 by American physicist Carl Anderson when looking at cosmic ray tracks, following on the heels of the 1928 prediction by British physicist Paul Dirac that such particles existed. As Dan Brown's own website says, "The first antiparticles were created in laboratories in the 1950s"—but not at CERN. In 1955 the antiproton was produced at the Berkeley Bevatron. If 1995 is considered recent, the fleeting creation of some antimatter atoms (not merely particles) was achieved at CERN. That is, an antiproton was joined with a positron for a brief instant to form an atom of antihydrogen. Nine such atoms were created. Using the CERN facility, the ATHENA consortium in 2002 achieved significant quantities of antimatter atoms, for research purposes, but still on an extremely small scale.

Page ix: "Until recently antimatter has been created only in very small amounts (a few atoms at a time)." Is Dan Brown accurate here?

It's true. It was only after *Angels & Demons* was published that production of antimatter atoms reached quantities in the hundreds or thousands of atoms—still extremely small amounts.

Page 3: "My name is Maximillian Kohler. I'm a discrete particle physicist." Is this what particle physicists call themselves?

No. Dan Brown's reference to "discrete" probably stems from the discussion begun in 1910 by Niels Bohr that led to quantum mechanics, or wave mechanics. It does not distinguish Kohler from other particle physicists (unless, of course, he is trying to indicate that he can be discreet and he merely misspelled the word). In proposing discrete particles and waves, Bohr departed from a commonly held belief that the fabric of the universe was continuous.

Page 4: " 'How did you get my number?' 'On the Worldwide Web. The site for your book.' Langdon frowned. He was damn sure his book's site did not include his home phone number. The man was obviously lying."

Langdon does not know about WhoIs. Does Dan Brown? When you register your domain name (as in www.danbrown.com), your domain name registrar typically publishes the registration information and it is accessible from lots of public WhoIs sites.

Some people don't give their real phone number, but that's a different matter. For instance, this is the administrative contact listed for www.danbrown.com:

Dan Brown
PO Box 1010

Exeter, NH 03833
US
Phone: 999-999-9999
Email: danbrown9@earthlink.net

Page 8: "The first hint of dawn was sifting through the birch trees in his [Langdon's] backyard." Is it really that dark?

It's a day in April. If we take the middle of April as the posited date, Daylight Savings Time is in effect in Boston (and Geneva and Rome). The sun rises at about 6:03 a.m.

There are three useful definitions of dawn. If you want time to observe the stars, then you count *astronomical dawn*, which is the time at which the sun is 18 degrees below the horizon in the morning, when the sun just begins to lighten the sky. Prior to this time, the sky is completely dark. If you are at sea, you may use *nautical dawn*, when the sun is 12 degrees below the horizon, and there is just enough light to distinguish objects. Finally, there is *civil dawn*, when the sun is 6 degrees below the horizon but now there is plenty of light for outdoor activities. Somewhere around this time, most people would have called it daybreak.

So even if Langdon is looking at nautical dawn, sunrise is only about forty minutes away. This creates a contradiction on page 9 when he arrives at Logan Airport around 6:00 a.m., since Langdon is said to perceive it as still dark.

Page 10: "The man led Langdon the length of the hangar. They rounded the corner onto the runway."

You cannot just walk onto a runway from a hangar. Runways are surfaces where the aircraft actually take off or land. No buildings abut any of Boston's runways. Customarily, the area of tarmac near a hangar is referred to as a *ramp* or *apron*, which leads to a *taxiway*, which leads to a *runway*.

Page 10: Langdon sees an "enormous" aircraft. "The wings were practically nonexistent—just two stubby fins on the rear of the fuselage. A pair of dorsal guiders rose out of the aft section. The rest of the plane was hull—about 200 feet from front to back—no windows, nothing but hull. . . . 'Two hundred fifty thousand kilos fully fueled,' the pilot offered, like a father bragging about his newborn. 'Runs on slush hydrogen. The shell's a titanium matrix with silicon carbide fibers. She packs a 20:1 thrust/weight ratio; most jets run at 7:1. The director must be in one helluva a hurry to see you. He doesn't usually send the big boy.' "

Dan Brown's description is a recognizable portrait of the X-33 through a layman's eyes. The terminology is imprecise (e.g., the "dorsal guiders" are properly called *vertical stabilizers* and *rudders*). However, the size of the aircraft is grossly overstated. The actual X-33 was to be only 69 feet long (not 200) and it would weigh about 130,000 kilograms fully fueled (not 250,000).

The construction of "titanium matrix with silicon carbide fibers" is just a string of nonsensical techie-sounding words. The X-33 never flew, and never even got its engines installed. But more important, it was never intended to be a manned aircraft at all, so no provision was made for a cabin or cockpit. As for the fueling reference, if he's just landed, how is he going to refuel? Do they sell "slush hydrogen" at Boston-Logan Airport? We don't think so! And as for the mock pilot-sounding talk, "She packs a 20:1 thrust/weight ratio; most jets run at 7:1," neither figure is at all plausible. (See my essay "The Technology of Toys" in Chapter 6 of this book.)

Page 11: "The pilot motioned up the gangplank. 'This way, please, Mr. Langdon. Watch your step.' "
Gangplank—are you kidding? What is this, a Jules Verne moon ship? In executive jets, you usually get an airstair door, combining a door with a set of steps.

Page 22: Kohler and Langdon pass a noisy hallway. "Free Fall Tube," Kohler says. They then get to view people cavorting in a vertical wind tunnel. They look through "four thick-paned portals . . . like windows in a submarine."
Most submarines do not have windows at all. But if they did, they would not have "portals," but rather *portholes.* (In marine construction, when fixed in place, they are technically *port lights.*)

Page 24: Kohler explains the acronym GUT as "General Unified Theory." Correct?
No, it should be "Grand Unified Theory."

Page 29: Vetra's apartment is so cold that there is a fog in it. (We later learn that Vetra's urine has become frosted.) "Freon cooling system," Kohler says. "I chilled the flat to preserve the body."
We don't know of any living space that has an air-conditioning system capable of reducing an apartment to freezing levels. Such a space has no practical use, and it would be a bad idea for the plumbing systems. Maybe as CERN director, Kohler could call upon some kind of equipment that could be quickly brought into the apartment. More important, an environmentally conscious organization like CERN would never use Freon, which was banned by European countries more than a decade ago. Freon is among a class of gases called chlorofluorocarbons, said to be destructive to the atmospheric ozone layer.

Page 31: Langdon is explaining, " 'Outspoken scientists like Copernicus—' 'Were murdered,' Kohler interjected. 'Murdered by the church for revealing scientific truths.' "
Copernicus was not murdered. Nicolaus Copernicus suffered a stroke at the age of seventy in 1543. No evidence exists that he was murdered, or even that

he had incurred disfavor with the church. Although his heliocentric theory had been circulating for years, it was not until the year of his death that his friends convinced him to publish it, as *De revolutionibus orbium coelestium*, (The Revolutions of the Celestial Orbits). Copernicus had suffered paralysis of one side of his body, lost his faculties, and lapsed into a coma. According to legend, he woke up long enough to see a copy of his book, pronounced it good, then died peacefully. Far from being in trouble with the pope, Copernicus in fact had dedicated the book to Pope Paul III. The most immediate opposition to his work came from the Protestants of the time, who said that it contradicted the Bible. Not until seventy years after his death, when the heliocentric theory was taken up by Galileo, did the Catholic Church come out against it. As numerous commentators in this volume point out, the church objected less to heliocentrism than to Galileo's handling of his criticisms of church doctrine.

Page 34: Langdon says the Vatican denounced the Illuminati as "Shaitan." He says it's "Islamic" for "adversary." He also says, "The church chose Islam for the name because it was a language they considered dirty.... Shaitan is the root of an English word ... Satan."

Uh-oh, call the language police! There is no language called "Islamic." The language at the beginning of Islam was Arabic. The Koran, for instance was written in ancient Arabic (before there were dots in the characters). But *Satan* is a word that was used in many books of the Hebrew Bible, long before Muhammad. Its root is indeed a word for *adversary*, but this was its ancient Hebrew definition, not Arabic. *Shaitan*, in Arabic, has the meaning of "a rebellious jinn (genie, or spirit) who leads men astray," which is certainly related to the concept of the devil, but *Shaitan* is not the root of the English word *Satan*.

Page 38: Langdon explains that when the Illuminati fled Rome, they took refuge with "another secret society ... a brotherhood of wealthy Bavarian stone craftsmen called the Freemasons."

If Brown's concept that Galileo was exposed as an Illuminati, was tortured, and gave up the identities of its members were true—which it's not—then these events ought to have occurred around 1633, when he was arrested by the Inquisition, but certainly no later than his death in 1642. This is at least 134 years too early for the Illuminati to have found refuge with Bavarian Freemasons. There is no evidence to suggest that there were Bavarian Freemasons until the mid-1700s. The first Blue Lodges of the Freemasons were founded in 1717 in London. Only later did Freemasonry spread to Europe. The Bavarian Illuminati, strongly rooted in Freemasonry, was founded on a specific date, May 1, 1776—134 years after Galileo's death.

Page 43: In Vetra's study, Langdon sees "a plastic Bohr model of an atom." What is that?

The Bohr model of an atom is a mathematical description and does not lend itself to a rendering in plastic. It predicts that the energy of electrons bound in an atom are to be found in quantized levels.

Page 63: "That's the Z-particle," Vittoria says. "My father discovered it five years ago. Pure energy—no mass at all. It may well be the smallest building block in nature. Matter is nothing but trapped energy."

Call the physics police! The Z particle, or Z boson, was detected in 1983 by Carlo Rubbia and Simon van der Meer of CERN, who jointly won the Nobel Prize in physics the following year. The Z boson not only has mass, but rather, has a lot of mass, relative to other particles. For instance, it is about a hundred times heavier than a proton. What Vittoria should have said if she really knew her stuff was that it has zero charge.

Page 69: Vittoria begins, "When the Catholic Church first proposed the Big Bang Theory in 1927 . . ."
She goes on to explain that a Catholic monk, Georges Lemaître, proposed the theory in 1927 and Edwin Hubble only confirmed it in 1929. Is this accurate?

Yes and no. When Lemaître proposed the theory, he was indeed a Catholic priest, but he was also a longtime scholar, having spent many years in academia as a student (earning a PhD at MIT) as well as a professor. He was, in fact, a professor of physics at the University of Leuven in Belgium when his theory was widely noticed. The Catholic Church did not immediately laud his efforts; not until 1936 did the pope induct him into the Pontifical Academy of Science, for instance. Einstein at first discounted Lemaître's ideas, but later realized that he had made a big mistake, and embraced them. In 1933, after Lemaître detailed his theory at a seminar, Einstein stood up, applauded, and said, "This is the most beautiful and satisfactory explanation of creation to which I have ever listened." "Big bang" was originally a derogatory nickname attached to the theory by its detractors, but it has lived on and they are long forgotten.

Page 74: The Hassassin is walking down a tunnel under the Vatican, counting in Arabic. "Wahad . . . tintain . . . thalatha . . . arbaa."

I am not schooled in Arabic, but scholars tell me the correct way to count is (1) *wâhid*, (2) *ithnân*, (3) *thalâtha*, (4) *'arbaa*. The Arabic word *tintain* is the feminine for "two" in many dialects, but counting in Arabic is masculine.

Page 75: Vittoria explains particles: "Everything has an opposite. Protons have electrons. Up-quarks have down-quarks. There is a cosmic symmetry at the subatomic level. Antimatter is yin to matter's yang. It balances the physical equation."

For a "bio-entanglement" physicist of Vittoria's reputed brilliance, this seems to be an overgeneralization. True, protons and electrons have opposite charges. In the Standard Model theory, however, the opposite of a proton is an antiproton, and the opposite of an electron is a positron. Quarks include up, down, charm, strange, top, and bottom as possible "flavors," and a quark has an antiquark.

Page 78: Vittoria describes her invention of antimatter canisters: "Airtight nanocomposite shells with opposing electromagnets at each end. . . . I borrowed the idea from nature. Portuguese man-o'-wars trap fish between their tentacles using nematocystic charges. Same principle here. Each canister has two electromagnets, one at each end. The opposing magnetic fields intersect in the center of the canister and hold the antimatter there, suspended in midvacuum."

This is more pseudo-technobabble. There is nothing specific to be gained from "nanocomposite" shells. In both *Angels & Demons* as well as *The Da Vinci Code*, Dan Brown adds the prefix *nano* (presumably a gratuitous allusion to nanotechnology) to technical words in a way to make them sound cooler or more leading edge. Nothing about a Portuguese man-o'-war tentacle applies here. This jellyfish does not trap fish between its tentacles, so much as it poisons them with its tentacles when the fish swim into them. The nematocysts are not "charged," but coiled, like natural springs.

Page 82: A sample of antimatter said to be "a few millionths of a gram" is annihilated and rocks the lab's vault. Vetra has been making occasional experiments of this nature for weeks or months. Later, Vittoria reveals that she and her father had made a quarter-gram of antimatter.

So how come no one at CERN has noticed these massive explosions going on beneath the facility? Don't they monitor seismic activity? The quarter-gram production effort required a significant expenditure of energy into the Large Hadron Collider. Didn't Kohler and CERN notice the amount of energy being consumed?

Page 90: "Antimatter was the ultimate terrorist weapon. It had no metallic parts to trip metal detectors, no chemical signature for dogs to trace, no fuse to deactivate if the authorities located the canister."

For security screening, it would not be possible to ignore the serious magnetic fields that are generated by the small but powerful electromagnets at the top and bottom of the canister.

Page 99: Kohler introduces Langdon to Vittoria as "a professor of art history at Harvard University . . . a specialist in cult symbology."

Langdon doesn't object, even though he himself says he is a professor of religious symbology, not art history.

Page 101: Kohler's secretary heard him in his office "on his modem, his phone, faxing, talking."

Kohler would have no need for an ordinary modem. At CERN, where the World Wide Web was invented, it would be unthinkable if everyone in the organization—particularly the director—did not have a hot, networked connection to the Internet.

Page 106: "The X-33 space plane roared into the sky and arced south toward Rome."
Flying due south from Geneva will take you to Toulon, France, and then over the western Mediterranean Sea. You need to fly southeast to get to Rome.

Page 115: The pilot has an odd costume. "His puffy tunic was vertically striped in brilliant blue and gold. He wore marching pantaloons and spats. On his feet were black flats that looked like slippers. On top of it all, he wore a black felt beret." 'Traditional Swiss Guard uniforms,' Langdon explained. 'Designed by Michelangelo himself.' " Later, on page 126, Langdon notes the Swiss Guards' weapon. "Each wielded the traditional 'Vatican long sword'—an eight-foot spear with a razor-sharp scythe."
Dan Brown does not remark on the brilliant red cuffs and red tassels of the Swiss Guard, which we find hard not to notice. What he describes as the "Vatican long sword" is actually a halberd. In most instances when the public sees Swiss Guards, this is what they are holding, although for certain ceremonies, they do wear broadswords. The broadswords, when worn, are readily recognizable as swords. The widely circulated claim that Michelangelo designed the uniforms seems to be a post-Renaissance legend, although he may have been tangentially involved. Raphael is owed some credit in this matter, as some of his paintings from that time period depict the basic elements of today's Swiss Guard uniforms.

Page 126: "The Great Castration, Langdon thought. It was one of the most horrific tragedies in Renaissance art. In 1857 Pope Pius IX decided that the accurate representation of the male form might incite lust inside the Vatican. So he got a chisel and mallet and hacked off the genitalia of every single male statue inside Vatican City. He defaced works by Michelangelo, Bramante, and Bernini. Plaster fig leaves were used to patch the damage. Hundreds of sculptures had been emasculated."
We know of no evidence that this event occurred in the reign of Pius IX during the mid-1800s. However, it is well known that Michelangelo had incurred the wrath of certain important churchmen for creating anatomically complete figures in the Sistine Chapel frescoes and elsewhere in statuary. These churchmen, Cardinal Carafa and Monsignor Sernini, attempted a censorship effort that became known as "the fig-leaf campaign." They were not successful until Michelangelo's death, when a law was passed to cover up the genitals. Daniele da Volterra, an apprentice of Michelangelo, created *perizomas* (briefs) to cover the genitals, and he was afterward called "Il Braghettone" (the breeches maker).

Page 154: The Illuminati caller lists the captured cardinals as "Cardinal Lamassé from Paris, Cardinal Guidera from Barcelona, Cardinal Ebner from Frankfurt and from Italy . . . Cardinal Baggia."

The selection of these four shows that the *papabili* (Brown incorrectly calls them *preferiti*) definitely were not chosen via a representative sample. If they had, at least one cardinal would definitely be from the Americas and probably one would be from Asia, Africa, or Oceana. It's true that about half of today's cardinals are from Europe, though they come from some twenty-seven different countries. Italians constitute about 20 percent of the total College of Cardinals and traditionally have had the inside edge in every modern conclave.

Page 154: "The camerlengo loosened like a tall ship that had just run sheets first into a dead calm."

Dan Brown reveals complete ignorance of sailing here. Landlubbers believe that a "sheet" is a sail. It is completely counterintuitive when they are told that a sheet is actually a line (rope) used to control a sail.

Page 155: Langdon recalls "la purga" in the year 1668. "The church branded four Illuminati scientists with the symbol of the cross. To purge their sins. . . . After the brandings, the scientists were murdered, and their bodies were dropped in public locations around Rome as a warning to other scientists not to join the Illuminati."

As far as we can tell from consultations with experts in many fields, almost every aspect of this story as rendered in *Angels & Demons* is fiction. That's exactly what a novelist is free to do—invent a "purge" that didn't occur, invent the "branding" of scientists that didn't happen, and invent the dropping of dead scientists' bodies as a warning. This all makes for strongly themed fiction. That it is at odds with Dan Brown's claims to base his work on fact is, of course, problematic. Our view is that *Angels & Demons* (as well as *The Da Vinci Code*) are novels—i.e, fiction, with many interesting historical, scientific, religious, artistic, and philosophical issues thrown in. One glaring plot flaw does appear here, however: if the 1668 event in question was supposed to have something to do with Galileo's arrest (as is alleged earlier in the book), that's hard to swallow—Galileo was arrested in 1633 and died in 1642. About "branding" and the Illuminati, maybe Dan Brown was thinking about the Affair of the Necklace, the well-known episode in European history, recently the topic of books and films. This real-life historical episode is set against the background of the Illuminati scare and the French Revolution. In a 2001 movie version, Hillary Swank is punished with the branding iron for having conspired with the Illuminati figure, played by Christopher Walken, to defraud Marie Antoinette. All of this takes place, of course, in the last years of the eighteenth century, not in 1668.

Page 159: The Hassassin says, "Your father? What is this? Vetra has a daughter? You should know your father whimpered like a child at the end. Pitiful really. A pathetic man."

The caller appears to be the person who surreptitiously invaded CERN, killed Vetra, and stole the canister. Why, with all his carefully orchestrated movements and well-researched assassination techniques, including knowing that he had to get Vetra's eyeball, would he not know Vetra had a daughter who worked with him? And especially since she owned the other set of eyeballs that would allow entry to the antimatter chamber?

Page 166: Olivetti argues against evacuating the Sistine Chapel. "Marching one hundred sixty-five cardinals unprepared and unprotected into Rome would be reckless." How many cardinals are in the chapel?

On page 185, Camerlengo Ventresca readily understands that the number cannot be 165, but 161 because four are missing. It is odd that Olivetti does not do the math on this. Dan Brown's figure of 165 does not reflect anything close to the actual situation. Taking the start of 2004 as a benchmark, there were 193 total cardinals, but 62 of them were already over eighty and could not act as electors in a conclave. Of the remaining 131 cardinals, 10 would become eighty years of age by the end of the year. So at any given time, it would be likely that only about 125 cardinals would assemble for the conclave.

Page 170: "The central office of the British Broadcast Corporation (BBC) is in London just west of Piccadilly Circus."

The British Broadcasting Corporation is headquartered at Broadcasting House. You would not go west from Piccadilly Circus to get there. It lies northerly, about half a mile up Regent Street from Portland Place.

Page 198: Langdon brings up the Diagramma della Verita, *or* Diagram of the Truth, *which he says was written by Galileo while under house arrest, smuggled to Holland, and published, becoming wildly popular with the European scientific underground. The church found out about it and went on a book-burning campaign.*

The *Diagramma* almost assuredly does not exist, and no Galileo scholar interviewed for this book believes it ever did. The description of the banned book, smuggled to Holland for printing, does, however, apply well to Galileo's *Discourses and Mathematical Demonstrations Relating to Two New Sciences* (1638).

Page 198: Langdon says, "Archivists rate documents one through ten for their structural integrity." He says the Diagramma *had a low "permanence rating" because it was "printed on sedge papyrus. It's like tissue paper. Life span of no more than a century. . . . This way any scientists caught with a copy could simply drop it in water and the booklet would dissolve." Is it likely that the document is papyrus, and does it dissolve in water? What about "permanence ratings"?*

SECRETS OF ANGELS & DEMONS

There is little likelihood that Galileo used papyrus. By the time he wrote, papyrus was long out of favor and would have been very hard to obtain, if it could be obtained at all. Galileo's age belonged to paper, of various kinds such as papers made of flax, linen, cotton, or wood pulp. Certain formal or special documents were written on parchment, which is made from animal skins. Papyrus enjoyed a long era of widespread use, originating in early Egypt and lasting thousands of years. It was even exported to other countries. But this changed by about AD 300 or 400 with an upsurge in the use of parchment in the eastern Mediterranean. In Europe, parchment ruled from around AD 900 until the printing of the Gutenberg Bible in AD 1456, which ushered in the widespread use of paper.

Papyrus from three thousand years ago is crumbly, but it still would not dissolve in water. The main fiber of papyrus is cellulose, which is not readily soluble in water. However, papyrus was traditionally made from strips of the papyrus plant that were laid horizontally and vertically with Nile water, then pressed and dried so that the juices of the plant became the main adhesive. Getting a sheet of papyrus wet would surely loosen the adhesion of the strips at some point. "Sedge papyrus" is apparently Langdon's attempt to appear more knowledgeable than he is. No other kind of papyrus exists, because papyrus is a member of the sedge family of grassy plants. By the way, when Dan Brown wants papyrus to dissolve in *The Da Vinci Code*'s ever-fascinating cryptex, he escalates the corrosive liquid to vinegar (dilute acetic acid). This makes it sound as though the liquid surely would dissolve papyrus. But that doesn't happen in reality, either.

No "permanence ratings" exist that would apply to papyrus. There are some standards for paper and cardboard media for libraries that want to order from trusted suppliers. These media are examined in accordance with the specified test methods of the American National Standards Institute, the American Society for Testing and Materials, and the Technical Association of the Pulp and Paper Industry. Generally, all the papers are expected to last at least five hundred years.

Page 204: Langdon describes the special atmosphere of the "hermetic vault." It has a "partial vacuum" in order to reduce the oxygen level, he says. It has only 8 percent humidity. It is "like going from sea level to 20,000 feet in an instant" when one steps inside. "Nausea and light-headedness were not uncommon. Double vision, double over, he reminded himself, quoting the archivist's mantra."

Libraries that have archives for rare books are lucky when they have rooms with temperature and humidity control. They do not have hermetically sealed vaults. Not even the Vatican Library. (See the discussion in my "Technology of Toys" piece in Chapter 6 for some of the atmospheric and bodily challenges that would be posed even if this kind of system could be installed.)

Page 207: Videographer Chinita Macri says that she can transmit live on "one point five three seven megahertz."

This is the same as 1537 KHz, a frequency within the band allocated to AM radio. Broadcasters would never use it for a television signal. In fact, it would probably "step on" the Vatican Radio broadcast at 1530 KHz.

Page 209: "Rummaging through a tray of archivist tools, Langdon found the felt-pad pincers archivists called 'finger cymbals'—oversized tweezers with flattened disks on each arm."

The "finger cymbals" idea is probably Dan Brown's invention. For handling papyrus, archivists may use tweezers, but they are flat, square-ended tweezers without pads. For handling paper documents, it is most common to find conservators using their hands (carefully washed, of course) or cotton gloves, which can sometimes cause problems of their own, such as snagging.

Page 217: " 'In the 1600s,' " [Langdon] said, talking faster now, 'English was the one language the Vatican had not yet embraced. They dealt in Italian, Latin, German, even Spanish and French, but English was totally foreign inside the Vatican. They considered English a polluted, free-thinkers' language for profane men like Chaucer and Shakespeare.' "

Although England officially turned to the Anglican Church after Henry VIII, there were still large numbers of Catholics in England. They would certainly have had clergy who spoke English, with a hierarchy that interacted with Rome. At times, England saw the rise of Catholic kings and queens. According to Stephen Greenblatt, one of America's leading Shakespeare scholars, Shakespeare's own father was a secret Catholic. It may have been from watching him practice Catholic ritual that the young Will developed his sense of the dramatic. Further, practically all of Ireland was Catholic and, again, there would have been lots of interaction with Rome by Irish speakers of English. The sixteenth century saw many efforts, primarily in German and English, to bring the Bible into the language of the common man, rather than keeping it locked in Latin. At first Rome had stiffly resisted this movement, but by about 1580 had begun to accept it. Getting the Bible translated into English was important enough that two Catholic translations were extant around the time that the King James Version (the Protestant Bible) was distributed in 1611.

Page 223: Langdon decodes "Santi" as the artist Raphael. He says Raphael was a child prodigy "who at the age of twenty-five was already doing commissions for Pope Julius II, and when he died at only thirty-eight, left behind the greatest collection of frescoes the world had ever seen. Santi was a behemoth in the art world." Langdon also says, "Raphael, like many other religious artists, was a suspected closet atheist."

Among art historians, Raphael is most commonly known by his Italian name of Raffaello Sanzio, but it is true he at times was called Raffaello Santi. He was born in 1483 and died on the eve of his thirty-seventh birthday on April 6, 1520. We find it odd that Dan Brown cites an inscription on his sarcophagus, "Raphael Santi, 1483–1520," yet could not correctly calculate thirty-seven years. Raphael's twelve years in Rome prior to his death were productive in frescoes, but this was by no means his total body of work. He painted many portraits and other paintings, and he created famous tapestries for the Vatican. Additionally, he had major architectural accomplishments and was for a time the architect of St. Peter's in Rome, as well as the original architect of the space within the Santa Maria del Popolo church that would become Bernini's chapel for the Chigi family. This is where Langdon and Vittoria in *Angels & Demons* discover the first, earth-themed, murder.

Page 238: It is about 7:48 p.m. in Rome and Langdon reflects that "six hours ago he had been sound asleep in Cambridge."
Since he was told it was shortly past 1:00 p.m. in Geneva when he landed (and presumably reset Mickey), he should know that he has been in Europe for nearly seven hours, and awake for about eight and a half hours.

Page 243: "The practice of 'god-eating'—that is, Holy Communion—was borrowed from the Aztecs. Even the concept of Christ dying for our sins is arguably not exclusively Christian; the self-sacrifice of a young man to absolve the sins of his people appears in the earliest tradition of the Quetzalcoatl."
True, these other cultures may have had parallel legends, but neither statement makes any sense if you accept a historical basis for the life of Christ and the Last Supper (when the Holy Communion was taught to the disciples). By AD 200 the early church included the communion rituals. The only way to explain it using Langdon's assertion supposes that Christ had learned the Aztec legends and was attempting to emulate them. But the Aztec culture did not rise until about nine hundred or a thousand years after Christ.

Page 245: Langdon mentions that the Pantheon was rebuilt in AD 119 by Hadrian. The Pantheon cicerone, or "guide," says, "It was the world's largest free-standing dome until 1960 when it was eclipsed by the Superdome in New Orleans!"
The span of the Pantheon dome is 43.3 meters. It was eclipsed in the 1400s. In building the cathedral at Florence beginning in 1420, Filippo Brunelleschi designed a dome—or cupola as it was called—that was 45.5 meters in diameter. The dome portion was completed in 1438, but Brunelleschi's work continued until his death in 1446. Construction of the cathedral continued for many years after that. Brunelleschi had conducted a thorough study of the Pantheon dome before coming up with his plan for Florence's cathedral. Michelangelo designed the dome at St. Peter's in Rome after looking at

Brunelleschi's dome. St. Peter's is 42.1 meters in diameter—slightly smaller. The Louisiana Superdome in New Orleans was not built in 1960. It was completed in 1975. Maybe Langdon was thinking of the Astrodome. Launched as an idea with the decision to start a major league baseball franchise in Houston in 1960, the Astrodome was not completed until five years later. In any event, although the New Orleans Superdome is big at 210 meters, the Georgia Superdome, completed in 1992, is the clear winner at 256 meters (840 feet).

Page 258: "Langdon and Vittoria's taxi completed the one-mile sprint up the wide Via della Scrofa in just over a minute. They skidded to a stop on the south side of the Piazza del Popolo just before eight." They look around the piazza, then seek out the church. "The Church of Santa Maria del Popolo stood out like a misplaced battleship, askew at the base of the hill on the southeast corner of the piazza."

This trip doesn't jibe with the real route in Rome. Although they might begin by going north up Via della Scrofa, this changes names to become Via di Ripetta and then Piazza Augusto Imperatore. Portions of this route are one-way in the southerly direction, and there is a traffic barrier at a crossing street, Via Tomacelli. You cannot put a church in a "corner" of an ellipse, but even if you go along with the thought, Santa Maria del Popolo is found in the northeast "corner" of the Piazza del Popolo, not the southeast.

Page 259: Langdon and Vittoria view the Porta del Popolo and see a symbol at the top center. Vittoria describes "a shining star over a triangular pile of stones" and Langdon agrees, calling it, "a source of Illumination over a pyramid." Vittoria recognizes this as describing the "Great Seal of the United States." Langdon agrees: "Exactly. The Masonic symbol on the one-dollar bill."

The symbol at the top of the Porta del Popolo is not at all what Langdon and Vittoria think they see. It is a well-known element of the family crest of Pope Alexander VII, who was definitely not a Mason. Born Fabio Chigi, of the wealthy Siena banking house of Chigi, Alexander VII wanted to leave behind signs of his greatness. He had artists create a number of elements that belonged to coats of arms of the Chigi family. He then had these symbols slathered all over Rome (and beyond) during his reign. He even got the symbol "six mountains and a star" added to structures that were not of his own time.

The Via Flaminia, a road into Rome, had been built in AD 220 and was the path used by many to enter the city over the centuries. In 1562 the pope of the time (Pius IV Medici) commissioned the gate, Porta del Flaminia, to impress pilgrims entering the city. It later became known as the Porta del Popolo (Gate of the People). Nearly a century later (in 1655) during the reign of Alexander VII, the queen of Sweden, who had embraced Catholicism, came through the Gate. The pope commissioned Bernini to decorate the structure in honor of this event. The gate already had Pius IV's crest on it, but Bernini surmounted it with Alexander VII's—the Chigi six mountains and a star.

The well-defined pyramid capped by an all-seeing eye, found on a one-dollar bill, is nothing like what Langdon and Vittoria see. The dollar's symbol, often attributed to Masonic influences, in fact comes from other sources that influenced the designers of the Great Seal of the United States. Nonetheless, Dan Brown has sprinkled it around two Langdon books already, and we expect to see it return when Brown's next book is released. Hints on the dust jacket of *The Da Vinci Code* make it clear that Brown will take Langdon to Washington, DC. There many bona fide Masonic symbols and structures can be found. Many more nefarious meanings can be conjured up as well, tying into Illuminati legends, conspiracy theories, and more. (Note that Langdon has begun to use "Illuminati" and "Masonic" interchangeably in his symbolic interpretations.)

Page 261: There is a side door on the church. "Langdon recognized it as the standard porta sacra— *a private entrance for clergy. Most of these entrances had gone out of use years ago . . ."*

Langdon is horribly misusing the term *porta sacra*, literally a sacred gate or doorway. A porta sacra is specifically found in each of four great basilicas in Rome: St. Peter's, St. John Lateran, St. Mary Major, and St. Paul-without-the-Walls. No mere "side door," it is not just for clergy. It is a special doorway that is plastered shut until the start of a jubilee year of the Catholic church. Jubilees were once intended to be at fifty- or hundred-year marks, but now customarily come at twenty-five-year intervals, as well as certain extraordinary years as determined by the pope. The pope opens the porta sacra at St. Peter's at Christmas time, and he deputizes three cardinals to do it at the other locations. At the appointed hour, the pontiff knocks thrice on the door with a silver hammer and, on the third blow, the plaster is rigged to fall away. Religious pilgrims who pass through the porta sacra of all four basilicas are rewarded with a special remission of sin known as an indulgence.

Page 263: "Every guard wore headphones connected to an antennalike detector that he waved rhythmically in front of him—the same devices they used twice a week to sweep for electronic bugs inside the Vatican. . . . The antennae would sound if they detected even the tiniest magnetic field. Tonight, however, they were getting no readings at all."

This is illogical. A wireless video camera is transmitting a picture of the canister at all times, so a constant signal is being transmitted. If this signal reaches the video system, it surely is detectable by the proper equipment.

Page 265: Vittoria finds "a decorative tile embedded in the stone" with a "pyramid beneath a shining star," next to a "grime-covered plaque" that says "Coat of Arms of Alexander Chigi, Whose Tomb Is Located in the Secondary Left Apse of this Cathedral." What's wrong with this picture?

First, the plaque, seems written in English—in an old Italian church. Second, the famous patron would not have been named Alexander Chigi. The Chigi Chapel was commissioned by the famous Agostino Chigi, who died in 1512. In the mid-1600s a famous member of the Chigi family, Fabio di Flavio became pope, taking the name Alexander VII. He launched the rehabilitation of the family chapel and asked Bernini to help renovate and decorate it. Third, the tomb of Alexander VII, a very famous monumental masterpiece in marble by Bernini, is found in St. Peter's Basilica, not in this church. Fourth, this is a church, not a cathedral. Fifth, the "decorative tile" is marble inlay. Sixth, although there are pyramids in the chapel, they are there for their imperial rather than mystical connotations. Langdon probably has again failed to recognize that at least one of the "pyramids" he sees is the six mountains and a star symbol of the Chigi family.

Page 268: Vittoria and Langdon enter the Chigi Chapel and see two large pyramids with "gold medallions" that are "perfect ellipses."
Indeed, the Chigi Chapel contains two pyramids with ellipses, but the ellipses are white marble, not gold. The chapel was paid for by the banker Agostino Chigi (died 1512) and his brother Sigismondo (died 1526). Both are buried in the chapel, and the elliptical medallions show their images. In a design by Raphael, their tombs have an unusual pyramidal form that was derived from Roman tombs and was carried out by Lorenzetto long before Bernini's time.

Page 269: They find the circular mosaic stone has been moved to reveal the "demon's hole" in the floor of the Chigi Chapel. Langdon sees the image of a skeleton depicting "death in flight." The skeleton is "carrying a tablet portraying the same pyramid and stars they had seen outside."
The Chigi Chapel does indeed contain a circular hole covered by the image of a skeleton with wings. This is a common symbol used on many tombs throughout Rome. The distinctive feature here is that the skeleton is holding a family crest, not a tablet. The inscribed banderole below the skeleton image reads "Mors aD CaeLos"—which means "death opens the way to heaven"— with the Roman numerals spelling out the jubilee year MDCL, or 1650, in capital letters. Below the skeleton lie the remains of women and lesser Chigis. Again, Langdon misinterprets the Chigi coat of arms, with the six mountains and star. This is odd, because, Langdon wonders to himself "how many generations of Chigis had been unceremoniously dumped in." The crest includes two repetitions of the six mountains symbol, and two of an oak tree, also a Chigi symbol.

Page 283: Vittoria and Langdon conclude that the sculptor Gianlorenzo Bernini was the Illuminati's secret master artist. Part of the logic is that Bernini, so well known as a Catholic religious artist, could never be suspected as an Illuminati. "A perfect cover. Illuminati infiltration." Another proof is a plaque that says "Art of the Chigi Chapel—While the architecture is Raphael's, all interior adornments are those of Gianlorenzo Bernini."

A small plaque exists in the real Chigi Chapel, but Dan Brown does not describe exactly what it says. Raphael was indeed the original architect, but he died in 1520. As indicated above, Lorenzetto worked on much of the decoration as well. Then, after Raphael's death, the project was abandoned for more than a century. Eventually, Bernini did come under the patronage of the Chigi Pope Alexander VII, who commissioned him to finish the job started so long ago. This is when Bernini created the statue *Habbakuk and the Angel*, as well as the skeleton inlay in the marble floor.

On this project Bernini worked for a Chigi pontiff who could foot the bill for extravaganzas in marble—the results were spectacular. The pyramidal tombs for the two Chigi brothers, however, were Raphael's design, only brought to fruition by Bernini. Bernini went to Mass every day and took communion twice a week, so he was really fooling the church if he was an Illuminati.

Page 285: They look at the Bernini sculpture Habakkuk and the Angel *and notice that both figures are pointing, but in different directions.*

Shouldn't they notice that the tip of the angel's index finger is broken off? It's pretty apparent to everyone who visits the sculpture in person.

Page 295: The Vatican guard describes a "block" of marble that he immediately calls "an ellipse." It has "the image of a billowing gust of wind." He goes on to talk about it as though it were a single tile in St. Peter's Square called the West Ponente (West Wind) or Respiro di Dio (Breath of God).

There are actually sixteen such ellipses, representing all the cardinal and intercardinal points of the compass. For the guard to remember just one of the sixteen tiles—as though the others didn't exist—is not plausible.

Page 297: At 8:54 p.m. "the springtime sun was setting behind St. Peter's Basilica, and a massive shadow spread, engulfing the piazza." What's wrong here?

The sun had set more than an hour earlier, if you are talking about the real Rome in April. But more important, it was back at 8:35 p.m. that Langdon viewed the sun "blotted" by St. Peter's Basilica, as he stood across town. A sun that is twenty minutes below the horizon cannot cast shadows across the square.

Page 305: Chinita Macri removes the "spent video cassette" from her camera. She thinks to herself, "Cellulose gold."

Chinita is supposed to be a veteran videographer with the BBC. She is either more ignorant than even a layman, or brilliant and should be promoted

1. It is probably not *cellulose* that she is thinking of. Cellulose is the fiber of a plant or tree, commonly found in paper.
2. She was probably thinking of *celluloid,* but that material was used in the movie industry from about 1895 to about 1948.
3. But wait—celluloid was made from cellulose! Maybe Chinita is brilliant, after all. At its earliest beginnings, the material called celluloid was chemically cellulose nitrate. Unfortunately, this cellulose was a highly flammable substance that caused a lot of movie house fires when the projector ignited it. Celluloid films in canisters also built up explosive vapors.
4. But wait—the movie industry moved on to *safety film* and that was actually cellulose acetate. So maybe Chinita is thinking of this material, still used in the film industry for making the prints of movies that are distributed to theaters.
5. But wait—it's a video camera. Videotape has no need for optical properties, so it is made on a base of polyester—nothing like celluloid.

So perhaps Chinita should have called it *polyester gold.*

Page 331: Vittoria and the camerlengo go to a sunken area beneath the main altar at the center of St. Peter's Basilica, where there is a "golden coffer," famous for holding "St. Peter's bones." The camerlengo explains that it holds "palliums—woven sashes that the Pope gives to newly elected cardinals."
A pallium is a sash woven of white lamb's wool. The plural of *pallium* is *pallia.* They are kept in the Niche of the Pallia in a silver coffer. They are bestowed upon newly made archbishops by the pope. There is an old folk myth about the coffer holding "St. Peter's bones," but the church does not hide the actual story.

Page 355: "The church is on Piazza Barberini," Olivetti said.
Olivetti is wrong. The church of Santa Maria della Vittoria is several blocks farther east, not on the piazza, but on the Via XX Settembre.

Page 367: Langdon and Vittoria get inside the church only to find a large bonfire in the dead center of the church, built of burning pews. The branded Cardinal Guidera is suspended over the fire by two incensor cables. Olivetti is not to be found.
Let's review what the Hassassin has had to accomplish in the past fifteen minutes or so. First, he had to arrive at the church with Cardinal Guidera in tow (but not in view of the churchgoers). He had to get them all to leave. Then he had to go out to his van—presumably—and bring Guidera into the church. Then he had to use a ladder to lower the incensor cable from the left wall and tie it to Guidera's hand. He had to take the ladder to the right wall to lower the incensor cable and tie it to Guidera's other hand. Then he had to go back

to the right wall and hoist Guidera by that cable, making sure that Guidera ended up in the middle of the church. Then he had to take the ladder to the left wall and hoist the left incensor cable. Then he had to build the bonfire and get it to burn well. He had to remember to throw the ladder on the pile. During his free time, he had to take a warning phone call from Janus, and then had to kill Olivetti when he showed up in the church about four minutes ahead of Langdon and Vittoria. Then he had to secrete himself in the back of the church so that he could surprise Vittoria after she walked by.

Page 377: Langdon needs both legs to shift the inverted sarcophagus, bringing it down onto the Hassassin's arm. Yet the Hassassin is able to extricate himself, even though he has only one free arm. How is this possible?

Perhaps Hassassins get superhuman strength from hashish.

Page 393: The fireman hears an electronic beeping sound coming from beneath the inverted sarcophagus. (It is Langdon's Mickey Mouse watch, of course.)

Langdon is forty years old. He had been given the watch during his child-hood, which we are free to guess was approximately age twelve—perhaps in the early 1970s. Mickey Mouse watches of that period were not electronic. The electric watches that were available then were expensive—above $300 at minimum. Mickey Mouse watches were just intended for kids, since we had not yet entered an era when it was thought camp for adults to wear a cartoon watch (or was it ever?). The early 1970s Mickey Mouse watch was a one-jewel, Swiss movement, wind-up watch with no alarm. (When alarms eventu-ally came into the Disney watches, by the way, the sound was usually not a beep, but a song, such as "It's A Small World After All.") Back in those days, Mickey couldn't swim, either—the watch was not water resistant nor "water-proof," as Dan Brown describes it on page 114.

Page 401: Langdon says the church of Saint Agnes in Agony was named for St. Agnes, "a ravishing teenage virgin banished to a life of sexual slavery for refusing to renounce her faith." Well, classmates, is anyone going to ask the professor to elaborate on this one?

Langdon gets lurid here, and is prone to exaggeration. According to the leg-end, during the reign of the emperor Diocletian in 304, the prefect Sempro-nius wished Agnes, thirteen, daughter of a noble, to marry his son. When she refused, he condemned her to death. Roman law did not permit the execution of virgins, so he ordered her to be raped beforehand, but her honor was mi-raculously preserved. According to some legends, her long hair miraculously grew to cover her naked body. When led out to die she was tied to a stake, but the faggots would not burn, whereupon the officer in charge of the troops drew his sword and struck off her head. By these accounts, there was no "life of sexual slavery." The refusal was in regard to marriage, not renunciation of faith. In any event, as noted elsewhere in this book, St. Agnes might well have been in agony, but she is known as St. Agnes not in Agony, but in Agone, the former name of the area housing the church in her memory. Today it is called the Piazza Navona and was previously a Roman athletic field.

Page 410: With Langdon hiding near the steps of St. Agnes, the Hassassin's van enters the piazza at 10:46 p.m., pulling up to the fountain so that its sliding door is "positioned only inches above the churning water."

Driving this close to the fountain is impossible. There are permanent obstructions around it.

Page 425: Langdon notes the Bridge of Angels with "twelve towering angels carved by none other than Bernini himself."

There are ten angels on the bridge, not twelve. The other two figures are the saints Peter and Paul.

None of the figures was carved to completion by Bernini, but rather by his pupils. The two exquisite marble angels carved by Bernini himself were so prized by Pope Clement IX that he did not want to put them outdoors. They remain in Rome's Sant'Andrea delle Fratte.

Page 425: Langdon says the "central arm" of the cross formed by the four obelisks passes directly through the center of the castle's bridge.

Not on our map of Rome.

Page 425: Langdon is speeding down Lungotevere Tor Di Nona with the Tiber River on his right, when he swerves right and slams into the barricades at the bridge.

The barricades are a blessing; he is no longer a threat to Roman drivers. He has been driving the wrong way down a one-way street again. But we should congratulate Langdon for his ability to navigate some tricky streets at night in a strange city, in record time. No Roman driver could have gotten there so fast.

Page 426: Langdon "donned his Harris tweed over his damp shirt, grateful for Harris's trademark double lining. The Diagramma *folio would remain dry." Does Langdon know his tweeds?*

No. Harris Tweed is not a brand name for clothing; it is a trademarked name for this type of cloth, from Scotland. Your tailor can give you a double lining if you like. That decision is not up to the weavers. Here's how to know Harris Tweed, taken from the Harris Tweed Authority website, www.harristweed.com: "Harris Tweed is cloth that has been handwoven by the islanders of Lewis, Harris, Uist and Barra in their homes, using pure virgin wool that has been dyed and spun in the Outer Hebrides."

Page 429: The Aussie tells Langdon that his satellite truck's arm can go up "fifteen meters." Why is this illogical?

A satellite truck works by aligning its dish with the satellite and then holding perfectly steady. A long-armed boom would make the dish unreliable in even a modest wind.

Page 492: "The camerlengo erupted through the doors of St. Peter's Basilica at exactly 11:56 p.m."

Wait a minute! It was only on page 472 that the camerlengo had gone into St. Peter's to get the canister at 11:42 p.m.. And it was 11:55 p.m. when he began his exit. Assuming he had spent one or two minutes praying at St. Peter's tomb, this still means that it took him about ten minutes to arrive at the canister from the steps of the basilica, but only one minute to make the return trip!

Page 514: "It was then that Langdon saw the ravaged shreds of parchment clinging all over the lining of his jacket. The folio from Galileo's Diagramma. *The last copy on earth had just dissolved."*

Wait another minute! Brown is getting sloppier as he races toward the end of the novel. Back on page 210 we were told it was papyrus, not parchment! Parchment is made of animal skin and is a lot more rugged than papyrus. It doesn't shred in water.

Page 569: Speaking of a "religious experience," Vittoria disrobes, saying, "You've never been to bed with a yoga master, have you?"

As our own patron saint, Paul Simon, once wrote, "If that's my prayerbook, Lord let us pray!"

WHAT'S IN A NAME?

BY DAVID A. SHUGARTS

The playful use of anagrammatical names that flowered in Dan Brown's *The Da Vinci Code* is only budding in his earlier *Angels & Demons*. There are only a few names that lend themselves to interpretation and rearrangement. Apparently, Dan Brown mined the faculty and alumni lists of his alma mater, New Hampshire's Phillips Exeter Academy, to arrive at names for the minor characters in *Angels & Demons*. The names of the major characters are only slightly more inventive. Here is a rundown:

Robert Langdon

On the acknowledgments page of Angels & Demons, *Dan Brown pays homage to John Langdon, who created the stunning ambigrams.*

An outstanding artist, John Langdon is one of two acknowledged masters in the genre of ambigrams, the other being Scott Kim, whose custom-made anagram for the word *secrets* can be seen in the next essay. Langdon and Kim's works may be viewed at www.johnlangdon.net and www.scottkim.com.

David A. Shugarts is a journalist of more than thirty years' experience. His skill as an investigative reporter led him to uncover the "names behind the names" of the main characters in Dan Brown's *The Da Vinci Code*, which he presented in *Secrets of the Code*.

Vittoria Vetra

In the novel, Vittoria Vetra is the adopted daughter of Leonardo Vetra, brilliant physicist at CERN. She is also a physicistor, as Dan Brown characterizes her, a "bio-entanglement physicist," and her father's partner in their private lab. Vittoria is described as lithe and graceful, tall with chestnut skin and long black hair. She is a strict vegetarian and CERN's resident guru of hatha yoga.

Vittoria is Italian for "Victoria," the Roman goddess of victory and the equivalent of the Greek goddess Nike. Vetra is a public square in Milan. This is the site where Maifreda, the proffered female pope of the Guglielmites, was burned by inquisitors in the year 1300.

In the thirteenth century, when the Gnostics and other groups had female clergy, a woman known as Guglielma of Bohemia came to Milan, Italy, and began to preach. After her death in 1281, as was not uncommon, a cult sprang up around her relics. Fanatics among Guglielma's followers believed she was an incarnation of the Holy Spirit and would return to depose the male pope, thus installing the first of a line of female popes and launching the "age of the spirit."

These fanatics eventually picked a young Milanese woman, Maifreda di Pirovano, and set the date of Guglielma's return, the Pentecost in the year 1300. When this date arrived, the forces of Pope Boniface VIII seized Maifreda di Pirovano and others, and burned them at the stake on the Piazza Vetra.

Leonardo Vetra

Leonardo Vetra is a week shy of his fifty-eighth birthday when he is tortured and killed at the outset of An-gels & Demons. He considered himself a theo-physicist.

We see "Leonardo" as the harbinger of the character Leonardo da Vinci in *The Da Vinci Code*. The last name, Vetra, is explained above. *Angels & Demons* has a general theme of religious martyrdom by gruesome deaths, which can be applied to Vetra's death.

Carlo Ventresca

The deceased pope's chamberlain, or camerlengo, is Carlo Ventresca, an orphan rescued by the pope, who had treated him like a son (because he was).

As our travel correspondent David Downie has discovered, the name Carlo Ventresca can be rather readily translated from Italian as "Charlie the Tuna."

Maximillian Kohler

Kohler is the fictional director of CERN, son of a well-to-do family from Frankfurt, Germany.

The German origin of *Kohler* can lead to *kohle*, which is German for "coal," but also to *kohl*, which is German for "cabbage" and also has the colloquial meaning of "rubbish," or in American, "hooey." A *kibler* in German is literally a "charcoal-burner."

Jaqui Tomaso

When Professor Langdon sees the plaque at the Vatican Secret Archives referring to "Padre Jaqui Tomaso," he thinks of "the toughest librarian on earth." The name evokes a mental image of "Father Jaqui in full military fatigues and helmet standing guard with a bazooka."

Now, we're not saying they're related, but Jacquelyn H. Thomas is the librarian at Phillips Exeter Academy and has been there for many years.

Tyler Tingley

As news of the crisis reaches the outside world, the principal characters in the Vatican flip television channels and hear one snatch about "conspiracy theorist Tyler Tingley."

Dr. Tyler C. Tingley is the thirteenth principal of Phillips Exeter Academy, appointed in 1997. He is a 1948 graduate of the school.

Richard Aaronian

In Angels & Demons, *a Harvard biology professor, Richard Aaronian, defends his genetic engineering work by depicting a Christian fish symbol with legs and the legend "DARWIN!"*

Richard Aaronian is the Harlan Page Amen Professor of Science at Phillips Exeter and is also an avid birdwatcher. He has led at least one student expedition to the Galapagos Islands, a spot near and dear to Darwin's heart.

Robert Brownell

Professor Langdon is dining with Harvard colleagues when physicist Bob Brownell comes in, raging about the cancellation of the US supercollider program.

Robert F. Brownell Jr. held a wide range of titles at Phillips Exeter. He was an instructor in science, director of scholarship students, acting dean of students, director of admissions, basketball coach, and dorm head.

Charles Pratt

A quiet man at the faculty dinner table is Charles Pratt, said to be Harvard's "Poet in Residence."

Charles Pratt was a 1952 graduate of Phillips Exeter.

Aldo Baggia

One of the slain cardinals in Angels & Demons *is Aldo Baggia.*

Aldo J. Baggia is a former head of the modern language department at Phillips Exeter, teaching Spanish, French, Italian, and German. He was known for traveling widely and for writing reviews on opera.

Bissell

Professor Langdon is flashing back to his own English class at Phillips Exeter, when "an animated schoolmaster named Bissell, leapt onto the table and bellowed, "Penta-meter!"

The late H. Hamilton Bissell, known as "Hammy" or "Mr. Exeter," was a fixture at Phillips Exeter for many years. He was a 1929 graduate and became the school's first director of scholarship students. Bissell had a forty-three-year career with the school and in retirement remained active on campus. He was an avid squash and tennis player. He had many famous sayings, one of which was "A teacher should put the heart before the course."

Peter Greer
Schoolmaster Bissell is pounding the meaning of iambic pentameter into the head of Peter Greer, school baseball star.

Peter C. Greer is the Bates-Russell Distinguished Faculty Professor and English instructor at Phillips Exeter Academy, as well as a 1958 graduate.

Hitzrot
A student dozing in the back of Professor Langdon's class at Harvard is a fellow named Hitzrot.

Lewis H. Hitzrot is an instructor in chemistry and physics at Phillips Exeter.

Kelly Horan-Jones
In Angels & Demons, *the "doe-eyed brunette" reporter for MSNBC, Kelly Horan-Jones, appears on television "live" from the Vatican with a bogus background shot.*

Kelly Horan Jones (sans hyphen) was a reporter for WMUR-TV in Manchester, New Hampshire, around 1997–1998 when Dan Brown was researching *Angels & Demons.* She went on to WCVB-TV in Boston and recently has been the managing editor at Foodline.com, a restaurant review guide in Boston.

Sylvie Baudeloque
In Angels & Demons, *Sylvie Baudeloque is the disgruntled executive secretary for Max Kohler, CERN director.*

Sylvie Baudeloque is listed in the acknowledgments of *The Da Vinci Code*, without further explanation. Also, there is a senior player of the French Federation of Badminton by that name.

Rebecca Strauss
Professor Langdon in Angels & Demons *recalls "a whirlwind of black velvet, cigarettes, and not so subtly enhanced breasts" by the name of Rebecca Strauss. The "onetime fashion model, now art critic from the* Times" *(presumably of New York) could become a love interest, but Langdon has not returned her phone calls.*

We searched for any Rebecca Strauss of note and came across a very interesting candidate. Like Dan Brown, she is a musician. Skilled at the viola and violin, she has played with the Boston Pops Esplanade Orchestra, the Boston Ballet Orchestra, the New England String Ensemble, and the Boston Lyric Opera. She is the creator and musical coordinator of the Riverview Chamber Players in Boston, which supplies classical music ensembles for corporate events and weddings. A specialty is weddings for gay and lesbian couples; Strauss is an acknowledged lesbian. She is an experienced teacher and holds a master's degree in early childhood education. And she is an acolyte of the Feldenkrais Method of somatic-movement awareness education.

The Secrets of Ambigrams

by David A. Shugarts and Scott Kim

One of the more stunning elements of *Angels & Demons* is the use of *ambigrams*, the words appearing in the novel's text that are readable either right side up or upside down; they are said to be the symbols emblazoned by Illuminati branding irons on the flesh of the murdered cardinals.

Ambigram is a relatively recent word, its definition still somewhat in flux. Having just one kind of symmetry, those found in *Angels & Demons* represent a relatively narrow definition. Even so, their effect is truly mind bending. See the ambigram on the next page of the word *secrets,* created for our series of books by artist Scott Kim.

The ambigrams found in *Angels & Demons,* representing each of the four elements—fire, earth, air, and water—plus a diamond-shaped combination of these, are an example of *rotational symmetry,* where an image can be rotated 180 degrees and still appear exactly the same. They were created by real-life artist John Langdon, credited as the first to discover and exploit this form in contemporary usage. Dan Brown not only draws on his work in this book but clearly admires him—after all, he named the novel's hero, Robert Langdon, after him. Robert Langdon, of course, continues on

David A. Shugarts is a journalist of more than thirty years' experience. His skill as an investigative reporter led to an evaluation of Dan Brown's plot flaws in *Angels & Demons.* He wrote a similar piece about *The Da Vinci Code,* which he presented in *Secrets of the Code.* Scott Kim is an independent designer of visual puzzles and games for the Web.

SECRETS

into Brown's next novel, although in *The Da Vinci Code* Brown becomes more interested in *anagrams*, the rearrangements of the letters in words or sentences to make other meaningful words or sentences, than in ambigrams.

Written languages have words and phrases that read the same backward and forward. These are called *palindromes*. A simple example is "mom," and perhaps the most famous classic palindrome is Napoleon's lament, "Able was I ere I saw Elba." An ambigram is not necessarily a palindrome, but it is related by notions of symmetry.

When you are looking for high artistry in ambigrams, with uncanny mastery of typographic forms and shapes, two contemporary artists stand out above the crowd: John Langdon and Scott Kim. Each is an accomplished artist with a large body of work to his credit, and each has been creating ambigrams for many years. Many corporate logos qualify as ambigrams, and over the years the two artists have produced numerous logos.

John Langdon gets the general nod as the first to "discover" ambigrams for contemporary purposes, although Langdon readily acknowledges that "Scott Kim had invented them, too, almost at the same time." Scott Kim sets the date of his first ambigram as 1975. Since these inventions did not yet have an accepted name, Kim called them "inversions," and was the first to publish, in a book titled *Inversions* (1981). Langdon eventually published a selection of his ambigrams in a 1992 book, *Wordplay*. Neither had any computer assistance in their early work.

Praise for each artist tends to be lavish. Reportedly, the famed science fiction novelist Isaac Asimov called Kim "the Escher of the alphabet," while one reviewer said of Langdon, "We'd like to thank John Langdon for being born in our lifetime." Readers can judge for themselves, since both artists have websites (johnlangdon.net and scottkim.com).

The coining of the word *ambigram* is generally attributed to Douglas R. Hofstadter, the author of *Gödel, Escher, Bach: An Eternal Golden Braid* (1979). That book, which won the Pulitzer Prize, was a complex explanation of metaphysical matters leading to an understanding of the challenge of creating an artificial intelligence program on a computer. Hofstadter used mathematics, art (including the works of M. C. Escher), science, and music to illustrate principles such as recursiveness, where a thing—whether it be a computer program, a musical or literary passage, or a strand of DNA—may be self-referencing.

Later, Hofstadter produced a series of articles for *Scientific American* that were gathered into a book, *Metamagical Themas*, published in 1983, where the word *ambigram* appeared. Hofstadter himself says he isn't sure which part of the word *ambigram* he coined, since he vaguely remembers it as part of a brainstorming session among friends.

While this is the modern history of ambigrams, it should be noted that some of the most ancient written languages readily lent themselves to ambigrams and palindromes. The hieroglyphs of Egypt had many characters that were symmetrical. The

Egyptians were actually free to string hieroglyphs in all four orientations (from left to right, right to left, up to down, or down to up). It therefore goes without saying that these ancients must have recognized palindromes and ambigrams, even if they did not have terms for them.

With all this history, we should perhaps point out that the real Illuminati were not particularly known for creating or using ambigrams or anything like them, although the ambigrams that appear in *Angels & Demons* look a bit like one of the standard German/Bavarian typography styles current in 1776. We could also find no historical basis for anyone branding anyone in seventeenth-century Europe with English-language words for the four primal elements of Aristotelian cosmology.

Scott Kim points out that he had seen at least one ambigram published in a 1902 book on puzzles, and he believes Doug Hofstadter did ambigrams in high school in the early 1960s. He also believes that Arabian artists, with their skill at calligraphy and love of symmetrical designs, were probably among the earliest to produce ambigrams.

In *Angles & Demons*, Professor Langdon widens the definition, saying symbology also has its ambigrams, such as "swastikas, yin yang, Jewish stars, simple crosses." Observations like these can be extended into surprising areas. Mathematicians, for instance, distinguish four kinds symmetrical transformation necessary to get from a simple shape to something like a swastika—translation, reflection, glide reflection, and rotation. And then the fun begins, as the discussion turns to dozens of kinds of crystalline shapes, each with symmetry of a kind. There follows an ever-widening explosion of ideas that are related, from patterns in nature, such as flower petals or DNA sequences, to geometric forms such as fractals or tessellations (mosaic-tile-like patterns).

Before long, cosmic questions arise, bringing us back, oddly enough, to *Angels & Demons*. For instance, one of the biggest puzzles for cosmologists is, What happened to the assumed symmetry of the big bang where, theoretically, equal amounts of matter and antimatter were produced, yet we now have a universe consisting of vast amounts of matter and very little antimatter? Where's the missing symmetry? It's a mystery!

ADVERBS & DEMONS: JUST HOW GOOD IS THE FORMER ENGLISH TEACHER'S ENGLISH?

BY GEOFFREY K. PULLUM

Many readers enjoy Dan Brown's novels immensely, yet find themselves maddened by some of the over-the-top prose, the cardboard characters, the descriptions of impossible action scenes, the incredible clichés, and other stylistic challenges to literary sensibilities. The reader may have a curiously mixed reaction to a Dan Brown novel. On the one hand, Brown's clever plotting and pacing combine brilliantly with his intellectual zeal for mixing and matching ideas, religion, science, art, history, anthropology, symbolism, occult mysteries, and twenty-first-century news items. On the other hand, there are those shockingly badly written sentences sticking out like sore thumbs throughout this adventurous chase through the catacombs of Western civilization. We asked a noted linguistics professor, Geoffrey Pullum, to help us decode Dan Brown's use of the English language in Angels & Demons. *Here is his report.*

For the sake of a good action-packed story I'll cut an author a lot of slack. For instance, I'll ignore Dan Brown's cluelessness about academia. He has his fictional Professor Robert Langdon in *Angels & Demons* spend weekends around Harvard "lounging on the quad in blue jeans, discussing computer graphics or religious history with stu-

---

Geoffrey K. Pullum, a linguist specializing in English grammar, is Professor of Linguistics and Distinguished Professor of Humanities at the University of California, Santa Cruz. He contributes frequently to the popular Language Log site (www.languagelog.com).

dents" (as if!), and eating an apple while lecturing (try it and you'll know why we professors don't do it). Langdon even complains that it's hard to make trips to Italy on "a teacher's salary." (Come on! The average pay for Harvard professors is now over $135,000. That would get him a few Boston–Rome round trips each year even if Harvard was stingy with travel grants, which it's not.)

Dan knows even less about the world of physics. He confuses "discrete particle physics" (that would be fluid mechanics applied to the flow of granular substances like sand) with elementary particle physics (the high-energy atom-smashing that Maximilian Kohler oversees); he thinks "GUT" (Grand Unified Theory) stands for "General Unified Theory"; and so on. But I'm prepared to set all that aside.

Even if some of the details of Rome's churches, passages, archives, and art were inaccurate, it would hardly spoil one's reading pleasure: *Angels & Demons* is driven by its plot action, and that is Dan Brown's forte.

What I just can't forgive is that Dan can't seem to write descriptive prose that makes sense. He drops phrases in front of the reader that simply boggle the mind with their confused klutziness. He does things to English that would be illegal if done to animals. And that really does interfere with the reading pleasure for some of us.

Direct contradictions, for example, always come as a bit of a shock. Maximilian Kohler is described as having "ventured" some remark "assuredly." To venture something is precisely to risk saying it when you are *not* assured that you're right. You simply cannot venture an opinion assuredly.

At another point we read: "It was once in a lifetime, usually *never*, that a cardinal had the chance to be elected Supreme Pontiff." Now which is it? Once? Or never? There's a big difference. Both statements are false, incidentally: plenty of cardinals see more than one papal election conclave, and could in principle have been candidates.

We run into flat-out ungrammaticality, too. I don't mean violations of those stupid old traditional usage prohibitions (split infinitives and sentences ending with prepositions and all that nonsense). I mean real descents into gibberish. Here's a relatively subtle example: "His reputation for secrecy was exceeded only by that of his deadliness" (from an early passage about the mysterious Hassassin). What does "that of his deadliness" mean? His reputation of his deadliness? Doesn't sound right. His reputation for secrecy of his deadliness? Worse. We can guess what was in Dan's mind (that his reputation for secrecy was exceeded only by his reputation for deadliness), but in its effort to avoid repeating *reputation* the sentence has blundered into a syntactic lobster trap and is unable to find the way out.

Much less subtle abuses of grammar abound. You could perhaps dismiss some as mere idiosyncrasies: Langdon experiences an "intense chill … raking through his body" (I'm not at all sure a chill can rake, but maybe) and when Vittoria heard of her father's death "grief strafed into her heart" (strafing is raking the ground from low-flying aircraft with close-range machine-gun fire, and I'm not sure grief can strafe). But others are much more clearly incorrect:

- Langdon is described as having had "a toned, six-foot physique that he vigilantly maintained." But your physique is the general state of musculature, proportions, and appearance of your body; it's abstract, it doesn't have a height. You may be six feet tall, but your physique isn't.

- We learn at one point that the Illuminati "had infiltrated English parliament" (British, actually, it's not just for England). But a phrase like "British parliament" needs the definite article: "had infiltrated the British parliament" is what he meant. Omitting *the* definitely makes the sentence ungrammatical.

- During the early stages of the hunt for the antimatter that is set to blow the Vatican and the entire College of Cardinals right up to heaven, Commander Olivetti of the Vatican Guard remarks optimistically, "I am faithful Captain Rocher will find the canister." But the adjective *faithful* doesn't take finite subordinate clause complements! No one says "I'm faithful Sally will be back soon with the groceries," no matter how much faith they have in Sally. Replace *faithful* by *sure* in either example and you have grammatical English, but as it stands, you don't.

Some of these wrong uses of words show unmistakable signs of incautious thesaurus use. Composition and rhetoric teachers sometimes unwisely recommend the practice of taking a grammatical and appropriate ordinary English word or phrase and looking it up in a thesaurus to find something more fancy to replace it. But if you do this, you must check whether the new word fits grammatically within the context. It may not, because *words of similar or identical meaning can have different grammatical behavior.*

For example, *shaking* and *quaking* are basically the same thing—the ground can shake and it can quake; but although we can talk about an earth tremor shaking a building, we can't describe it as quaking a building. (To get technical for a second, *shake* takes a direct object; *quake* doesn't.) So you can't randomly replace *shake* by *quake* just because they are both mentioned in the same thesaurus entry.

I am pretty sure Dan Brown has occasionally substituted fancy words without checking. Consider the passage where Vittoria is explaining to Kohler that her father solved the problem of creating and storing antimatter: "Kohler spoke as though emerging from a fog. His voice sounded suddenly precarious." Now, I don't know the exact timbre the voice acquires when one is emerging from a fog, but I do know that a voice can't be precarious. Things that are precarious depend on chance, or unknown conditions, or uncertain future developments. There's simply no such thing as a voice sounding precarious.

Dan simply meant that Kohler sounded uncertain. Vittoria was enlightening him about some facts of physics he didn't know. But Dan opened up a thesaurus at some word like *uncertain* and looked for an alternative word.

A good thesaurus will separate the words out into groups with particular senses, but many just jumble together a long list of possible equivalents. *Uncertain* can mean doubtful or dubious, but it can also mean unstable or variable. *Precarious* means something like the latter, but not the former. So you can't just replace random occurrences of *doubtful* by occurrences of *precarious*! Langdon and Kohler are traveling way down in an elevator to Vetra's lab: " 'Six stories,' Kohler said blankly, like an analytical engine." How do you speak like an analytical engine? The phrase is an odd anachronism: "analytical engine" was the name Charles Babbage gave to the mechanical calculating device he endeavoured to build in the nineteenth century. It had cogs and gears and spindles, it didn't work, and it sure didn't talk.

The Hassassin gets a puzzling voice simile too. "His words were as hard as the rock walls," says Dan. The Hassassin has just gotten through saying "Si; perfettamente." So the Italian words for *yes* and *perfectly* are like a rock wall? I hope you can hear that in your mind's ear, because I can't.

Vittoria gets an even stranger voice description. She says something to Commander Olivetti with "her voice like boiling lava." Think about that. What does lava sound like? Was she rumbling? Hissing? Belching steam and ash?

Olivetti's arrival shortly before, however, had involved even more dramatic pyrotechnics: "The door of the Swiss Guards' security center hissed open. The guards parted as Commander Olivetti entered the room like a rocket." No wonder the guards parted. Rockets travel at speeds that reach thousands of miles per hour, spewing flame behind them as they rise.

Later on, having ceased flying about like a rocket, the commander is in the presence of the pope's chamberlain, and we read: "Olivetti stood rigid, his back arched like a soldier under intense inspection." Well, it would certainly attract some intense inspection if he arched his back, because is head would be down near his knees. Soldiers' backs are meant to be straight. It is frightened cats who arch their backs.

And so it goes on. So many of the similes, metaphors, and other descriptive devices in *Angels & Demons* fall between the wincingly hopeless and the positively ludicrous. They tell us what we don't need to know and conceal what we do need. The weirdest examples in the book have to do with strange eyeball tricks. The camerlengo's eyes, for example, can ask questions ("His green eyes demanding an explanation") or fill up with flames ("His green eyes seemed filled with a new fire"). Commander Olivetti's eyes perform a particularly unusual array of stunts. We learn first that Olivetti's eyes "burned with the kind of hardened determination only obtainable through years of intense training." I can't recall ever seeing that hardened, highly trained, determined burning, but it sounds impressive.

Then someone says something he doesn't like, and we read, "Olivetti's pupils seemed to recede into his head. He had the passionless look of an insect." What kind of insect does that trick with the pupils? A praying mantis? The book doesn't say. It also doesn't say whether the pupils came back out again. We can assume they did. But they're soon gone again: Langdon asks him an innocent question (whether he's heard of the Illuminati), and "his eyes went white, like a shark about to attack." Scary!

A few pages on, "Olivetti's eyes stabbed like bayonets." Ouch! After that he fixes his dangerous ocular weapons on Vittoria, and "his eyes bored through her." Yow!

And still we are not done with the commander's visual special effects. Slightly later, "Olivetti wheeled to the camerlengo, his insect eyes flashing rage."

Let's take stock at this point. Olivetti has insect eyes (possibly those compound ones that you see in *The Fly?*) that can flash like lights, stab people like daggers, bore holes in people like drills, and go white like those of an attacking shark. And these strange insectoid/ichthyoid visual appendages have pupils that can recede into the skull. Either this man is a space alien or Dan Brown cannot write a sensible description of someone's appearance to save his immortal soul. It's interesting that as the pace picks up, the writing gets much less distractingly bad. Dan Brown's strength is in story-line twists and action sequences. His plotting, like Langdon's crisscrossing of Rome to try to save cardinals from horrible deaths, is guided by angels from above; but some-times his prose seems to be in the grip of dark forces from the other place, his adverbs selected by demons.

Novelistic Metaphysics

BY GLENN W. ERICKSON

Some novels seem to have uncannily parallel premises, as for instance Joseph Conrad's *Nostromo* and Malcolm Lowry's *Under the Volcano*, but others seem to possess outright equivalences, as in the case of Dan Brown's *The Da Vinci Code* and *Angels & Demons*. Although *Angels & Demons* was written first (published in 2000), the vast majority of its readers come to it second, only after getting interested in the blockbuster *Da Vinci Code* (2003). Reading the earlier book after the later one, what was in fact a rough draft seems more like déjà vu all over again. For the similarities between the two are manifold.

The protagonist, R. Langdon (not to be mistaken for Liv Tyler's hubby, of the rock group Spacehog), spans both novels. In the transition between the first and second versions of this story, the brotherhood of the Illuminati and the Vatican become the Priory of Sion and Opus Dei; Geneva and Rome become Paris and London; Leonardo and Vittoria Vetra become Jacques Sauniére and Sophie Neveu; the Hassassin becomes Silas; Commander Olivetti and Captain Rocher become Captain Bezu Fache and Lieutenant Collet; Bernini becomes Leonardo da Vinci; Camerlengo Carlo Ventresca becomes Sir Leigh Teabing; and so on.

Glenn W. Erickson is a philosopher who has taught at leading universities in the United States, Brazil, and Nigeria. He has published philosophical works on a wide range of subjects, including many of the topics alluded to in Dan Brown's novels.

The two books share the same opening statement about how the major art, architecture, and historical elements are supposed to be factual, yet they also share the authorial willingness to play with facts, as well as making a legion of outright mistakes in each case.

An illustrative review of errors of fact or opinion in *Angels & Demons* might include the following: The Hassassins did not so much take drugs to "celebrate" their terrorist deeds, as Brown suggests (p. 14), but to prepare themselves for them. Doric columns are not the "Greek counterparts" (p. 26) of Ionic columns, because one is as Greek as the other. "Jewish stars" [sic] are not ambigrams (p. 31), because they are not legible in the relevant sense. For the learned, an "ancient brotherhood" (p. 30) would not be founded in the late sixteenth century (p. 31), because this would make it in fact late Renaissance, which no Harvard professor would describe as "ancient." Italian Renaissance scientists did not found "the world's first scientific think tank" (p. 32), for Pythagoras, Plato, Aristotle, the Ptolemies all had their own; G. Bruno, not Copernicus (p. 51), who published posthumously, was outspoken, and executed for it. The Nazis did not borrow the swastika from the Hindis (p. 40); certainly, a similar symbol exists in Eastern cultures, but the derivation of the Nazi symbol is more likely to have come from the Finnish air force. The Florence of Dante, Machiavelli, Ficino, Pico della Mirandola, Leonardo da Vinci, and Michelangelo, far more than Rome, was "the cradle of modern civilization" (p. 117). No *Renaissance* paintings portrayed Galileo and Milton together in 1638 (p. 219), because the Renaissance was over by then except, say, for the Germanies and points east. Holy communion was not borrowed from the Aztecs (p. 243), whose civilization was at its high tide long after the practice of communion began in Europe and around the same time Brown (incorrectly) suggests the Illuminati arose.

Dan Brown's factual contortions make it hard for the high-brow not to knot his brow in disbelief at the Harvard don and the CERN fellows. Two things might be said to justify this string of outré pronouncements. First of all, the middle of brow, who are the novel's target market, never feel brow-beaten by the Brown book. Wittgenstein says in the *Philosophical Investigations* that philosophers of his ilk can invent natural histories to suit their own purposes; and according to conventions of verisimilitude over truth, the same goes for novelists.

Second, the work might be taken as a kind of science fiction in which the world is somehow different than it is in fact, and in which this "somehow" includes all the funny business of the previous discussion. What is more, it includes the antimatter glob (manufactured by Leonardo Vetra) and the antimatter globe (invented by Vittoria Vetra) to put it in. Such science fiction might be termed Jules Vernesque, because its premise is the modest introduction of some foreseeable technological innovation, such as clean-machine submarines or whiz-bang balloons, and not the wholesale abandonment of reality testing, as when Mars invades or when warp engines render intergalactic journey routine.

To be sure, the science fiction aspect might also be reflected in the way the Illuminati story is told. Brown's historical fiction suggests that Rome gave birth to the brotherhood of the Illuminati in the fifteenth century. Then in the early sixteenth, the brotherhood spread throughout Italy to a broader doctrinal base, and then eventually it spread to Europe and joined with strong intellectual currents such as Masonry and so on.... Perhaps it is even alive today in hypersecret and supersinister form. Actual historical movements labeled Illuminist include the Hesychasts, ascetic mystics of the Eastern Church (fourteenth to eighteenth century), especially the Palamist followers of Gregory Palamas (c. 1296–1350) at Mount Athos; the Alumbrados of fifteenth- and sixteenth-century Spain; the Rosicrucians, the Perfectibilists of eighteenth-century Germany, especially followers of Adam Weishaupt (1748–1830) in Bavaria from 1776 who later changed their name to the Illuminati; the French and Russian Martinists; the Jeffersonian spin on Masonry, etc. Of these historical Illuminisms, the only one that Brown seems to utilize in his narrative is the Bavarian connection (see pp. 38, 99), although he overlays it on the Rome of Bernini and Galileo almost two centuries earlier. Here the distortion lies not just in the differences between the several historical movements that were termed *Illuminist* (usually by their critics) and the story told in the novel, but the idea that such movements somehow continue to exist from century to century rather than being reinvented periodically, typically in substantially different forms. The reality is that there are multiple Masonries, alternative Rosicrucianisms, various Illuminisms, differing Cabalas.

Yet the real difference in quality between Brown's two novels of historic religious mystery and conspiracy seems to be at the level of thought. The Mother Goddess, a key theme of *The Da Vinci Code*, is excellent mythological material, and so, too, is the Illuminism theme of *Angels & Demons*, but the latter develops its theme less adequately. In order to appreciate these shortcomings, it is useful to touch on some of the highpoints of the mythopoetic identification of mind and light.

Promethean, all too Promethean: fire was surely numinous even before old-style man dominated its manufacture and sustenance, becoming therein godly in his turn. And if we're to judge by the Brahmins and Druids and Flamens, the old Indo-European religion was centered in fire cults. Heraclitus, of Ephesus, styled the Obscure, reflects this prediluvian tradition in his identification of fire with its light as the principle of the material elements.

In the West, the locus classicus for the concept of divine illumination was the Myth of the Cave in Plato's *Republic*. In the state of nature, man is in darkness, but the world of truth is bathed in light; and man can glimpse aspects or fragments of truth through unpredictable flashes of illumination. Stoicism follows Heraclitus and Plato in seeing in man a spark of universal reason.

The Gospel of John identifies truth, light, and God; and by dint of this scriptural sanction, in an early Christian sense, someone was one of the Illuminati, or the "enlightened," if he were baptized. Neoplatonism regards light as both a physical and a spiritual element. This double meaning of light reflects itself notably in St. Augustine, Proclus, and Dionysius Areopagite. These Neoplatonizing themes are adopted and adapted by certain Scholastic philosophers, including William of Moerbeke (1215–1286), Witelo (ca. 1230–1275), Robert Grosseteste (ca. 1168–1253), St. Bonaventura (1221–1274), and Henry of Ghent (ca. 1217–1293). Among Protestants, Anabaptists, and Quakers, notably George Fox (1624–1691), make particular use of the metaphor of divine illumination.

Even though in the end of *Angels & Demons*, the brotherhood of the Illuminati turn out to be a red herring laid down by the papal chamberlain to throw investigators off the track of his Vatican coup d'état, Robert Langdon's exploration of Illuminati motives and deeds is one main focus of the novel. And that exploration seems to turn on whether the Illuminati were nonreligious or antireligious. In this regard, it is important to note the difference between the absence of something and the opposite of something. In contrast, for example, to the number one, or to any other number for that matter, the absence is nothing, represented as zero, but the opposite of one is more appropriately understood as the number negative one. There is, curiously, an affinity between one and negative one that does not obtain between one and nothing, insofar as both one, that is, positive one, and negative one are both one; whereas zero does not stand over against one as its absence any more than it does over against two or three or any other member of that sheepish flock.

Psychoanalysis, for illustration, recognizes this logic in the concept of reaction formation. For it does not particularly matter if a person is very neat or very untidy, very clean or very dirty, in that these extremes are manifestations of the selfsame preoccupation. The opposite of fastidiousness is willful disorder, but its absence is just not being overly involved with that dimension of being. Thus in the defense mechanism labeled *reaction formation*, a compulsion is transformed into its opposite while the underlying complex remains the same.

In theology, we might say (following Søren Kierkegaard) that the opposite of theism is demonic despair, in which God is willfully rejected, but the absence is the case where one is oblivious to God. This distinction is what we hear, say, in the dictum of Christ about swallowing the hot or the cold but not the lukewarm. It is also a rationale for Friedrich Nietzsche's judgment that Lord Byron is superior to Goethe: whereas Faust sells his soul to the Devil, Childe Harold, and Don Juan are just blissfully ignorant of that whole question.

Now in several modern European languages, *Illuminism* is used interchangeably with *Enlightenment* (or their equivalents) to name the centuries of light, that is, the seventeenth and eighteenth centuries, as a period of occidental civilization or culture. In this sense, Illuminism names the moment of the scientific revolution, especially the advances in physics and astronomy. Galileo's identification of terrestrial and celestial mechanics and his application of algebra to develop mathematical models of physical systems, as well as his reflections on the experimental methodology, are all monumentally important to this Enlightenment. (These factors are rather even more important than what *Angels & Demons* stresses, to wit, Galileo's acceptance of Copernican heliocentrism, or his improvement of the refracting telescope.)

In this sense, Galileo was the paradigmatic Illuminatus, but these deeds do not require that he or his followers were demonic, even in the eyes of the universal church. In fact it was not the opposition to Christian theism that was characteristic of the age of Illuminism, but rather its absence as a theme of culture or science. Illuminist intellectuals in Bavaria, France, and among the American founding fathers had, in fact, a growing tendency to embrace deism, a doctrine that does not deny God's existence, because he made sense of creation, but only that he takes an active part—that is, an interventionist (read: "miracle-making") role—in providence.

In *Angels & Demons*, Galileo Galilei (1564–1642) is the antitype of Leonardo Vetra. Whereas Galileo, according to Dan Brown, "held that science and religion were not enemies, but rather allies—two different languages telling the same story," Vetra "hoped that science and religion are two wholly compatible fields—two differing approaches to finding the same truth." And Vetra is supposed to prove, through his antimatter experiments, the truth of religion by showing that the creation (of something like the universe) from nothing is possible. Yet such experiments fail to work in this way for manifold reasons.

First, after Karl Popper, we believe that experiments do not confirm even *scientific* theories, but at most fail to falsify them (and hence give them some support).

Second, if matter and antimatter emerge from some concentration of energy, this is not a case of "something coming from nothing," as is said in the novel, but rather, it is a case of developing matter arising from energy, which conversion is already posited in Einstein's "energy equals matter times the speed of light squared." The discussion of Vetra's science seems to waffle among three possible oppositions to matter:

1. Antimatter is the opposite of matter (in another sense, antimatter is a form of matter).
2. Energy is the opposite of matter (but is convertible with matter).
3. Nothingness is the opposite of matter (where matter and energy are taken conjunctly as what has material existence).

Third, the creation of something from nothing would not serve to make plausible the notion that God lies somehow behind or before the nothing and caused the something to appear, because God-talk does not even enter into the lexicon of science.

Fourth, even if the Vetra experiment made some conception of God more plausible, it would be the deistic God who, to use a billiard hall metaphor, broke the rack and then checked out, not the theistic God of orthodox Christianity, who presumably keeps watch over the table.

Fifth, even if, indeed, the Vetra experiment made theism more plausible, this would not show that science and religion are allied approaches to the truth, because the novel seems to equivocate among at least four senses of religion:

1. Science is the opposite of religion (understood as superstition).
2. Atheism is the opposite of religion (understood as Christiantheism).
3. Satan is the opposite of religion (understood as true religion).
4. Antipapism is the opposite of religion (understood as the universal church).

The uptake of these brief reflections is that "religion" does not seem to be a sufficiently precise term to serve usefully in this kind of discussion.

That does not, of course, answer the question of whether intellectual discussions at this level of profundity might not be novelistically effective, even in the kind of novel that seeks its effects in the sphere of thought. Unfortunately, while *Angels & Demons* offers its readers many interesting allusions and ideas, it remains up to the reader to learn the real history of these ideas and to contemplate their relevance to any system of philosophical, cosmological, religious, or scientific thought.

VOX POPULI: COMMENTARY ON ANGELS & DEMONS FROM CULTOFDANBROWN.COM

BY LEIGH-ANN GEROW

The Web is the ideal global "town square" for exchanging opinions about Dan Brown and his novels. And, sure enough, in less time than it takes to go from Harvard to the Vatican in an X-33, googling Angels & Demons *provided links to dozens of sites. Who could resist one called cultofdanbrown.com? When contacted, Leigh-Ann Gerow and her partner (who were managing Internet message boards prior to the creation of cultofdanbrown.com) told us the name came from a chance encounter with a bookstore clerk who told them that fans of Dan Brown were so consumed with the novels that it reminded him of a cult. An idea—and a Web-based message board—were born. (Unlike instant messaging or an Internet chat room where interaction happens in real time, you don't need a second person to be present in order to have a discussion on a message board. A message is posted and can be commented upon today, tomorrow, or any time in the future. Rather than use their real name, many participants adopt a special identity.) Through search engines and word of mouth they invited Dan Brown readers from all over the world to come and sound off about his novels. And talk they did.*

Angels & Demons sat on my bookshelf, unread, for many months. I knew little of Dan Brown other than the media hype behind *The Da Vinci Code*, and assumed *Angels &*

Leigh-Ann Gerow is a freelance writer and Web designer. She and her partner, Nancy Ross, are the owners and webmasters of cultofdanbrown.com.

Demons would be another bland mass-market paperback with a predictable story line. By the time I read the first few pages, however, I was transfixed and enthralled and absolutely in love. I was smitten by glimpses into the secret Vatican Library, and by the historical descriptions of Italy. My mind raced with exciting questions about factual content versus fictional content; I wondered how much of the novel could possibly be true. I immediately begged my partner to read the book so I could talk to her about the all the wonders of Italian art and Vatican history and modern physics and chemistry. After she finished reading it, we both wanted our friends and family members to buy copies of the book so we could discuss the content with them. It was soon obvious that Dan Brown's novels in general, and *Angels & Demons* in particular, would be the perfect subject for an Internet message board.

Once the conversations started, it immediately became obvious that a majority of readers found the same central themes and controversies of interest. This is fascinating because our message-board users have come from not only the United States, but from Australia, Canada, Mexico, Singapore, Turkey, among other countries. No matter where they're from, people want answers to the same questions.

- Some of the most popular topics fall into the broad category of, what did Dan Brown mean by . . . ? Perhaps the most common question has been, what is the correct translation of *Novus Ordo Seclorum*? Is it "New World Order" or "New Secular Order"? Is the word *seclorum* a traditional Latin word, or one simply invented in the modern day to "sound Latin"? If it's the latter, what meaning did its inventors intend it to have? There seem to be endless translation possibilities for this word, and a number of Latin scholars have posted messages giving their interpretation. It is a key point to ponder because if the proper translation of the phrase is not "world" but "secular," it takes away part of the foundation for the conspiracy theories posed in *Angels & Demons*. Message-board member Hinge of Fate claims that a "secular" translation is inaccurate when he posts, *"Brown is wrong when he implies that FDR and his vice president created Novus Ordo Seclorum. The Great Seal was added to the dollar bill in 1935. However, the Continental Congress approved the Great Seal of the United States on June 20, 1782. According to the* Congressional Record, *novus ordo seclorum means "a new order for the ages."* However, board member Galen responds, *"I studied Latin for three years and, like others who have studied it, I can assure you that the* Congressional Record *is wrong, or quite possibly the worst translation I've ever seen."*

- People also wonder about Dan Brown's facts. They express their skepticism by asking questions such as, Can a man really fall from the sky and survive? Why does Langdon's mechanical Mickey Mouse watch have an alarm? Why does Vittoria's cell phone have a dial tone? and Is it true that a computer can't be programmed to make an ambigram? No possible plot error seems too insignificant to be explored.

- Many discussions pose searching questions, such as, Does the church have the duty to withhold information for the greater good? Does the church have valid reasons to protect its followers from the information stored in the Vatican Library? Might the church be corrupted by power? Says Sephia, *"The church and priests are not really obligated to tell the 'truth' per se—only the religious truth of their particular religion. I am all for freedom of information, but I am also thinking about the normal Joe Catholic who doesn't want to hear any of this and prefers to go on in life secure in his knowledge that by doing X, Y, and Z and by avoiding A, B, and C, he can get into heaven."* Should the church actively work to prevent scientific advancement if it threatens the credibility of creation theory? Arras comments on what he'd do if given the chance to release scientific documents that challenge religious beliefs: *"I'd certainly be tempted. But I also know that the truth cannot be forced on people—if they don't want to hear it or embrace it, they'll always find a mental mechanism to avoid doing so."*

- An interesting take on the Illuminati has been the posting of the question, Would you join the Illuminati if they still existed today? Given the choice of working with the Illuminati to protect scientific interests, or to work against them to protect religious interests, the majority of board members are firmly in the science camp. Packer Fan wonders what decision he would have made if he lived at the time of the Illuminati, saying, *"I would like to think I'd join, given the logical way in which I think about science. But I wonder if I would've had the courage and strength to believe in the scientific data of that time, especially in light of public opinion and the beliefs of the majority. What I'm saying is that today, with hindsight as my guide, it'd be a simpler decision."* It's also noteworthy that the majority of posters share a common interest in furthering science and a gentle skepticism about organized religion. Readers who find *Angels & Demons* blasphemous haven't been flocking to the board to defend their point of view. While many board members seem to hold some religious beliefs, they express a general desire that organized religion grant more freedom to scientific expression.

- From the spiritual to the superficial—what should an *Angels & Demons* movie be like? Who would be cast in the roles of Langdon, Vittoria, and the camerlengo? What aspects of the plot are essential to the screenplay and what should be left out? Colin Firth is a popular choice to play Langdon, but so is Russell Crowe. Or should it be George Clooney? FtLouie34 is entirely skeptical about a possible screenplay, saying, *"I'm not a big fan of it being made into a movie. Unless it's as long as all hell, all of the information cannot be included. Of course, since it's Hollywood, the writers couldn't possibly care less about the historical aspect of it."*

- Fans of Dan Brown enjoy speculating on the board about the plot of Brown's next novel, given the similarities between *Angels & Demons* and *The Da Vinci Code*. As Dave Shugarts reported in Dan Burstein's bestseller, *Secrets of the Code*, the puzzle encoded into the dust jacket of *The Da Vinci Code* gives readers the clue that the next novel is likely to include a conspiracy involving the Freemasons. Our participants also speculate about the involvement of the CIA, the Illuminati, the Knights Templar, and the Priory of Sion. Dark Anise is one of many who feels that the novel will involve yet another conspiracy with implications reaching far into government, religious circles, and the art world. And there will also be a woman sidekick: *"I'm pretty sure he'll have a beautiful woman by his side whose father figure (or close male relative) was murdered. Question is, will he keep this one?"*

• To summarize, here are the top ten questions we have seen addressed on cultofdanbrown.com:

  1. Will science and religion ever be united in a common goal?
  2. What is the correct translation for *Novus Ordo Seclorum*?
  3. Are there other clues to Masonic influence in American history?
  4. What is your reaction to seeing ambigrams?
  5. Do you support or oppose the actions and motivations of the Illuminati?
  6. Do the Illuminati still exist and are they related to the Masons?
  7. Is there a role for religion in modern technological society?
  8. Are Brown's story lines about matter, antimatter, and CERN scientifically accurate?
  9. How much of history does the church still hide from public view?
  10. Do Dan Brown's books cause more harm than good?

The message board clearly serves as a springboard for the enquiring reader. Perhaps Poia puts it best when she describes the true value of Dan Brown's work: *"An extremely large number of people affirm that Dan Brown is not a good writer. Yet the impact his books have had on ordinary people is amazing. His work has made them seek and enjoy."* That summarizes our philosophy as well: if a book encourages people to think, question, and read more, it surely must be a good thing.

ANGELS & DEMONS AND THE EMERGING LITERARY GENRE OF ART FICTION

BY DIANE APOSTOLOS-CAPPADONA

In writing Angels & Demons *in the late 1990s, Dan Brown knew he wanted Robert Langdon to be a Harvard professor with expertise in art and religious iconography. But Brown had not yet crystallized the idea of making Langdon a professional "symbologist," the academic title Professor Langdon would receive in* The Da Vinci Code.

Diane Apostolos-Cappadona, a professor of religious art and cultural history at Georgetown University, basically does academically and professionally what we presume Robert Langdon would do if he were a real professor during those times when he wasn't doing crime scene investigations and solving murders. Elsewhere in this volume, she has written about the mismatch between her scholarly work on Gianlorenzo Bernini, and Dan Brown's use of Bernini in Angels & Demons. *In the following commentary, she addresses a different issue: the proliferation of novels that deal with the lives of artists and their artworks—and how Dan Brown's fiction does and doesn't fit into this burgeoning genre of "art fiction."*

Diane Apostolos-Cappadona is Adjunct Professor of Religious Art and Cultural History in the Center for Muslim-Christian Understanding and Adjunct Professor of Art and Culture in the Liberal Studies Program of Georgetown University. She is a widely published cultural historian specializing in religious art.

Just about five years ago, as I rushed through the shop at the National Gallery in London, on my way to Waterloo Station for the Chunnel trip to Paris, I discovered the existence of a new literary genre: art fiction. At the time, however, I did not yet realize how important that genre was to become in my own research and lectures. As I picked up the paperback edition of Katharine Weber's *The Music Lesson, A Novel* (1999) to read on that train ride, I noted the shelf filled with books including Tracy Chevalier's *Girl with a Pearl Earring* (1999) and Susan Vreeland's *Girl in Hyacinth Blue* (1999). I remembered, and momentarily mused upon, my first encounters with art-related fiction in the then seeming profusion of Caravaggio-inspired texts, such as Peter Watson's *The Caravaggio Conspiracy* (1984) and Oliver Banks's *Caravaggio Obsession, A Novel* (1984), which led to Margaret Truman's *Murder at the National Gallery* (1990).

Slowly over the last five years, I have watched this shelf in the National Gallery shop grow into a bookcase burgeoning with new titles, and the inclusion of similar bookshelves or cases in museum shops around the United States and Europe. My momentary "train read" had expanded exponentially into an international literary phenomenon even before anyone had heard of *The Da Vinci Code* (2003), let alone *Angels & Demons* (2000), which was resurrected in 2004 as a bestselling prequel to the bestselling *Da Vinci Code*.

Little did I realize that, by the summer of 2004, I could easily list more than two hundred published books ranging from pseudo-biographies to historical fiction to art history mysteries within my identified genre of art fiction. Or that I would have directed an innovative master's thesis at Georgetown University by a student writing on the cultural valuing implicit to "Vermeer fiction." Or that I would be lecturing on the art historical, religious, and cultural aspects of this literary category. Or that I would frequently be asked to comment on the artworks and symbolism used so blithely by Dan Brown in *The Da Vinci Code*. Or that I would consider writing about my own concept of what art fiction is and why it has appeared with such a flourish!

Nonetheless, here I am putting pen to paper (yes, pen to paper!) in the café at the Edinburgh International Book Festival between author talks. As I perused the book displays at the book festival shop and some of literary Edinburgh's finest bookshops, I confess that I remain amazed by the profusion of interest in and publication of art fiction. Of course, today the question has become, Would anyone have considered art fiction as a literary genre before the phenomenon of *The Da Vinci Code*? The further question becoming, Has any writer been as serious about such a genre prior to Dan Brown? The reality is simple: *The Da Vinci Code* is an enormously successful book in terms of initial reviews and continuing sales. Part of that success must be credited to Brown's inclusion of well-known works of art and artists, and the compelling, if often invented, stories he tells about them.

Now, whether either *Angels & Demons* or *The Da Vinci Code* is a work that conforms to what I see as this new genre of art fiction is a more difficult question. As with a success in any field of endeavor, critics and imitators enter into the fray—perhaps more quickly now, given the technology of the computer and the internet. However, I was cognizant of the existence of an earlier body of literary texts—many influential and critically (and financially) successful—which I identify as art fiction. Do these works have marked differences from both *Angels & Demons* and *The Da Vinci Code*?

As I became fascinated—as both a reader and a cultural historian—with this genre of art fiction, I wondered, where does it begin? For me, being a cultural historian is something like being an archaeologist of symbols, images, and myths. I seek out connectors and origins all the time in my work. My initial thought was that art fiction began with the now classic novels turned into successful motion pictures, in particular, Irving Stone's *Lust for Life* (1934) about van Gogh and *The Agony and the Ecstasy* (1961) about Michelangelo. However, as I began to research library catalogues and websites, I recognized this genre was a nineteenth-century phenomenon, beginning with Honoré de Balzac, *The Unknown Masterpiece* (1834) and Nathaniel Hawthorne, *The Marble Faun*, (1860), and culminating in the works of Henry James, especially *The Golden Bowl* (1904) and *The Outcry* (1911). Early philosophers, such as Plato and Aristotle, and authors like Homer and Dante, discuss works of art, their influences, and their effects on artist, audience, patron, or collector. However, "my" genre of art fiction is most likely rooted in these nineteenth-century books. As I read and interpret the genre of art fiction, the central role and place of art is that related to the process of cultural valuing—a role and place that earlier Western culture would have proscribed to religion, especially in everyday life.

The range of this new genre—from biography to history to mystery to romance—is tempered by the mode in which art as specific works, as representative of an artist, as object of a theft or political scandal, as a biographical statement or historical event, or merely as a prop is incorporated into the story line of the book. In my opinion, those authors who use art as a prop or "come on" to a story which has very little to do with art, artist, or artwork are on the periphery of art fiction.

For a clear example of the art fiction genre, one should look at the novels of Tracy Chevalier. Her fictionalized narratives about the persons in the paintings (*Girl with a Pearl Earring* and *The Lady and the Unicorn*) rest on the premise of the significance of a work of art and its ability to entrance a viewer to imagine a world from a painted image. However, she is cognizant, as are her readers, that this is only one of the stories the paintings tell and that these stories are intuitive, yet profound, statements of what it means to be human.

Similarly, Iain Pears's series of "art history mysteries" intertwine a significant work of art—his artists have included Raphael, Titian, and Bernini, among others—with the modern reality of art theft, and its ensuing questions of authenticity and ownership in the contemporary world in which the financial value of art has increasingly been detached (distinguished) from traditional values. The human thread running through Pears's series of seven novels is the romantic relationship between the Italian art investigator Flavia di Stefano and the British art historian Jonathan Argyll. Other art mystery series have been developed by Thomas Banks, Robertson Davies, Arturo Pérez-Reverte, and Thomas Swan. This genre I identify as "art fiction," then, can be composed not simply of wide-ranging modes of art (art, artworks, or artist) or literary categories (romance, thriller, mystery, historical novel, or biography), but further can be a single work, several unconnected works, or a clearly developed series by the same author.

When I first read the review of *The Da Vinci Code* in the *New York Times*, I confess to an aura of excitement in light of my growing interest in the genre of art fiction, my admiration for Leonardo's art, and my scholarly research on Mary Magdalene, not to mention my work with symbols and symbolism. A quick visit to amazon.com revealed that this was the second in a series of "Robert Langdon mysteries," so I promptly ordered both *Angels & Demons* and *The Da Vinci Code*. Scholarly modes of investigation have always informed my life as well as my own research, so I try to read any series of books in the order in which they have been written. With great anticipation, I entered the world of the fictional character, Robert Langdon, the Harvard professor, who, in *Angels & Demons*, had not yet matured into the professional "symbologist" he would become in *The Da Vinci Code*, but who was still described by Dan Brown as the leading scholar in the more traditional fields of art history and religious iconography. I began at the birth of the Langdon character in his first decoding adventure with the murder of a renowned scientist in Switzerland and then fell headfirst into his escapades throughout the baroque world Gian Lorenzo Bernini created in Rome.

As I have written about my reactions to Brown's discussions of Bernini's works elsewhere in this collection, suffice it to say here that my concern is that Brown treated art, at least in *Angels & Demons*, not as a concept, idea, or object reflecting cultural or religious values as they might be interpreted by art historians, iconographers, and church historians. Rather artworks in this novel are tools for solving a puzzle—a series of clues—that lead Langdon forward in his quest for the identity of a murderer.

The Robert Langdon mysteries are primarily about conspiracy theories, not art. Art becomes a key tool to these conspiracies because of the visualization of codes and symbols it can offer. Langdon's role as a symbologist is enhanced by his ability to read both textual and visual symbols, to connect them, and to decode them. In *Angels & Demons*, Bernini's sculptures become the visual formula for a map on the route to a series of murders, a conspiratorial lair, and the identity of the villains. Good thrillers must be premised upon believability, and without doubt, Brown's engaging descriptions of Bernini's sculptures and their hidden meanings enhance the believability of this story. As a result, it is a good read. However, is it, then, good art fiction?

We don't necessarily learn anything factually substantial about art, artists, or artworks, nor do we garner an appreciation of art as a cultural value in either of Brown's art-related thrillers. Rather, readers are enthralled by the coded messages Langdon alleges are legible in the sculptures of Bernini in *Angels & Demons*, or the paintings of Leonardo in *The Da Vinci Code* without recognizing that these readings of "the code" are Dan Brown's own or various occult sources' invention. This code is, of course, immensely useful in solving the mysteries, and in both *Angels & Demons* and *The Da Vinci Code* the coded messages in the artworks provide intriguing thought provocations and interesting speculations. Do they offer the general reader any new insight into the artworks or into history?

Consider what we know of Dan Brown's own view of the line he is walking between fact and fiction as reflected in the following excerpt from the author's note in *Angels & Demons*: "References to all works of art, tombs, tunnels, or architecture in Rome are entirely factual (as is their exact locations). They can still be seen today." Now compare Brown's opening statement to Iain Pears's author's note in *The Raphael Affair* (1970): "Some of the buildings and paintings in this book exist, others do not, and all the characters are imaginary. There is no National Museum in the Borghese Gardens, but there is an Italian art squad in a building in central Rome. However I have arbitrarily shifted its affiliation from the Carbinieri to the Polizia, to underline that my account bears no relation to the original."

The difference between Brown's claim to historical fact and Pears's disclaimer telling us that he is deliberately mixing fact and fiction is telling for both individual readers and their interpretations of the text. Without doubt, Pears incorporates his admiration for art, artists, and artworks into his stories, as his art historical training coalesces with his recognition that his novels are fiction. Thereby, even the most casual reader recognizes that Pears is not writing history. Meanwhile, Brown's claim to truthtelling and to the mantle of authenticity that comes with his statement about "facts," poses a series of troubling questions, especially since so many readers are learning about the historical, theological, and art historical issues in *Angels & Demons* and *The Da Vinci Code* from Brown's books alone, rather than from traditional sources of knowledge.

Careful readings of *Angels & Demons* and *The Da Vinci Code* result in multiple red flags for scholars and critics as Brown mixes fact and fiction with such even-handedness and so liberally that the nonexpert is easily confused. Similarly, neither Brown nor his lead character, Robert Langdon, appear interested in viewing paintings or sculptures or architectural works for their intrinsic artistic value. Rather, the attraction is their use as clues and the intellectual games played in his plots as he transforms Bernini, a subtle, complex artist, into a sculptor who would incorporate a series of obvious coded messages into the middle of his works.

For me, however, it is in this claim to be reporting fact, that Brown does a disservice to both art and to his readers. He confuses a literary genre and the elements of fiction with scholarly research and historical facts, and, in doing so, opens himself to critical scrutiny that should not normally be applied to works of fiction. As more and more critical eyes focus their attention on his texts, the extent to which he has commingled his fictions with his facts will become apparent. This scrutiny is not being performed simply by critics and scholars, but increasingly by general readers intrigued by the ideas and interpretations that appear in Brown's texts as factual. Such readers are often disappointed when they come to learn that Bernini was not a member of the Illuminati and that Bernini's use of symbols and symbolism was reflective not of ancient occult mysteries but rather of mainstream Roman Catholic theology of the baroque era. Without doubt there is a place in all our lives for thrillers, mysteries, and romance novels. However, the caution is for the reader as well as the author to be aware of the fictional elements of those stories based on facts and to be able to separate them from factualizing fiction.

There is no innocent eye for readers or for authors; we all come with preconceptions, as did I with my understanding of Bernini, religious symbolism, and church history. We all have our personal histories through which we filter what we read. Brown's art fiction provides affirmation for those who live outside the walls of institutional religion but hunger for belief or spirituality, as well as those outside the boundaries of art criticism and art history who respond to art and want to know more but don't want to subject themselves to the aloofness of scholars. For this larger collective, then, art has been "Art" with its distinctive character of "being for the elite," especially that elite which has had the leisure and the financial resources to study and to travel to see artworks in a variety of locations. Such an elitist reading and appreciation of art, especially in terms of the "secret codes" of images and symbols, enhances Brown's claims to an elite conspiracy that rules the larger culture, and does so by retaining that so-called secret code for the symbols and images in works of art. Similarly, for many readers of *Angels & Demons* and *The Da Vinci Code* institutional religion is a "secret gnosis"—with hidden meanings in its rituals and disguised messages in its teachings. Thus, the fundamental distrust of religion and specifically of religious institutions so common among our Founding Fathers continues perhaps more overtly today in the United States.

This aura of conspiracy in institutional religion weighs even more heavily with the clerical abuse scandal in the Roman Catholic Church. Such unfortunate realities have reaffirmed the common misperception of the conspiratorial nature of Christianity, thereby strengthening the context of Brown's conspiratorial thrillers. After over a year on the *New York Times* bestseller list, even Brown's most severe critics recognize that his texts are wildly popular and that his popularity has spread throughout the world. While popularity does not make a work of art or literature historically relevant, it does permit the cultural historian to consider the mindset and interests of the populace. This is what Brown has done so well—he has recognized that the educated general reader enjoys the thrill of uncovering secret meanings previously "hidden" in these artworks, garnering snippets of history, and deciphering the "secret" meaning of visual symbols.

Sadly, I have the impression that Brown is content with the extraordinary popularity of *Angels & Demons* and *The Da Vinci Code*. At the same time, he appears to be blasé about any responsibility he may have to provide his readers with a clear recognition of the lines of demarcation between art history and his regular use of intriguing speculation as he expands the boundaries of his initial literary genre of conspiracy thrillers into the realm of art fiction. I recognize that far more readers will come to learn about Bernini and his sculptures from *Angels & Demons* than from all the outstanding academic studies of Bernini's work combined. Thereby, I wonder, would it be too much to expect from Dan Brown that he modify his claim to historicity toward the more nuanced approach of Iain Pears?

CONTRIBUTORS

Dan Burstein is the coeditor, with Arne de Keijzer, of *Secrets of Angels & Demons: The Unauthorized Guide to the Bestselling Novel.* He was also the editor of *Secrets of the Code: The Unauthorized Guide to the Mysteries Behind* The Da Vinci Code, which spent more than five months on the *New York Times* bestseller list in 2004 and has so far appeared in nineteen foreign-language editions.

The founder and managing member of Millennium Technology Ventures Advisors, a New York–based venture capital firm, Burstein's day job is as an investor in innovative new technology companies. He is also an award-winning journalist and author of numerous books on global economics and technology, including a forthcoming book on the blogging phenomenon, *BLOG! How the Web's New Mavericks Are Changing Our World.*

Yen!, Burstein's first book, focused on the rise of Japanese financial power. It was an international bestseller in more than twenty countries in the late 1980s. His 1995 book, *Road Warriors,* was one of the first books to analyze the impact of the Internet and digital technology on business and society. His 1998 book, *Big Dragon,* written with Arne de Keijzer, outlined a long-term view of China's role in the twenty-first century. Burstein and de Keijzer launched their own publishing enterprise, Squibnocket Press, and are currently working on a variety of pathbreaking new projects in the "Secrets" series, as well as other topics.

Burstein was a longtime senior adviser at The Blackstone Group, one of Wall Street's leading investment banks. He is also a prominent corporate strategy consultant and has served as an adviser to CEOs, senior management teams, and global corporations including Sony, Toyota, Microsoft, Boardroom Inc., and Sun Microsystems.

Arne de Keijzer's published work reflects his wide-ranging interests. He has written and edited books and articles spanning many disciplines, from business to travel and from religion to boating. He was managing editor of the previous book in this series, the *New York Times* **bestseller** *Secrets of the Code: The Unauthorized Guide to the Mysteries Behind The Da Vinci Code.* He and Dan Burstein were the coauthors of *Big Dragon,* an innovative look at China's economic and political future and its impact on the world, and *The Best Things Ever Said About the Rise, Fall, and Future of the Internet Economy.* During his career as a China business consultant, he wrote *China: Business Strategies for the '90s,* and the *China Guidebook.* He resides in Weston, Connecticut, and Martha's Vineyard, Massachusetts, with his wife, Helen, and daughter, Hannah.

Amir D. Aczel, PhD, was a professor of mathematics and statistics at Bentley College in Waltham, Massachusetts, from 1988 to 2003. His works of nonfiction include the international bestseller *Fermat's Last Theorem,* translated into nineteen languages. His other books include *The Mystery of the Aleph, God's Equation, The Riddle of the Compass,* and *Entanglement: The Greatest Mystery in Physics,* all of which have appeared on various bestseller lists in the United States and abroad. Aczel is a frequent guest on the lecture circuit, radio, and television. He recently received a John Simon Guggenheim Memorial Foundation Fellowship to support the writing of his forthcoming book, *Descartes' Notebook.*

Diane Apostolos-Cappadona is an adjunct professor of religious art and cultural history at the Center for Muslim-Christian Understanding and an adjunct professor of art and culture in the Liberal Studies Program of Georgetown University. A widely published cultural historian specializing in the study of religious art, she is currently completing a book, *Mary Magdalene Imaged Through the Centuries, Or How the Anonymous Became the Magdalene.* She contributed the foreword for the reprint edition of *Sacred and Profane Beauty: The Holy in Art* by Gerardus van der Leeuw, and is editing two anthologies of sources and documents in the history of Christian art and symbolism. Professor Apostolos-Cappadona also contributed to the previous book in this series, *Secrets of the Code*.

Michael Barkun is a professor of political science in the Maxwell School at Syracuse University. He has written widely on conspiracy theories, terrorism, and millennial and apocalyptic movements. His book *A Culture of Conspiracy: Apocalyptic Visions in Contemporary America* was published by the University of California Press in 2003 and published in Japan a year later. He has also written *Religion and the Racist Right, Crucible of the Millennium,* and *Disaster and the Millennium.* Barkun has served as a consultant to the FBI and is the recipient of fellowships and grants from the Harry Frank Guggenheim Foundation, the Ford Foundation, and the National Endowment for the Humanities.

Paul Berger is a British freelance writer and journalist based in Brooklyn, New York. He is a former reporter for the *Western Morning News,* in Cornwall, England, where he won the Society of Editors' Award. In the United States he has contributed to the *Washington Post, US News & World Report,* and the *Gotham Gazette.*

Amy D. Bernstein is a writer and academic who specializes in Renaissance literature and history. A graduate of Wellesley College, she earned her doctorate from Oxford University in sixteenth-century French literature. Her doctoral work, completed in 2004, comprised a new edition of the sonnets of Jacques de Billy de Prunay, a Benedictine monk, author, and translator of Gregory of Nazianzus and other patristic writers. She has also written for *US News & World Report,* contributed to *Secrets of the Code,* and edited *Quotations from Speaker Newt: The Red, White and Blue Book of the Republican Revolution.*

Peter W. Bernstein, a partner with Annalyn Swan in ASAP Media, was a contributing editor for this book. Founded in 2003, ASAP Media is a media development firm whose clients include *Reader's Digest Association, US News & World Report,* and the *Boston Globe,* as well as other companies and nonprofit organizations. Before founding ASAP he served as an editor at *US News & World Report* and *Fortune* magazine. He was also publisher of Times Books, a division of Random House, Inc. In addition, he is a bestselling author. He is the editor and publisher of *The Ernst & Young Tax Guide,* the country's number one annual tax guide. He coauthored the *Practical Guide to Practically Everything* and, with his wife

Amy, edited *Quotations from Speaker Newt: The Red, White and Blue Book of the Republican Revolution.*

James Carlisle, PhD, is a venture capital investor, an adviser to CEOs, a scientist, and a serial entrepreneur. Jim has done defense research funded by ONR, DARPA, NSF, the RAND Corporation, and the Department of Defense. He has designed advanced decision support systems for executives of major corporations as well as the US secretary of defense. He has an engineering degree from Princeton and a PhD from Yale. Jim's current investing and research activity includes biometrics applications for homeland defense, access, home automation, medical diagnosis, product marketing, and inventory control. He is a managing partner at Graystone Capital.

Jennifer Carlisle, the author of *B.I.S. Biometric Identification System: A Radical Proposal for Solving the Identity Problem in a Time of Heightened Security,* is an expert in biometrics, international security, and economics. She is CEO of Anzen Research, which recently completed a study on the use of biometric identity verification of passengers and employees for access control at airports. She graduated with honors degrees in international relations and economics from the University of Southern California. She has taught science and history to probation students and worked in marketing for Credit Suisse and for a dot-com later acquired by Answerthink Consulting. She is currently a graduate student at the London School of Economics.

John Castro is a New York City–based writer, editor, and researcher. He has worked on publications by civil rights leader Jesse Jackson, financial journalist Marshall Loeb, and Internet entrepreneur Charles Ferguson. John is also a theater director, actor, and playwright, with a particular love of Shakespeare. John contributed to the previous book in this series, *Secrets of the Code.*

John Dominic Crossan, a monk for nineteen years (and a priest for the last twelve years of that time), was also a university professor for twenty-six years. He has written more than twenty books on early Christianity and has been translated into ten foreign languages, including Korean, Chinese, and Japanese. He lectures to lay and scholarly audiences across the United States as well as in Australia, England, Finland, Ireland, New Zealand, Scandinavia, and South Africa. He is interviewed regularly about religious matters by both print and electronic media.

Paul Davies is professor of natural philosophy at the Australian Center for Astrobiology at Macquarie University in Sydney, Australia. He previously held academic appointments in astronomy, physics, and mathematics at the universities of Cambridge, London, Newcastle upon Tyne, and Adelaide. His research has spanned the fields of cosmology, gravitation, and quantum field theory, with particular emphasis on black holes and the origin of the universe. He has written more than twenty-five books, including *Other Worlds*, *The Edge of Infinity*, *God and the New Physics*, and *The Mind of God*. He was awarded the Templeton Prize in 1995.

Richard Dawkins, the International Cosmos prizewinner for 1997, is the first holder of the newly endowed Charles Simonyi Chair in the Public Understanding of Science at the University of Oxford. Professor Dawkins's first book, *The Selfish Gene*, became an immediate bestseller and *The Blind Watchmaker* won the Royal Society of Literature Award and the *Los Angeles Times* Book Prize. Among his other bestsellers are *Climbing Mount Improbable*, *Unweaving the Rainbow*, and *The Ancestor's Tale*. Professor Dawkins's awards have also included the Silver Medal of the Zoological Society of London, the Royal Society's Michael Faraday Award, the Nakayama Prize for Achievement in Human Science, and the Kistler Prize. He has honorary doctorates in both literature and science and is a fellow of the Royal Society of Literature as well as a fellow of the Royal Society.

Hannah de Keijzer attends Swarthmore College, where she pursues her interests in cognitive science, religion, and dance. She is also a published poet.

Judith DeYoung is a reporter-researcher for *Vanity Fair* magazine. She is also a freelance writer whose work has appeared in *Marie Claire*, *McCall's*, *PC Magazine*, and *Working Woman*. She has been on staff at such magazines as *Lear's* and *Connoisseur*. She studied art history at the Sorbonne in Paris.

David Downie is a Europe-based freelance writer, editor, and translator. His topics are European culture, travel, and food, and his articles have appeared in more than fifty magazines and newspapers worldwide. He is the author of several fiction and nonfiction books. HarperCollins USA published his latest, critically acclaimed cookbook, *Cooking the Roman Way: Authentic Recipes from the Home Cooks and Trattorias of Rome*. He is currently at work on a collection of travel essays entitled *Paris, Paris* and a food lover's guidebook to Rome, where he has spent part of each year since childhood. Downie also contributed to the previous book in this series, *Secrets of the Code*.

Glenn W. Erickson has taught philosophy at Southern Illinois University, Texas A&M University, Western Carolina University, and the Rhode Island School of Design, as well as at five federal universities in Brazil and Nigeria, sometimes as a Fulbright Scholar. He is author of a dozen works about philosophy (*Negative Dialectics and the End of Philosophy*), logic (*Dictionary of Paradox*, with John Fossa), literary criticism (*A Tree of Stories*, with his wife Sandra S. F. Erickson), poetry, short fiction, art history (*New Theory of the Tarot*), and the history of mathematics. Erickson also contributed to the previous book in this series, *Secrets of the Code*.

Leigh-Ann Gerow is a freelance writer and graphic artist, and the webmaster of CultofDanBrown.com. She and her partner, Nancy Ross, design and administrate a number of Internet websites. They live in Las Vegas, Nevada, with thousands of books and far too many pets.

Owen Gingerich is research professor of astronomy and of the history of science at Harvard University and a senior astronomer emeritus at the Smithsonian Astrophysical Observatory. He is a leading authority on German astronomer Johannes Kepler and on Nicolaus Copernicus. Professor Gingerich has edited, translated, or written twenty books and hundreds of articles and reviews. He is the author of *The Book Nobody Read: Chasing the Revolutions of Nicolaus Copernicus*, the result of a three-decade-long personal survey of Copernicus's book *Revolutions*. He and his wife live in Cambridge, Massachusetts, and are avid travelers, photographers, and rare book and shell collectors.

Marcelo Gleiser is the Appleton Professor of Natural Philosophy in the Department of Physics and Astronomy at Dartmouth College. He has been a research fellow at Fermilab as well as at the Institute of Theoretical Physics at the University of California. He is the recipient of a Presidential Faculty Fellows Award from the White House and National Science Foundation, one of only fifteen scientists to receive the award. He has been featured in numerous television programs, including the PBS documentary *Stephen Hawking's Universe*. Gleiser is author of *The Prophet and the Astronomer: Apocalyptic Science and the End of the World*, and *The Dancing Universe: From Creation Myths to the Big Bang*. He is currently working on a historical novel based on the life and work of Johannes Kepler.

Deirdre Good is a professor of the New Testament at the General Theological Seminary in New York City. She reads Greek, Coptic, Latin, Hebrew, and some Aramaic. She has a special interest in the Greek language found in the book of Matthew and its use of both Greek idioms from the Greek translation of Hebrew scriptures (the Septuagint) and Hebrew idioms that are rendered into Greek by the author of Matthew. Her recent publications include an essay on Mary Magdalene in *Secrets of the Code* and an essay for the April 2004 issue of *Episcopal Life*: "A Visual Narrative: Is Mel Gibson's Passion a Gospel for Our Time?" Her book *Jesus the Meek King* appeared in 1999 and she is presently finishing *Mariam, the Magdalen, and the Mother*, to be published in the spring of 2005.

Dean Hamer has done work on the biology of sexual orientation, thrill seeking, anxiety, anger, and addiction. His books on these topics, *Science of Desire* and *Living with Our Genes*, were bestsellers in the science category. Recently, Dr. Hamer has become interested in spirituality. In his new book, *The God Gene*, he argues that our inclination toward religious faith is no accident; it is hardwired into our genes. Chief of gene structure and regulation at the National Cancer Institute in Bethesda, Maryland, Hamer has worked at the National Institutes of Health for more than two decades. He has appeared in national and international newspapers, magazines, and documentaries. Dr. Hamer is also a frequent TV guest.

Steven J. Harris received his BA in physics and PhD in the history of science. He has taught at Harvard University, Brandeis University, and Wellesley College, winning two awards for outstanding teaching. His main areas of interest are the scientific revolution, the history of astronomy and cosmology, and especially the scientific activity of members of the Society of Jesus in the sixteenth through eighteenth centuries. Harris is coeditor of a two-volume collection of essays on Jesuit cultural history and is the author of several

essays on the history of Jesuit science. Several of the points made in his interview in this book are developed in his essay "Roman Catholicism and Science Since Trent," in *The History of Science and Religion in the Western Tradition*.

Michael Herrera is a freelance writer based in Denver, Colorado. He has an undergraduate degree in history and spent several years pursuing a PhD in early Christianity before leaving academia for a career in high-tech public relations.

Stephan Herrera is a New York–based journalist with eighteen years of experience writing about science and technology for the likes of *The Economist*, *Nature*, *Forbes*, *Red Herring*, and the *Acumen Journal of Science*. At present he is life sciences editor at MIT's *Technology Review* magazine in Cambridge, Massachusetts. His book, *Closer to God: The Fantastic Voyage of Nanotechnology*, will be published in the fall of 2005. Stephan earned his undergraduate degree in economics and management at Colorado State University and his master's degree at Columbia University in the Graduate School of Journalism.

Anna Isgro is a freelance writer and editor based in northern Virginia. She was formerly an associate editor at *Fortune* magazine and editor of the corporate newsletter *US News Business Report*. She has worked on a variety of book projects, including serving as managing editor of the *Practical Guide to Practically Everything* and as an editor of a scholarly work on Robert Southwell, the sixteenth-century Jesuit poet.

George Johnson writes about science for the *New York Times* from Santa Fe, New Mexico, and is winner of the AAAS Science Journalism Award. His books include *Fire in the Mind: Science, Faith, and the Search for Order* and *Architects of Fear: Conspiracy Theories and Paranoia in American Politics*. He is codirector of the Santa Fe Science-Writing Workshop and can be reached on the Web at talaya.net. His seventh book, *Miss Leavitt's Stars*, will be published in the spring of 2005.

Scott Kim has been a full-time independent designer of visual puzzles and games for the Web, computer games, magazines, and toys since 1990. His puzzles are in the spirit of Tetris and M. C. Escher—visually stimulating, thought provoking, broadly appealing, and highly original. He has created hundreds of puzzles for magazines and thousands for computer games. He is especially interested in designing daily, weekly, and monthly puzzles for the Web and for portable devices.

Gwen Kinkead, an award-winning journalist, has contributed to the science pages of the *New York Times*. While an editor at *Fortune*, she specialized in international affairs. She co-won the prestigious 1980 George Polk Award for cultural reporting.

George Lechner is an adjunct professor at the University of Hartford, where he teaches courses on Italian art and culture. He earned his master's degree in art history at Bryn Mawr, specializing in religious symbolism. As a Whiting fellow in Rome, he spent two years researching Andrea Sacchi, a baroque painter and contemporary of Bernini, who was commissioned by Pope Urban VIII to create an astrology-themed fresco for his palace ceiling. Lechner discovered that the mystical images in the fresco were designed to induce good fortune and protect the pope and the Catholic Church against the challenges posed by the Protestant Reformation. His thesis on the subject was published in *Art Bulletin*.

Tod Marder is Professor II (distinguished professor), chair of the Department of Art History, at Rutgers University, and a fellow of the American Academy in Rome. He studied art history at UC Santa Barbara and received MA and PhD degrees from Columbia University in New York, studying with Howard Hibbard and Rudolf Wittkower. He has published two books on Bernini's work: *Bernini's Scala Regia in the Vatican Palace, Architecture, Sculpture, and Ritual* and *Bernini and the Art of Architecture*. The latter book won the Borghese Prize for the best book on a Roman topic by a foreigner in 1998. Dr. Marder is currently writing a book about new developments in Bernini studies.

Jill Rachlin Marbaix is a freelance writer and editor who covers a wide variety of topics, from business to education to entertainment. During the course of her twenty-year career, she has worked as a writer and editor at several national magazines, including *TV Guide*, *People*, *US News & World Report*, *Ladies' Home Journal*, and *Money*.

Richard P. McBrien is Crowley-O'Brien Professor of Theology at the University of Notre Dame, having formerly served three terms as chair of the Department of Theology. He is also past president of the Catholic Theological Society of America. The author of twenty books, including *Catholicism*, *Lives of the Popes*, and *Lives of the Saints*, he appears regularly on network television as a commentator on Catholic events, and will be an ABC News on-air commentator for the next papal election. Father O'Brien was also a contributor to the previous book in this series, *Secrets of the Code*.

Mark Midbon is a senior programmer and analyst at the University of Wisconsin. As a computer programmer during the early 1990s, Mark automated campus libraries at the University of Wisconsin. During this time he wrote articles for *Computers and Society*, a journal of the Association of Computing Machinery. His pieces focused on Israel's computer models for the 1967 War and the rise of the computer firm IBM. Later, he worked for the Y2K project at Arizona State University, when he became more interested in pure science. It was during this time that he wrote a number of Internet articles about the priest-geologist Pierre Teilhard de Chardin and the priest-astronomer Georges Lemaître.

Tom Mueller is a writer based in Italy. His work has appeared in the *New York Times*, *Atlantic Monthly*, *New Republic*, *BusinessWeek*, *Best American Travel Writing*, and other US and European publications. He is completing a novel about the building and rebuilding of St. Peter's Basilica, as well as what he calls a "user's guide" to underground Rome—the vast realm of temples, palaces, brothels, and humble homes that lie buried beneath the modern city.

John W. O'Malley, a Jesuit priest, teaches church history at the Weston Jesuit School of Theology in Cambridge, Massachusetts. He has lectured widely in the United States, Europe, and Southeast Asia. Among his prize-winning books are *The First Jesuit* and *Trent and All That*, both from Harvard University Press. A fellow of the American Academy of Arts and Sciences, he is also past president of the American Catholic Historical Association and the Renaissance Society of America. His most recent book is *Four Cultures of the West*.

Geoffrey K. Pullum is a linguist specializing in English grammar. He lives in Santa Cruz, California, and is a professor of linguistics and a distinguished professor of humanities at the University of California, Santa Cruz. He contributes frequently to the popular Language Log site www.

languagelog.com, where, if you dig through the archives, you can find a hysterically funny piece called "The Dan Brown Code" about Brown's use of language in *The Da Vinci Code*. He has also authored or coauthored more than two hundred articles and a dozen books. The funniest of his books is *The Great Eskimo Vocabulary Hoax*, and the most serious is a large-scale English reference grammar, *The Cambridge Grammar of the English Language*, which in 2004 won the Leonard Bloomfield Book Award.

Alexandra Robbins is a *New York Times* bestselling author and lecturer whose books include *Pledged: The Secret Life of Sororities; Secrets of the Tomb: Skull and Bones, the Ivy League, and the Hidden Paths of Power;* and *Conquering Your Quarterlife Crisis: Advice from Twentysomethings Who Have Been There and Survived.* She has written for *Vanity Fair, The New Yorker,* the *Atlantic Monthly,* and the *Washington Post,* among other publications. She regularly appears in the national media and lectures frequently to groups about secret societies, twentysomething issues, Greek life, and writing. She can be contacted at www.alexandrarobbins.com.

Wade Rowland is the author of *Galileo's Mistake: A New Look at the Epic Confrontation Between Galileo and the Church,* and more than a dozen other books. He is an award-winning journalist and television producer of news and documentary programs. He is a former Maclean-Hunter Chair of Ethics in Communications at Ryerson University in Toronto and currently lectures in the social history of communications technologies at Trent University in Peterborough, Ontario. Rowland is completing a book about corporations and the eclipse of morals entitled *Ethics and Artificial People.* He lives near Port Hope, Ontario. Dr. Rowland can be reached via www.waderowland.com.

Susan Sanders is the cofounder and executive director of the Institute of Design and Culture in Rome. She received her MA in architecture from Georgia Tech and her BA in art from the University of Georgia. Over the past decade Susan has taught architectural design for the Universities of Arkansas and Kansas, and the Savannah College of Art and Design, in addition to holding the Hyde Chair of Excellence for the University of Nebraska. She was also creative director for Carrier Johnson Architects in San Diego, California. She currently resides in Rome.

David A. Shugarts is a journalist with more than thirty years' experience, having served on news-

papers and magazines as a reporter, photographer, desk editor, and editor-in-chief. He was reared in Swarthmore, Pennsylvania, and obtained a BA in English from Lehigh University, followed by service in Africa in the Peace Corps, then received an MS in journalism from Boston University. His fields of expertise include aviation and marine writing. He was the recipient of five regional and national awards from the Aviation/Space Writers Association. Shugarts was the founding editor of *Aviation Safety Magazine* in 1981 and of *Powerboat Reports* magazine in 1988. As a writer, he has contributed to a dozen books, including *Secrets of the Code.* As an editor and production manager, he has produced hundreds of books. He lives in Newtown, Connecticut.

Annalyn Swan, a partner with Peter Bernstein in ASAP Media, was a contributing editor for this book. Founded in 2003, ASAP Media is a media development firm whose clients include *Reader's Digest Association, US News & World Report,* and the *Boston Globe,* as well as other companies and nonprofit organizations. Swan has been a staff writer at *Time* magazine, music critic and arts editor of *Newsweek,* and editor-in-chief of *Savvy.* With the art critic Mark Stevens, she has also written a biography of the artist Willem de Kooning, just published by Knopf.

Greg Tobin is an author, editor, journalist, and scholar who is currently the publisher of the *Catholic Advocate,* the newspaper of the archdiocese of Newark, New Jersey. He has written fiction and nonfiction books about the Catholic Church, including *Conclave* and *Council,* two novels about the papacy of the near future; *The Wisdom of St. Patrick,* meditations about the beloved patron saint of Ireland; *Saints and Sinners,* an anthology of writings by American Catholics in the latter half of the twentieth century; and *Selecting the Pope: Uncovering the Mysteries of Papal Elections,* a handbook about the history and future of the papal elections for Catholics and non-Catholics alike.

Neil deGrasse Tyson, an astrophysicist, was born and raised in New York City, where he attended the Bronx High School of Science. Tyson went on to earn his BA from Harvard and his PhD from Columbia. His professional research interests include star formation, exploding stars, dwarf galaxies, and the structure of the Milky Way. He has served on two presidential commissions on America's future in space. Dr. Tyson is a monthly essayist for

Natural History magazine. Among the books he has written are his memoir *The Sky Is Not the Limit: Adventures of an Urban Astrophysicist,* and *Origins: Fourteen Billion Years of Cosmic Evolution.* He is the director of New York City's Hayden Planetarium and recently served as host for NOVA's *Origins* miniseries.

Alex Ulam is a freelance writer who specializes in cultural issues. His work has appeared in *Discover, Archaeology, Wired, Architectural Record,* the *National Post of Canada,* and other publications. He lives in New York City.

Steven Waldman is the editor-in-chief and co-founder of beliefnet.com. Previously he was the national editor of *US News & World Report* and a national correspondent for *Newsweek.* He has also served as editor of the *Washington Monthly,* an influential political magazine. Waldman was senior adviser to the CEO of the Corporation for National Service, the government agency that runs Ameri-Corps and other volunteer programs.

James Wasserman is a lifelong student of esotericism. His writings include *Art and Symbols of the Occult,* and *Aleister Crowley and the Practice of the Magical Diary.* His Chronicle Books edition of *The Egyptian Book of the Dead,* edited by Dr. Ogden Goelet, features a full-color papyrus with an integrated English translation. His *The Templars and the Assassins* has thus far been published in five languages. His controversial *The Slaves Shall Serve* defines political liberty as a spiritual value and analyzes modern trends toward collectivism. He is currently collaborating with Jon Graham on a translation of *The Bavarian Illuminati and German Freemasonry* and writing *The Illuminati in History and Myth.*

Cyril H. Wecht is certified by the American Board of Pathology in anatomic, clinical, and forensic pathology. He serves as the elected coroner of Allegheny County in Pittsburgh, Pennsylvania, and is chairman of the Advisory Board of the Cyril H. Wecht Institute of Forensic Science and Law at Duquesne University School of Law. He has personally performed approximately 15,000 autopsies and has supervised, reviewed, or been consulted on approximately 35,000 additional postmortem examinations. Dr. Wecht is author of more than 475 professional publications and editor of thirty-five books. He frequently provides expert testimony in court cases. He also appears regularly on national TV and radio shows and has written several books about cases in the news, including *Cause of Death, Grave Secrets,* and *Who Killed Jon Benet Ramsey?*

Mark S. Weil, PhD, a leading expert on the art of sculptor Gianlorenzo Bernini and baroque imagery, teaches at the University of Washington. He wrote his dissertation on Bernini's decoration of the Ponte Sant'Angelo (the Bridge of Angels that Robert Langdon crosses in search of the Illuminati lair), which led to his book *The History and Decoration of the Ponte S. Angelo.* For the past thirty years Weil has gone to Rome each year to conduct research at the Vatican Library and Archives. Weil is also the director of the Mildred Lane Kemper Art Museum at Washington University and the director of the university's Sam Fox Arts Center.

Robert Anton Wilson is an acclaimed author of more than thirty books. He was associate editor at *Playboy* in the late 1960s and is a futurist, playwright, poet, lecturer, and stand-up comic. With Robert Shea, Wilson coauthored the *Illuminatus! Trilogy,* which the *Village Voice* called "the biggest sci-fi cult novel . . . since *Dune.*" The trilogy has been reprinted in many languages and adapted into a ten-hour epic theater piece. In 1986, only ten years after its publication, *Illuminatus!* won the Prometheus Award as a classic of science fiction. Wilson stars in *Maybe Logic: The Lives and Ideas of Robert Anton Wilson,* a film by Lance Bauscher, which won the Best Documentary award at the San Francisco Film Festival in 2004. Wilson teaches online courses at the Maybe Logic Academy.

Josh Wolfe is a managing partner of Lux Capital, where he focuses on investments in nanotechnology. He previously worked at Salomon Smith Barney and Merrill Lynch and now sits on Merrill's TechBrains advisory board. He conducted cutting-edge AIDS research and published in *Nature, Cell Vision,* and the *Journal of Leukocyte Biology.* Josh is the author of the five-hundred-page "The Nanotech Report." He is also editor of the *Forbes/Wolfe Nanotech Report,* and writes a column at *Forbes* magazine. As a founder of the NanoBusiness Alliance, Josh joined President Bush in the Oval Office for the signing of the 21st Century Nanotech Research and Development Act. *Red Herring* has called him "Mr. Nano." Steve Forbes has called him "America's Leading Authority of Nanotechnology." He has appeared in *BusinessWeek,* the *New York Times,* the *Wall Street Journal,* and is a regular guest of CNBC. Josh graduated with distinction from Cornell University.

ACKNOWLEDGMENTS

Secrets of Angels & Demons, like its predecessor, *Secrets of the Code*, is an amazing publishing story. In a few months' time we have been able to go from concept to bookstore, producing a book filled with the knowledge of great thinkers and brilliant writers. We have captured world-class expertise on a diversity of subjects that range from science to art and from history to religion. People familiar with the normal constraints imposed by the charming but antiquated publishing business often ask us how we can do these books so quickly. The answer—aside from no sleep and great support from our families—is that these books rely on the cooperative efforts of a large number of talented people. We would like to acknowledge the contributions of many of them.

First of all, our publisher, CDS Books, stood by us as a true partner every step of the way, offering all the attention, ideas, resources, publishing acumen, and distribution strength that any author could hope for. In particular, we would like to thank Gilbert Perlman for sharing our vision and showing us how to realize it. David Wilk was again our able guide, tireless master of ceremonies, and cheerful chief enforcer from inception to finished book. Donna M. Rivera, managing editor of CDS Books, was the master juggler of ever-changing copy. We would also like to thank Steve Black and the great sales team at CDS; their efforts ensured the success of *Secrets of the Code* and paved the way for this book. The all-star team assembled to work on many aspects of the design and production of the book included George Davidson, Leigh Taylor, Lisa Stokes, Gray Cutler, and David Kessler. A very special thanks to Paul J. Pugliese for his maps and to Elisa Pugliese for her illustrations. We missed Jaye Zimet's creativity and energy on this book, but her spirit was with us and we remember her fondly.

We also benefited from the tireless work of a terrific team of editors, interviewers, and writers. Our thanks to David A. Shugarts, Paul Berger, Peter Bernstein, Annalyn Swan, John Castro, Judy DeYoung, Anna Isgro, Gwen Kinkead, Jill Rachlin Marbaix, and Alex Ulam.

The core of *Secrets of Angels & Demons* is the specialized knowledge of our many experts. We deeply appreciate the efforts they all made to answer our questions and to provide important and timely contributions that enrich the book at every turn. A huge thank-you to Amir D. Aczel, Diane Apostolos-Cappadona, Michael Barkun, Amy Bernstein, James Carlisle, Jennifer Carlisle, John Dominic Crossan, Paul Davies, Richard Dawkins, Hannah de Keijzer, David Downie, Glenn Erickson, Leigh-Ann Gerow, Owen Gingerich, Marcelo Gleiser (with special thanks for letting us borrow the "pious heretic" phrase), Deirdre Good, Dean Hamer, Steven Harris, Michael Herrera, Stephan Herrera, George Johnson, Scott Kim (with special thanks for creating the *Secrets* ambigram), Paul Kurtz, George Lechner, Tod Marder (with thanks for cartography help as well as Bernini expertise), Richard McBrien, Mark Midbon, Tom Mueller, John W. O'Malley, George Pullum, Alexandra Robbins, Wade Rowland, Greg Tobin, Neil deGrasse Tyson, Steven Waldman, James Wasserman, Cyril Wecht, Mark Weil, Robert Anton Wilson, and Josh Wolfe.

Thanks for their assistance in Rome to Sergio Caggia of Nerone & Rome Made to Measure; Susan Sanders, Executive Director, Institute of Design and Culture; Mauro Scarpati; and the Hotel Exedra.

Many people have worked behind the scenes to advise us, encourage us, share a great idea with us, help us find a key piece of information, or otherwise assist in myriad ways to make the *Secrets* series the blockbuster success it has become. Our thanks to Danny Baror, Elkan and Gail Blout, David Burstein, Mimi Conway, Helen de Keijzer, Steve de Keijzer and Marni Virtue, Jelmer and Rose Dorreboom, Marty Edelston, Brian Flynn, Michael Fragnito, Peter Kaufman, Clem and Ann Malin, Lynn Northrup, Julie O'Connor, Cynthia O'Connor, Joan O'Connor, Michael Prichinello, Bob and Carolyn Reiss, Dick and Shirley Reiss, Stuart Rekant, Amy Schiebe, Sam Schwerin, Allan Shedlin, Bob Stein, Kate Stohr, Brian and Joan Weiss, Sandy West, and Joan Wiley. We also tip our hats to the staffs of the Chilmark Public Library and the Weston Public Library as well as to Mike Keriakos, Nerissa Wels, Ben Wolin, and the rest of the Waterfront Media team.

—Dan Burstein and Arne de Keijzer